BEYOND NORMS: STRATEGIES FOR EXCELLENCE

BEYOND NORMS: STRATEGIES FOR EXCELLENCE

Editors

RAKESH CHOPRA
JAYANTHI RANJAN
SANDEEP PURI
NEERAJ AWASTHY

BLOOMSBURY

LONDON • NEW DELHI • NEW YORK • SYDNEY

First Published, 2013

BLOOMSBURY PUBLISHING INDIA PVT. LTD.
London New Delhi New York Sydney

ISBN: 978-93-82563-45-7

Published by Bloomsbury Publishing India Pvt. Ltd.
VISHRUT Building, DDA Complex, Building No. 3, Pocket C-6 & 7
Vasant Kunj, New Delhi 110 070

Laser Typeset by FORTUNE GRAPHICS
WZ-911/2, Shankarlal Street, Naraina, New Delhi

Printed at Anvi Composers
1 DDA Market, Block A-1B, Pachim Vihar, New Delhi 110 063

Acknowledgements

The editors are grateful to the management and Dr. Bibek Banerjee (Director) of IMT, Ghaziabad, India without whose support it would not have been possible to bring out this volume. We would like to thank Dr. Rajendra Nargundkar (Sr. Dean) and Dr. Suresh Bedi (Dean) for their guidance and help in numerous activities to organize FOBE 2012. We specially thank our knowledge partners Mazagon Dock Limited, for their support in making FOBE 2012 a big success.

Research is a painstaking business and we cannot overemphasize the importance of carefully researched papers in contributing to a volume of this type. A large number of distinguished authors from academia and practicing managers from industry have shown a keen interest in the subject area and have contributed well researched papers. Thanks to their interest that this volume has been possible. We would like to thank our colleagues from academia for their valuable time, support and guidance. The support came in many forms: review and re-review, suggestions and modifications and observations to make this volume more focused and relevant.

Our thanks are also due to Bloomsbury Publishing, their editors, production experts and their entire staff for their cooperation in bringing out this volume. We would also like to thank all the faculty colleagues, officers and staff members at IMT, Ghaziabad in extending their support for FOBE 2012. Special thanks are due to Mr. Krishna Murari Sinha for his contribution in the progress of this volume.

We value your feedback and suggestions on this volume. We look forward to your comments on emails: jranjan@imt.edu; rchopra@imt.edu; spuri@imt.edu in order to bring out a better innovative volume in future.

Finally, deep thanks go to our family members for their understanding, patience and support for this endeavor.

Rakesh Chopra
Jayanthi Ranjan
Sandeep Puri
Neeraj Awasthy

Acknowledgements

The editors are grateful to the management and Dr. Bibek Banerjee (Director) of IMT, Ghaziabad, India without whose support it would not have been possible to bring out this volume. We would like to thank Dr. Rajendra Nargundkar (Sr. Dean) and Dr. Suresh Bedi (Dean) for their guidance and help in numerous activities to organize FOBE 2012. We specially thank our knowledge partners Mazagon Dock Limited, for their support in making FOBE 2012 a big success.

Research is a painstaking business and we cannot overemphasize the importance of carefully researched papers in contributing to a volume of this type. A large number of distinguished authors from academia and practicing managers from industry have shown a keen interest in the subject area and have contributed well researched papers. Thanks to their interest that this volume has been possible. We would like to thank our colleagues from academia for their valuable time, support and guidance. The support came in many forms: review and re-review, suggestions and modifications and observations to make this volume more focused and relevant.

Our thanks are also due to Bloomsbury Publishing, their editors, production experts and their entire staff for their cooperation in bringing out this volume. We would also like to thank all the faculty colleagues, officers and staff members at IMT, Ghaziabad in extending their support for FOBE 2012. Special thanks are due to Mr. Krishna Murari Sinha for his contribution in the progress of this volume.

We value your feedback and suggestions on this volume. We look forward to your comments on emails: jranjan@imt.edu; rchopra@imt.edu; spuri@imt.edu in order to bring out a better innovative volume in future.

Finally, deep thanks go to our family members for their understanding, patience and support for this endeavor.

Rakesh Chopra
Jayanthi Ranjan
Sandeep Puri
Neeraj Awasthy

Preface

Thinking beyond the box is to think differently, unconventionally, or from a new perspective 'to investigate the unexploited path. It is thinking beyond the constraints of human consciousness and experience – to see beyond the norm. "Thinking beyond norms Strategies" provides an authoritative review of the concepts of new approaches to management in the age of globalization and knowledge economy.

FOBE 2012 – International Conference Facets of Business Excellence – Thinking beyond the Box is organized by IMT Ghaziabad after the successful FOBE 2011- International Conference Facets of Business Excellence – Leveraging Information Technology for Strategic Advantage.

The primary goal of the FOBE 2012 is to bring together creative academic and industrial experts in the field of Business Administration to discuss, exchange views and experiences on thinking beyond the box to help today's business organizations to exceed their goals and expectations while pursuing their full growth and earning potential. This conference is a platform for discussing contemporary issues in Strategy, IT, Management and Marketing and for exchanging views and experiences on various issues related to out of box thinking in business management.

It contains rich resources from the vast experiences of researchers, academicians, and practitioners in the industry. This premier reference source contains a very comprehensive knowledge on beyond norms management practices and provides an all-encompassing perspective on the importance of innovation in management practices.

Hope this volume finds space in the minds of the practicing world of business and IT and draws new landscapes in future.

Rakesh Chopra
Jayanthi Ranjan
Sandeep Puri
Neeraj Awasthy

The Editors

PROF. RAKESH CHOPRA

Dr. Rakesh Chopra is a professor in the area of Economic Environment & Strategy. He is a Ph. D and M.Phil from Mumbai University in Strategic Studies & International Relations focusing on Energy Security, M.Sc. from Madras University, and an MBA from JBIMS, Mumbai. He was Senior Visiting Research Fellow with the "Oxford Leverhulme Programme on the Changing Character of War" at Oxford University. He is an alumnus of the Harvard Kennedy School. Prior to joining IMT, he was a Professor of Strategy at XLRI Jamshedpur. He served in the Indian Navy for 38 years. He has commanded three ships including a ship in the 1971 Indo Pak war in the Eastern Theatre, and has held various operational appointments. He is an alumnus of the National Defense Academy, and the Defense Services Staff College, Wellington, where he has been on the Directing Staff. He was the Chief Instructor and Dean of the College of Naval Warfare at Karanja, Mumbai, and Chief Instructor of the Navigation & Direction School where officers specialize in the planning and conduct of maritime operations. He was mentioned in 'Mention in Dispatches' for gallantry during military operations in Sri Lanka and was awarded the Vishisht Seva Medal by the President of India for exemplary service.

DR. JAYANTHI RANJAN

Jayanthi Ranjan is a Professor in IT Management area at IMT, Ghaziabad. She is also Associate Dean-International Relations, IMT Ghaziabad. She has more than 19 years of teaching experience. She has published various papers on Data clustering, Data Mining, Database security, business intelligence, educational technologies that appeared in various international refereed journals. She has over 110 publications till date. She has over 53 publications in various International Journals, 15 national conference proceedings and 10 International conference Proceedings till date. She has published 14 edited books. She has published research papers with refereed publications like in World Scientific, Emerald, Inderusceince, ANSINET, GIFT society. She is the recipient of 'Best Teacher Award' from AIMA-Ghaziabad Management Association, India for her contribution to teaching and research. She is also the recipient of Best Management Researcher award, from Association of Management Scholars AIMS.

She is serving on the editorial board for the international journal "Information Technology Journal", Asian Network for Scientific Information. She is also the editorial member of "Indersceince-International Journal of E-CRM". She is the Editorial member of "Inter disciplinary journal of information knowledge and management", Informing Science Institute, UK. She is the associate editor of "Journal of Applied and Theoretical Information Technology". Her Teaching and Research interests include Data Mining & Building Data Warehouses, Information Systems Design, Information Agents Building and Business Intelligence. She can be reached at jranjan@imt.edu

PROF. SANDEEP PURI

Sandeep Puri is working as a faculty in Marketing at IMT, Ghaziabad. He is pursuing his Ph. D on Private labels. He is Gold Medalist during B. Pharmacy. He has over 19 years of experience in Industry & academics. He has held senior level positions in Marketing and Sales Management in Trident & Novartis. He has 24 publications till date. He has 5 publications in various International Journals and 9 in magazines and newspapers. He is also having 2 publications in International conference proceedings and 2 in national conference proceedings. He is also a visiting faculty at prestigious business schools like S P Jain, Singapore, Fachhochschule Vorarlberg, Austria and Great Lakes His teaching, research and training interests include Customer Relationship Management, Sales Management & Service Marketing. He has published six edited books He can be reached at spuri@imt.edu.

DR. NEERAJ AWASTHY

Dr. Neeraj Awasthy is a Manager Academic Programs at IMT, Ghaziabad and works in the area of rural innovation as a part of Centre for Rural Innovation, Capacity Building, Knowledge Management, Social Entrepreneurship and Technology (CRICKET). He holds Ph. D in Finance from H.P. University and has worked in the area of rural finance. He has over 15 years of experience in Entrepreneurship and social sector. His research interest includes microfinance and working capital management. He can be reached at nawasthy@imt.edu

Contents

A Structural View of the Eco-friendly Supply Chain Management (ESCM) in Indian Computer Manufacturing Industries

Sushanta Tripathy and Satyabrata Aich

School of Mechanical Engineering, KIIT University, Bhubaneswar, Orissa

ABSTRACT

In order to enhance the performance of eco-friendly supply chain management (ESCM) in computer manufacturing organizations, the supply chain managers need to identify the internal as well as the external factors and they need to understand the interdependencies of these factors. This paper has attempted to identify the success factors for eco-friendly supply chain management in Indian manufacturing firms and provides an interpretive structural model (ISM) to develop a map of the complex relationships and magnitude among identified success factors. The results represent that Indian computer manufacturing industries should be equipped with proper management strategy based on customer focus to achieve the long-term objective such as performance of marketing and communication of ESCM in most efficient way within a short span of time. In addition to that the proposed ISM model acts as good guideline in order to improve the performance of ESCM in the computer manufacturing organizations in India.

INTRODUCTION

Supply chain management (SCM) is the integration of all activities associated with the flow and transformation of goods and raw materials to the end user through improve supply chain relationship to achieve a sustainable competitive advantage (Handfield and Nicholas, 1999).In 21st Century, manufacturing and service organizations are focusing themselves under pressure to eco-friendly their supply chain activities. This pressure derives from different stake holders i.e. customers, suppliers, and policy formulators etc for competitive and strategic advantage. Due to the increase in cost of material and energy, the manufacturers and service providers find new directions to reduce their cost of production and continue their competitiveness in the global market. This has made Eco-friendly supply chain management (ESCM) a key strategic tool (Kangangi,2011).Therefore the scope of ESCM starts from monitoring the general environmental management programme and continues with various activities such as reduce, reuse, rework, refurbish, reclaim, recycle, remanufacture and reverse logistics etc (Srivastava, 2007).

It is important that ESCM gets its pace within the supply chain management due to impact and connectedness in between supply chain management and natural environment. ESCM is also defined as the summation of environment purchasing, environment manufacturing/ environment procurement, environment Marketing/distribution, and reverse logistics (Hervani et al., 2005).To satisfy the primary and secondary markets, the eco-friendly supply chain management is directing bidirectional activities, i.e. forward (Procurement, design, manufacture and distribution) and backward (inspection, disassembly for the purpose of reuse, reprocessing and redesign) (Wang, 2009).According to Wang (as shown in Fig. 1), restriction of hazardous substance (RoHs) by vendor. energy using products (EuP) by designer, environment product declaration by manufacturers, and waste electrical and electronic equipment are the forward activities for the demand of 21st century global market.

Therefore ESCM has been considered as an important proactive strategy by top electronic manufacturing organizations i.e. Dell, HP, IBM, SONY, Panasonic, Hitachi and Toshiba. (Zhu and Sarkis, 2006). The WEEE, RoHS and EuP directives recognizes that electronic equipment needs specialist handling and disposal. Among these electronics equipment, computer contributes most of the hazardous material like lead, hexavalent chromium and mercury and hazardous waste. An average personal computer contains plastic (23%), ferrous metals (32%), non-ferrous metals (18%), electronic boards (12%) and glass (15%).A single computer can contain up to 2kg of lead, and the complex mixture of materials make personal computers very difficult to recycle.

As per the new legislation come into force in 2007 to cover waste electrical and electronic equipment (WEEE), the users must store, collect, treat, recycle and dispose of WEEE separately from other waste. It is now a requirement that all businesses obtain and keep proof that their WEEE was given to a registered waste management company, and has been treated and disposed of in an environmentally sound way. Environmental protection and conservation of natural resources has become a key essential objective at national and international levels. Management of hazardous waste is key target in achieving environmental protection throughout the world. Reducing the productions of hazardous waste, recovery of the valuable materials from the waste and protective to the environment degradation are some critical issues which need to be focused. (Kannan et al., 2010).

The objective of this paper is to discover various key factors to implement ESCM in computer manufacturing industries, to discover further the contextual relationship among the identified factors to implement in ESCM, to separate these key factors depending upon their driving and dependence power and finally to develop ISM based model of these key factors. In this study we have selected 13 key factors from the review of literature, i.e., Environmental procurement, Environmental Accounting, Environmental Design, Environmental Manufacturing, Environmental Logistics, Economic Performance, Environmental Performance, Life Cycle

Management, Customer Focus, Management Vision and Direction, Operational Performance, Supplier Management and Performance of marketing and communication.

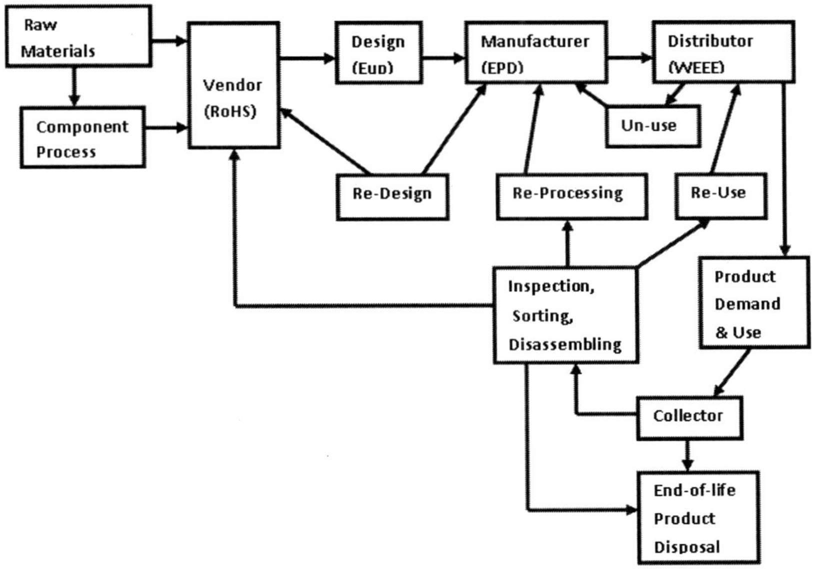

Fig. 1. Framework of Eco-friendly Supply Chain with the Involved Forward and Reverse Activities and their Corresponding Directives

The structure of the paper is as follows: Section 2 summarizes, in a tabular form, the conclusions drawn from the past works on different success factors affecting ESCM. Key success factors for implementation in ESCM relevant to computer manufacturing industry have been identified and described in section 3. Section 4 presents the proposed ISM methodology which develops a structure of interrelationship among the identified critical success factors. Section 5 presents results and discussions and Section 6 discusses the conclusions drawn based on the ISM.

LITERATURE REVIEW

Identification of critical success factor reflects the organization's unique values and vision (Caralli and Richard, 2004). These key areas are unique to the organization and the industry in which it competes can be defined as the organization's success factors. Table 1 gives different success factors for ESCM activities from earlier studies.

Table 1. Success Factors for ESCM Identified by Previous Researchers

Important Factors for Implementation of ESCM	*Researcher*
Environmental procurement	Sanjeev Kumar et al (2012); Faith-Ell et al (2006); Yuelei Zhang et al(2012);Salam M(2008).
Environmental Accounting	Sanjeev Kumar et al (2012); Žaneta Stasiškienė(2001); Mehenna Yakhou (2004)
Environmental Design	(Ninlawan et al, 2010); Sanjeev Kumar et al (2012); Kee-hung Lai et al(2008);Rajesh Kumar et al(2012)
Environmental Manufacturing	Samir K. Srivastava(2007); Sanjeev Kumar et al (2012); L. H. Shih et al(2007); Namdev Vishal(2012); M. Atlas(1998); (Ninlawan et al, 2010)
Environmental Logistics	Ninlawan et al, 2010);Sanjeev Kumar et al (2012); R. Glenn Richey(2000); Pietro Evangelista et al(2010); Rodrigue, J-P et al. (2012)
Economic Performance	Sanjeev Kumar et al (2012); Zhu et al. (2007); Diane Holt et al (2005); Shih et al (2007); (Fuentes-Fuentes, et al., 2004).
Environmental Performance	Sanjeev Kumar et al (2012); Ninlawan et al, 2010);Shih et al (2007);Ru-Jen Lin(2011);
Management Vision and Direction	Hu et al (2010); Sanjeev Kumar et al (2012); Rajesh Kumar et al(2012); Shih et al (2007)
Life cycle Management	Hu et al (2010);Hsu et al (2008).
Customer Focus	Ninlawan et al, 2010);Sanjeev Kumar et al (2012);Luthra et al(2011)
Operational Performance	Maruf Hasan(2006); Sanjeev Kumar et al (2012); (Zhu et al., 2008a).
Supplier Management	Hu et al (2010);Hsu .C.W, 2008)
Performance of Marketing and Communication	Sanjeev Kumar et al (2012); Nimawat Dheeraj(2012)

IDENTIFIED SUCCESS FACTORS

Environmental Procurement: Environment procurement is a solution for environmentally concerned and economically conservative business, and a concept of acquiring a selection of products and services that minimizes environmental impact (Salam, 2008).The Environment procurement activities are (1) Purchase of materials that are either recyclable or reusable, or have already been recycled. (2) Conceive suppliers, certified with ISO-14001, OHSAS 18000 and or RoHS directives. (Ninlawan et al, 2010).

Environmental Accounting: Environmental Accounting is an essential component of ESCM. Environmental cost accounting directly places a cost on every environmental aspect, and determines the cost of all types of related action.(Mehenna Yakhou, 2004).It includes (1) Accounting the costs to the customers associated with the use and disposal of products. (2) Environmental costs associated with operation and processes (monitoring equipment, waste disposal etc). (Sanjeev Kumar et al, 2012).

Environmental Design: Environmental design or design for environment is a helpful, emerging tool to improve companies' environmental performance and help organizations close the supply chain loop by addressing product functionality while simultaneously minimizing life-cycle environmental impacts.(Zhu et al, 2008). The key aspects that taken into accounts are (1) Design of products for reduced consumptions of material /energy. (2) Design of products for reuse, recycle, recovery of material, component parts. (3) Design of products to avoid or reduce use of hazardous of products and/or their manufacturing process. (4) Design of product for support regulation. (5) Design the products to be easy set up for the users in the most energy saving way. (Ninlawan et al, 2010).

Environmental Manufacturing: Environmental manufacturing is defined as manufacturing processes which use inputs with relatively low environmental impacts, which are highly efficient, and which generate little or no waste or pollution (Atlas M, 1998).The key aspects of Environment manufacturing are (1) Reduce the amount of hazardous material that are mentioned in WEEE (Waste Electrical and Electronic Equipment) and RoHS (Restriction of Hazardous Substances Directive) used during the production of product. (2) Use of energy efficient technology in the production process. (Ninlawan et al, 2010) and (Sanjeev Kumar et al, 2012).

Environmental Logistics: Supply chain management practices and strategies that reduce the environmental and energy footprint of freight distribution. It focuses on material handling, waste management, packaging and transport. Rodrigue, J-P *et al.* (2012) The key aspects of Environment logistics are (1) Deliver the product directly to the user site (2) Use of alternate fuel vehicle to reduce the pollution (3) Distribute products together, rather than in smaller batches. (Ninlawan et al, 2010).

Economic Performance: Environmental protection activities can have a positive effect on a corporation's economic performance. The effects of ESCM on economic performance are (1) Efficient waste disposal methodology for reducing the cost. (2) Increase the market share growth because of energy efficient technology. (3) Reduction in cost of energy consumption. (Zhu and Sarkis, 2004) and (Fuentes-Fuentes, et al., 2004).

Environmental Performance: Environmental performance is defined as the environmental impact that the corporation's activity has on the natural surroundings (Sharma and Vredenburg, 1998). The effects of ESCM on economic performance are (1) Establish an environmental risk management system for ESCM (2) Environmental policy for ESCM. (3) Reduction of air emission (4) Reduction of waste water. (5) Reduction of solid wastes (6) Decrease of frequency for environmental accidents (7) Decrease of consumption for hazardous/harmful/toxic materials. (Ninlawan et al, 2010).

Management Vision and Direction: Management vision and Direction is an essential parameter for implementing ESCM in a corporation. The key aspects of management vision are (1) Top management support (2) Cross-functional cooperation for environmental improvements. (3) Effective communication platform within companies and with the suppliers. (4) Manpower Involvement (5) Effective communication platform within companies and with suppliers. (Hu et al, 2010)

Life Cycle Management: This parameter will help to identify the environmental impact throughout the life cycle of the product. The key factors of Life Cycle Management (LCM) on ESCM are (1) Applying life cycle Assessment to carry out eco-report (2) Establish an environmental database of products. (Hu etal. 2010).

Customer Focus: Customer demands have now become the most important type of external pressure (Doonan, et al., 2005).To obtain more sustainable solutions, the environmental properties of products and services must meet customer requirements (Zhu and Sarkis, 2006).The key factors that need the cooperation from customer are (1) Cooperation with customers for eco-design (2) Cooperation with customers for cleaner production (3) Cooperation with customers for Environment packaging. (Ninlawan et al, 2010).

Operational Performance: Operational performance relates to the manufacturing plant's capabilities to more efficiently produce and deliver products to customers (Zhu et al., 2008a).The key benefits of operational performance are (1) Cost saving and increased efficiency (2) Product quality improvement (3) Reduced lead times. (Sanjeev Kumar et al , 2012).

Supplier Management: Suppliers contribute to the overall performance of a supply chain, and poor supplier performance affects the performance of the whole chain (Sarkar and Mohapatra, 2006). Supplier–manufacturer relationships are considered important in developing a sustainable competitive advantage for the manufacturer (Sheth and Sharma, 1997); Cannon and Homburg, 2001). Screening of suppliers for environmental performance has now become a key deciding factor in many organizations (Clark, 1999).The key factors that taken into consideration are (1) Environmental auditing for suppliers, (2) Supplier environment questionnaire, (3) Requesting compliance statement, (4) Asking for product testing report, (5)Demanding bill of material.(Hu et al, 2010).

Performance of Marketing and Communication: The performance of marketing and communication gives a huge boost to an organization. The benefits are (1) Export demand (2) Improve sales to foreign customers (3) Country's environmental awareness (4) Establishing company's eco-friendly image. (Sanjeev Kumar et al., 2012) and (Nimawat Dheeraj, 2012).

THE PROPOSED ISM METHODOLOGY

Identification of the structure within a complex system is of great value in dealing efficiently and effectively with the system and better decision making. Waller (1983), Sage (1977) and Warfield (1973a) have described Interpretive Structural Modelling (ISM) as context free in that it can be used in any complex situation, irrespective of the content of the situation, provided that a set of elements can be identified and an appropriate contextual relation defined.

Furthermore, the elements may be qualitative or quantitative, permitting items to be included which are not measurable on anything other than ordinal scales of measurement. In this sense ISM is much more flexible than many conventional quantitative modelling approaches which require variables to be measurable on ratio scales. ISM thus offers a qualitative modelling language for structuring complexity and enables a group of users to map their thinking on an issue by building an agreed structural model through expert opinion.

13 factors have been identified by early literature review and it is essential to develop a structure of interrelationship among the identified critical success factor using an interpretive structural model.

The ISM methodology consists of the following important steps.

(a) Development of Structural Self-Interaction Matrix

(b) Construction of Reachability matrix.

(c) Carrying out Level partitions.

(d) Obtaining Classification of factors

(e) Formation of Interpretive Structural Model.

Contextual Relationships Among Main Influence Factors

For the sake of analyzing the main influence factors, here a contextual relationship of "leads to" is chosen. For developing the contextual relationships among the main influence factors, the factors affecting ESCM of computer manufacturing industries are analyzed on the basis of expert opinion.

For developing contextual relationships among variables, the opinion of total 17 experts, thirteen from nine different computers manufacturing industries and four from academia from SCM area have been taken. For expressing the relationship between different key success factors, four symbols are used to denote the direction of relationship between parameters i and j (here i < i). (1) A: parameter j will lead to i; (2) V: parameter i will lead to j; (3) X: parameters i and j will lead to each other; (4) O: parameters i and j are unrelated. Based on the contextual relationships, the Structural Self Interaction Matrix (SSIM) is developed in Table 2.

Table 2. Structural Self Interaction Matrix

SL.NO.	Factors for implementing GSCM	Notation	EPR	EA	ED	EM	EL	EP	EVP	MVD	LCM	CF	OP	SM	PMC
1	Environmenatal Procurement	EPR	1	A	X	V	X	V	A	A	A	A	V	A	V
2	Environmental Accounting	EA		1	V	V	V	V	V	A	O	A	V	O	V
3	Environmental Design	ED			1	V	X	V	A	A	A	A	V	A	V
4	Environmental Manufacturing	EM				1	A	V	A	A	A	A	V	A	V
5	Environmental Logistics	EL					1	V	A	A	A	A	V	A	V
6	Economic Performance	EP						1	A	A	A	A	A	A	V
7	Environmental Performance	EVP							1	A	A	A	V	A	V
8	Management Vision and Direction	MVD								1	V	X	V	V	V
9	Life Cycle Management	LCM									1	A	V	O	V
10	Customer Focus	CF										1	V	V	V
11	Operational Performance	OP											1	A	V
12	Supplier Management	SM												1	V
13	Performance of Marketing and Communication	PMC													1

Construction of Reachability Matrix

The SS1M has been converted into a binary matrix, called the initial reachability matrix by substituting A, V, X, O by 1 and 0. The substitution of 1s and 0s are as per the following rules:

1. If the (i, j) entry in the SSIM is V, the (i, j) entry in the reachability matrix becomes 1 and the (j, i) entry becomes 0.
2. If the (i, j) entry in the SSIM is A, the (i, j) entry in the reachability matrix becomes 0 and the (j, i) entry becomes 1.
3. If the (i, j) entry in the SSIM is X, the (i, j) entry in the reachability matrix becomes 1 and the (j, i) entry also becomes 1.
4. If the (i, j) entry in the SSIM is O, the (i, j) entry in the reachability matrix becomes 0 and the (j, i) entry also becomes 0.

The reachability matrix for the success factors is shown in Table 3, developed by using the above rules.

Table 3. Reachability Matrix

SL.NO.	Factors for implementing GSCM	Notation	EPR	EA	ED	EM	EL	EP	EVP	MVD	LCM	CF	OP	SM	PMC	Driving Power
1	Environmental Procurement	EPR	1	0	1	1	1	1	0	0	0	0	1	0	1	7
2	Environmental Accounting	EA	1	1	1	1	1	1	1	0	0	0	1	0	1	9
3	Environmental Design	ED	1	0	1	1	1	1	0	0	0	0	1	0	1	7
4	Environmental Manufacturing	EM	0	0	0	1	0	1	0	0	0	0	1	0	1	4
5	Environmental Logistics	EL	1	0	1	1	1	1	0	0	0	0	1	0	1	7
6	Economic Performance	EP	0	0	0	0	0	1	0	0	0	0	0	0	1	2
7	Environmental Performance	EVP	1	0	1	1	1	1	1	0	0	0	1	0	1	8
8	Management Vision and Direction	MVD	1	1	1	1	1	1	1	1	1	1	1	1	1	13
9	Life Cycle Management	LCM	1	0	1	1	1	1	1	0	1	0	1	0	1	9
10	Customer Focus	CF	1	1	1	1	1	1	1	1	1	1	1	1	1	13
11	Operational Performance	OP	0	0	0	0	0	1	0	0	0	0	1	0	1	3
12	Supplier Management	SM	1	0	1	1	1	1	1	0	0	0	1	1	1	9
13	Performance of Marketing and Communication	PMC	0	0	0	0	0	0	0	0	0	0	0	0	1	1
Depedence Power			9	3	9	10	9	12	6	2	3	2	11	3	13	

Table 3 also shows the driving power and dependence of each variable is also shown. Driving power for each variable is the total number of variables (including itself), which it may help to achieve. On the other hand, dependence is the total number of variables (including itself), which may help in achieving it. These driving power and dependencies will be later used in classification of variables into the four groups: autonomous; dependent; linkage; and driver variables (independent).

Carrying out Level partitions

From the final reachability matrix (matrix M), the reachability set, the antecedent set and the intersection set for each factor can be found. The factor for which the reachability and intersection sets are the same is the top-level factor. Once the top-level factor is found, it should be separated out from the other factors.

After that, the next level of factor is identified by the same process. These identified levels help in building the diagraph and final model. In Table 4,

it is shown that the overall performance improvement of the ESCM of computer manufacturing companies is found at level 1. So it would be positioned at the top of ISM hierarchy. This iteration is repeated till the levels of each factor are found out as shown in Table 4 to Table 11. The identified levels help in building the final model of ISM.

Table 4. Iteration 1

Factor	Reachability set	Antecedent Set	Intersection Set	Level
1	1,3,4,5,6,11,13	1,2,3,5,7,8,9,10,12	1,3,5	
2	1,2,3,4,5,6,7,11,13	2,8,10	2	
3	1,3,4,5,6,11,13	1,2,3,5,7,8,9,10,12	1,3,5	
4	4,6,11,13	1,2,3,4,5,7,8,9,10,12	4	
5	1,3,4,5,6,11,13	1,2,3,5,7,8,9,10,12	1,3,5	
6	6,13	1,2,3,4,5,6,7,8,9,10,11,12	6	
7	1,3,4,5,6,7,11,13	2,7,8,9,10,12	7	
8	1,2,3,4,5,6,7,8,9,10,11,12,13	8,10	8,10	
9	1,3,4,5,6,7,9,11,13	8,9,10	9	
10	1,2,3,4,5,6,7,8,9,10,11,12,13	8,10	8,10	
11	6,11,13	1,2,3,4,5,7,8,9,10,11,12	11	
12	1,3,4,5,6,7,11,12,13	1,8,10,12	1,12	
13	13	1,2,3,4,5,6,7,8,9,10,11,12,13	13	1

Table 5. Iteration 2

Factor	Reachability set	Antecedent Set	Intersection Set	Level
1	1,3,4,5,6,11	1,2,3,5,7,8,9,10,12	1,3,5	
2	1,2,3,4,5,6,7,11	2,8,10	2	
3	1,3,4,5,6,11	1,2,3,5,7,8,9,10,12	1,3,5	
4	4,6,11	1,2,3,4,5,7,8,9,10,12	4	
5	1,3,4,5,6,11	1,2,3,5,7,8,9,10,12	1,3,5	
6	6	1,2,3,4,5,6,7,8,9,10,11,12	6	2
7	1,3,4,5,6,7,11	2,7,8,9,10,12	7	
8	1,2,3,4,5,6,7,8,9,10,11,12	8,10	8,10	
9	1,3,4,5,6,7,9,11	8,9,10	9	
10	1,2,3,4,5,6,7,8,9,10,11,12	8,10	8,10	
11	6,11	1,2,3,4,5,7,8,9,10,11,12	11	
12	1,3,4,5,6,7,11,12	1,8,10,12	1,12	

Table 6. Iteration 3

Factor	Reachability set	Antecedent Set	Intersection Set	Level
1	1,3,4,5,11	1,2,3,5,7,8,9,10,12	1,3,5	
2	1,2,3,4,5,7,11	2,8,10	2	
3	1,3,4,5,11	1,2,3,5,7,8,9,10,12	1,3,5	
4	4,11	1,2,3,4,5,7,8,9,10,12	4	
5	1,3,4,5,11	1,2,3,5,7,8,9,10,12	1,3,5	
7	1,3,4,5,7,11	2,7,8,9,10,12	7	
8	1,2,3,4,5,7,8,9,10,11,12	8,10	8,10	
9	1,3,4,5,7,9,11	8,9,10	9	
10	1,2,3,4,5,7,8,9,10,11,12	8,10	8,10	
11	11	1,2,3,4,5,7,8,9,10,11,12	11	3
12	1,3,4,5,7,11,12	1,8,10,12	1,12	

Table 7. Iteration 4

Factor	Reachability set	Antecedent Set	Intersection Set	Level
1	1,3,4,5	1,2,3,5,7,8,9,10,12	1,3,5	
2	1,2,3,4,5,7	2,8,10	2	
3	1,3,4,5	1,2,3,5,7,8,9,10,12	1,3,5	
4	4	1,2,3,4,5,7,8,9,10,12	4	4
5	1,3,4,5	1,2,3,5,7,8,9,10,12	1,3,5	
7	1,3,4,5,7	2,7,8,9,10,12	7	
8	1,2,3,4,5,7,8,9,10,12	8,10	8,10	
9	1,3,4,5,7,9	8,9,10	9	
10	1,2,3,4,5,7,8,9,10,12	8,10	8,10	
12	1,3,4,5,7,12	1,8,10,12	1,12	

Table 8. Iteration 5

Factor	Reachability set	Antecedent Set	Intersection Set	Level
1	1,3,5	1,2,3,5,7,8,9,10,12	1,3,5	5
2	1,2,3,5,7	2,8,10	2	
3	1,3,5	1,2,3,5,7,8,9,10,12	1,3,5	5
5	1,3,5	1,2,3,5,7,8,9,10,12	1,3,5	5
7	1,3,5,7	2,7,8,9,10,12	7	
8	1,2,3,5,7,8,9,10,12	8,10	8,10	
9	1,3,5,7,9	8,9,10	9	
10	1,2,3,5,7,8,9,10,12	8,10	8,10	
12	1,3,5,7,12	1,8,10,12	1,12	

Table 9. Iteration 6

Factor	Reachability set	Antecedent Set	Intersection Set	Level
2	2,7	2,8,10	2	
7	7	2,7,8,9,10,12	7	6
8	2,7,8,9,10,12	8,10	8,10	
9	7,9	8,9,10	9	
10	2,7,8,9,10,12	8,10	8,10	
12	7,12	1,8,10,12	12	

Table 10. Iteration 7

Factor	Reachability set	Antecedent Set	Intersection Set	Level
2	2	2,8,10	2	7
8	2,8,9,10,12	8,10	8,10	
9	9	8,9,10	9	7
10	2,8,9,10,12	8,10	8,10	
12	12	1,8,10,12	12	7

Table 11. Iteration 8

Factor	Reachability set	Antecedent Set	Intersection Set	Level
8	8,10	8,10	8,10	8
10	8,10	8,10	8,10	8

CLASSIFICATION OF FACTORS

The success factors defined and described earlier are classified into four clusters as shown in Figure 2.

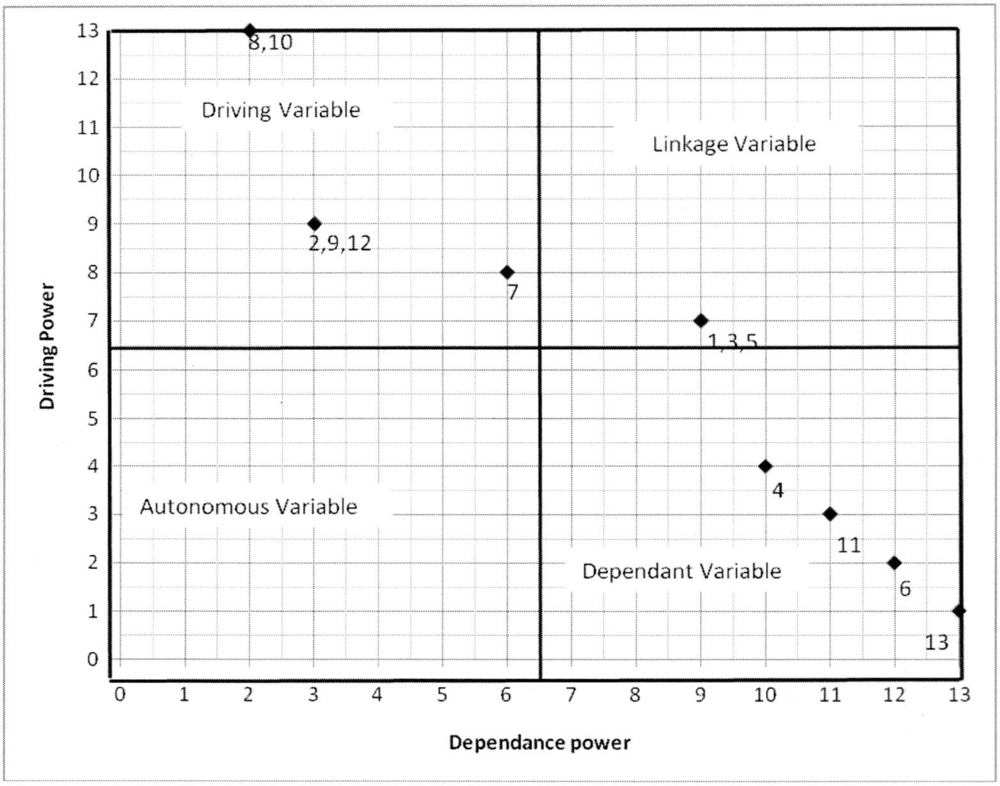

Fig. 2. Cluster of Factors for Implementing ESCM in Indian Computer Manufacturing Industries

The first cluster consists of the "autonomous factors" that have weak driving power and weak dependence. These factors are relatively disconnected from the system, with which they have only few links, which may not be strong. The "dependent factors" constitute the second cluster which has weak driving power but strong dependence. Third cluster has the "linkage factors" that have strong driving power and strong dependence. Fourth cluster includes the "independent factors" having strong driving power but weak dependence. The driving power and dependence of each of these factors are shown in Table 3.

In Table 3, an entry of "1" added along the columns and rows indicates the dependence and driving power, respectively. Subsequently, the driver power-dependence diagram is constructed as shown in Figure 2. For illustration, the factor 4 having a driving power of 4 and dependence of 10 is positioned at a place corresponding to driving power of 4 and dependency of 10 in Figure 2. Similarly all other factors considered in this study are positioned on different quadrants depending on their driving power and dependency.

Formation of Interpretive Structural Model

The interpretive structural model is generated by means of vertices or nodes and lines of edges from the final reachability matrix (Table 3). If there is a relationship between factors i and j, this is shown by an arrow which points from I to j. This graph is called a directed graph or digraph. After removing the transitivities, the digraph is finally converted into ISM as shown in Figure 3.The interpretive structural model represents the structural relationship among the different success factors.

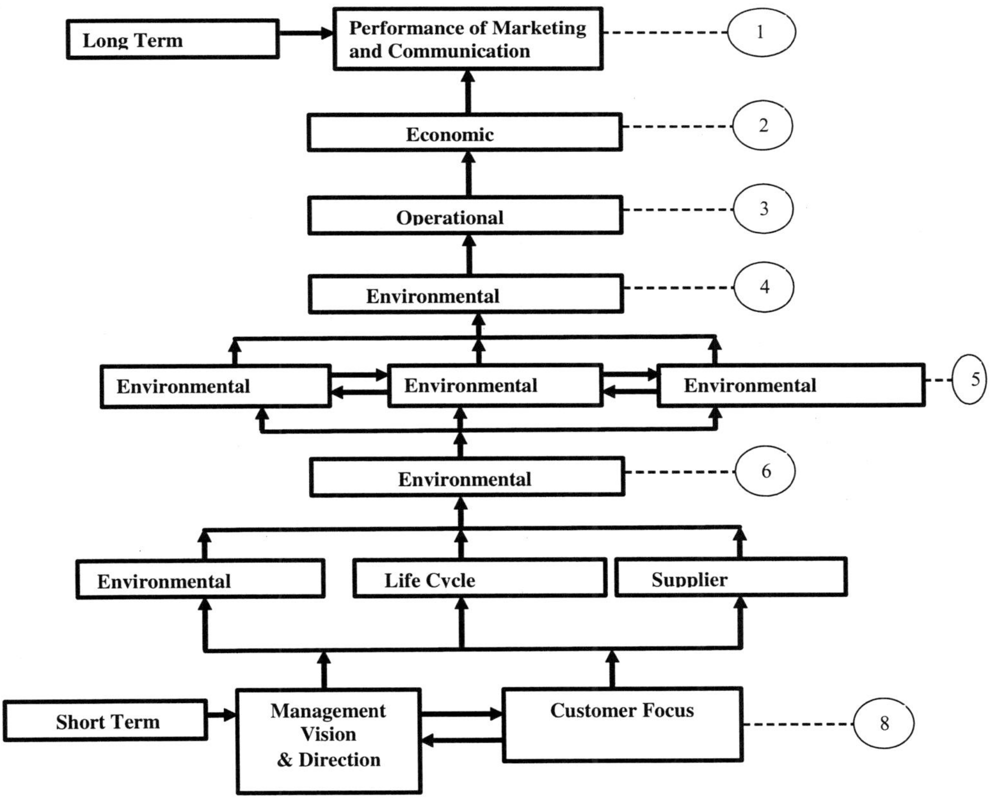

Fig. 3. ISM Model of Factors for Implementing ESCM in Indian Computer Manufacturing Industries

RESULTS AND DISCUSSIONS

Eco-friendly supply chain management (ESCM) performance of manufacturing organizations in India has the potential for improving their performance dramatically and contributes to the local as well as global society. For improving the performance of ESCM of manufacturing organizations in India, the managers of computer manufacturing industries need to identify critical factors, so that management may effectively incorporate these factors at their organizational level. Further, these factors should be structured to find out the factors which are prerequisite for the success and which facilitates the achievement of others. The analysis of interaction among the factors is provided by ISM. It identifies the hierarchy of actions to be taken by management in order to improve the performance of their organization. The driver power-dependence matrix (Figure 2) gives some valuable insights about the relative importance and interdependencies among success factors. Major findings of this study are as follows:

(i) There is no autonomous factor. Autonomous factors generally appear as weak driver as well as weak dependant. These factors do not have much influence on the other factors of the system. There are relatively disconnected from the system and do not have influence on other variables and have only few links, which may not be strong.

(ii) Four factors fall under the dependent category. These are performance of marketing and communication, economic performance, operational performance, and Environment manufacturing. These factors are weak drivers and strongly dependent on other factors. They are seen at the top of ISM hierarchy (Figure 3). These factors represent desired objectives for any organization and are classified as dependant factors. The results focus that performance of marketing and communication, economic performance, operational performance, and Environment manufacturings are the long-term objectives of ESCM in computer manufacturing industries.

(iii) Linkage factor have strong driving power and strong dependence. These factors are unstable due to the fact that any change occurring to them will have an effect on others and also a feedback on themselves. Thus it can be inferred that among all the thirteen variables chosen in this study, three variables are unstable. These variables are Environment design, Environment procurement, and Environment logistics. Therefore the managers should focus these factors to get the consistency performance of ESCM.

(iv) Seven factors are termed as drivers, such as management vision and direction, customer focus, suppler management, life cycle assessment, environmental accounting, and environmental performance. These factors are at the bottom of the model having strong driving power. These factors will help organizations to achieve their desired objectives and are classified as independent factors or drivers. The factors with higher driving powers are more of the strategic orientation. Thus, performance can be improved by continuously improving the driving factors. The results represent that management vision and direction and customer focus are the most important success factors and has a great influence on the other success factors. Though management vision and direction and customer focus are the short-term objectives, Indian computer manufacturing industries should be equipped with proper management strategy to achieve the long-term objective such as performance of marketing and communication of ESCM in most efficient way within a quick time frame.

CONCLUSIONS

Although managers of Indian computer manufacturing industries are aware of various success factors, a systematic approach is required for identifying key success factors, and as these factors may have complex interrelation between them for analyzing ESCM performance in computer manufacturing industries, it is essential that such an approach is in place. The hierarchy based ISM further defines those factors which are really critical and need more focus on the root causes of the success. This has enormous feasibility of strategic decision for ESCM policy formulation for the organization considered for study. Therefore, when actualizing performance of ESCM in manufacturing firms, the SCM manager should pay more attention to these thirteen main critical factors and their relationships and interaction. In addition to that the proposed ISM model acts as good guideline in order to improve the performance of the ESCM in manufacturing organizations in India.

REFERENCES

[1] A. A., Hervani, M. M., Helms, J., Sarkis, (2005),*"Performance measurement for green supply chain management"*, Benchmarking: An International Journal, Vol. 12 Iss: 4 pp. 330 – 353.

[2] A., Hu, C., Hsu, (2010*),"Critical factors for implementing green supply chain management practice: An empirical study of electrical and electronics industries in Taiwan"*, Management Research Review, Vol. 33 Iss: 6 pp. 586 – 608.

[3] A., Sarkar, P.K.J., Mohapatra, (2006*) "Evaluation of supplier capability and performance: A method for supply base reduction"*, J. Purch. Supply Manage., 12, p.148-163.

[4] Caralli, Richard, (2004), "The Critical Success Factor Method", *Carnegie-Mellon SEI*

[5] C., Ninlawan, P., Seksan, K., Tossapol, and W., Pilada (2010*)"The Implementation of Green Supply Chain Management Practices in Electronics Industry"* Proceedings of International Multiconference of Engineers and Computer Scientists Vol. III, IMECS,Hong Kong.

[6] D., Clark, (1999). *What drives companies to seek ISO 14000 certification?* Pollut. Eng., 14-15.

[7] FAITH-ELL, C. (2005) *The Application of Environmental Requirements in Procurement of Road Maintenance in Sweden.* Land and Water Resources Engineering. Stockholm, Royal Institute of Technology.

[8] G., Kannan, P., Sasikumar, K., Devika (2010), *"A genetic algorithm approach for solving a closed loop supply chain model: A case of battery recycling"*, Applied Mathematical Modeling, volume 34, issue 3, pp655-670.

[9] Handfield, R. B., Nichols, E. L. (1999): *Introduction to Supply Chain Management*, New Jersey: Prentice-Hall.

[10] H., Wang, S.M., Gupta,(2009) Green supply chain Management .

[11] J., Doonan, P., Lanoie, B., Laplante, (2005) *"Analysis determinants of environmental performance in the Canadian pulp and paper industry: an assessment from inside the industry"*, Ecol. Econ., 55, 73-84.

[12] J.N., Sheth, A., Sharma, (1997) *Supplier relationships*, Ind. Market. Manage., 26, p.91-100.

[13] J.P., Cannon, C., Homburg (2001). *Buyers–supplier relationships and customer firm costs. J. Marketing,* 65(1), p.29-43.

[14] J., Rodrigue, B., Slack, C., Comtois (2012) *The Geography of Transport Systems*, Department of Global Studies & Geography, Hofstra University.

[15] Kenneth W. Green Jr, Pamela J. Zelbst, Jeramy Meacham, Vikram S. Bhadauria, (2012*), "Green supply chain management practices: impact on performance"*, Supply Chain Management: An International Journal, Vol. 17 Iss: 3 pp. 290 – 305.

[16] M., Atlas, and R., Florida,(1998) *"Green manufacturing,"* Handbook of Technology Management.

[17] M., Chien; L., Shih (2007*) "An empirical study of the implementation of green supply chain management practices in the electrical and electronic industry and their relation to organizational performances"* Int. J. Environ. Sci. Tech., ISSN: 1735-1472, 4 (3): 383-394.

[18] M.M., Fuentes-Fuentes, C.A., Albacete-Saez, F.J., Llorens-Montes, (2004), *"The impact of environmental characteristics on TQM principles and organizational performance"* Int. J.Manage. Sci., 32, 425-442.

[19] M.T., Kangangi, *"Green Supply chain Implementation: Best Practices and Challenges"*, School of Business, University of Nairobi.

[20] M.A. Salam (2008) *"Green procurement adoption in manufacturing supply chain"* Proceedings of the 9th Asia Pacific Industrial Engineering & Management Systems Conference (APIEMS2008), Indonesia, pp.1253-1260.

[21] M., Yakhou, V., Drowsier (2004). *"ENVIRONMENTAL ACCOUNTING: AN ESSENTIAL COMPONENT OF BUSINESS STRATEGY"* Business Strategy and the Environment Bus. Strat. Env. 13, p.65–77.

[22] N., Dheeraj, N., Vishal (2012) *"An Overview of Green Supply Chain Management in India"* Research Journal of Recent Sciences, ISSN 2277-2502 Vol. 1(6), p.77-82.

[23] Q., Zhu, J., Sarkis, K., Lai, (2001) *Green supply chain management implications for "closing the loop"*Transportation Research Part E 44, p 1–18.

[24] Q., Zhu, J., Sarkis,(2004) *"Relationships between operational practices and performance among early adopters of green supply chain management practices in Chinese manufacturing enterprises"* Journal of Operations Management, 22: 265-289.

[25] Q., Zhu, J., Sarkis, (2006) *"An inter-sectoral comparison of green supply chain management in China: Drivers and practices"*, J. Clean. Prod., 14, 472-486.

[26] Q., Zhu, J., Sarkis, and K., Lai (2008a), *"Conrmation of a measurement model for green supply chain management practices implementation"*, International Journal of Production Economics, Vol. 111 No. 2, pp. 261-73.

[27] R., Kumar, R., Chandrakar, (2012) *"Overview of Green Supply Chain Management: Operation and Environmental Impact at Different Stages of the Supply Chain"* International Journal of Engineering and Advanced Technology (IJEAT) Volume-1, Issue-3, ISSN: 2249 – 8958.

[28] Sage,A.P., 1977, Interpretive structural modeling. In Methodology for Large Scale System, *McGraw-Hill*, New York, 91-164.

[29] S., Kumar, S., Chattopadhyaya, V., Sharma (2012) *"Green Supply chain Management: A case study from Indian Electrical and Electronics Industry"* International Journal of Soft Computing and Engineering (IJSCE) Volume-1, Issue-6, ISSN: 2231-2307.

[30] S., Sharma, H., Vredenburg, (1998), *"Proactive corporate environmental strategy and the development of competitively valuable organizational capabilities"* Strategic Manage. J. 19 (8), 729-753.

[31] S., Srivastava, (2007) *"Green supply-chain management: A state-of the-art literature review"* International Journal of Management Reviews Volume 9 Issue 1 pp. 53–80.

[32] Walter, R. 1, 1980, Contextual relations and mathematical relations in interpretive structural modeling, *IEEE Trans Syst. Man. Cybern*, SMC-10, 143-145.

[33] Warfield, J.N., 1973a, Binary matrices in system modeling, *IEEE Trans. Syst. Man. Cybern.*, SMC-3,441-449.

[34] W., Yan, Y., Zhang (2012*)"Research on factors of green purchasing practices of Chinese"* E3 Journal of Business Management and Economics Vol. 3(5). pp. 222-231.

[35] Ž., Stasiðkienë, (2001) *"Environmental Accounting in Lithuanian Industry: Analysis of Necessity, Possibilities and Perspectives"* Environmental research, engineering and management, No.2 (16), P.25-31.

A Study to Assess Impact of Mergers and Acquisitions on Organizational Culture and Development

Bhupesh Malhotra and Vandana Sharma

Department of Management, Birla Institute of Technology, Ranchi, Mesra

ABSTRACT

Whenever a merger or any acquisition is announced in any industry and in any geography of the world, the first question that comes to mind whether it the economists or industry specialist or the employees themselves – is how much is the financial gain?

There is no or little argument on the impact on the organizational culture and development perspective that would also be changing with any merger or acquisition. Companies do pay considerable attention to financial and strategic issues during mergers and acquisitions, but they frequently neglect human resource issues. The role of people and the organizational cultures is often placed in a marginal position, and most of the energy is invested in strategic and financial planning. It will be argued here that problems of human resources and organizational cultures should, however, be given a high priority, along with strategic issues, to increase the likelihood of a successful combination. Literature review on this topic along with a small sample study is undertaken to assess the impact.

INTRODUCTION

It is widely known that roughly half of all the mergers and acquisitions (M&A) fail to create the shareholder value and that about one quarter actually destroy it. It is also no secret that there are tried and tested methodologies for successfully integrating companies. So why do so many deals – especially those that appear to offer substantial cost and revenue synergies – produce such disappointing results?

There are numerous research studies to indicate that the most common reason why organizational mergers so often fail is lack of attention by the top leaders to the cultural dynamics involved in this change such as relationships, identity, roles of the senior team of future structures. Culture, learned, shared and tacit assumptions so easy to refer to but so difficult to measure cannot be painted on after the event. Once the operational plans are put into place and rolled out, it is thereafter so often assumed that the people and the culture will follow, and the old cultures will blend together with little effort or attention. This is rarely the case.

Definition

Organizational culture tends to be unique to a particular organization, composed of an objective and subjective dimension and concerned with tradition and the nature of shared beliefs and expectations about organizational life (Buono et al., 1985, p.482)

Organizational Culture

Differences in the two organizational cultures involved in a merger or acquisition and how they are managed are crucial to the success or failure of the process. An organizational culture is comprised of 'the patterns of shared beliefs and values that give the members of an institution meaning, and provide them with the rules for behavior in their organization' (Davis 1994, 1). The culture is not generally recognized within organizations, because 'basic assumptions and preferences guiding thought and action tend to operate at a preconscious level' (Sathe 1985, 30). Nevertheless, this preconscious level affects many areas within the organization, including, 'performance, cooperation, decision making, control, communication, commitment, perception and justification of behavior' (31).

Organization culture is described in the literature as a typical profile of a group of people with regard to standards, values, behavior and institutions. If an organization decides to merge with another organization or takes it over, then it has to deal with a difference in organizational culture. This difference in culture can lead to consistent decrease in performance of both companies' employees after the merger (Weber & Camrer, 1996).

Strong versus Weak Cultures

Three elements determine the strength of corporate culture:

1. The number of shared beliefs, values, and assumptions. The higher the number of shared assumptions, the 'thicker' the culture. In 'thin' cultures, there are few commonly held assumptions and values.
2. The number of employees who accept, reject, or share in the basic beliefs, values, and assumptions. If employee acceptance is high, a strong corporate culture will emerge.
3. The higher the number of shared beliefs, values and assumptions, the stronger the culture of the organization. (Nahavandi and Malekzadeh 1993, 19)

Organizational culture can be seen as a lasting and only gradually changing characteristic of an organization and refers to implicit aspects of an organization. It reflects core values that are cherished and assumptions in the organization that are often not under discussion. It is recognized by the dominant leadership styles, language and symbols, procedures and fixed rules, and definitions of success that makes an organization unique (Cameron & Quinn, 1999). Organizational culture develops itself through the years and it is created and maintained by the owners of the company (Cameron & Quinn, 1999). If a new employee enters the organization he or she immediately gets aware of the organizational culture, which happens consciously as well as unconsciously. Also, the country of origin determines the culture. The norms and values of a nation can also have an influence on the culture of each and every organization operating or located within it. "Culture refers to the norms, values and beliefs the members of an organization maintain about the purpose of work and how they are expected to go about doing the work" (Tentenbaum, 1999 p.5). The norms and values of a country can determine what kind of Organizational Culture attitudes and behavior are appropriate or acceptable. Likewise, in an organization the norms and values of a company determine the way people work together.

EMPIRICAL EVIDENCES OF ORGANIZATION CULTURE:

Roger Harrison has Defined four Main Types of Organizational Culture, this is Listed Below

Power Cultures	In organizations with power cultures, power rests either with the president, the founder, or a small core group of key managers. This type of culture is most common in small organizations. Employees are motivated by feelings of loyalty towards the owner or their supervisor; these types of organizations foster a sense of tradition in both the physical and spiritual sense. Power cultures tend to have inequitable compensation systems and other benefits based on favoritism and loyalty, as well as performance.
Role Cultures	Role cultures are highly autocratic. There is a clear division of labor, and authority figures are clearly defined. Rules and procedures are also clearly defined, and a good employee is one who abides by them. Organizational power is defined by position and status. These organizations respond slowly to change; they are predictable and risk averse. This type of culture thrives in industries which employ mass production techniques, in automobile manufacturing, for example.
Task/Achievement Cultures	Task/achievement cultures emphasize accomplishment of the task; research and development is an example. The employees usually work in teams, and the emphasis is on what is achieved rather than how it is achieved. Employees are flexible, creative, and highly autonomous.
Person/Support Cultures	Organizations with a person/support culture have minimal structure and serve to nurture personal growth and development. They are egalitarian in principle, and decision making is conducted on a shared collective basis. This type of culture is rarely found in profit making corporations; it is more typical of professional partnerships such as law firms.

Source: Types of Organizational Cultures, Roger Harrison (Cartwright and Cooper 1992, 58-68).

Dan Archer has Listed Common Cultural Challenges Faced by Leaders During a Merger or Acquisition as below

Impatience	Organizational cultures are resistant to change for numerous reasons. The legacy of their history and technologies, not to mention the stories, heroes and symbols of the past mean that programmes premised upon the notion that the past can be erased inevitably fail. An organization's history cannot be erased. A good change programme will acknowledge this, and build upon it.
The effects of conflict within the senior leadership group	One of the most common causes of disillusionment amongst subordinates is conflict within the senior leadership team, not least because it is rarely possible to hide this from others.
Rivalries, fiefdoms and silos	Existing tensions between units and departments can often be aggravated by an acquisition. Ignoring these or hoping that they will be addressed by an assertive top down approach rarely works.
Preaching the new but rewarding the old	Organizations continuing to promote people who display 'old' cultural values long after investing significant time and effort in conveying a new cultural message
Organizational Disillusionment	The stronger the hope generated at the start, the stronger the disillusionment if leaders let them down.
Plans for change are too static and inflexible	This means that strategies inevitably need to constantly evolve to meet the demands of the external context.
Blind faith in a formula	Any prescription that advocates a step-by-step approach without recognizing the complexity of organizational behavior and the uniqueness of each organization is destined to failure.

Source: Archer, Dan (October 2007), "Mergers and acquisitions: change, culture and the "leaderful" organization", Leadership Trust, UK.

EXPERT OPINION ON IMPACT OF MERGER AND ORGANIZATION ON ORGANIZATION CULTURE AND DEVELOPMENT

An organization culture (OC) cannot be drafted as a standard operating procedure in a manufacturing company or as a process document. There is no procedure to list what follows what, which action has what reaction in an organization. It is like air, you can't see – but feel it.

Organization culture is something that people make it and carry it on. Typically the action and policy maker's decision trickle it down to the rest of the organization.

Organization culture can differ by regions, demographics, average age of the people working, time of people spent in the same organization and definitely industry scenarios. It is not common. OC and development can be different in the same industry as well. Some elements can be common but not all. A marketing company, a manufacturing company, a BPO, IT and even retail – they all have it differently.

On the other hand even a BPO setup in the same state of a country, like Maharashtra – two cities namely Mumbai & Pune will have different kind of culture.

Different components of culture & development:

- Policies of HR
- Future prospects
- Respect of junior staff
- Training
- Compensation policy
- Openness
- Honesty

Some organizations have the culture of openness and they encourage people to come forward and discuss things/issues, typically in organizations having total workforce strength of not more than 300 to 400 people and primarily in the same location. Comparatively to Government organizations wherein there are lots of procedural formalities to be completed for any task, a very big hierarchy and probably the culture of high regards and respect at every level. This is the culture which governmental organizations have established.

Another example being of software/ITES wherein two broad categories of BPO and IT companies – the culture differs a lot. In BPO – a lot of young crowd works – typical average age of the employee is anywhere in between 21 to 30yrs.

There is a lot of energy and fun element. People are dressed casually, work in shifts and have a lighter attitude. In fact there are BPO's wherein people listen to music in the background to create a good working atmosphere. Lot of periodic rewards is given to encourage employee's productivity. Even the food served in the cafeteria comprises of fast food items rather than traditional meals. Parties and get together are organized every month, birthdays are celebrated.

In the organization itself arrangements are made for their further studies (like MBA courses), concierge services to do odd jobs like bill payments, travel booking etc. The culture is also to have small teams and produce results.

But quite opposite in IT – where typically software engineers, MBA and experienced people are recruited. The culture is vey client oriented that requires proper discipline. The average age of employees is between 21 to 50yrs and that makes a lot of difference. People have to be more formal in their approach, by not only being presentable but having presentable skills that looks promising in front of the client. The culture is more formal.

Impact of Merger on Culture

In the world where M&A has become very common, people are also becoming very adaptive to this change in culture. With even tier 2 cities in India being exposed to IT industries, BPO's and even large banks and manufacturing units setting up their plants – more and more people are being exposed to this fact of M&A.

As mentioned above the variety of culture in existence and is being carried out in different forms – definitely there is impact on OC and development.

Example: If company "A" (employee strength of over 1 Lakh employees) acquires company "B" (employee strength of 300 employees) – considering "B" is a smaller organization as compared to "A" – generally the parent company has all head of departments and "B" has to obey the instructions.

Culture will not change as on day 1 of the merger. It is not like signing the contract copy with an effective date. It takes time – typically one full calendar year to experience and react to changes. When two companies merge, three things can happen: a complete new culture emerges; the organizational culture of the most dominant organization overrules the organizational culture of the less dominant counterpart; or the new organization includes best of both worlds, in other words the cultures merge nicely (Guns, 2006).

Some examples of organizational culture and development changes / pointers:

- Communication: In the changed scenario it is just done directly through an email – however earlier people were used to listen it from the director in person. Obviously the larger the organization, it is easier to communicate through an email to all at one go.
- Opportunities were given to people for handling cross functional roles irrespective of the actual knowledge but based on the capability – but now only well trained & experienced people are considered – primarily because of the volume of work and the credibility & buy in factor of the client.
- Autocratic nature of the seniors / bosses as against the open nature.
- Money being spent on team get-together and even on their families, but now it is only for employees and limited.
- A culture of providing feedback to employees and discussing future needs and roles were encouraged. However in the new setup only once a year feedback is considered and future decisions are made.
- Managers are not easily approachable.
- Working from home culture being encouraged to facilitate employees, as otherwise a compulsion to be in office. This behavioral adjustment takes time.
- Employees are considered as "Resources" however previously they were considered as "associates".
- Everything is formal and letters are issued – as against informal discussions happening and being honored.
- Retention of employees is a preference as against the policy of letting them go and replacing with a fresher or lower designated and to be trained – leading to cost savings as well.

Vendors/Suppliers

Old vendors & suppliers are replaced and people now have to work with new companies / suppliers. Rapport building takes some time and might impact decision making. The policies to deal with customers and tightening of norms impact the quality of the end product or service.

Regional and local cultures are also impact some decisions. If the company is headquartered say in French capital but the acquired company is in one of the tier 2 cities of India – there is going to be a lot of impact of thinking process and getting the policies implemented.

Acquisition and Organizational Culture

Most of the acquisitions suffer due to the culture clashes. The literature has explained culture in the form of "value" having both similarities and differences Riseberg 1997. According to Jemison and Sitkin 1986, cited in Riseberg 1997 to make the acquisitions work; it is very important to find fits between the combining companies. E.g. similarities in corporate culture and management styles Nahavandi and Malekzadeh, 1988.

The most fundamental hypothesis is that to make the acquisition work. The two organizations must be integrated in such a way that they become as similar as possible in order to attain a mutual corporate culture Nguyen and Kleiner 2003. According to Haspeslagh and Jemison 1991 cited in Riseberg 1997 that these hypothesis does not fully describe integration in all acquisitions. So, it indicates that, various degrees of integration should be used according to the nature of acquisition.

However, researchers such as Napier et al 1989 argues that, the acquired company mostly forced to adapt to the acquiring company's culture and routines which may lead to complications in their adjustment to the parent company. The other way round should also be implemented, it is just a question that which of the two organizations have a better organizational culture. According to Martin and Meyerson 1991 cited in Riseberg 1997 p. 258 "A culture viewed from an ambiguity perspective cannot be characterized as being either in harmony or conflict. Instead, individuals share some viewpoints, disagree about some and are ignorant of or indifferent to others." According to Fines 1991 that still in existing organisational theories, the acquired company should be integrated into the acquiring company's culture which does not account for cultural differences within the organization.

Inside the organization many different cultures exist due to people's belonging to different ethnic group gender or nationality Risberg, 1997. Martin and Meyerson 1991 elucidate that according to these organizational theories culture is viewed as something which can homogenize both the organization and its members. Thus, when the two cultures are merge together, the existing theories which often assume that one of the two should integrate into the other existing organizational culture to make the new organization work Berry, 1980, Nahavandhi and

Malekzadeh, 1988 cited in Risberg 1997. However, an organizational culture rarely has values, norms, expectations and assumptions which unite all organizational members. According to

Schein 1993 organization may consist of different subcultures that may have quite conflicting assumptions about reality.

CULTURE DIFFERENCES

Cultural differences, which is considered as to be the most prominent issue for the lack of predicted performance, loss of key employees, and time consuming conflicts in merging of business Bijilsma-Frankema, 2002. According to Bijilsma-Frankema 258 2002 the term 'Culture clash' could be used to describe the conflict between the merged organizations; which may include differences in their styles, norms, sanctions, philosophies, and objectives. This may, in fact, be the most dangerous factors when two companies decide to combine. Covin et al 1997 argues that even, if the conditions for M&A are favorable, still mergers can so change the nature; orientation and character of one or both of the merged partners; which means it will require five to seven years where employees can feel whether they have truly understood one another's culture.

Many adjustment problems have been witnessed during the post-merger period Mirvis and Marks, 1992. According to Mirvis and Marks 1992, these problems arise due to employee's fear of losing the job and financial debt due to job loss. Also, fears that arise due to the loss of close team members, appointment of new team members and new supervisors can lead the organizations into an ambiguous situation. By forcing employees to deal with new supervisors and new team members, they could build up worries of taking certain risks and raising sensitive issues. This can lead to develop 'us versus them' scenario, where trust for new members will be nominal Mirvis and Marks, 1992. Organizations, having this kind of situation may find themselves in dilemma due to loss of collaboration and interest among the employees of the new business amalgamation. It will be difficult to achieve the synergies that were initially sought; it will also be difficult to resolve conflicts and sensitive issues, if at all, this resistance arises often. Post-merger can be the most difficult time for the new team to move forward as a whole Appelbaum et al, 2004.

EMPIRICAL STUDY ON IMPACT OF MERGER & ACQUISITION ON ORGANIZATION CULTURE AND DEVELOPMENT IN AN IT INDUSTRY – SURVEY RESULTS

A sample survey was conducted on this topic with one IT company which has recently acquired 2 other IT companies, one in 2007 & other in 2011. A set of 821 employees who were from the acquired organizations, were sent the questionnaire, of which 227 people responded. This is part of a larger research which is still underway on the broader topic and is in progress.

However the relevance of the topic questions is shortlisted for this paper. The respondents were asked to answer as one of the options mentioned below and all the questions were compulsory.

Company A: This company was of the total strength around 6500 employees across the globe when acquired in 2007. Of which now only 1302 employees are left in India while conducting the survey in July 2012. The survey was responded by 159 employees out of 618 to which this questionnaire was sent.

Company B: This company was of the total strength of 300 employees when acquired in 2011. Of which now only 203 employees are left in India while conducting the survey in July 2012. The survey was responded by 75 employees out of 203 to which this questionnaire was sent.

Likert Scale	Strongly Agree	Agree	Somewhat Agree	Neutral	Somewhat Disagree	Disagree	Strongly Disagree	No Response
For Mean Calculations	7	6	5	4	3	2	1	0

*Results are rounded off to the next whole number post the two decimal places crosses .50

Demographic Information of the Respondents

For both the Company "A" & "B": 227 respondents:

- 51% of the respondents were between the age group of 31 – 40yrs and hold the position as middle level in the hierarchy. Followed by 31% of respondents between the age group of 26 – 30yrs.
- The average work experience of the respondents is 9.5yrs (between 6 to 11yrs).
- 82% male and 17% female employees responded to the survey. 1% People skipped some questions and did not answer all.

The results are interesting and the following inferences can be drawn:

Inferences: Strongly agree, agree, somewhat agree is considered positive response and somewhat disagree, disagree and strongly disagree is considered as negative response.

As per responses received from 227 employees, the mean Mean calculations, results for the communication, policy & processes, culture & value & training development related questions are:

"Communication" Related Questions

HR Issues during merger & acquisition - "Communication" related questions:				
Questions	*Mean Score of Response to Rating scale 1-7*	*Associated Definition*	*Response Count*	*Correlation*
Question 1	4.25	Neither Agree Nor Disagree	210	0.67
Question 2	4.19	Neither Agree Nor Disagree	210	0.74
Question 3	4.60	Somewhat Agree	210	0.87
Question 4	4.29	Neither Agree Nor Disagree	210	0.81
Question 5	4.91	Somewhat Agree	210	0.99
Question 6	5.27	Somewhat Agree	210	0.96
Question 7	4.86	Somewhat Agree	210	0.99
Question 8	5.04	Somewhat Agree	208	0.92
Question 9	4.32	Neither Agree Nor Disagree	208	0.92
Question 10	4.49	Neither Agree Nor Disagree	208	0.81
Question 11	5.76	Agree	208	0.81
Question 12	4.76	Somewhat Agree	208	0.95
Question 13	4.17	Neither Agree Nor Disagree	208	0.83
Question 14	4.27	Neither Agree Nor Disagree	208	0.89
Overall	4.65	Somewhat Agree		

- A Mean score of **4.91 out of 7** means that most of the respondents "somewhat agree" that the communication received now as compared a year ago prior to merger / acquisition on company's strategies and its ongoing accomplishments is better.
- A Mean score of **5.27 out of 7** means that most of the employees "somewhat agree" that they receive all the relevant information in the company newsletter periodically.
- A Mean score of **4.19 out of 7** means that respondents "Neither agree nor disagree" that communication about the merger activities was an issue even after 6 months of the merged date.
- A Mean score of **4.49 out of 7** means that respondents "Neither agree nor disagree" that they prefer communication from their manager rather than grapevine
- A Mean score of **4.86 out of 7** means that respondents "somewhat agree" on that they are satisfied with the overall communication mechanism in the organization.

"Policy & Processes" Related Questions

HR Issues - "Policy & Processes" related questions:				
Questions	*Mean Score of Response to Rating scale 1-7*	*Associated Definition*	*Response Count*	*Correlation*
Question 1	4.80	Somewhat Agree	194	0.93
Question 2	5.36	Somewhat Agree	194	0.86
Question 3	4.23	Neither Agree Nor Disagree	194	0.92
Overall	4.80	Somewhat Agree		

- A Mean score of **4.80 out of 7** means that respondents "Somewhat agree" that they are clear about the company policies and processes as compared to pre-merger or during the merger activities.
- A Mean score of **5.36 out of 7** means that respondents "Somewhat agree" that there are no differences in race, religion, gender, educational background & departments and are overall content / no complains.
- A Mean score of **4.23 out of 7** means that respondents "Neither agree nor disagree" that the company understands family responsibilities of the employees.

"Culture & Value" Related Questions

HR Issues - "Culture & Value" related questions:				
Questions	*Mean Score of Response to Rating Scale 1-7*	*Associated Definition*	*Response Count*	*Correlation*
Question 1	4.84	Somewhat Agree	192	0.99
Question 2	4.65	Somewhat Agree	192	0.96
Question 3	4.58	Somewhat Agree	192	0.97
Question 4	5.49	Somewhat Agree	192	0.96
Question 5	5.14	Somewhat Agree	192	0.98
Question 6	5.08	Somewhat Agree	192	0.99
Question 7	4.80	Somewhat Agree	192	0.97
Question 8	4.26	Neither Agree Nor Disagree	192	0.94
Question 9	4.57	Somewhat Agree	182	0.99
Question 10	4.61	Somewhat Agree	182	0.87
Question 11	4.73	Somewhat Agree	182	0.93
Question 12	3.94	Neither Agree Nor Disagree	182	0.76
Question 13	5.09	Somewhat Agree	182	0.78
Question 14	4.60	Somewhat Agree	182	0.98
Question 15	4.24	Neither Agree Nor Disagree	182	0.95
Overall	4.72	Somewhat Agree		

- A Mean score of **5.49 out of 7** means that most respondents "Somewhat agree" that their colleagues help in case of any difficulties while performing any job in the new merged organization.
- A Mean score of **5.08 out of 7** means that most respondents "Somewhat agree" that the company has the culture of helping each other, which is satisfactory.
- A Mean score of **5.14 out of 7** means that most respondents "Somewhat agree" that their supervisors helps the subordinates for effective delivery and overall has a good culture.
- A Mean score of **4.80 out of 7** means that respondents "somewhat agree" that their managers and the people at higher designation are approachable in the new merged organization.
- A Mean score of **4.26 out of 7** means that respondents "Neither agree nor disagree" and see that the company has the culture of developing the career's of the employees as compared to their previous organization.
- A Mean score of **4.60 out of 7** means that respondents "somewhat agree" that the people trust each other in the organization, which is part of a good culture.
- A Mean score of **3.94 out of 7** means that respondents "Neither agree nor disagree" that there is no disparity among the merged and erstwhile employees of the organizations.

"Training" Related Questions

HR Policies: "Training" related questions:				
Questions	*Mean Score of Response to Rating scale 1-7*	*Associated Definition*	*Response Count*	*Correlation*
Question 1	4.58	Somewhat Agree	175	0.98
Question 2	4.95	Somewhat Agree	175	0.98
Question 3	5.10	Somewhat Agree	175	0.99
Question 4	3.98	Neither Agree Nor Disagree	175	0.80
Overall	4.66	Somewhat Agree		

- A Mean score of **4.58 out of 7** means that respondents "Somewhat agree" that the organization plans their training annually.
- A Mean score of **5.10 out of 7** means that respondents "somewhat agree" that there are opportunities provided to upgrade skills via new industry certified programs in the new merged organization.
- A Mean score of **3.89 out of 7** means that respondents "Neither agree nor disagree" that they get opportunities once they are trained in a particular area.

DISCUSSION AND CONCLUSION

With all the above the conclusion driven is that although historically people involved in the activities of mergers and acquisitions did not pay enough attention to the impact on organizational culture and development – it has started over the period of time. The sample study above is just one such indicator wherein employees are also happy if things done to improve the working environment are taken care.

Based on the survey results, we can conclude that: Overall for both the companies, 227 respondents:

- Communication questions: A Mean score of 4.65 out of 7 means that most of the respondents "somewhat agree" that overall communication during and post merger to the employees were good enough.
- Policy & Process questions: A Mean score of 4.80 out of 7 means that respondents "somewhat agree" that the policy & processes were fairly understood by employees and are still not clear.
- Culture & Value questions: A Mean score of 4.72 out of 7 means that most of the respondents "somewhat agree" that overall organization culture and values both during and post merger to the employees are good.
- Training questions: A Mean score of 4.66 out of 7 means that most of the respondents "somewhat agree" that the training opportunities in the new organization is good.

RECOMMENDATIONS

Based on the survey results and all the literature review, the following can be recommended for good impact of mergers and acquisitions on the organizational culture and development:

Communication is no doubt very very important factor in mergers and acquisitions, not only pre, but during and post initial 6 months phase. Although people have rated & responded on a relatively good score – people have agreed that communication becomes and issue during the first 6 months post merger. These turn out to be very important not only financially but emotionally for the new comers in the post merger scenario. It is very much recommended to have a company newsletter that periodically highlights the merger benefits and keep all informed about new changes that touch all the employees. This will definitely kill the grapevine communication that is the usual indirect way of getting the insider news about the overall health of the organization.

Policy & process are the enablers for human resources departments across any organization and this plays all the more significant role when two new organizations come together to form one consortium. The survey score definitely supports to the thought that these have remain uniform. It is recommended that ways only wherein there are no individual differences considered among the erstwhile and the newly integrated employees. The employees should be felt comfortable and feel part of the organization and nothing different. Whether it is the annual appraisal or the basic policies related to benefits or location changes. It is recommended that uniformity is the key to make sure these elements do not become roadblocks for any kind of integration.

For Culture & Value, the survey scores and the history around it suggests it playing a key element in the loss of key employees. It has always been observed that whenever a new merger or acquisition is announced, the key people in the higher designations tend to lose confidence and moreover if they have spent longer tenure in the erstwhile organization. The feeling is that things will change drastically and they do not want to get into a position wherein people are being to ask to be the change driver affecting their authorities – hence they leave. It is recommended that a good orientation program is devised for the new joiners that cover the basics of culture and the values of the organization. If it requires to add certain new levels of values that were pre-existing in the yet to be merged organization, then those good things should be considered. People should not just be imposed with the all new culture that may lead to group'ism of old and new employees. Rather it is recommended that when it comes to new opportunities, there should be a healthy competitive environment built so that there is no such thing as old and new employee.

Training gives an extra edge to employees to build their competencies and be ready for any new upcoming opportunities, thus building their careers effectively. It is recommended that the organizations take active interest in investing in the training programs linked to their industry and giving people enough opportunities to learn at all the levels. Again the merged employees will be happy to see that their career aspirations and knowledge is not losing its sheen with the announcement of the merger or acquisition. In today's world where the technology changes rapidly and there are no geographical boundaries to outperform any work – the newly integrated employees should be highlighted with these kind of benefits that lead to certifications that will be helpful not only within the organization but also in their careers.

REFERENCES

[1] Mohibullah, (2009), "Impact of Culture on Mergers and Acquisitions: A Theoretical Framework", *International Review of Business Research Papers,* Vol.5 No. 1 January 2009 pp. 255-264.

[2] Archer, Dan (October 2007), "Mergers and acquisitions: change, culture and the "leaderful" organization", Leadership Trust, UK.

[3] Chun, Rosa (2009)," A corporate's responsibility to employees during a merger: organizational virtue and employee loyalty", Emerald Group Publishing Limited, ISSN 1472-0701, VOL. 9 NO. 4 2009, pp. 473-483.

[4] Pikula, Deborah A., (1999), "Mergers & Acquisitions: Organizational Culture & H R Issues", ISBN: 0-88886-516-3 © 1999, Industrial Relations Centre Printed and bound in Canada.

[5] Soroghan, S, Kippenberger, T, Gould, B, (1998),"Company cultures in M&A (mergers and acquisitions)", The Antidote, Vol. 3 Iss: 2 pp. 31-33 (Emerald).

[6] Kabiraj, Sajal (2010), "Examining Strategic Issues in Merger of Asian and Western MNCs: Holistic Cross Cultural Imperatives", ASIAN JOURNAL OF MANAGEMENT RESEARCH, ISSN 2229–3795.

[7] Mike Schraeder, Dennis R. Self, (2003),"Enhancing the success of mergers and acquisitions: an organizational culture perspective", Management Decision, Vol. 41 Iss: 5 pp. 511 – 522 (Emerald).

[8] Bhansing, Neeta (2010), "Change in perception of organizational culture after merger: The influence of Motivation, Acceptance and Knowledge", University of Twente, Enschede.

[9] Majidi, Mehdi (2007), "Cultural Factors in International Mergers and Acquisitions", International Journal Of Knowledge, Culture And Change Management, ISSN: 1447-9524, Australia.

[10] Appalbaum, S.H., et al 2004, "Anatomy of a merger: behavior of organizational factors and process throughout the pre-during-post-stages", Management decision, Vol.38, No.2, pp. 649-62.

[11] Bijilsma-Frankema, K. 2002, "On managing cultural integration and cultural change processes in mergers and acquisitions," Journal of European Industrial Training, Vol.25, April, pp. 192-207.

[12] Covin, T.J., Kolendo, T.A., Sighter, J.W. and Tudor, R.K. 1997, "Leadership style and Post-merger satisfaction," Journal of management development.

[13] Mirvis, P.H. and Marks, M.L. 1992, "Rebuilding after the merger: Dealing with survivor sickness," Organizational Dynamics, Vol. 21. No.2, pp. 18-23.

[14] Nahavandi, Afsaneh, and Ali R. Malekzadeh. 1993. *Organizational culture in the management of mergers*. Westport, CT: Quorum Books.

[15] Nahavandi, A. Malekzadeh, A.R. 1988, "Acculturation in mergers and acquisitions", Academy of Management Review, vol, 13, pp. 79-90.

[16] Quinn,R.E., Quinn, K.S. (1999). Onderzoeken en veranderen van organisatiecultuur. Academic Service.Den-Haag.

[17] Tentenbaum, T.J. (1999). Beating the Odds of Merger & Acquisition: Seven Key Practices That Improve the Chance for expected Integration and Synergy Organizational Dynamics.

[18] Buono, A.F., Bowditch, J.L. and Lewis, J.W (1985), "When cultures collide: the anatomy of a merger", Human Relations, Vol. 38 No. 5, pp. 477-500.

[19] Haspeslagh, C. Jemison, B. 1991a "Managing Acquisitions-Creating Value through Corporate Renewal," New York, The free press.

[20] Jimson, D.B. Sitkin, S.B. 1986. "Acquisitions: the process can be a problem." Harvard business review, March-April, 107-16.

[21] Nguyen.H, Kleiner Brain H. 2003 "The effective management of mergers" Leadership and organizational development journal 24/8, 447-454.

[22] Riseberg. A 1997 "Ambiguity and communication in cross-cultural acquisitions: towards a conceptual framework." Leadership and organizational development journal volume 18 issue 5. 257-266.

[23] Schein. E 1993 "On dialogue, culture, and organizational learning", Organizational Dynamics, Vol. 22. No. 2, Fall, pp. 40-51.

[24] Weber, A., Camrer, C.F. (1996). Cultural conflict and merger failure: An experimental approach. *Management Science*. Vol. 49. No. 4, pp. 400-415.

[24] Guns, T. (2006). De Impact van fusies en overnames op de bedrijfscultuur: literautuurstudie en empirisch onderzoek. Universiteit Gent. Faculteit Economie en Bedrijfskunde.

[25] Sathe, Vijay. !985. *Culture and related corporate realities.* Homewood, IL: Richard D. Irwin.

[26] Davis, Stanley M. 1994. *Managing corporate culture.* Cambridge, MA: Ballinger.

[27] Cartwright, Susan, and Cary L. Cooper. 1992. *Mergers and acquisitions: The human factor.* Oxford: Butterworth-Heineman.

[28] Napier, N.K. Simmons, G. Stratton, K. 1989. "Communication during merger: the experience of two banks." Human resources planning, 12, 2.

[29] Martin and Meryson.D J.1991 "Organizational cultures and the denial, channelling and acknowledgement of ambiguity", in Ponday L.R.Boland, R.J. and Thomas. H. EDS "Managing ambiguity and change", John Wilay and Sons, New York, NY.

[30] Capgemini Repository Archives, (October 2008), "Our Point of View: Post Merger Integration Framework and Tool Box".

Websites

www.mercer.com – Impact of culture on M&A

www.nasscom.com - NASSCOM's 'Strategic Review 2010' report

An Analysis of Deal Characteristics of Large Cross-Border Acquisitions by Developed and Emerging Market Acquirers

Dipali Krishnakumar and MadhviSethi[1]

Symbiosis International University
[1]Symbiosis Institute of Business Management

ABSTRACT

This study investigates large cross border deals above USD 1 billion during the 2000 to 2011 time frame to explore whether deal values, valuation multiples and payment methods differ with the economy of the acquirer and target firm; for diversified acquisitions v/s non diversified acquisitions;or during recession. This study also investigates the impact of deal characteristics on the mode of payment.

We find that mean deal values differ with the economy of the acquirer and target (emerging market/developed market).Contrary to expectations, valuation multiples are not impacted by either the economy of the acquirer and target or during recession. Bidders pay similar premiums when they make related and unrelated acquisitions. Payment is more likely to be in the form of stock for higher deal values and it is more likely to be in the form of cash for unrelated acquisitions. Recession and economy of acquirer and target do not impact the payment method.

There are several research studies which have looked at characteristics of acquirers / targets and market reactions to acquisition announcements. However, understanding emerging market firms' deal characteristics vis-à-vis developed market firm's deals and understanding the impact of recession on deal characteristics raises a significant research question which we explore.

INTRODUCTION

Markets react differently when developed and emerging market firms make cross border acquisitions depending on whether the acquirer and target is developed or developing (Chari, Ouimet, Tessar(2010), Gubbi, Aulakh Ray, Sarkar, Chitoor(2010)). The characteristics of acquirers and target have been studied in several research studies. However, given that acquisitions by emerging market firms have grown from a meager 2% of worldwide cross border deal volumes in 1999 to 29% of worldwide cross border deal values in 2010, understanding of emerging market firms' deal characteristics vis-à-vis developed market firm's deals raises a significant research question. This study investigates cross border deals above USD 1 billion during the 2000 to 2011 time frame to explore whether deal values, valuation multiples and payment modes (cash/stock) differ depending on whether the acquirer or target is from a developed market or emerging market. We also examine the impact of related and unrelated acquisitions on deal characteristics. Our data period helps us to cover another question which is whether deal characteristics are impacted by recession during the recession phase of 2001 and 2008-2009.

Figure 1 plots the cross border deal values along with the share of developed and emerging market acquirers. We clearly see that recession has had an impact on the value of cross border Mergers and Acquisitions(M&A) causing it to decline in the years of recession. Hence, we make a hypothesis that recession has an impact on deal value.

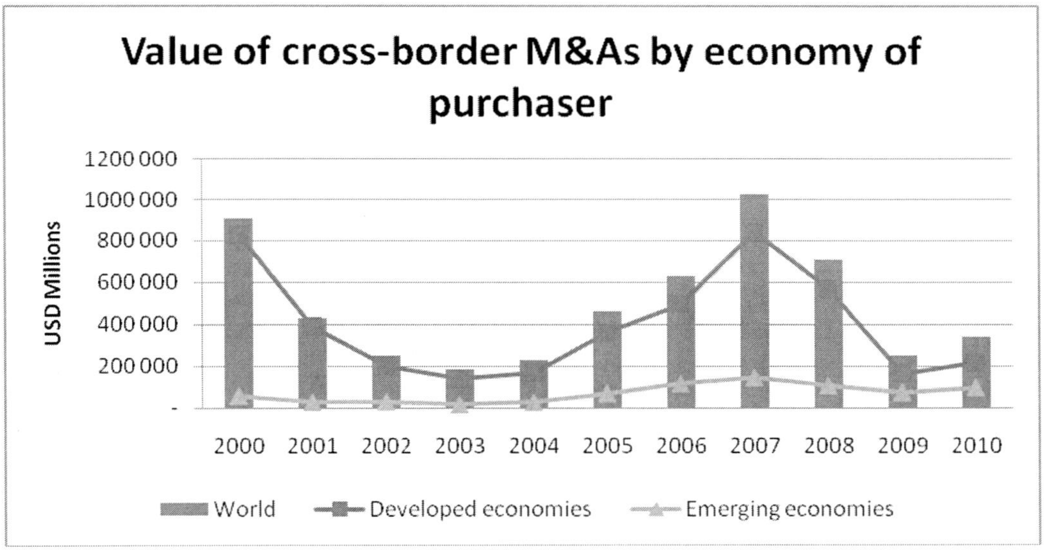

Fig. 1. Computed from UNCTAD World Investment Review 2011

THEORY AND HYPOTHESIS

Our research question is motivated by several studies on internationalization. The review of these studies can primarily be divided into several categories. Reasons for going cross border (Dunning, 1988; Teece, 1985; Teece 1986, Buckley and Cason, 1976), characteristics of acquirers and targets (Barkema and Vermeulen, 1998;Brouthers&Brouthers, 2000), and value effects of going cross border (Jensen and Ruback , 1983; Andrade, Mitchell, and Stafford, 2001; Chari, Ouimet&Tesar, 2009). We place our study in the literature for cross border deals where acquirers and targets belong to different kinds of economies and whether these differences in deal characteristics are significant.

Chernykh, Liebenberg and Macias, (2011) document the growth of acquisitions byemerging market firms during the period 1990 to 2007. They report a sharp increase in the number and size of acquisitions by emerging market firmsand note specifically the growth of acquisition of developed market targets by emerging market firms. In this study, we analyze cross border deals during the 2000 to 2011 time frame to explore whether deal values, valuation multiples and payment modes (cash/stock) differ depending on whether the acquirer or target is from a developed market or emerging market.

Hypothesis 1: There are differences between deal values, valuation multiples and payment modes between the different Acquirer-Target pairs

Our study also finds its place in literature where major economic events like recession impact the decision to go cross border for an acquisition. Acharya, Shin and Yorulmazer (2007), Aguiar, Mark, andGopinath (2005) have described how assets in an economy undergoing a crisis are sold off at low rates. This study tries toexplore whether individual deal characteristics are impacted by recession during the recession phase of 2001 and 2008-2009. Aguiaret. al. have found that median price to book value ratios declined during the Asian financial crisis for acquisitions of Asian firms. We extend this logic to state that it is likely that worldwide assets are sold off at low valuation multiples during a recession.

Hypothesis 2: There are differences between deal values, valuation multiples and payment modes between the different Acquirer-Target pairs before and after recession

Jahera, Hand &Lloyd (1985), study various factors that impact acquisition premiums in controlling stake acquisitions and find that diversification hasa negativeinfluence on acquisition premium. King, Dalton and Daily(2004) in their review of M&A literature found that related acquisitions have a positive impact on performance. On the basis of these studies we test the hypothesis that acquisition of controlling stakes in related industries would involve a higher valuation multiple paid out.

Hypothesis 3: Acquisition of controlling stakes in related industries would involve a higher valuation multiple paid out

Faccio and Masulis, (2005) find that the method of payment cash, stock or combination of payments is influenced by deal characteristics such as shareholding of majority owners; relative size of bidder and target, leverage of bidder; whether the deal is in the same industry or not etc. Facciao and Mausilis (2005) report that the probability of a cash financed deal decreases when the bidder and target are in the same industry. Martin (1996) studies the impact of various factor that influence the method of payment in a deal including growth opportunities of bidders, managerial stock ownership, cash levels with acquirers, institutional share ownership and business cycles. They find that an increase in stock market values is associated with an increase in stock financed deals. We study the impact of deal characteristics such as deal value, industry of acquirer and bidder, economy of bidder target pairs, percentage ownership sought and recession on the method of payment.

HYPOTHESIS4 :The choice of payment mode might depend on whether the deal is in a diversified or same industry, business cycle, economy of the target and percentage ownership sought.

DATA AND METHODOLOGY

We analyze large value cross-border deals above USD 1 billion listed in the Bloomberg database from 2000 to 2011. Bloomberg lists 2309 cross-border deals for the 2000 to 2011 time frame with deal values above USD 1 billion. The reason we choose 1 billion USDdeals is to understand the capital flows between the economies in a more representative way. After dropping deals that are not complete or deals where the acquirer or target nation is not mentioned, we are left with a sample of 1367 observations. Acquiring and Target countries are categorized as Developed (D) or Emerging (E) on the basis of UNCTAD classification. The 1367 deals comprise of 1118 deals by developed market acquirers and 249 deals by emerging market acquirers. We classify deals by acquirer and target country pairs to arrive at 964 deals where both acquirer and target are from developed nations (DD) and 154 deals where the acquirer is developed while the target is from an emerging market.(DE) There are 131 deals where the acquirer is from an emerging county and the target is from a developed country (ED) and 118 deals by an emerging market acquirer in an emerging market target(EE).

Table 1. Description of Acquirer-Target Pairs

	Target-Developed	*Target-Emerging*	*Total*
Acquirer-Developed	DD 964	DE 154	1118
Acquirer-Emerging	ED 131	EE 118	249
Total	1095	272	1367

This table documents the number of completed deals classified by acquirer and target economies on the basis of Bloomberg data.

We collect data from Bloomberg on various deal particulars such as target and acquirer industry sector, target and acquirer nation, percentage sought, percentage owned before deal, total announced value of deal, deal status and valuation multiples paid for the deal namely book value multiple, revenue multiple, and net income multiple.

Table 2 summarizes the deal characteristics for acquirer and target pairs. We observe that the mean deal value for DD (developed acquirer and developed target) is the highest 3.6 billion USD, followed by ED when Emerging market firms acquire Developed market targets at 2.9 billion. The percentage sought in cases where the target is from a Developed country is higher, median value 100% for both DD and ED compared with cases when the target is emerging, median values are 58% for DE and 60% for EE deals. We also observe differences in the valuation multiples paid between different acquirer target pairs.

Table 2. Descriptive Statistics

Acquirer Target Pair	*Statistics*	*Deal Value USD Million*	*% Sought*	*Book Value Multiple*	*Revenue Multiple*	*Net Income Multiple*
DD	mean	3,615.82	82.28	11.12	10.85	50.77
	median	2,008.77	100.00	3.56	2.35	25.91
	std deviation	4,860.21	29.85	78.15	77.92	144.11
DE	mean	2,512.20	59.29	24.79	21.66	62.37
	median	1,816.00	57.65	3.09	2.56	24.83
	std deviation	2,087.10	36.21	189.11	139.67	139.79
ED	mean	2,929.24	71.38	5.19	3.88	31.48
	median	1,765.00	100.00	3.08	2.06	19.49
	std deviation	2,814.04	38.43	7.57	6.32	35.06
EE	mean	2,086.87	61.69	3.57	3.42	25.54
	median	1,568.87	59.85	2.88	2.45	19.78
	std deviation	1,259.12	35.89	2.71	2.95	27.55

We observe from Figure1 that there has been a dip in worldwide acquisition activity during and after recession in 2001 and then again during 2007 to 2009 time frame. We investigate the impact of the recessionary phase on mean deal values, taking the official recession phase as announced by National Bureau of Economic Research (NBER). The 9 month period from March 2001 to November 2001 and 18 month period from December 2007 to June 2009 was identified as a recessionary phase by NBER.Since, it is difficult to determine the duration of the post recession impact phase; we have ignore that period, and only consider the official recession period for our study. We create an additional variable called recession, coded 1/0 for the recessionary phases as defined by NBER.

Table 3 describes the number of acquisitions in each target industry sector during the period 2000 to 2011 by acquirer and target country pairs. We find that acquisitions during the period in terms of numbers were lead by acquisitions in the financial sector for both developed and emerging market acquirers. The next priority for developed market acquirers was consumer non cyclical firms such as pharmaceuticals and healthcare firms. While, next to financial sector firms emerging market firms chose to acquire basic material firms such as metals and plastics from developed markets and communications sector firms from emerging markets. Priority of emerging market acquirers seems to be resource seeking when they acquire in the developed world and market seeking when they acquire in the emerging markets.

Table 3. Industrywise Description of the Acquirer-Target Pairs

Target Industry Sector	*No. DD*	*% of DD*	*No. DE*	*% of DE*	*No ED*	*% of ED*	*No. EE*	*% of EE*	*No. Total*	*% of Total*
Basic Materials	75	8%	20	13%	21	16%	12	10%	128	9%
Communications	125	13%	21	14%	6	5%	29	25%	181	13%
Consumer, Cyclical	80	8%	11	7%	10	8%	3	3%	104	8%
Consumer, Non-cyclical	194	20%	26	17%	18	14%	8	7%	246	18%
Diversified	12	1%	1	1%	3	2%	6	5%	22	2%
Energy	64	7%	14	9%	33	25%	18	15%	129	9%
Financial	192	20%	40	26%	12	9%	31	26%	275	20%
Government		0%	2	1%		0%		0%	2	0%
Industrial	118	12%	7	5%	18	14%	4	3%	147	11%
N.A.	7	1%	2	1%		0%	1	1%	10	1%
Technology	35	4%	3	2%		0%	1	1%	39	3%
Utilities	62	6%	7	5%	10	8%	5	4%	84	6%
	964		154		131		118		1367	

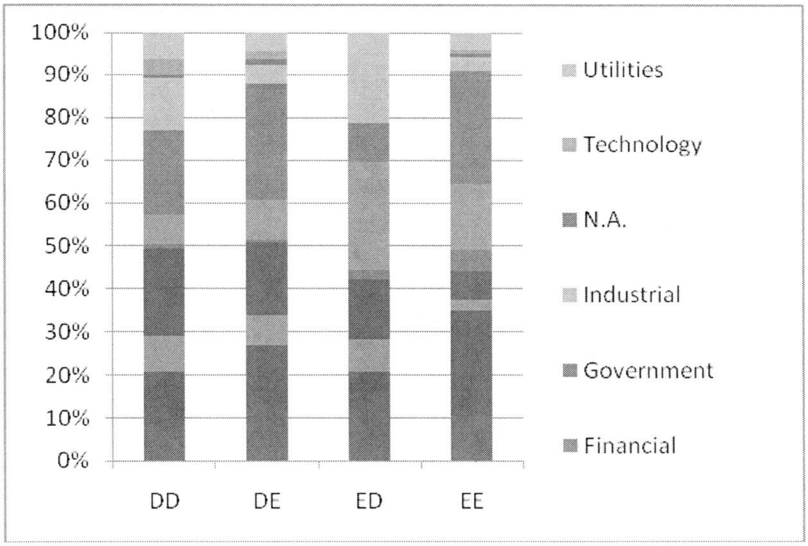

Fig. 2. Shows the Deal Numbers in Target Industry Sectors.

Table 4 summarizes the deals values in each target sector by acquirer target pairs. Interestingly, when we look at the deals in terms of value of deals in a particular industry sector, for all completed deals above USD 1 billion, we find that financial sector does not have the highest number of deals. Consumer non cyclical deals are of the highest value followed by financial sector deals. When developed acquirers acquired firms in developed markets the highest total deal value was in consumer, non cyclical sector, while they spent the maximum amount on financial sector targets when they made acquisitions in emerging markets. Acquisitions by emerging market firms in developed markets were resource seeking as they have spent 25% in value terms on energy sector followed by 20% on basic materials. Emerging market acquisitions in other emerging markets were with a view to expand markets as they have made the largest acquisitions in communications sector.

Table 4. Deal Values of Acquirer-Target Pairs-Industrywise

Target Industry Sector	*Bn USD DD*	*% of DD*	*Bn USDDE*	*% of DE*	*Bn USD ED*	*% of ED*	*Bn USD EE*	*% of EE*	*Bn USD Total*	*% of Total*
Basic Materials	337	10%	65	17%	76	20%	20	8%	499	11%
Communications	540	15%	50	13%	28	7%	68	28%	685	15%
Consumer, Cyclical	175	5%	22	6%	16	4%	7	3%	220	5%
Consumer, Non-cyclical	843	24%	53	14%	56	15%	16	6%	967	21%
Diversified	22	1%	3	1%	4	1%	8	3%	37	1%
Energy	198	6%	31	8%	96	25%	47	19%	372	8%
Financial	660	19%	101	26%	35	9%	60	24%	857	19%
Government	0	0%	8	2%	0	0%	0	0%	8	0%
Industrial	279	8%	27	7%	51	13%	6	2%	363	8%
N.A.	13	0%	6	2%	0	0%	1	0%	20	0%
Technology	95	3%	4	1%	0	0%	3	1%	102	2%
Utilities	323	9%	16	4%	22	6%	10	4%	372	8%
Total	3486		387		384		246		4503	

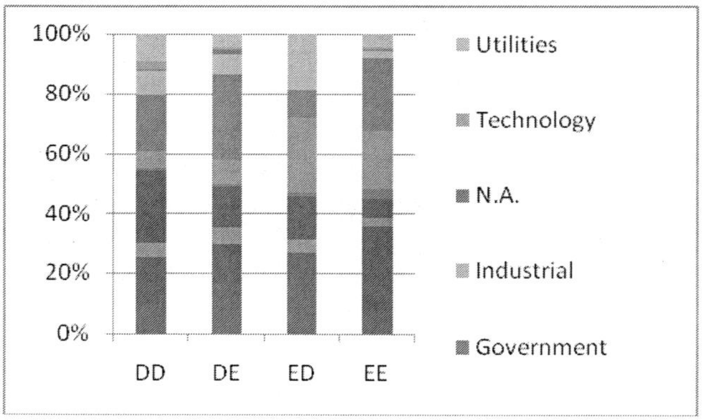

Fig. 3. Deals in Value Terms in Target Sectors

Next, we examine the type of deals (diversified/non diversified) made by developed and emerging market firms. Figure 4 provides the distribution of diversified and non diversified deals for each of the acquirer target pair. We observe that the proportion of same industry deals is similar for all acquirer target pairs at around 70% of deals.

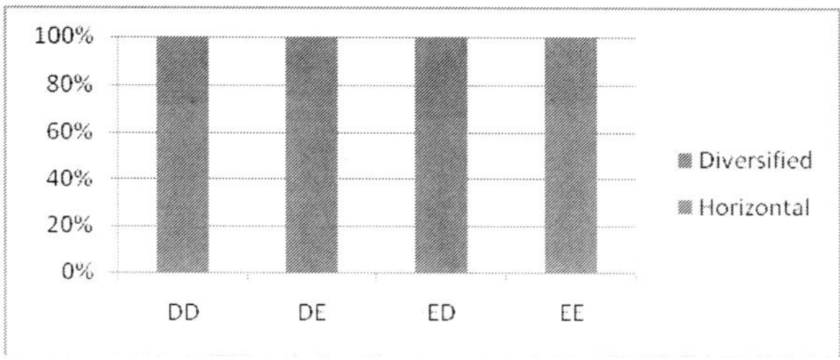

Fig. 4. Illustrates the Percentage of Diverisfied and Horizontal deals for Acquirer Target Pairs

Morck, Shleifer&Vishney, (1990) found that acquiring firms suffered negative abnormal returns when they made diversifying acquisitions. We analyze acquisition multiples paid to test whether they are influenced by whether the deal is diversified or horizontal.

For testing the first three HYPOTHESiS, we adopt a multifactor analysis of variance (ANOVA) test. We use the ANOVA test to test the hypothesis that the mean announced deal values, deal multiples do not vary with deal characteristics such as acquirer-target pairs, recession, diversification.

For our fourth HYPOTHESiS, we use a multinomial logistic model. We have three categories of payment modes – stock, cash and combination. Since they are unordered, we can use multinomial logit model. The probability in other categories is compared to the probability of payment in the reference category. In our case, the reference category is payment by cash.

$$Ln(\frac{P(payment = stock)}{P(payment = cash)}) = \beta_{10} + \beta_{11}(\text{diversified}) + \beta_{12}(\text{dealvalue}) + \beta_{13}(control) + \beta_{14}(\text{countrypair}) + \beta_{15}(recession)$$

$$Ln(\frac{P(payment = combination)}{P(payment = cash)}) = \beta_{20} + \beta_{21}(\text{diversified}) + \beta_{22}(\text{dealvalue}) + \beta_{23}(control) + \beta_{24}(\text{countrypair}) + \beta_{25}(recession)$$

RESULTS

We test for the analysis of variance in deal characteristics and analyze whether they are influenced by the economy of target and acquirer, by whether the acquisition is diversified or in the same industry sector, and during recession.

Table 5. This Table States the Results of a Multi Factor Anova with the Log of Knnounced Deal Value as the Dependent Variable

Source	*Partial SS*	*df*	*MS*	*F*	*Prob> F*
Model	29.76	5	5.95	11.98	0.00***
pair_no	13.42	3	4.47	9.00	0.00***
diversified	16.53	1	16.53	33.28	0.00***
recession	0.23	1	0.23	0.46	0.50
Residual	676.24	1361	0.50		
Total	705.99	1366	0.52		

(*** p<0.01, ** p<0.05, * p<0.1)

Deal value is impacted by acquirer target pairs and by whether the deal is diversified or horizontal. however, surprisingly mean deal values are not impacted by recession. Hence we find that though number of deals fell during recession as depicted in figure 1, the mean deal values for large deals above USD 1 billion were not impacted by recession.

Table 6. Summary of Announced Total Value

	Mean (USD million)	*Std. Dev.*	*Freq.*
Horizontal Deals	3626.028	4677.821	976
Diversified Deals	2464.209	2909.14	391
\Total	3293.715	4279.098	1367

We find that there is a significant difference in mean deal values between diversified and non diversified deals. Mean deal values of horizontal deals during the 2000 to 2011 time frame are 3.6 billion while diversified deals are for 2.4 billion.

Next we study the impact of acquirer target economies, diversification and recession on three valuation multiples – book value multiple, revenue multiple and net income multiple for controlling stake acquisitions defined as cases where percentage acquisition sought is more than 50%. We also limit our analysis to cases where all three multiples are available for a deal. The analysis of variance results for valuation multiples are tabulated in Table 7. We find that the economy of acquirer and targets, diversification and recession have no impact on valuation of deals. This seems to indicate that emerging market economies stand at par with developed market acquirers in large acquisitions. Similarly the hypothesis that assets may have been sold at fire sale prices during recession is not true in the case of high value asset sales. Also, the sector of the acquirer and target whether same or diversified does not impact deal valuation multiples.

Table 7. This Table States the Results of a Multi factor Anova with the Deal Multiples as the D ependent Variable

Book Value Multiple

Source	*Partial SS*	*Df*	*MS*	*F*	*Prob> F*
Model	12783.1626	5	2556.6	0.59	0.7114
Pair_no	1900.42059	3	633.47	0.14	0.9329
Diversified	8796.54839	1	8796.5	2.01	0.1566
Recession	1120.1937	1	1120.2	0.26	0.6129
Residual	1926895.25	441	4369.4		
Total	1939678.41	446	4349.1		

Revenue Multiple

Source	*Partial SS*	*df*	*MS*	*F*	*Prob> F*
Model	336.061242	5	67.212	0.33	0.8958
Pair_no	304.154672	3	101.38	0.5	0.6856
Diversified	9.08560265	1	9.0856	0.04	0.8332
Recession	18.2361838	1	18.236	0.09	0.7654
Residual	90236.8119	441	204.62		
Total	90572.8731	446	203.07819		

Net Income Multiple

Source	*Partial SS*	*df*	*MS*	*F*	*Prob> F*
Model	29764.3504	5	5952.9	0.54	0.7459
Pair_no	23175.1862	3	7725.1	0.7	0.5519
Diversified	5548.11759	1	5548.1	0.5	0.4784
Recession	399.709156	1	399.71	0.04	0.849
Residual	4860024.31	441	11020		
Total	4889788.66	446	10964		

Payment Type: Next we investigate whether the payment type (cash/Stock/ combination of stock/cash is influenced by whether the acquirer and target are from developed or emerging countries, deal values, percentage sought and whether the deal is diversified or not.

We code deals with 1 for cash deals, 2 for stock deals and 3 for cash and stock combinations, debt, debt combinations, etc, 117 deals do not have payment data which are excluded from our analysis.

The deals break up by payment type and acquirer target economy is as follows

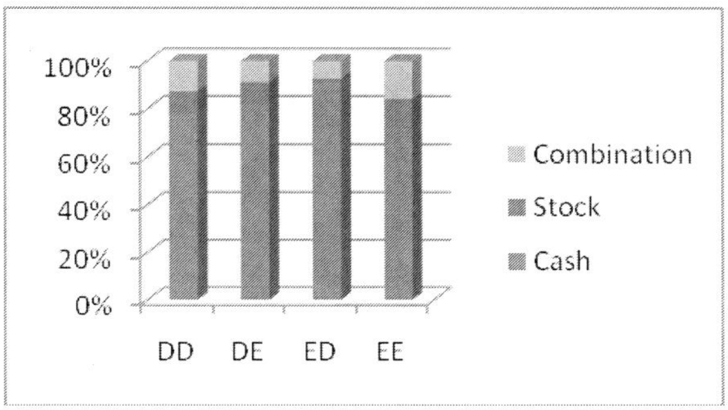

Fig. 5. Illustrates the Breakup of Payment type for Acquisition Target Pairs

We observe that cash is the primary mode of payment in most deals. However, in case of emerging markets acquisition of developed market targets the largest proportion of deals are in cash followed by combination deals. The proportion of stock deals for emerging market acquisitions in developed market targets is very low. This seems to be arising from the reluctance of developed market targets to hold shares in emerging market firms or from regulatory and listing issues.

We run a multinomial logit with the base outcome as cash deal, second outcome as stock deal and the third as combination deals to determine the factors that would impact the lilelyhood of a a firm going for a cash or stock or combination deal depending on the deal characteristics.

We find that deals are more likely to involve stock payment if announced deal values and percentage of the target sought to be acquired is higher.

Table 8. This Table Presents the Results from a Multi Nominal Logit test with Payment in Cash as the base Outcome, and Payment in Stock and Combination of Cash and Stock and Other Payment modes as the Alternate Outcome

Deal Characteristics	*Stock*	*Combination*
diversified	-1.429***	-0.745***
	-0.329	-0.231
log_dealvalue	0.295**	0.497***
	-0.13	-0.111
percentsought	0.0136***	0.0123***
	-0.00405	-0.00343
pair_no	-0.0211	0.0163
	-0.0297	-0.0233
recession	-0.155	-0.254
	-0.283	-0.251
Constant	-5.059***	-6.786***
	-1.161	-0.998
Observations	1,250	1,250

Standard errors in parentheses (*** p<0.01, ** p<0.05, * p<0.1)

We interpret these results to mean that if the deal is diversified then the log odds for a stock deal decrease by 1.429 units and a combination deal decrease by 0.745 units keeping all other deal characteristics constant. While if the log of the deal value is increased by 1 unit then the log odds of the deal being a stock deal increase by 0.295 units and by .497 units for a combination deal. If the percentage sought is increased by 1 unit, then the log odd of the deal being a stock deal increase by 0.0136 units and a combination deal increase by .0123 units. Whether the acquirer and target are developing or emerging and whether there is a worldwide recession does not impact the payment mechanism.

CONCLUSIONS

Cross border deals have gained in importance over the last decade, with an exponential growth in acquisition by emerging market firms. Researchers have studied characteristics of acquirers and targets and announcement effect of acquisitions. However, there has been a limited focus on understanding emerging market firm deal characteristics vis-à-vis developed market firms. There has been a dip in acquisitions during recession phases during 2000 to 2010. Research on exploring the impact of recession on mean deal values has been limited.

Our results indicate that mean deal values differ between acquisition target pairs. As per expectations the highest mean deal values are for developed market acquisitions of developed market targets. We also observe that diversification impacts deal values; horizontal deals have higher mean deal values then diversified deals. Contrary to expectations, mean deal values during recession are not significantly different from values during a non recessionary phase. This result needs to be analyzed further as there could be a post recession impact phase which has been ignored in our study.

It is interesting to note that deal valuation multiples are not significantly impacted by either the economy of the acquirer or target, by whether the deal is diversified of not and whether the deal took place during recession. This seems to indicate that emerging markets are not worse off than developed markets with respect to negotiations on price, and should be explored further.

Cash has been the primary form of payment for all acquirer target pairs, however the probability for stock payments increases for larger deal values and cases where a higher percentage of ownership is sought. The likelihood of cash payment is higher for diversified acquisitions which is in line with expectations.

Our study bring out some interesting stylized facts about mergers and acquisitions over the 2000 to 2011 time frame. We address a few research questions on deal characteristics and raise questions for further research in this area. The way forward could be to look at the universe of all the cross border deals and then test the robustness of our results. In future research we would also like to explore other characteristics of acquirer and target like the different characteristics of the countries and the value created for each kind of pair. The results in this study motivate us to further our study in understanding the regulations of the countries which might be one of the reasons for the payment mode adopted by the firms. However, this study brings forth a new dimension to the cross border deals literature and provides an incremental path in this area for further exploration.

REFERENCES

[1] Acharya, V., Shin, H. and Yorulmazer, T (2007). 'Fire-sale FDI'. *CEPR Discussion Paper no. 6319. London, Centre for Economic Policy Research.*

[2] Aguiar, Mark, and GopinathG., (2005), Fire-Sale FDI and Liquidity Crises, *The Review of Economics and Statistics,* 87(3): 439-542.

[3] Andrade, G., Mitchell M., and Stafford E. (2001).New evidence and perspectives on mergers.*Journal of Economic Perspectives,* 15, 103-120.

[4] Barkema, H.G., Vermeulen, F., (1998). International expansion through start-up or acquisition: a learning perspective. Acad. Manage. J. 41, 7–26.

[5] Brouthers, K.D., Brouthers, L.E., (2000). Acquisition or greenfield start-up? Institutional, cultural and transaction cost influences. *Strategic Management Journal,* 21, 89–97.

[6] Buckley, P. J., &Casson, M.,(1976). The future of the multinational enterprise. London: Macmillan.

[7] Chari, A., Ouimet, P., andTesar, L., (2010). The Value of Control in Emerging Markets.*Review of Financial Studies,* vol. 23, No. 4, pp. 1741-1770.

[8] Chernykh, L., Liebenberg, I.A., and Macias, A. J., (2011) Changing Direction: Cross Border Acquisitions by Emerging Market Firms. Retrieved October 31 2012 from *SSRN: http://ssrn.com/abstract=1540260.*

[9] Dunning, J. H, (1988). The eclectic paradigm of international production: A restatement and some possible extensions. *Journal of International Business Studies,* 19(1): 1–31.

[10] Faccio, M., and Masulis, R.W., (2005).The Choice of Payment Method in European Mergers & Acquisitions.*Journal of Finance,* Vol. 60, No. 3, pp. 1345-1388, 2005.

[11] Gubbi, S.R., Aulakh P.S., Ray S. Sarkar M.B., Chitoor R., (2010).Do international acquisitions by emerging-economy firms create shareholder value? The case of Indian firms.*Journal of International Business Studies*41**,** 397–418.

[12] Jahera, J. S., Hand, J., & Lloyd, W. P. (1985).An Empirical Inquiry into the Premiums for Controlling Interests.*Quarterly Journal of Business and Economics,* 67-77.

[13] Jensen, M.C., and Ruback, R. S. (1983). The market for corporate control: The scientific evidence. *Journal of Financial Economics,* 11, (1-4), 5-50.

[14] King, D, Dalton, D, Covin J, Daily C, (2004). Meta-Analyses of Post-Acquisition Performance: Indications of Unidentified Moderators. *Strategic Management Journal, 25*(2), 187-200.

[15] Martin, K. J.,(1996). The Method of Payment in Corporate Acquisitions, Investment Opportunities, and Management Ownership.Journal of Finance, (51) 4, 1227-1246.

[16] Morck, R., Shleifer, A., &Vishney, R. W. (1990). Do Managerial Objectives Drive Bad Acquisitions. *Journal of Finance,* 45(1), 31-48.

[17] Teece, D., J., (1985). Multinational Enterprise, Internal Governance, and Industrial Organization, *American Economic Review* 75 (2), 233–238.

[18] Teece, D. J., (1986). Transaction Cost Economics and the Multinational enterprise. *Journal of Economic Behaviour and Organization,* 7:21-45.

An Experiment on Effect of Anchoring Bias in Financial Decision Making

Arindam Banerjee, Parijat Upadhyay[1] and Prithiraj Banerjee[2]

Asia-Pacific Institute of Management, New Delhi
[1]Institute of Management Technology, Ghaziabad
[2]Globsyn Business School, Kolkata

ABSTRACT

The psychological aspects of financial decision-making are an interesting and emerging area of contemporary research. The objective of this study is to investigate the role of the anchoring (bias)*(Tversky and Kahneman, 1974) in perceiving financial and economic information. Anchoringbias may be defined as popularbent to form estimates for diverse categories, primarily starting from anavailable, and may be an irrelevant value. Presence of anchoring bias leads to inadequately adjusting final judgmentsfrom this starting value. Under this study, we carried out an experiment involving a group of post-graduate students. We asked torecall a number of latestfinancial and economic indicators, with half of the participantsreceiving actual information about some unrelated indicators (anchors), before answering thequestions. During the experiment,vast majority of the participants exhibits significant anchoring bias.*

INTRODUCTION

Anchoring also called focalism is a cognitive bias. Anchoring bias describes the general human tendency to rely too deeply on the first piece of information offered, i.e. the "anchor" at the time of decision-making. During decision-making, anchoring occurs when individuals use an initial piece of information to make subsequent judgments. After setting the anchor,other judgments are made by adjusting around that anchor, and thus creating a bias toward interpreting other information around the anchor.

This phenomenon wasfirst proposed by Tversky and Kahneman(1974). In this study, we analyze the effect ofanchoring in perceiving financial and economicdata. Under this study, we carried out an experimentinvolving a group of post-graduate students, askingthem to recall a number of recent economicand financial indicators for Indian economy,in general (interest rate, rates of inflation, currency exchange rates etc.),and National Stock Exchange of India, in particular(stock and bond market index values andreturns, yield to maturity rates ongovernment bonds). In this study, we adopt theexperimental design consistent withJacowitz and Kahneman (1995). Werandomly created two groups out of the participants:

(i) "Control" group (GroupC): Participants in this group are asked to provide their best estimate for each of the questions. However, noadditional information is given to them.

(ii) "Anchoring" group (Group A): Participants in this group are asked the *same* questions as in group C. However, before each question they are provided with *unrelated* financial or economic indicators ("anchor indicators"), of the sameorder of importance and expressed at thesame scale.

We expect from this experiment that the answersgiven by participants in Group A should be closer to anchor indicators than the answersgiven by participants in Group C.

In our experiment, significant anchoring bias is exhibited.

The rest of the paper is structured as follows. In Section 2, literature on anchoring is being reviewed. Experimental design and research approach is described in section 3. Section 4 defines the hypotheses and provides the empirical tests and the results. Section 5 makes the conclusion to this paper.

LITERATURE REVIEW

Human judgments are subject to a variety of systematic biases and distortions (Kahneman, et al. (1982)).Tversky and Kahneman (1974) propose that in assessing the likelihood of uncertain events and predicting or recallingcertain values or outcomes, people rely on a number of simplifying rules of decision-making,called heuristics. *Anchoring* (or *anchoring bias)* is one of theheuristics. They arguethat in many situations people makeestimates by considering an initial value thatthey adjust upwards or downwards to yielda final estimate. Such adjustments are ofteninsufficient, leaving judgments biased in thedirection of the initial "anchor" value.

Anchoring effects have proved to be a truly omnipresent experience that has been observed in a broad array of different critical domains (Mussweiler and Strack (1999a), English (2008)).Jacowitz and Kahneman (1995) ask students a number of general knowledge questions (like length of Mississippi or height of Everest), and report that participants who are given high anchors provide higher estimates than those who are given low anchors. Strack and Mussweiler (1997) and Mussweiler and Strack (1999b) also obtained similar results. Cervone and Peake (1986) document that people receiving high anchors subsequently estimate their own capabilities higher than those who are given low anchors. Plous (1989) argues that the anchoring bias affects people's probability assessments. Furthermore, Chapman and Johnson (1994) ask people to evaluate a number of lotteries varying in their expected values and ranges, and find that the higher the anchor they are given, the higher the minimal sum for which they would sell the lottery. Anchoring effects are well-documented in legal judgment. Markovsky (1988) reports that subjects exposed to large monetary anchors suggest higher rewards for a witness who comes forward to testify about a crime. Chapman and Bornstein (1996) ask their experiment participants to act as jurors and to decide on the amount of personal injury compensation for a specific case, and find that the higher the requested compensation, serving as a random anchor, the higher the compensation actually awarded by the "jurors". This may constitute a really interesting result, implying that the more people ask for, the more they get. In the same spirit, English and Mussweiler (2001) carry an experiment involving a group of professional judges, and conclude that sentencing decisions are anchored towards the sentences demanded by prosecutors. The magnitude of this influence proves to be dramatic, as judges who consider a high demand of 34 months give final sentences (for the same crimes) that are almost 8 months longer than judges who consider low demand of 12 months. The effect appears to be independent of judges' experience.

EXPERIMENTAL DESIGN

In our experiment, we ask our participants to recall a number of recent economic and financial indicators for Indian economy, in general, and National Stock Exchange of India, in particular. The participants are majorly post-graduate management students. To introduce and to control for the effect of anchoring, we randomly attribute our participants to one of the two groups2:

- "Control" group (Group C): No additional information are given to the participants belonging to this group. They were asked to provide their best estimate for each of the respective indicators. There were 36 participants in Group C (21 males and 15 females, with mean age of 23.3),
- "Anchoring" group (Group A): Same questions were asked to the participants in this group. However, before each question they receive unrelatedeconomic or financial indicators("anchor indicators"), of the same orderof magnitude and expressed at the samescale. For example, we provide thecurrent value of S&P 500 Index and the participants were asked to provide their bestestimate for the current value of Nifty-50. Clearly, these two figures are unrelated. There were 45 participants in Group A (29 males and 16 females, with mean age of 24.2).

The questionnaire is presented to Group A. Since anchoring bias is supposed, "to draw people's estimates closer to the anchor", thegeneral intuition says that the answers given by participants in Group A should be closerto anchor indicators than the answers given by participants in Group C.

RESEARCH QUESTIONEER

The purpose of this questioner is to measure presence of anchoring bias in financial decision-making. Please do not consult your colleagues during filling up this questioner. Finding of this questioner will be used for research purposes only.

Below you will find a number of real financial data. Please fill in the missing numbers, according to your best estimation.

1. The current value of S&P 500 Index is 3625 points.

   I suppose that the current value of Nifty-50 Index is ____________.

2. The S&P 500 Index annual return at 2011 was 6.58%.

   I suppose that the Nifty - 50 Index annual return at 2011 was _________%.

3. The average annual return of S&P 500 Index over the years 2007-2011 was-9.50%.

   I suppose that the average annual return of the Nifty - 50 Index over the years 2007-2011 was _________%.

4. The current value of S&P 500 Index differs from the Index's historical high by 35.11%.

   I suppose that the current value of the Nifty - 50 Index differs from the Index's historical high by _________%.

5. The manufacturing production in India increased in 2009 relatively to 2008 by 8.50%.

   I suppose that the the Nifty - 50 Index annual return at 2009 was _________%.

6. The average annual rate of increase in the manufacturing production in India over the years 1998-2008 was 3.55%.

   I suppose that the average annual return of Nifty 100 Index over the years 2007-2009 was _________%.

7. The major increase in the manufacturing production in India in the last decade took place in 2000. The manufacturing production increased by 11%.

   I suppose that the current value of Nifty 100 Index differs from the Index's historical high by _________%.

8. The DAX Index annual return at 2009 was 23.85%.

   I suppose that the Mid-Cap-50 Index annual return at 2009 was _________%.

9. The current value of DAX Index differs from the Index's historical high by 32.81%.

   I suppose that the current value of Nifty MidCapIndex differs from the Index's historical high by _________%.

10. The agricultural output in India increased in 2008 relatively to 2007 by 7.45%.

    I suppose that the Nifty 500 annual return at 2009 was _________%.

We followed the method consistent with methods proposed by Jacowitz and Kahneman (1995). First of all, we calculate the anchoring measure for each answer given by each participant in group A in the following way:

$$A_n^i = 1 - \left\| \frac{RA_n^i - In}{DCn} \right\| \quad \ldots (1)$$

where:

A_n^i – Anchoring (bias) measure for question *n* and person *i*,

RA_n^i – Actual answer (Response) to question *n* given by participant *i* from Croup A,

I_n– Anchor Indicator (anchor) for question *n*,

DC_n- Mean Deviation from the anchor for question *n*, in Group C, which, in its turn, is calculated as:

$$DC_n = \frac{\sum_{j=1}^{NC} \left\| RC_n^j - In \right\|}{NC} \quad \dots (2)$$

where:

RC_n^j - Actual answer (Response) to question *n* given by participant *j* from Group C,

NC - Number of participants in group C (36 participants).

HYPOTHESIS TESTING

The objective of our paper is to analyzethe relevance of anchorson the degree of anchoring bias. To meet this objective, we first calculate mean anchoringmeasures for each of the questions and foreach of the participants, and then analyzethe differences in these measures fordifferent groups of questions, by types ofanchors provided.

Firstly, we calculate theanchoring measuresfor each questionand for each participant, and subsequently,the mean (over 46 participants from GroupA) anchoring measures (AQ_n) for each of the experimental questions. If we believe in existence of anchoring bias, the participants in Group A will, on average,provide answers that will be closer to therespective anchor indicators than those byparticipants in Group C.

Table 1: Measuring Bias: (A_n^i)

Question No.	*Anchoring Measure (A_n^i)*						*AQ_n> 0: t – statistic (p- value,%)*
	Mean (AQ_n)	*Median*	*Standard Deviation*	*Maximum*	*Minimum*	*No. of Positive*	
1	0.654	0.356	0.547	0.874	-0.458	34	10.75 (0.00)
2	0.731	0.654	0.258	0.987	-0.325	33	2.57 (1.48)
3	0.695	0.258	0.471	0.854	0.254	34	11.26(0.00)
4	0.458	0.547	0.647	0.657	0.365	36	14.17(0.00)
5	0.654	0.458	0.254	0.785	0.214	35	0.20 (83.92)
6	0.698	0.745	0.478	0.854	0.365	38	4.51 (0.01)
7	0.745	0.752	0.658	0.854	0.452	39	3.92(0.04)
8	0.632	0.642	0.985	0.854	0.363	34	0.90(37.52)
9	0.564	0.587	0.478	0.698	-0.254	26	20.72(0.00)
10	0.674	0.635	0.254	0.785	0.354	36	3.78 (0.06)

Now for each of the 10 experimental questions, we hypothesize the following:

Hypothesis 1:

H0: $AQ_n = 0$ (no anchoring bias for question *n*)

H1: $AQ_n > 0$ (positive anchoring bias for question *n*)

As may be observed from table 1, the results strongly indicate presence of anchoring bias. All the ten mean anchoring measures are positive, and majority of them significantly.

CONCLUSION

The objective of our paper is to explore the role of anchoring in perceiving financial and economic information. We employed an experimental questioner before a learned and competent audience. The result shows significant presence of anchoring bias.

The results have important implications for decision-making in various fields of real life. We showed that decision-making may be influenced by some arbitrary anchors.

REFERENCES

[1] Beggs, A., and K. Graddy, 2009, AnchoringEffects: Evidence from Art Auctions,*American Economic Review*, 99, 1027-1039.

[2] Biswas, A., and S. Burton, 1993, ConsumerPerceptions of Tensile Price Claims inAdvertisements: An Assessment ofClaim Types across Different DiscountLevels, *Journal of the Academy ofMarketing Science*, 21, 217–229.

[3] Blank, H., J. Musch, and R. F. Pohl, 2007,Hindsight Bias: On Being Wise after theEvent, *Social Cognition*, 25, 1-9.

[4] Blank, H., G. von Collani, V. Fischer, and S.Nestler, 2008, How Many HindsightBiases are There? *Cognition*, 106, 1408-1440.

[5] Bowman, N. A., and M. N. Bastedo, 2010,Anchoring Effects in World University

[6] Rankings: Exploring Biases inReputation Scores, *Higher Education*,Forthcoming. Cervone, D., and P. K. Peake, 1986, Anchoring,Efficacy, and Action: The Influence of Judgmental Heuristics on Self-EfficacyJudgment and Behavior, *Journal ofPersonality and Social Psychology*, 50,492–501.

[7] Chapman, G. B., and B. H. Bornstein, 1996, TheMore You Ask for, the More You Get:Anchoring in Personal Injury Verdicts,*Applied Cognitive Psychology*, 10, 519–540.

[8] Chapman, G. B., and E. J. Johnson, 1994, TheLimits of Anchoring, *Journal ofBehavioral Decision Making*, 7, 223–242.

[9] English, B., 2008, When Knowledge Matters—Differential Effects of AvailableKnowledge in Standard and BasicAnchoring Tasks, *European Journal ofSocial Psychology*, 38, 896-904.

[10] Englich, B., and T. Mussweiler, 2001,Sentencing under Uncertainty:Anchoring Effects in the Courtroom,*Journal of Applied Social Psychology*,31, 1535–1551.

[11] Ehrbeck, T., and R. Waldman, 1996, Why areProfessional Forecasters Biased? Agency Versus Behavioral Explanations, *Quarterly Journal of Economics*, 111, 21-40.

[12] Erdfelder, E., M. Brandt, and A. Broder, 2007, Recollection Biases in Hindsight Judgments, *Social Cognition*, 25(1), 114-131.

[13] Fisher, K. L., and M. Statman, 2000, Cognitive Biases in Market Forecasts, *Journal of Portfolio Management*, 27, 72-81.

[14] Galinsky, A. D., and T. Mussweiler, 2001, First Offers as Anchors: The Role of Perspective-Taking and Negotiator Focus, *Journal of Personality and Social Psychology*, 81, 657–669.

[15] Gruen, D. K., and M. C. Gizycki, 1993, Explaining Forward Discount Bias: Is It Anchoring? Princeton University Woodrow Wilson School Discussion Paper in Economics, 164.

[16] Jacowitz, K. E., and D. Kahneman, 1995, Measures of Anchoring in Estimation Tasks, *Personality and Social Psychology Bulletin*, 21, 1161–1166.

[17] Kahneman, D., P. Slovic, and A. Tversky, 1982, Judgment under Uncertainty: Heuristics and Biases, New York: Cambridge University Press.

[18] Kudryavtsev, A., and G. Cohen, 2010, Anchoring and Pre-Existing Knowledge in Economic and Financial Settings, *American Journal of Social and Management Sciences*, Forthcoming.

[19] Markovsky, B, 1988, Anchoring Justice, *Social Psychology Quarterly,* 51, 213-224.

[20] Mussweiler, T, 2001, The Durability of Anchoring Effects, *European Journal of Social Psychology*, 31, 431–442.

[21] Mussweiler, T., and F. Strack, 1999a, Comparing is Believing: A Selective Accessibility Model of Judgmental Anchoring, In W. Stroebe& M.

[22] Hewstone (Eds.), *European review of social psychology* (Vol. 10, pp. 135–167). Chichester, UK: Wiley.

[23] Mussweiler, T., and F. Strack, 1999b, Hypothesis-Consistent Testing and Semantic Priming in the Anchoring Paradigm: A Selective Accessibility Model, *Journal of Experimental Social Psychology*, 35, 136–164.

[24] Mussweiler, T., and F. Strack, 2000, Numeric Judgment under Uncertainty: The Role of Knowledge in Anchoring, *Journal of Experimental Social Psychology*, 36, 495–518.

[25] Northcraft, G. B., and M. A. Neale, 1987, Experts, Amateurs, and Real Estate: An Anchoring-and-Adjustment Perspective on Property Pricing Decisions, *Organizational Behavior and Human Decision Processes*, 39, 84–97.

[26] Pohl, R.F., 2004, Hindsight Bias, In R.F. Pohl (Ed.), *Cognitive Illusions: A Handbook on Fallacies and Biases in Thinking,Judgment and Memory*, Hove, UK: Psychology Press, 363-378.

[27] Plous, S, 1989, Thinking the Unthinkable: The Effects of Anchoring on Likelihood Estimates of Nuclear War, *Journal of Applied Social Psychology*, 19, 67–91.

[28] Simonson, I., and A. Drolet, 2004, Anchoring Effects on Consumers' Willingness-to- Pay and Willingness-to-Accept, *Journal of Consumer Research*, 31, 681-690.

[29] Strack, F., and T. Mussweiler, 1997, Explaining the Enigmatic Anchoring Effect: Mechanisms of Selective Accessibility, *Journal of Personality and Social Psychology*, 73, 437–446.

[30] Tversky, A., and D. Kahneman, 1973, Availability: A Heuristic for Judging Frequency and Probability, *Cognitive Psychology,* 4, 207-232.

[31] Tversky, A., and D. Kahneman, 1974, Judgment under Uncertainty: Heuristics and Biases, *Science*, 185, 1124-1131.

[32] Wilson, T. D., C. Houston, K. M. Etling, and N. Brekke, 1996, A New Look at Anchoring Effects: Basic Anchoring and its Antecedents, *Journal of Experimental Psychology: General*, 4, 387–402.

[33] Zielonka, P., 2004, Technical Analysis as the Representation of Typical Cognitive Biases, *International Review of Financial Analysis*, 13, 217-225.

Commercial Significance of Menthol Mint Cultivation in Uttar Pradesh

Shaili Vadera

Amity Business School, Amity University, Lucknow

ABSTRACT

Medicinal and Aromatic plants (MAPs) are recently emerging not only as the natural source of new drugs and valuable compounds but also as the green bio- resource alternatives offering viable business opportunities. India is leading producer of menthol in the world with 13,000mt produced in 2008. Between 1965 and 2006, the Indian mentha oil market grew from 2 MT to 32,000MT, registering an incredible production increase. India now dominates 80% of the world market. Anticipating huge demand for mentha crystal and flakes in both overseas and domestic markets, pharmaceutical companies in the northern region have planned to take up mentha cultivation under contract farming. The crop is grown in large tracts of Uttar Pradesh which supplies not only India's requirement but also the bulk of the global requirement.

INTRODUCTION

Agriculture is considered to be the mainstay of the Indian economy. In India, about 72% of the population resides in rural India out of which about 65% of the population is solely dependent on agriculture for their livelihood. The 2020 vision specially focuses on agriculture and food processing as a very important area for assured growth in Gross Domestic Product. The World Health Organization *(WHO)* has estimated that the global trade in herbal medicines is likely to be $5 trillion by the year 2050. India has a reputation of a low-cost manufacturer of high quality generic drugs in the global market *(Mashelkar RA 2005)*. Importance of medicinal plants to rural development and livelihood improvement of the poor communities has also been emphasized as the overall goal of the sector development *(Jason Holley and Kiran Cherla 1996)*. According to Assocham "Indian herbal industry is likely to register a compound annual growth rate of 20 per cent by 2012. Major trade destinations for India's export of Ayurvedic medicines include Unites States of America, Germany, Russia, United Kingdom, Taiwan, the United Arab Emirates, Hong Kong and Malaysia. Medicinal and Aromatic plants (MAPs) are emerging as the green bio-resource alternatives offering viable business opportunities. According to a study *(Kate, Laird 1999),* 18% of the world's top 150 prescription drugs are derived from plant sources. Medicinal plants have the potential to fill these needs as they provide green health alternatives and a number of other eco-friendly products of domestic and industrial usage *(Bordeker, 2002).*

BACKGROUND

India is an active participant in the global medicinal plants market (Patnaik G 1994). The Indian System of Medicines include Ayurveda, Siddha, Unani and Homeopathic system which predominantly use plant based raw materials in most of their preparations and formulations. Modern pharmacopoeia also contains at least 25% drugs derived from plants (Planning commission 2000). Indian exports of medicinal plants have increased from 1.5% in 2001 to 8.31% in 2009 which is indeed promising. Investors from all over the world are making more and more investments in this particular sector for unleashing its existing potentialities as well as for exploring the untapped areas.

India has emerged as the leading producer and exporter of Menthol Mint in the world. India now meets about 80 percent of the global requirement. India has not only overtaken China which earlier met 60 percent of world demand, but has also begun exporting Menthol Mint oil to Beijing as well as Brazil which used to be another major producer and exporter of the same. In India, state of Uttar Pradesh mainly accounts for about 90 per cent of total area under mentha cultivation, whereas the rest of the production comes from Punjab districts like Jalandhar, Ludhiana and Hoshiarpur.

Central Institute of Medicinal and Aromatic Plants, a CSIR laboratory at Lucknow has developed a new cultivar of *mentha arvensis* which provides three harvests a year. The new varieties have been named 'Himalaya' and 'Kosi'. These varieties are early maturing, disease and pest resistant and give higher yield and oil.

Mentha oil is used for several purposes like in the food, perfumery, flavouring and pharmaceutical industry. It is used in manufacturing of products like lozenges, toothpaste, pain balm, cold balm etc. Strong industrial growth over two decades and increasing off-take from tobacco industry has pushed up the consumption of menthol. Menthol flakes and its constituents and derivatives are used in food, pharmaceutical, perfumery and flavoring industry. Its main constituent, menthol, is used in the manufacture of lozenges, toothpastes, pain balms, cold balms, Dabur Pudin Hara, etc. Pharmaceuticals and tobacco industry consume more than 50% of the total mentha oil followed by oral hygiene and confectionary industry.

DOMESTIC SCENARIO OF MENTHOL MINT IN INDIA

Uttar Pradesh is India's largest producing state, contributing almost 80-90%, to the country's total production, followed by Bihar, Punjab, Haryana and Himachal Pradesh. Cultivation of mint in India starts from February - March every year and the crop takes around 90 days to mature and produces first flowers, which is the best stage to harvest. First harvesting is done during May - June. Farmers undertake at least two harvestings from the crop. Menthol flakes production in India begins from mid-June and steady arrivals are seen till November. The major production/trading centers of Menthol flakes cover the districts of Moradabad, Rampur, Barabanki, Sitapur and Lucknow in the Central Uttar Pradesh; Chandigarh & Jalandhar in Punjab.

The large scale commercial cultivation of Mentha is done in different states of Uttar Pradesh (Bilaspur, Rampur, Chandausi, Sambhal, Barabanki , Bareilly , Sitapur etc.), Punjab (Jalandhar), Haryana (Ambala) , Himachal and Bihar (Muzuffarpur). India produces about 27,600 tons of mentha crude oil per annum (avg. for last five years). The output is increasing in recent years and a record production close to 32,000 tons is estimated for the current year.

Medicinal plants like menthol mint (Mentha arvensis) transform the socio-economic status of poor farmers with all round improvement in quality of their life. India has thus been able to produce over 15,000 tonnes of menthol mint oil in a year. This yield comes from an area of one lakh twenty five thousand hectares. About 35 per cent of mint cultivators plant this after the harvest of traditional winter crops of mustard, potato, lentil and wheat. About one million persons are employed in the mint sector, of which 3 lakh joined in the last three years. These developments have greatly benefitted the areas in the Indo-gangetic region and rural prosperity is looking up among other areas around Lucknow, Sitapur, Badaun, Moradabad and Udham Singh Nagar. In fact, commercial agriculture has begun to take roots and the Indian farmers are resolutely taking advantage of the opportunities opened up by globalisation. Also, Japanese mint is considered as bonus crop providing leadership to India in world market.

Table 1. Total Area Under Menthol Cultivation in India

S.No.	*Area/State*	*% of Total Crop in India*
1.	Barabanki (include the area as Sitapur, Faizabad, Gonda & Baraich	60%
2.	Sambal, Chandosi, Moradabad, Bareilly, Rampur and Bilaspur	30%
3	Punjab, Haryana, Rajasthan	10%

Source: National Multi-Commodity Exchange of India 2011

90% crop of India, grown in Uttar Pradesh, rest 10% in Punjab, Haryana and Rajasthan. In recent years Mentha Herb was developed in Madhya Pradesh & Gujarat but in little quantity.

Table 2. Economics of Cultivation of Mint

1. I)	*ITEMS* *Estimated Returns from Cultivation*	*Sucker Planted*	*Transplanted*
A)	Expenditure for Cultivation		460
	Raising of nursery	2000	2000
	Preparation of land	6,200	5,500
	Manures and fertilizers	2,500	500
	Cost of planting material	6000	3,600
	Weeding and hoeing	3000	2,400
	Irrigation	1,500	750
	Harvesting	6,000	4,500
	Distillation cost@Rs. 30/kg oil, miscellaneous charges (including pesticides)	1,000	1,000
	Total	28,200	20,710
B).	Gross return		
	Oil yield	200 kg	150 kg
	Oil price (Rs./kg)	400	400
	Cost of Oil produced (Rs.)	80,000	60,000
	C) Net Return (Rs./ha)	51,800	39,290
II)	Additional income generation from vermicompost		
A)	Expenditure for vemicomposting (utilizing 15t of deoiled herbage) involving cost of labour, worms, and thatched shed.		
B)	Returns Yield of 3t vermicompost from 15t of distillation waste, price of vermicompost @Rs. 3/kg	Rs. 9000	Rs.9000
C)	Additional Profits/Income	Rs.6000	Rs.6000
	Total net Profit with Vermicompost IV+IIC	Rs.57,800	Rs. 45,290

Khanuja SPS et al 2006, Central Institute of Medicinal and Aromatic Plants

(i) By intercropping of mint with okra, onion, and radish an additional net return of Rs. 15000-18000/ha can be obtained.

(ii) By intercropping menthol mint in sugarcane, an additional net return of Rs. 10,000-12,000/ha can be obtained.

(iii) The sale price of the menthol mint oil varies from season to season and year to year based on the international supply and demand situation.

(iv) The above calculations are based on market prices as prevailing during 2005-06.

Crop Combination for Higher Profitability of Mint

Box: 1

Maize	Potato	Mentha
Paddy	Potato	Mentha
Basil	Potato	Mentha
Paddy	Lahi	Mentha
Paddy	Wheat	Mentha

Khanuja SPS et al 2006, Central Institute of Medicinal and Aromatic Plants

Table 3. Estimated area and Production of Menthol Mint in India During 1995 – 2009

Year	*Approx. area (ha)*	*Approx. Production of Mentha oil (tonnes)*
1995	80000	7000
1996	120000	9000
1997	170000	14000
1998	133000	12000
1999	125000	11000
2000	150000	14000
2001	155000	14500
2002	150000	14000
2003	150000	15000
2004	150000	15000
2005	160000	16000
2006	160000	16000
2007	170000	17000
2008	180000	18000
2009	180000	180000

Source: Singh and Khanuja (2009-2010)

GLOBAL SCENARIO OF MENTHOL MINT

Presently, India is the largest producer of mentha oil in the world contributing about 80% of total production. Rest 20% of global production, comes from China (9%), Brazil (7%) and US (4%).

India meets the global demand by exporting nearly 20,000 to 21,000 tonnes per annum. The major exports are directed to countries like China, France, Germany, Japan etc. About 50% of total Menthol flakes production is exported to China, whereas menthol crystals are exported to US and European countries. The global output from India alone was close to 32,000 tons in 2009-10. Exports of mint products from India are increasing over the years, which include menthol flakes, menthol crystals, mint oils. This could mainly be attributed to rising overseas demand for India produce. The major destinations of export for India includes countries such as Argentina, Brazil, France, Germany, Japan, UK, USA etc.

Table 4. Worldwide consumption of menthol, by industry, (based on 2009 data)

Oral hygiene	28.0%
Pharmaceuticals	26.6%
Tobacco	25.3%
Confectionaries	11.0%
Shaving products	7.0%
Miscellaneous	2.1%

Source: http://www.leffingwell.com

KEY PLAYERS IN MENTHOL MARKET IN INDIA

India is leading producer of menthol in the world with 13,000mt produced in 2007. China and Brazil are other significant manufacturing nations. Between 1965 and 2006, the Indian mentha oil market grew from 2 MT to 13,000MT, registering an incredible production increase. India now dominates 80% of the world market.

Price trend

Currently prices of menthol are ruling around ₹ 640/ Kg for Crystal Bold, ₹ 630/Kg for Crystal Medium and Rs 580/Kg for Flakes. Increase in international demand, augmented by poor crop returns of Menthol from China and Brazil, is responsible for this increased price.

Anticipating huge demand for mentha crystal and flakes in both overseas and domestic markets, pharmaceutical companies in the northern region have planned to take up mentha cultivation under contract farming. These companies have already upgraded their processing facilities in order to meet the demand for mentha derivatives. Menthol crop has a made a tiny and an uncertain beginning in Tamil Nadu near Sriperambudur, near Chennai. The crop is grown in large tracts of Uttar Pradesh which supplies not only India's requirement but also the bulk of the global requirement.

To reduce the volatility in pricing, and reduce freight costs, industry users are encouraging production of the same in the South, to the mutual benefit of farmers and industry. Market demand for the product is growing at the rate of 10 to 15 per cent annually within and outside the country. Five years ago China used to be a major producer and exporter, but the country removed the subsidies on the product. Middlemen of disrepute reduced farmer's returns further and the industry collapsed. With no serious competition on the global front and no synthetic substitute for menthol, the future seems to be bright for the cash crop.

According to a pain balm manufacturer, menthol could be grown in the South even though the area does not face extreme cold. There are no pest threats to the crop. It could be sown in February and harvested once in June and again by October in time for the next different crop.

Chandigarh-based Surya Pharmaceuticals Ltd, which is procuring mentha oil from Uttar Pradesh, plans to bring 5,000 acres under contract farming in Punjab in the next season. Surya is one of the largest exporters of mint/menthol derivatives like flakes and crystal and exports to countries like China, Europe and the US. The company, last year, commissioned its unit at Baddi in Himachal Pradesh with a processing capacity of 10,000 tonne per month. It expects a turnover of Rs 180-200 crore in the very first year of operation on the back of growing demand for crystal and flakes.

Another Chandigarh-based firm Ind Swift Laboratories too is planning to take up mentha cultivation from the next season to avoid price fluctuation, which is currently purchasing crude mentha from Uttar Pradesh in the form of crystals and flakes to cater to domestic as a well as overseas market. The company has an installed capacity of 750 tonne per month. Total global market is estimated at US$ 250mn-300mn, of which Nectar Life Sciences specializes in manufacture and sale of menthol flakes, menthol crystals, and mint oils and captures roughly 25% share. Sales of menthol crystals account for 70% of Phyto-chemicals revenue, with menthol flakes 20% and mint oils accounting for the balance. Over 90% of Nectar's revenue in this segment is generated from exports. Key competitors in the organized market are Jindal Drugs (Mumbai) and Sharp Menthol (Delhi) who collectively hold 45% market share. Key export markets for these products are U.S.A, China, Japan, and Southeast Asia.

Similarly, Nectar Lifesciences Ltd is contemplating entering the venture of mentha cultivation under contract farming. India is the largest producer of mentha, so there is huge potential." Nectar has facilities in Jammu and Derabassi with an installed capacity of 12,000 tonne per annum. Mint growers consider mentha as a bonus crop as it does not disturb or replace the cultivation of any major winter (rabi) or rainy season (kharif) crop.

Medicinal and Aromatic Plants can be viewed as an important commercial item for sustainable economic development of the country. To meet the demand of prominent industries producing herbal plants, pharmaceuticals, cosmetics, neutraceuticals, and other confectionary items etc, it has become imperative to produce the quality raw materials in significant quantities by devising organised cropping schedule and processing technological of harvested produces.

REFERENCES

[1] World Health Organization (WHO), WHO Traditional Medicine Strategy 2002-2005 [online]. Geneva, 2002 [cited 10 October 2003].

[2] Mashelkar RA. India's R & D: reaching for the top. Science. 2005;307:1415–1417. doi:10.1126/science.1110729. [PubMed]

[3] Jason Holley and Kiran Cherla 1996, The Medicinal Plants Sector in India: A State of the Art Review, World Bank and SARO, IDRC.

[4] www.financialexpress.com, march 28, 2008 /Herbal/Assocham/United States

[5] Patnaik, G. 1994. Information Management for the Marketing of Medicinal and Aromatic Plants. Unpublished Manuscript. APEDA, New Delhi.

[6] Planning Commission 2000- Report of the Taskforce on Medicinal Plants in India. Planning Commission, Government of India, Yojana Bhawan, New Delhi, India

[7] Rawat A.K.S. 2004, Karki, M. Sustainable forest management In Encyclopedia of Forest Sciences, pp. 1357–1367.Amsterdam, the Netherlands, Elsevier Adulteration & Substitution of Herbal Drugs in Indian Market, CMHHP

[8] Malla SB, Shakya PR,1984 Medicinal plants. In: T.C. Majupuria (Ed). Nepal - Nature's Paradise. Bangkok, Thailand; White Lotus Co. Ltd. pp. 261-297

Comparative Analysis of Family Run and Professional Conglomerates – Case Study of ITC Ltd and Godrej Group

Ankit Bansal, Priyanshi Kejriwal and Arin Chakraborty

Institute of Management Technology, Ghaziabad

ABSTRACT

The business environment around the world has been dominated by conglomerates which have formed the backbone of countries. Indian economy has been one of the fastest growing nations owing to contributions by huge conglomerates. This paper brings about the types of conglomerates based on the leadership and cultural model. The broad classification has been based into family managed and non family managed conglomerates and a comparison has been made on value creation, growth, profitability and risk. The paper compares two conglomerates of each category i.e. ITC Ltd. and Godrej group. It also gives a brief account of business environment conducive to the growth of family managed and non family managed conglomerates.

INTRODUCTION

Conglomerates are corporations that are involved in a number of different and unrelated/ related lines of business in which one company owns a controlling stake in a number of smaller companies conducting business separately. The smaller business operates independently of other divisions but report to senior management of parent company. The main motive of a conglomerate is diversification of risk by investing in different companies. The approach of conglomerate business enables them to reduce cost by using fewer resources.There can be several criteria for classification of conglomerates; the type of leadership models a conglomerate if following. Under this criterion, conglomerates can be classified as family run conglomerates and professionally run conglomerates. In this paper we attempt to put forward the comparative analysis of these two types of conglomerates: family run conglomerates like Godrej Group versus professionally run conglomerates like ITC. The paper brings about a contrast of the value system and mode of working of the two types of conglomerates. In family run conglomerates, the members are closely associated with each other which lead to good mutual understanding. Although family run conglomerates are always treated with gratuitous criticism, but pertaining to Indian economy they are akin to stabilizer of the system. Companies like Tata, Birla and Mahindra have carried the country through good and bad times. The senior level management is composed of the founders and heirs,which may sometimes play to disappointment of shareholders as they are complex to manage and family dynamics makes the decision making process complex. In family run conglomerates it is difficult to bring about radical cultural changes because of the powerful hegemony of family dominance. In a professionally run conglomerate, the senior management is composed with unrelated individuals who run the company on behalf of shareholders. The professionally run conglomerates may sometimes, suffer from lack of drive and commitment from the managerial class due to lack of ownership. The paper brings about the comparison of the two types of conglomerates based on a three parameter analysis: Relational distance, corporate finance decisions and value systems.

METHODOLOGY

The main objective of a family run business is creation of shareholder value which may encompass increasing cash flows, building equity and increasing share prices or giving dividends. Business strategy literature by Brandenburg and Stuart gives the following definition of value creation by a business.

Value created = Willingness of Buyer to Pay - Opportunity Cost of the Supplier

This equation is a simple market perspective where value created is difference of what a company gives to customer and what it takes to produce the product. A more deterministic way of calculating value produced is generating return on investments that exceeds the cost of capital. Financial ratios are useful indicator of the financial performance of firms. The four major dimensions of comparisons are value creation, growth, profitability and risk.

1. Shareholder's value creation: this is defined as ratio of market capitalization to average total assets. A low Q value represents an undervalued company and high Q value is a mark of overvalued company.
2. Growth: This is measured in terms of Compounded Annual Growth Rate (CAGR).
3. Profitability: Profitability is evaluated using Return on Assets (ROA), Return on Net worth (RONW), Return on Capital Employed (ROCE), Profit Margin and Earnings per Share (EPS).
4. Risk: It is usually evaluated by the capital structure of the company and interest coverage ratios.

COMPARATIVE ANALYSIS AND INTERPRETATION

Shareholder's Value Creation

The current trend shows the Tobin Q ratio (market capital/ Average Total Assets) is greater than 1 for both the companies so it can interpreted that both the companies are overvalued.

But according to the graph, a stock of NFMB is more expensive than the replacement costs of its assets when compared to FMB.

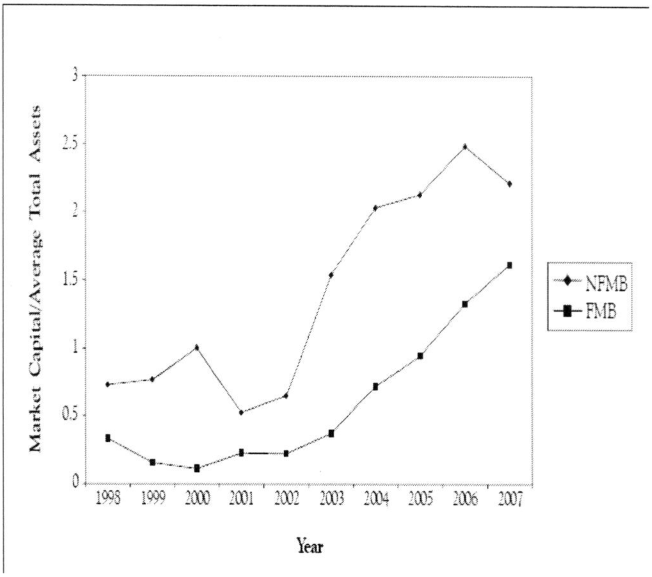

Fig. 1. Tobin's Q Ratio for performance and value creation: NFMB vs FMB

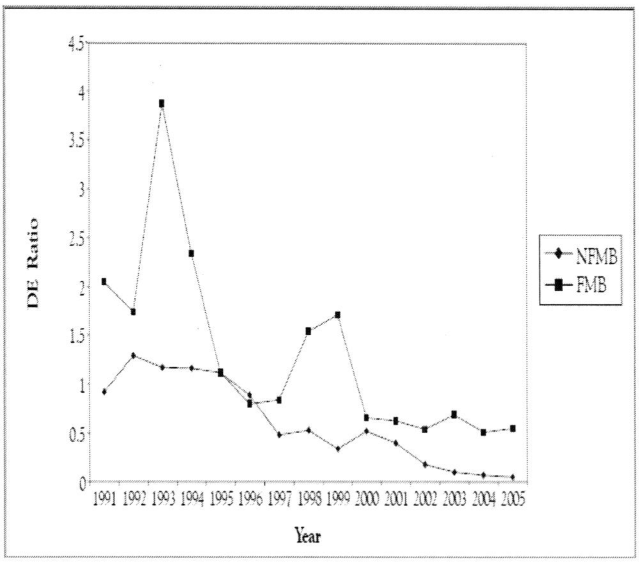

Fig. 2. Debt Equity Ratio: NFMB vs FMB

Risk

The risk factor evaluation of the two types of business can be determined by analyzing their debt equity ratio. The FMB types of businesses started with high D/E ratio which has gradually reduced over time; it can be attributed to the fact that they started as family businesses using debt as a financing mode which gradually reduced over time as the businesses expanded over time and generated equity. The NFMB have maintained a decent level of debt to equity which has gradually reduced overtime and most of the businesses have become near zero debt.

Growth

The growth of the business can be evaluated using CAGR approach. The two main areas of evaluation are net assets and growth in sales. The net assets of FMB have always been higher than the NFMB because they have primarily indulged in brick and mortar industries. The net sales of the NFMB business has increased over time but owing to large number of FMB in India the net sales of those types of business has always been higher than NFMB as evident from the figure 3 and 4.

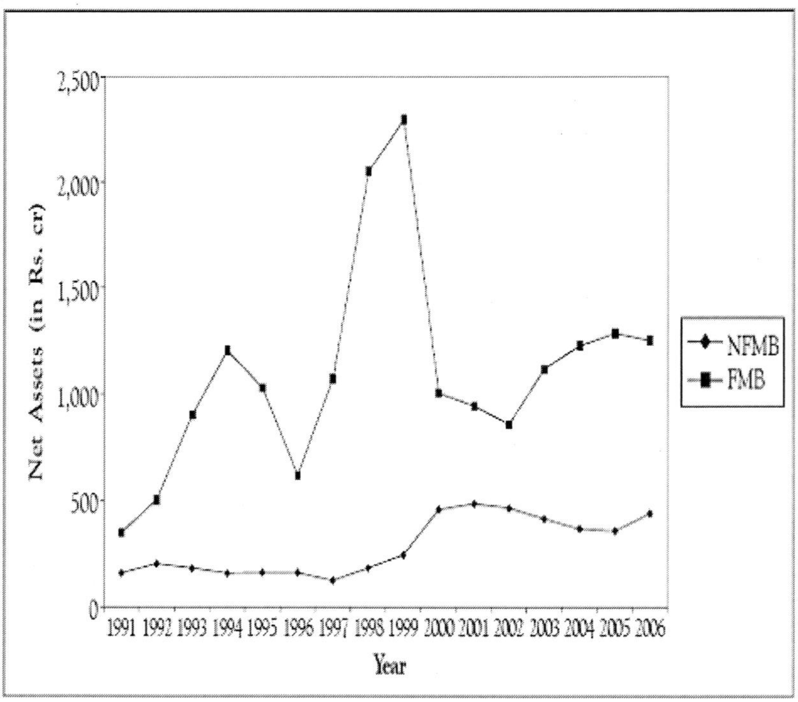

Fig. 3. Net Assets: NFMB vs FMB

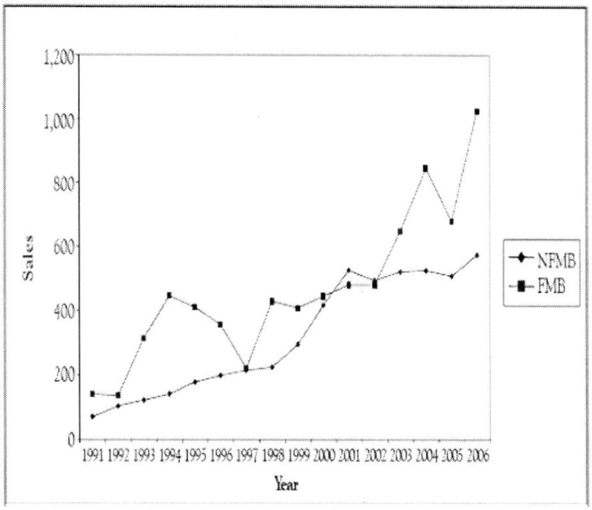

Fig. 4. Sales: NFMB vs FMB

Profitability

The profitability of the two types of business has been evaluated on the basis of the following factors: ROA, RONW, Profit Margin and EPS.

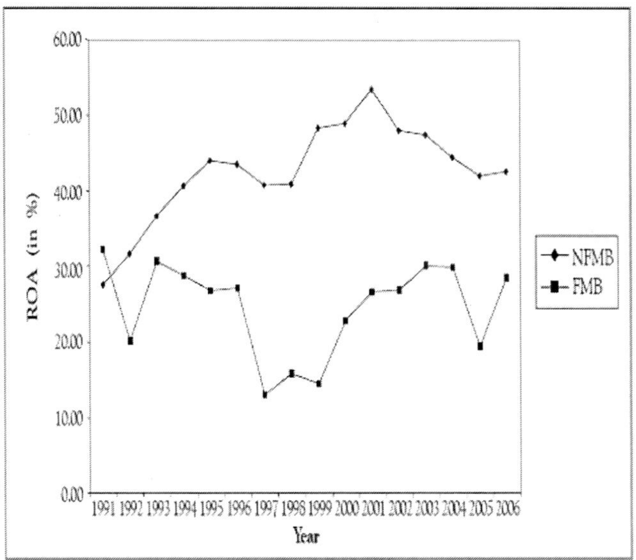

Fig. 5. ROA: NFMB vs FMB

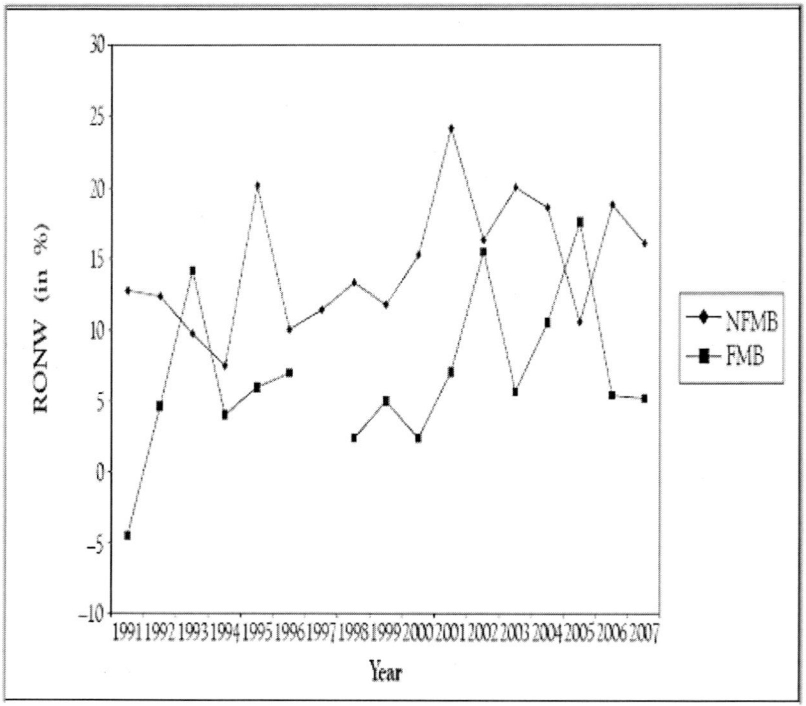

Fig. 6. RONW: NFMB vs FMB

a. ROA: The ROA figure gives an idea of how effectively the company is converting the money it has to invest into net income (Figure 5). The higher the ROA %, the better the company is in earning money on less investment. NFMB of India has higher ROA, meaning high earning on less investment.

b. RONW: The net worth of a business is the sum of equity and reserves of the business. In this criteria also, the NFMB has higher RONW, as they have amassed high equity and reserves as suggested by the D/E ration too.

c. Profit Margin: The profit margin for NFMB has always been higher than that of FMB because of higher levels of cost controls in the businesses. The NFMB has been very professional in their business management aspects where little emphasis is given to the emotional quotient.

d. EPS: The major motive of FMB has been to liberate the economy from slums in the initial years whereas NFMB has always laid emphasis on the profitability to the shareholders. So the EPS of NFMB has always been higher than FMB. The difference in the EPS is mainly due to the difference in value system of the company.

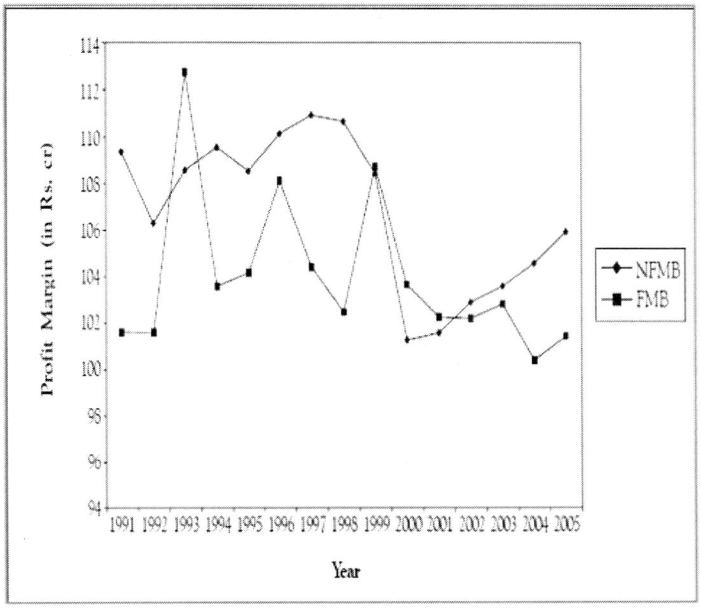

Fig. 7. Profit Margin: NFMB vs FMB

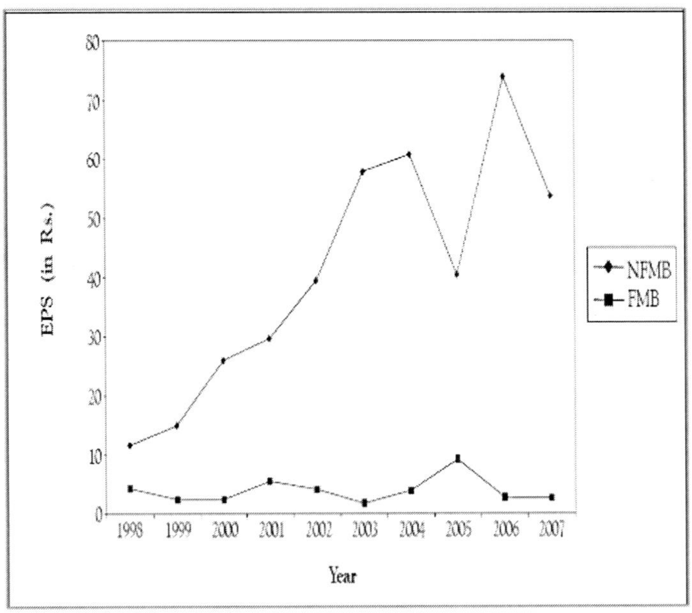

Fig. 8. EPS: NFMB vs FMB

The finding of the study shows that the NFMB has been more successful in creating shareholder's value. Both types of conglomerate business are overvalued, but the value creation is more for NFMB because of the expensive stocks and comparatively lesser level of assets. The professionally managed conglomerates are more successful in cost management so they have high levels of ROA. The family run conglomerates have started from scratch using more debt than owner's money which is suggestive from the D/E ratio. The net worth and growth is considerably higher for FMB because of their market capitalization and diversification is a large number of sectors.

THREE FACTOR ANALYSIS

Differentiation between the family-run and professionally-run conglomerates can be done on following parameters:

1. Relational distance;
2. Corporate finance decisions; and
3. Value system.

Relational Distance

Relational distance is the relationship between companies in a conglomerate setting. Family-controlled conglomerates will exhibit complex cross-holdings between group companies as compared with professionally-run conglomerates.

Generally, in a family-controlled conglomerate, at least one family member will directly or indirectly control each affiliated firm. Hence, the relational distance in the case of a family-controlled conglomerate is lower than professionally-run conglomerates.

Smoother internal markets: can be used as a tool to tunnel funds from firms where the family has low ownership to firms where the family has high ownership.

Of the Godrej empire, the wholly-owned Godrej & Boyce is a holding company, and in the two publicly listed companies — Godrej Industries and Godrej Consumer Products — promoters hold 88.4% and 68.2%, respectively. Godrej Industries Ltd has several subsidiaries, joint ventures, associates and equity investments some of which in turn have strategic holdings in their acquired subsidiaries. It gives a lot of independence to its affiliate companies and subsidiaries in decision-making. However, the control of Godrej family exists with family members having full control or as board members in some of the companies.

Family Business Model: The Godrej family holds a majority shareholding (ranging from 50% to 100%) in most of its companies. The role of the family members have been more of a trusteeship one in growing the business and the group has never experienced a single split, in its 100-year old history. The group's senior management consists mostly of the family members, predominantly from the third generation of the family. The fourth generation has just commenced entry into the business.

The young generation of the family has to join at the lowest executive levels like any other executive and be trained and found good before climbing up the corporate hierarchy. A strong and systematic succession plan is in place and the younger generation of the family is groomed under the guidance of the senior family members and outside professionals

The group companies are more like Strategic Business Units (SBUs), chaired by the family members. Each company is given a lot of independence. The CEO of the companies have maximum freedom to devise the strategy of the company, though, there is a consultation both at the family and business levels. This model of governance seems to have worked well for Godrej as is evident from the steady growth in the recent years after the economy has been opened up.

Corporate Finance Decisions

In the case of professionally-controlled conglomerates, managers who control each firm are relatively independent and hence their proposed ventures are stringently accountable and each manager competes for budgetary approval for his her ventures. Hence, most of their corporate financing decisions need to be economically viable. Such an environment will naturally curtail the empire-building exercises of the managers.

However, in a family business context, often new venture decisions are based on the availability of a kin or the ambitions passion of the family and hence it could result into an empire-building exercise. In a way, for family-controlled conglomerates, family wealth maximisation could be the motivation behind corporate finance decisions and for professionally-run conglomerates it could be shareholders' wealth maximisation.

It is imperative to mention, in this context that most of the public limited companies face considerable amount of pressure from shorter investment horizons by investors along with pressure from hedge funds. Compared to this, family firms who enjoy a strong controlling position can contemplate long term strategies like M & A options more easily as well as increased capex investments.

Small, Nimble, and Quick to React: By virtue of the fact that there are fewer decision-making gates to deal with, family businesses, both small and large, tend to be quick to react to threats as well as opportunities. Very often, the survival of the family depends on the survival of the business. This results in sharp and decisive action in the face of threats that could be potentially fatal for the business.

Godrej Context: Godrej has survived in the open economy, when most other local businesses have closed down, primarily because they never allowed majority ownership to any of their foreign partner. It is a closely held family group and neither the Indian financial institutions nor the Foreign Institutional investors hold any share of its company.

The downside of this model seems to be that such close holding by the promoters might affect expansion of the company. For instance, in 1974 when Jamshyd Godrej joined the company, Godrej and Boyce was a much bigger company than even Larsen & Toubro. Today, L&T is much bigger.

Value System

The value system of a typical family is survival and progeny. Research evidence supports this in the case of family-controlled conglomerates. Recent research evidence on Indian family business groups found that family-controlled firms help each other during financial distress with an objective to protect family reputation and to co-insure each other for better survival. However, in a professionally-run conglomerate, as the decisions are mainly based on economic viability, there is more likelihood that a financially distressed company would be closed than unnecessarily propping up the internal capital market. Hence, economic viability is more valuable than firm survival.

In the following sections we shall compare the two conglomerates: ITC and Godrej. Beginning by their introductions, their evolution over the years, the mergers and acquisitions patterns and eventual comparison.

COMPANY INTRODUCTION

ITC Limited is an Indian public conglomerate company, 25.4% owned by British corporation, British American Tobacco. It is headquartered in Kolkata. ITC was formed on August 24, 1910 under the name Imperial Tobacco Company of India Limited. ITC is a board-managed professional company, committed to creating enduring value for the shareholder and for the nation. Its diversified business includes four segments: Fast Moving Consumer Goods (FMCG), Hotels, Paperboards, Paper & Packaging and Agri Business. ITC is today, a diversified multi-business conglomerate with a market capitalisation of over US $ 33 billion and a turnover of over US $ 7 billion. Currently the ITC group employs more than 26,000 people in its manufacturing facilities, offices and hotels at more than 60 locations across India.ITC is rated among the World's Best Big Companies, Asia's 'Fab 50' and the World's Most Reputable Companies by Forbes magazine .

Godrej Group is an Indian conglomerate headquartered in Mumbai, Maharashtra, India. It was founded by Ardeshir Godrej and Pirojsha Godrej in 1897. It operates in diverse sectors such as real estate, consumer products, industrial engineering, appliances, furniture, security and agricultural products. The Godrej conglomerate consists of companies like Godrej Consumer products,Interio, Properties, Efacec, Saralee, Agrovet, Infotech, Godreg Industries and Godrej & Boyce. The Company has a network of 38 Company owned Showrooms, more than 2,200 Wholesale Dealers, and morethan18,000 Retail Outlets. The Company has Representative Offices in Sharjah (UAE), Nairobi (Kenya), Colombo (Sri Lanka) and Riyadh (Saudi Arabia).

Swot Analysis	*ITC Limited*	*Godrej*
Strength	Leading brand reputation, Customer loyalty, Product innovation, Supplier integration, Low production damage rate, Customer intimacy	Wide range of product line, Trained and efficient management, Well developed R&D capability, Huge distribution network
Weakness	Low depth and width in product, Low R&D budget, Need for sales personnel training, Higher price	Lack of advertisements, Absence of effective selling schemes like instalment payments
Opportunity	New distribution channel, Exploring international market , Expansion into 2 tier and 3 tier cities, Seasonal fashion influence	Increasing consumer offers, Huge market share
Threats	Changing customer lifestyle and preferences, Competition from local producers, Changing technology, Political and economic instability	Strong competition, Products are not unique

EVOLUTION AND GROWTH

ITC was incorporated on August 24, 1910 under the name Imperial Tobacco Company of India Limited. As the Company's ownership progressively Indianised, the name of the Company was changed from Imperial Tobacco Company of India Limited to India Tobacco Company Limited in 1970 and then to I.T.C. Limited in 1974. Though the first six decades of the Company's existence were primarily devoted to the growth and consolidation of the Cigarettes and Leaf Tobacco businesses, the Seventies witnessed the beginnings of a corporate transformation that ushered in momentous changes in the life of the Company.

ITC's Packaging & Printing Business was set up in 1925 as a strategic backward integration for ITC's Cigarettes business. ITC chose the Hotels business for its potential to earn high levels of foreign exchange, create tourism infrastructure and generate large scale direct and indirect employment. In 1979, ITC entered the Paperboards business by promoting ITC Bhadrachalam Paperboards Limited. In 2004, ITC acquired the paperboard manufacturing facility of BILT Industrial Packaging Co. Ltd (BIPCO), near Coimbatore, Tamil Nadu. In 1985, ITC set up Surya Tobacco Co. in Nepal as an Indo-Nepal and British joint venture. In August 2002, Surya Tobacco became a subsidiary of ITC Limited and its name was changed to Surya Nepal Private Limited. In 1990, leveraging its agri-sourcing competency, ITC set up the Agri Business Division for export of agri-commodities.

ITC's foray into the Foods business in August 2001 is an outstanding example of successfully blending multiple internal competencies to create a new driver of business growth. It began with the introduction ofKitchens of India' ready-to-eat Indian gourmet dishes which extended to confectionery and staples segments. ITC's philosophy of contributing to enhance the competitiveness of the entire value chain lead to its entry into Safety Matches, Agarbatti and even in personal care business. Throughour ITC's growth and evolution, Its philosophy of all-round value creation has been backed by strong corporate governance policies and systems.

Godrej group was founded in 7th May, 1897 in Mumbai by Ardeshir and Pirojsha Godrej. Godrej Introduced the first lock with lever technology in India. After achieving indisputable success in the Safes and Locks business, Godrej Soaps Limited was incorporated in 1918 with the launch of Chavi Bar- a soap made entirely with vegetable fats. The first verseas Godrej factory was set up in Johore-Bahru in Malaysia in 1965 for the manufacture of Office Equipment. Godrej started manufacturing refrigerators in 1958 and washing machines in 1996.

In 1990, Godrej Properties Limited, a real estate development company was established within the Godrej Group of businesses. In 1994 Transelektra Domestic Products was acquired which forged a strategic alliance with Sara Lee USA which ultimately lead to the incorporation of Godrej Infotech Ltd in 1999. In 2001, Godrej Consumer Products was formed as a result of the demerger of Godrej Soaps Limited. Godrej Soaps renamed Godrej Industries Limited. In 2002, Godrej Tea Limited was set up and in 2003 Godrej entered the BPO solutions and services space with Godrej Global Solutions Limited. In 2006, the Foods business was merged with Godrej Tea which was renamed as Godrej Beverages & Foods Limited. Then in 2007, Godrej Beverages & Foods Limited formed a JV with The Hershey Company of North America and the company was renamed Godrej Hershey Foods & Beverages Limited.

In 2011, Godrej Consumer Products Ltd (GCPL) announced that it has entered into an agreement for the rights to acquire 51% stake in Darling Group Holdings that operates in 14 countries across sub-Saharan Africa. The Darling Group manufactures and distributes the full range of hair extension products - which is among the largest hair care categories in Africa. The group continues to learn from its mistakes and understands the challenges it has of making the organization more dynamic and harnessing its vast pool of assets, strong brand, a wide network of loyal suppliers and distributors, loyal employees and resources, cherishing the vision and values of the family.

THE ENVIRONMENT THAT MADE FAMILY OWNED CONGLOMERATES THRIVE

Family-run business has a specific role in India's history. "The Indian family business dates back to the latter half of the 19th century, which also marks the beginning of business in India. Family businesses in India initially started in the 1890s as a means to promote import substitution and attain economic freedom from the British. These enterprises were an integral part of India's freedom struggle, and as part of the Swadeshi movement, got special treatment and subsidies from the government. The businesses consolidated their positions as near monopolies under the protective environment of the license Raj and their inefficiencies did not get exposed to the indefatigable market realities". The idea of Indian family-run business has always been revered, respected, and protected in India.Though many of the top world companies are run by families, Indian businesses have the highest percentage.

CONCLUSIONS

Though it is evident from the findings that the net worth and net assets is high for the Family managed businesses for this study, all the other performance indicators are in favor of professionally managed businesses.

In a professionally run conglomerate, the senior management is composed with unrelated individuals who run the company on behalf of shareholders. The decisions are mainly based on economic viability there is more likelihood that a financially distressed company would be closed than unnecessarily propping up the internal capital market.

The value system for a typical family owned conglomerate is survival and progeny. They usually take sharp and decisive action in the face of threats that could be potentially fatal for the business, and their eventual survival.New venture decisions are often based on the ambitions passion of the family and family wealth maximisation is usually the motivation behind corporate finance decisions.A strong controlling position can contemplate long term strategies like M & A options more easily as well as increased capex investments.

REFERENCES

[1] http://lindsayleaver.blogspot.in/2009/12/family-research-report.html

[2] http://en.wikipedia.org/wiki/Godrej_Group

[3] http://www.godrej.com/godrej/godrej/index.aspx?id=1

[4] http://www.scribd.com/doc/13581740/Godrej-Group

[5] http://www.itcportal.com/

[6] http://en.wikipedia.org/wiki/ITC_Limited

[7] http://firstindiaschoolofbu.articlealley.com/swot-analysis-of-itc-limited-100-years-journey-1798649.html

[8] Sindhuja P N* "Performance and Value Creation: Family Managed Business Versus Non-Family Managed Business"

[9] http://www.economist.com/sites/default/files/special-reports-pdfs/20111022_business_in_india.pdf

[10] http://www.businessworld.in/en/storypage/-/bw/the-search-for-successors/301362.0/page/0

[11] Evaluation of a Family Business – Godrej Group [http://edumall.pxq.in/wp-content/uploads/2011/01/Entrepreneurship/Evolution of a Family Business – Godrej Group.pdf]

[12] http://www.firstpost.com/business/why-family-business-conglomerates-will-shrink-588.html

[13] http://www.dnaindia.com/money/comment_is-tata-group-better-or-itc_1186692

Comparative Study of Human Resource Strategies of Manufacturing Companies and BPO's

Shreya Dhingra and J.K. Tandon

Jaipur National University, Rajasthan

ABSTRACT

Strategic human resource management is the process of linking the human resource function with the strategic objectives of the organization in order to improve performance. 'An organization's [human resource management] policies and practices must t with its strategy in its competitive environment and with the immediate business conditions that it faces.' A strategy is a course of action planned to be undertaken to achieve desired goals. Whereas an HRD strategy indicates the desired course of action planned by an organization to Achieve HRD goals or HRD outcomes. The course of action may deal with the choice of various means to achieve the desired goal and a plan for implementing the chosen Activity or action. Thus HRD strategy adopted by an organization may deal with the following dimensions.

INTRODUCTION

People are the real asset of an organization. If treated with their best interest they can take the organization to commanding heights. Organizations are, generally driven by a set of pre determined goals. They employ physical, financial and human resource in order to achieve the goals. These goals have no meaning unless people understand the underlying philosophy, translate them into concrete action plans and put their heart while realizing the targets. Organization depend on people for their survival and growth, similarly people also need organization.

The growth of the Indian BPO industry has been accompanied by political, cultural, and social interventions under a wide framework of media and law. With news on lifestyle, social interaction, safety and security of the BPO employees pouring every now and then, it has become quite compulsive for the BPO organizations to ensure effective and judicious people management. The way BPO firms manage their people should be apparent in their HRD practices. The results here imply modifications in the existing HRD system; better use of opportunities; and strengthening the people-policies, which can consider the demographics of the employees while framing strategies to satisfy them. Employee satisfaction leads to employee retention and thus their satisfaction level can be further utilized to ensure prolonged and stronger organizational commitment by the employees. The findings imply the need of introducing adjustments and adaptations to people management strategies and practices by taking into account any discrepancies that exist according to demographic characteristics of employees.

The meaning of HRD differs among HRD professionals and among managers in the respective Departments. While some see HRD in a broader and holistic sense as an investment in human capital to meet the organization's strategic agenda, others see HRD as merely training that is delinked from its effect on performance and productivity. The perception of HRD is reflected in the manner in which it is organized and perceived in organizations.

LITERATURE REVIEW

A growing trend in HRD in recent years has seen a steady increase in the number of training tasks being undertaken by external providers (Ardichvili and Gasparishvili, 2001; Woodall et al., 2002). This practice of outsourcing carries benefits such as cost reduction, increased service quality and increased access to experts in specialized areas (Csoko, 1995). Others, however, believe that outsourcing exposes organizations to opportunistic behavior by contractors, limiting the ability of firms to develop distinctive competencies within the workforce, and creating inefficiencies because of a lack of familiarity with the organizations' strategy and culture (Ulrich, 1996).

The BPO industry is typified by a host of job-related characteristics that is typical to it, some of which eventually become the reasons for employees' dissatisfaction from a typical BPO job – high stress levels (Mirchandani, 2004; Mehta et al., 2006); monotonous nature of the job (Taylor and Bain, 2004, 2005, 2006; Budhwar et al., 2006; Ofreneo et al., 2007; Batt et al., 2006), demand-supply disparity and lack of career growth potential on the professional front (Mehta et al., 2006; Batt et al., 2006); loss of identity (Mirchandani, 2004); mismatch with normal cycle, complete change of life style and lack of comfort on the personal front (Budhwar et al., 2006). All such reasons lead to mounting dissatisfaction in BPO employees. Increased dissatisfaction leads to reduced motivation, which in turn results in diluted efficiency because of which employees are not able to give their expected output which eventually results in their leaving the job (Sengupta and Gupta, 2008).

HRD at Macro and Micro Level

HRD as stated earlier is mainly concerned with developing with developing the competences of people. The main objective; however is to develop the newer capabilities in people so as to enable them to tackle both present and future challenges while realizing organizational goals.

HRD at Macro Level At Macro level, HRD is concerned with the development of people for the nation's well being. It takes health, capabilities, skills, attitudes of people which are more useful to the development of the nation as a whole. While calculating the national income and economic growth, the prospective HRD concept examines the individual potentialities, their attitude, aspiration, skills, knowledge's etc. and establishes a concrete base for economic planning.

HRD at Micro Level HRD has concern for grass root developments in the organization. Small wonder, then that HRD was well received by companies' managements as they realized its importance and foresaw its future contribution for the individual and organizational development. Generally, HRD at micro level talks of the organizations manpower planning, selection, training, performance appraisal, development, potential appraisal, compensation, organizational development etc. HRD's involvement in all these areas is mainly with an objective to develop certain new capabilities in people concerned to equip them to meet the present job challenges and to accept future job requirement.

The strategy used to explain the issue is mentioned through some case studies of some organizations. Organizations that have attempted to develop HRD are chosen and brief descriptions about these organizations and their decisions to implement HRD are presented below. The case studies presented here are based on the actual HRD experiences written and presented by senior managers for their respective organizations. These case studies were presented and discussed in two of the annual conferences of the National HRD Network. The HRD experiences narrated in this unit reflect the HRD practices existing at that time in these organizations. It is believed that the HRD activities undertaken by these organizations had some impact in terms of the functioning of the organization. As explained, the organizational outcomes (output, profit, productivity, etc.) are influenced by a variety of factors. The HRD climate and HRD culture is only one of the several significant factors affecting the organizational effectiveness. Therefore, an excellent HRD profile, excellent HRD practices and excellent HRD climate at a given point of time may not guarantee continued effectiveness of the organization for all times at come. HRD profiles need to be constantly upgraded and HRD climate needs continuous strengthening and renewal. These case studies therefore, should be taken as illustrations of HRD activities and not necessarily as examples for blind imitation. The case studies are intended to facilitate learning about various aspect of HRD for an interested learner.

HUMAN RESOURCE STRATEGIES OF MANUFACTURING COMPANIES

(Larsen & Tubro) L&T is probably the first organization in India to introduce an integrated HRD system HRDS. The HRD system was suggested by consultants while they were looking at the performance appraisal system for officers. The consultants felt that a development oriented performance appraisal system may not achieve developmental objectives unless accompanied by other sub-systems like potential appraisal, employee counseling, career planning and development, training and OD. HRD system was introduced by L & T in the year 1975 with the introduction of Performance Appraisal and Feedback and Counseling sub-systems like; potential appraisal, employee counseling, career planning and development, training and OD. A high level task force was constituted to implement the HRDS. The L & T had a strong training department which was conducting a large number of training programmes and occasional OD exercises prior to this. These were further strengthened with the introduction HRDS by linking training and performance appraisals and by stepping up OD activities. The starting of HRDS was also marked by the bifurcation of the Personnel Department into Personnel and HRD departments. The critical attributes required for various jobs were also identified but a potential appraisal system is yet to be finalized.

The top management of Voltas always believed that their people are their strength. This belief has been brought to focus in the last few years through mechanisms like performance appraisal, counseling, management development, communication policy, potential appraisal, training, etc. Voltas did not have a department separately for HRD apart from their training and manpower development unit which was a part of the Personnel Department. However, HRD culture was attempted to be brought in the company in a variety of ways. In 1977 itself while reviewing the reasons for its poor performance, the Managing Director identified the inadequate attention paid to the development of human resources as one of them. In order to ensure development of human resources and generate a healthy organization climate, a communication policy was evolved. This policy aimed at wider participation in a decision-making, openness and regular flow of information. Voltas have revised their performance appraisal systems from time to time. In 1982-83 they redesigned the managerial appraisal system focusing it sharply on management development. It had the multiple objectives of strengthening managers as individual, developing them for higher level positions, strengthening working relationships providing a basis for OD exercise and increasing accountability. Voltas also have a strong base in training and OD.

HUMAN RESOURCE STRATEGIES OF BPO'S

Skilled employees are the foundation of true, long-lasting competitive differentiation—companies have to attract and retain these key resources, and manage them effectively. More and more companies are turning to business process outsourcing (BPO) to ensure their HR function operates at peak. Accenture HR BPO Services deliver next-generation benefits, pairing business outcomes with cost savings to drive high performance.

Some big BPOs focus more on employee engagement as a practitioner influence, and many research studies (barring a few like Rothbard, 2001; May, 2004; Schaufeli and Bakker, 2004) have proven this in this area. This paper examines both the aspects in the literature. We first deal with practitioner-oriented definitions and then move to academic research. According to CEO Speak in the Hewitt Best Employers Survey (2004), among the many key people challenges one is to build a fierce employer brand equity (Fitz-enz, 2003), and one way to do that is to retain employees. This would be possible if organizations provide them with a passion to work, and an engrossing environment which maximizes their performance and gives a continuous work experience that is difficult for competitors to replicate. Managers are an important key in this equation (Banumruk, 2006; Lockwood, 2006). Further, an employer of choice recruits and engages talent through practices that address both tangibles and intangibles, with a focus on the long-term as well as the short term, and are tailored to the organization (Branham, 2005). A recent survey of HR professionals in BPO companies reflects that the most important issue anticipated in 2006 involved retaining and developing key employees (75 percent of responses); the next issue was of employee engagement and enhanced productivity (60.7 percent of responses cited this issue), followed by leadership training and development. Effective talent management policies and practices demonstrate commitment to human capital, resulting in more engaged employees and lower turnover. Consequently, employee engagement has a substantial impact on employee productivity and talent retention. Employee engagement, in fact, can make or break the bottom line (Lockwood, 2006), Martel (2003) is of the opinion that, "in order to obtain high performance in postindustrial, intangible work that demands innovation, flexibility, and speed, employers need to engage their employees Engaging employees – especially by giving them participation, freedom, and trust – is the most comprehensive response to the ascendant postindustrial values of self-realization and self-actualization".

NEED FOR NEW HRD INSTRUMENTS

From an analysis of the HRD experiences of these companies, the source of inspiration for introducing new HRD system seem to come from one or more of the following :

1. To support the structural and strategic changes made by the organization to orchestrate its growth and expansion.
2. Recognition by the top management of the importance of HRD and their responsibility to promote it for the goods of the organization.
3. To prepare employees to respond to the increasing problems faced by the organization both internally (dissatisfaction, delays, fall in productivity, etc.) and externally (high competition and falling market situation, etc.)
4. To keep the image of the company up by adding such modern instruments to its structure.

From this, it may be concluded that most companies seem to perceive HRD as an instrument to orchestrate the growth of the organization by preparing its people to strive for/or facilitate such growth or at least maintain internal stability.

Overview of HRD Instruments and Sub-systems

The HRD function itself has been initiated in most organizations in the last few years only. Some of them are yet to make their presence felt. It also reveals that no organization has yet introduced, all the HRD mechanisms presented. Several organizations have just few of these and even thee are being evolved or experimented with. Therefore, it is difficult to conclude whether any organizations have comprehensive and complete system of HRD at all. Probably L & T comes closer to having a comprehensive system but its synergistic effects are yet to be experienced by the company. There is a danger of these organizations taking a long enough time to dilute the spirit of HRD existing today, if they do not act fast. More vision, leadership and dynamism are required for implementing various sub-systems and creating a HRD culture.

CONCLUSION

The most neglected group in HRD is the line mangers. The HRD effect will become visible and stronger only when the line managers start accepting and internalizing their own role. The success of HRD will be the day when every employee sees himself as a developer of his subordinates. The HRD departments will not be need when such a situation arises. In other words, HRD people should work towards their dispensability.

The second neglected group in HRD is the unionized categories of employees. HRD for them also need to be attended last as they are in large numbers and form the foundation of the organization. The nature of HRD instruments may bee to be different. Organizations have neglected this so far. Part of the reasons may be unions.

HRD the union leaders also have a role to play. For their members they should probably play the role HRD managers are playing today for supervisory staff and managers. The HRD managers should assist the unions and promote the spirit of collaboration. Thirdly there should be more research in this filed to answer several of the questions raised earlier in this unit.

REFERENCES

[1] Ardichvili, A. and Gasparishvili, A. (2001), "Human resource development in an industry in transition: the case of the Russian banking sector", Human Resource Development International, Vol. 4 No. 1, pp. 47-63.

[2] Branham, L. (2005), "Planning to become an employer of choice", *Journal of Organizational Excellence*, Vol. 24 No.3, pp. 57-68.

[3] Budhwar, P., Varma, A., Singh, V. and Dhar, R. (2006), "HRM systems of Indian call centres: an exploratory study", International Journal of Human Resource Management, Vol. 17 No. 5, pp. 881-97.

[4] Baumruk, R., Gorman, B. Jr, Gorman, R.E., Ingham, J. (2006), "Why managers are crucial to increasing engagement", *Strategic HR Review*, Vol. 5 No.2, pp. 24-7.

[5] Fitz-enz, J. (2003), "Human capital branding: the new organizational effectiveness model", *Heads Count: An Anthology of the Competitive Enterprise*, Peoplesoft, Inc., Pleasanton, CA,

[6] Lockwood, N.R. (2006), "Talent management: driver for organizational success HR content program", *SHRM Research Quarterly*, available at: www.shrm.org/research/quarterly/2006/0606RQuart.asp, .

[7] Martel, L. (2003), "Finding and keeping high performers: best practices from 25 best companies", *Employee Relations Today*, Vol. 30 No.1, pp.27-43.

[8] Mirchandani, K. (2004), "Practices of global capital: gaps, cracks and ironies in transnational call centers in India", Global Networks, Vol. 4 No. 4, pp. 355-73.

[9] Rothbard, N.P. (2001), "Enriching or depleting? The dynamics of engagement in work and family roles", *Administrative Science Quarterly*, Vol. 46 pp.655-84.

[10] Sengupta, S. and Gupta, A. (2008), "Vicious circle of attrition in the BPO industry", The ICFAI Journal of Organizational Behavior, Vol. 8 No. 2, pp. 57-66.

[11] Taylor, P. and Bain, P. (2004), "Call centre outsourcing to India: the revenge of history", Labour and Industry, Vol. 14 No. 3, pp. 15-38.

Comparative Study of the Emerging Superpowers of Asia

Nimish Varma and Geoff Mathew

IMT Ghaziabad

ABSTRACT

China has risen in an exponential manner in the past few decades. Even the recent financial recession was tackled brilliantly by China but have they ensured the development of their citizens as well? India on the other hand also stood firm during the recession but has it utilized its resources in the best manner to ensure the maximum development for the nation as a whole? Indian Foreign policy seems to have been unable to forge a coherent response towards China despite the fact that it is India's nearest rival for geo-political influence. Still, does India have an upper hand in becoming the next superpower? This paper is a comparative study of the strengths, resources, policy and framework followed by both the emerging superpowers in the race for global dominance to emerge as numero uno.

THE CHINA STORY

It all started with the cheap lending of money that a country with the largest population in the world transformed from a nation with conservative government policies to a competitive nation engulfing global trade & commerce. Bank interest rates dropped to a real low and the money supply was increased. China had planned some major changes, starting from 2003, in its policies to boost infrastructure and metamorphose into a manufacturing giant. Companies had been offered capital on low interest rates. This meant that lesser the interest rates the more profitable it became for the companies to take money from the banks than to lend them. Companies had better financial leverage along with a cheap and disciplined labour force. The companies were quick to capitalize the opportunity to score big. China's government planned to set up great infrastructures to establish manufacturing and real estate industries to enhance exports (See Current Account Balance of China in Exhibit) and provide better standard of living to its people or that is what it claimed.

CHINA'S GOVERNANCE

China is governed by a republican form of government. . A republican form of government looks for economic welfare more than social welfare. It would not be wrong to say that the

Chinese government aimed to arm their people with economic prowess. It so happened. Chinese government hit the nail on the head when it reduced interest rates. China's industrial sector was encouraged to spread their wings in and out of the country.

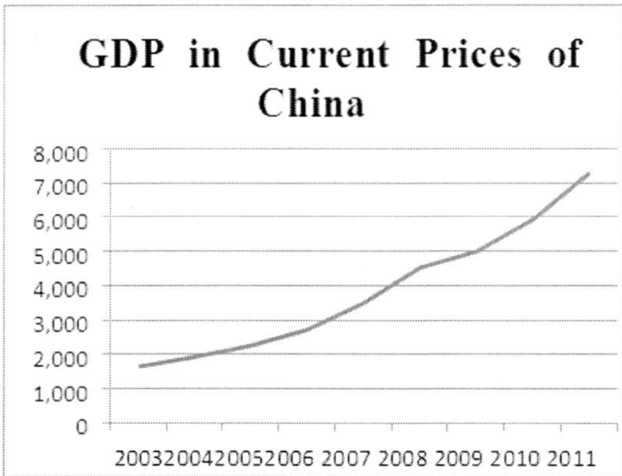

Source: IMF Data in US Billion$

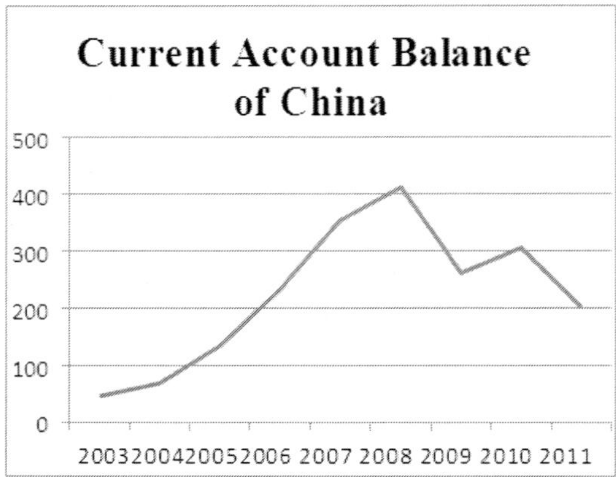

Source: World Economic Outlook Data, April 2012 In US Billion$

China started to find economic stability and this started to reflect in their Gross Domestic Product (GDP: Exhibit). People drifted from rural lands to urban part of the societies in search of jobs. Infrastructure has always been a large opportunity to find occupation. People turned to manufacturing from the agriculture sector in search of jobs. The income levels began to increase.

The increasing levels of income were driving demand for homes for the increased urban population. As a result, from 2005 to 2008, the Chinese real estate prices rose to great heights. The property rates were gradually increasing. The infrastructural companies continued to find buyers and the cycle went on to become bigger. The companies began using the initial funds from the people to invest again into new buildings.

These buildings were not only homes but also commercial offices and industrial zones. The demand was increasing with the increase of buying power of the people. However critics of the bubble theory had been justifying the rise in property rates with the rise in income levels. People believed that the rising rates were backed with greater income.

FINANCIAL CRISIS

Year 2008 brought devastating tremors across borders. The financial crisis had gripped the money markets in many countries. It was evident that this super power was also jolted due to the financial turmoil in the Western World. The impact of the crisis was obvious on the Chinese government as the Chinese exporters majorly found the West as the buyer. The crisis had the markets low but Chinese products held an edge over the others in terms of price, ability to meet demands, faster servicing to customers etc. as they had mastered the art of modern day trade.

Chinese companies had achieved economies of scale across diversified product ranges which proved to be a trump card for them. Where western industrialists were fighting with high per unit production cost, costly transportation, lesser capacities to meet demands there were the Chinese race of businessmen which had economically optimized production, a concrete supply chain system, huge capacities to meet demands.

Chinese government responded to the situation predictably. The government came up with a stimulus package to counter the crisis and hence defend the economy from a contagion effect. The economy was deluged with $586billion (4 trillion Yuan) to encourage investments on infrastructure. The scenario was precarious but competitive. Countries around the world were looking for bare minimum measures of survival and there was China ready to take a bold step. Considering the standpoint of the Chinese government, the measure was justifiable. Its competitors had grown financially weak and Chinese had their model working before the crisis. The time was ripe to capitalize by investing more into the economy in order to outperform the others. The Asian markets responded positively to the news about the package but there persisted a fraction of economists who believed that the radical step would swell up the economy even more.

As a result, the economy did expand. Chinese products flooded the markets worldwide. Since the demand for cheap, readily available Chinese exports were high the Chinese exporters were charging money in hedging their foreign exchange risk. The foreign importers had to agree to their terms. China became a super power with its exports reaching out to many nations (Exhibit).

China surpassed countries in terms of trade and exports. It evolved into a manufacturing giant by achieving economies of scale. But is that everything? The governance in China focused on economic empowerment but did China achieve the same? The nation, now, faces an internal imbalance.

The property prices in China have been rising. The people have started to fall short of money. The country stands on the verge of another stimulus but it cannot encourage further investment as it has already exceeded its limits.

The urbanized population is living life on expanding concrete lands but the rural opulation is being pushed inwards. The cities like Shanghai, Beijing, Hong Kong, Guangzhou etc., have been expanding but at the same time there are the farmers in the rural lands who are made to sell off their lands. Farmers are losing their farms to industrialists who set up manufacturing plants in these lands. Poor farmers are looking for occupation and eventually reach to industries to contribute their bit to the manufacturing sector. This imbalance is making rich richer and the poor poorer.

ROLE OF CHINESE GOVERNMENT IN THIS SOCIAL ISSUE

The measures taken by the government were inclined towards making China a progressive and competitive nation. The competitive approach of running a nation may push the economic stature of a nation to a high but the onus is still on the government to bring equal opportunities to the poor. In the contemporary society, it is unlikely that a country can provide a sustainable economic model which will provide equal opportunities to all and sundry and yield befitting benefits to different sections of the society. It may always happen that the strong snatches a larger share of the pie from the weak. And that's exactly the issue which China is currently dealing with.

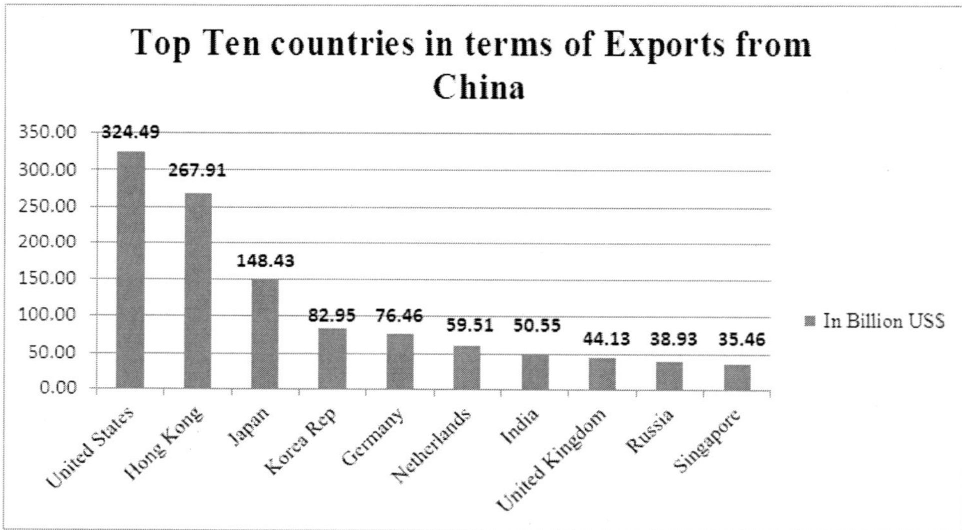

Source: China Customs Statistics 2011

Unlike democratic countries where media and people have differences in opinions, China's societal model has held itself back in voicing sentiments of the poor. The superficial stable life of urban areas does not etch the entire portrait of the world's second most populated nation. A lot still lies beneath that phony notion of China's economic supremacy. Lower middle and lower classes have to be supported. The economically backward and rural population have to be made a part of China's success story. But building an approach comprised of competitiveness and inclusivity is like walking on a tight rope.

SO IS INDIA DISMAL? NOT YET!

Be it approach, or the lack of it, in the Indian economy, the future prospects of India look bright similar to that of China. Although the two countries are neighbours but the dissimilarities in culture, work ethics, social system, governance (and the list is never ending) etc., make it sound interesting that economists believe that China and India both are bound to have a neck to neck competition in the future. Although it is evident that Chinese have a stronger trade, sturdy banking system, process oriented engineering, a glitch free power infrastructure, a demand fulfilling investment, a more balanced economy than India but the latter too has promising prospects. Although Indian economy has been undergoing a rough phase in the recent past but the future is speculated to hold good for it too. There are many aspects on which India stands ahead of its neighbouring country China.

DEMOCRACY

It is the call of the hour to have an approach to question whatever is prevalent. India's political infrastructure is one such symbolic representation of this approach. The governance of the seventh largest nation in the world boosts of democracy. It is certainly tough to manage, but not rule, a country with almost 16% of the world population. It certainly makes policy implementation sometimes chaotic and slow but it's essential for a government to have an opposition which provides a differing point of view from the government. China being a one party system doesnot support an opposition, making implementation faster but on the cost of a single minded view.

CHINA'S SOCIAL PROBLEM

India being a democracy has varying options to choose from. Media and entertainment industry in India, for instance, has the freedom to express thoughts and perceptions for and against the government. The viewers too have the freedom of choosing their preferences from the offered. However in China, options are restricted as the government regulations are unavoidable.

LOW LANGUAGE BARRIER IN INDIA

India is a diverse nation. It has a rich cultural diversity which has helped Indians to be open to different cultures, traditions and perspectives. Impact of this factor has certainly made Indians open to English. Indians are willing to learn English which happens to make Indians more globalised than Chinese. Since English is the second most widely spoken language globally, penetration of this language is more in India than China.

INNOVATION IS A CLICHÉ

The small and medium enterprises in India are known for their innovation in product engineering. The demand for Indian equipment, medical appliances, textiles, agro products etc. brings considerable innovation in its manufacturing with diversified product lines. On the other hand, China has an expertise in using innovative technology to manufacture products with known process definition in large-scale.

ON THE THRESHOLD OF CONSUMER BOOM

India has its mammoth population of 1.21 billion on the verge of a swelling consumption demand. The foreign investors are standing on Indian doorsteps for flushing the moolah into the economy as they see India as a lusty opportunity to make money. Likes of IKEA, Carrefour, Walmart etc. look to invest in India in the future. Moreover, many sectors in India have already seen foreign direct investment come their way like infrastructure.

India's middle class is a broad segment of the nation's society with eager buyers making India a bright prospective market complimented with cheap labour reducing input costs for companies.

POPULATION: A BOON OR A BANE

India's rising population was once seen as a big problem. Once considered a liability is now gradually turning into an asset. India is a young nation with an average age close to 25 and a rapidly expanding population whereas China has a stable but ageing population. This might give India a better shape in the times to come.

China has certainly made it big in the recent years by conquering international trade. Its huge exports supported by the hefty investments have poised China in a comfortable position in terms of economic growth. India but then has had shaky economic growth and an underperformed government in the past. But the future still remains promising for the Indian economy as the race is still on between the two.

USA: AN INDIAN ALLY

India's potential in the economic and the energy sector encouraged USA to look at India as an important ally which led to the signing of the Indo-US civilian nuclear cooperation agreement. It became a testament to the growing strength of the US-India ties. USA had declared its ambition in helping India achieve status of world power. China reacted swiftly and since then has been referring to India as a global power as opposed to a regional one, a formulation China preferred before.

INDIA'S WEAKNESSES

There have been some problems which India has been facing from a long time. As a country, India needs to overcome these issues in the future so as to emerge as a global superpower:

LACK OF LEADERSHIP

Being the world's largest democracy, India's sovereign governance has had no single leader in the past. Only two of the 13 Indian prime ministers have leaded the country for more than 10 years in 65 years of its independence. Indian governance lacks the visionary virtue of a leader which could instil synchronous policies in the internal and external affairs of the country. On the contrary, Chinese leaders are known for their focussed approach. The average years served by the Chinese president is more than 10 years in office. Therefore relatively long periods have brought stability in the policies of Chinese government.

LACK OF NATIONAL INTEREST

Although India is on its path of an economic superpower but it faces some serious issues upfront. The 2011 World Bank report clearly states that 32.7% of Indians are below the poverty line and 68.7% earn less than 2 US$ a day. National security has also been India's major concern since ages. The Maoist Naxalite insurgency, affecting large swathes of the country, has rightly been identified by the government as India's most serious security concern. Violence saps the government's authority to take the country forward in India's many states. Apart from internal imbalance, India has questionable external ties. Historical conflicts with Pakistan and China have not been completely been dealt with.

The role of China's modern leaders stands out in contrast. In his first interaction with the media, one of India's previous chief of the Naval Staff, Adm. Sureesh Mehta, said: "China, we believe, is shaping the maritime battlefield in the region. It is making friends at the right places. If you don't have the capability to operate in those waters, for a length of time, then you need friends who will support your cause, when the time comes, so definitely China is doing that, as there are Pakistan Bangladesh, Myanmar, Sri Lanka, and down below, Africa. So it is a known fact that we are ringed by states, which may have a favourable disposition towards China. They are looking 20 years ahead." In other words, China has dealt with its external security tactfully.

Lack and delay in policy implementation Bureaucracy, on one hand, offers streamlined and process oriented work flow but on the other hand it vests power on the hands of many layers. The turnaround time of processes not only increase, bureaucracy also creates power centres which make the policies of Indian government majorly ineffective. The reach of government policies to the poor has become a rarity now. Chinese government, being a communist one, has implemented policies in an efficient and disciplined way. Infrastructure projects have been implemented in a rampant manner in China. Development has reached to the different levels of society. Industries big and small have been benefitted from gove rnment policies.

INDIA'S WAY FORWARD

The challenges which India faces need to be corrected in the future. The way forward for India should implement the following:

EMPOWERING NATIONAL SECURITY COUNCIL

The National security council (NSC) was established in the late 1990's to analyse the military, economic and political threats to the nation and to advise the government on meeting these challenges effectively. However, it has failed to deliver its key responsibilities due to government intervention and lackof institutionalization. It can be empowered by institutionalizing the same. For that, the power of the national security advisor should be de-centralized from being the most powerful authority on national security. An effective foreign policy institutional framework needs to be designed as it will not only identify the challenges, but also develop a coherent strategy to deal with it, organize and motivate the bureaucracy, persuade and inform the public thus enhancing and ensuring the proper functioning of NSC

BI-PARTY SYSTEM

India is a multi-party political system. India has six national parties and 59 state parties. With each party advocating a different school of thought, India's political system lacks focus. Every party in India has its own vested interest and miss out on India's growth as their vision. A bi-party system will make political activities more disciplined by instilling focus towards India's growth. If there would be only one party focussing on questioning government's rule, people will have a better conviction in choosing their representative.

PRESIDENTIAL FORM OF GOVERNMENT

The major advantage of a presidential form of government is that it ensures a united collective and is not impeded by the collective's indecisive natures. The authority is vested in one hand and it leads to better stability and prevents greater strife. As time passes, the system evolves enough to sate the dissenting voices by making them heard through the legislature and also indicates a limited interference by the executive and legislature in each other's affairs.

COLLECTIVISM IN INDIA

As Moyra Grant says in his book, Key Ideals in Politics:

A belief that some kind of group or collective is the most important unit in the social structure and that people function better, both ethically and efficiently, in cooperative groups rather than selfish or self-seeking, competitive individuals. Collectivism includes both 'left wing' concepts of communitarian equality and 'right wing' concepts of organic hierarchy.

Indian society needs collectivism in their approach. Once if Indians see societal benefit over individual benefit the occurrence of vested interests will fade away. What will also fade away are the political parties taking advantage of distressed segments of societies. A belief of this sort will bring India's national interest into the forefront. Once if individuals look towards social coherence, political coherence will prevail. The vision to see India as a global superpower will emerge above the rest only if people of India agree to look beyond their own interests and incline towards social interdependence.

CONCLUSION

As 50 years go by Sino-India War, India's race with China remains somewhat unsettled. As India faces some innate problems in its governance, economy and society, China seems to have done everything right. But deep down under China too has been challenged by fundamental complications. Gone are the days when other nations used to blame India for being a corrupt nation. With the innovation in media and its far reaching capabilities, corruptions in other countries are no longer a hidden fact.

In his recent and the last speech to the Congress, China's ruling communist party president told the nation that corruption is a very integral part of the party and the party must make unremitting efforts to combat corruption, promote integrity and stay vigilant against degeneration. His exact words were

"If we fail to handle this issue well, it could prove fatal to the Party, and even cause the collapse of the Party and the fall of the state."

Although India lags China in terms of economic growth, China faces increasing social challenges like these. China's attempts to increase its influence in India's neighbouring countries like Nepal, Bangladesh, Myanmar, its claims on parts of India as its own like Arunachal Pradesh, its lack of support for India's membership to the United nations Security council and other regional and global organizations, all point towards China's attempts at preventing the rise of India as a regional and global power and China has continuously pursued this strategy. All this clearly proclaims that China has realized India's potential to rise as a super power and it is now up to India to work it out as to how soon it can achieve this.

The war between Asia's two biggest economies to become a global superpower will bring a promising climax!

REFERENCES

[1] Leng Peter, 2006: Documentary: Race to the top of the World- China vs India BBC Network

[2] Barbosa David: "China unveils $586 billion stimulus plan" (2008, Nov. 10), NY Times Available: http://www.nytimes.com/2008/11/10/world/asia/10iht-10china.17673270.html

[3] Bradsher Kieth: "Affirming slowdown China reports second month of scant economic growth" (2008, Sept. 4), NY Times Available: *http://www.nytimes.com/2012/06/10/business/global/chinese-economy-shows-a-second-month-of-anemic-growth.html*

[4] Oliver, Chris: "World Bank sees no property bubble in China" (2009, Nov. 04). Market Watch. Available: *http://www.marketwatch.com/story/world-bank-sees-no-bubble-in-chinese-real-estate-2009-11-04*

[5] Bradsher Kieth: "Main Bank of China is in need of capital" (2008, Sept. 4), NY Times

[6] Economist Intelligence unit: China Economy: Underwhelming stimulus, (2012, July 17)

[7] Yongrong Chen, Zhengfu Zhang and Lili Wang:"China's Real estate bubble, a heated debate" (2010, Jan. 04), Window of China. Available: *http://news.xinhuanet.com/english/2010-01/14/content_12808553.htm*

Consumer Analysis: Emerging Trends in Brazil

Rakesh Chopra and Astha Gupta

Institute of Management Technology, Ghaziabad

ABSTRACT

No matter where we are, there are consumers...consumers...consumers..and it does not matter whether they are rich or not. USA's Walmart, Britain's Tesco, and India's Pantaloon have all grown from being small businesses, mainly selling value-for-money merchandise to the masses. At the same time, the Modis and others are beginning to sell expensive goods from global luxury brands, and growing these new businesses. It is important to realize that the emerging countries of the world like Brazil and India which seem promising as never before have long been an aspirational society, the kind that the western countries have only become in the last 150 years. Consumers aspire to better lives, better possessions and better experiences. And with more money in their hands, more people in these countries are turning into consumers. These countries also have a significant young population profile among the other countries of the world. There are a lot of young people, in different income segments and locations who are influencing their parents' spending, or spending their own money. Hence the companies have a lot to capitalize on this segment which poses a lot of potential.

After having spent three months in the city of Rio de Janeiro, Brazil, it was an interesting observation to note the buying behavior, shopping mentality and general attitude of the people. I found it quite similar to that of our own country and the most surprising observation was the immense opportunities both these places provide and almost in a similar way. This paper highlights the consumer behavior of the Brazilian population which I found to be quite similar to the Indian context as well and this paper would help understand the reason to some extent atleast of the reasons behind why these economies are the significant emerging economies of the world.

INTRODUCTION

Brazil, Russia, India and China (BRIC) markets have huge potential for the development of a stable consumer society that can be profitably targeted by consumer packaged goods players across the globe. Although the BRIC region requires further social cohesion and economic development to fully stabilize, players that act quickly and tailor their offering can reap significant rewards.

Many demographic and lifestyle trends that are associated with developed Western markets are increasingly applicable to consumers in the BRIC region. For instance, aging populations and changing family dynamics are trends playing out in at least 3 of the 4 countries. The core consumer trends of convenience, health and sensory orientated consumption are also beginning to emerge. This suggests that successful branding concepts from Western markets have the potential to appeal to the huge consumer base that exists via the BRIC nations. The insights and actions within this paper provide a foundation for this with prime focus on Brazil.

Emerging markets are the source of many of the world's most recent economic success stories. A growing middle class and booming corporate sector have helped make them the next great battleground for global companies.

Emerging economies presently account for around half of the total global output, and they continue to experience great growth levels in comparison to many of their more established peers.

It has been estimated that by 2025, the BRIC nations – Brazil, Russia, India and China – along with Indonesia and South Korea will together make up over 50% of global economic growth. Other developing economies are thriving, too: in 2010, Turkey enjoyed a GDP growth rate of 9% – similar to that of China – while Poland was the sole member of the European Union to not dip into recession during 2009. Opinions vary as to precisely how many emerging economies exist around the planet today, but what is clear is that they are growing fast and becoming more and more significant.

Emerging markets are at the heart of global trade growth, with China set to account for around 13% of global trade revenues by 2025, at approximately $6.3 trillion. The development of these markets has helped to create a landscape at which it is increasingly difficult to look in terms of tiers – the economy is now very much a global one, and progressive internationally-operating companies need to treat it as such.

Now the question arises why are countries like India and Brazil important ?

- Emerging economies comprise well in excess of half of the world's population
- They boast increasingly consumerized societies, demanding access to state-of-the-art products and related services
- The four BRIC nations are all present in the top eight of the global GDP rankings
- Information and Communication Technology is growing at an exponential rate in the emerging markets – the telecoms sector is predicted to exceed $220 billion by 2013

THE DEMOGRAPHICS AND CONSUMER BEHAVIOR-BRAZIL

The Gross Domestic Product (GDP) in Brazil was worth 2476.65 billion US dollars in 2011, according to a report published by the World Bank. The GDP value of Brazil is roughly equivalent to 3.99 percent of the world economy. Historically, from 1960 until 2011, Brazil GDP averaged 469.51 Billion USD reaching an all time high of 2476.65 Billion USD in December of 2011 and a record low of 15.17 Billion USD in December of 1960. This GDP was achieved despite significant parts of the population being at very low income levels and thus falling outside the consumer bracket for most of the relevant markets.

Population Evolution

The Largest Population in Latin America

With over 196 million people, Brazil ranks as the sixth largest in the world and the largest in terms of the region as far as the population of the country is concerned. Population is estimated to be growing at approximately 1.3% per year.

Brazil is the only Latin American country which is a Portuguese speaking nation. English is the foreign language mostly used by the business community.

The majority of the Brazilians are of European or African descent. Apart from the original Portuguese settlers, others who have settled in Brazil and significantly influenced its culture include Germans (mainly in the southern states), Italians and Japanese (mainly in the state of Sao Paulo). In the larger cities, there are many other smaller ethnic communities representing most nationalities. There are also some sparse indigenous tribes in the Amazonian regions.

About 42% of the population is under 20 years of age and less than 7% is over 65. The average life expectancy is 69 years. More than 80% of the population in Brazil is urban and approximately 30% live in the ten principal metropolitan areas. The metropolitan areas of Sao Paulo and Rio de Janeiro have populations of around 19 million and 12 million, respectively. Some 14 other metropolitan area have populations of more than 1 million. The population growth is fairly evenly spread over all regions, but the North and Centrewest are expected to grow at faster rates.

% of Total Population	*1999*	*2004*	*2009*
Urban	80.5	83.5	86.1
Rural	19.5	16.5	13.9

Income/Buying Power

Income per capita in Brazil has increased during the past years and is expected to continue to grow in the medium term, as a result of the expected economic growth.

Region	*GDP per Capita (BRL)*
North	4,939
Northeast	3,694
Southeast	10,086
South	9,157
Centrewest	8,166
Total average	7,704

Source: Institute Brasileiro de Geografia e Estatistica 2002/ no updated information available

GDP per capita varies from BRL 3,694 in the Northeast to BRL 10,086 in the Southeast. Purchasing power is also expected to grow as a consequence of the decrease in the interest rates and of credit expansion- the latter, as a result of partnerships among financial institutions and the main retail players.

Income concentration is still a challenge for the Brazilian governments. Data from the World Bank point to a decline in the Brazilian income inequality and poverty levels from 1993 to 2009.

A Growing Middle Class

According to research conducted by Instituto Target/FGV, in the next 5 years the Brazilian middle class is expected to grow its share in the consumer market by 5.6 points, from 60.8-66.4% of the total consumption. For this research, middle class is defined as having household/ family income between BRL 2,230 and BRL 3,750 per month, in addition to other characteristics such as level of education, consumption pattern, occupation etc. The number of urban households is expected to increase by 8.3% over 2009.

Consumer Behaviour

No Coherent Consumption Pattern

Despite the fact that 80% of the Brazilians live in urban areas, this apparent uniformity does not reflect homogenous consumption habits. As mentioned before, as a result of a historical inequality in income distribution, different classes of consumers are encountered in the Brazilian consumer market, like for instance, the typical basic needs patterns in lower income classes, where household spending is higher on food and beverage items, or the ascendant middle class pattern that normally shows an increase in the participation of expenditure in transport and communications. Upper classes reveal an increase in the share of goods and services, like durable goods, leisure activities, education and healthcare, and expenditure with luxury items.

The main retail and consumer players currently target each of these groups in the Brazilian Consumer market, as long as they are sizeable and have a significant consumption potential likely to grow both in volume and value.

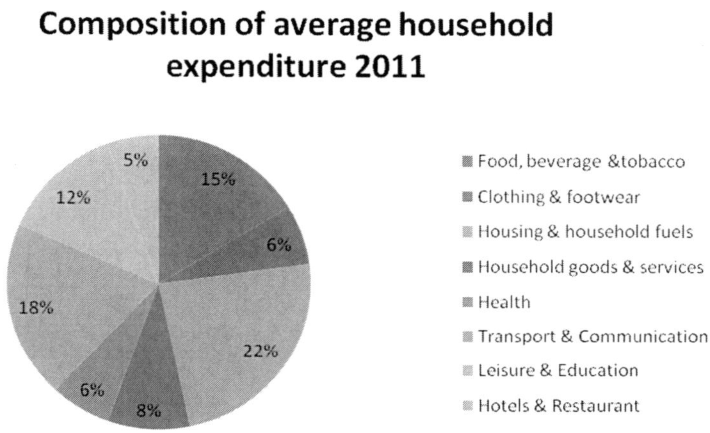

Source: EIU

Consumer behavior has seized being stable since globalization, communication and internet have played an important role in consumer habits. In Brazil, trends connected with the principles of "quality of life", convenience, price-consciousness, brand loyalty and others are very present in the market.

In fact, many companies in Brazil already provide products and services that meet the consumer needs derived from those trends. For example, Nestle has announced another new unit in the North of the country, for the demand of the lower income, that is, the C/D/E classes, which will probably include the development of new products to meet their specific needs.

Lifestyles/Shopping Habits

Shopping for Leisure in Urban Areas

Shopping is definitely integrated into the lifestyle of the Brazilian urban population, as a usual and necessary activity and as an entertainment program.

Shopping malls, outlets, hypermarkets, supermarkets and convenience stores have been designed to fit the profile of the relevant customer. Regardless of whether the consumer's profile is of high or low consumption, quality-service or price-oriented, or attracted to branded or private labels, in most developed cities it is possible to find places that best meet these characteristics.

Many of these places are designed to offer a wide range of services (for example, restaurants, coffee shops, fitness centres, beauty parlours, shoe repairs, post offices, bank services and dry cleaners among others) and to provide some entertainment with cinemas, cyber-cafes and play areas for children.

Brand/Price Sensitivity

Well Developed Brand Awareness

The Brazilian consumers distinguish products by the brand, associating them with concepts of high quality, trust, loyalty and status. The Brazilian consumer market has plenty of examples of local or international brands that have historically maintained a significant market-share.

Despite the fact that Brazilian consumers recognize distinct brands, they are influenced by those brands in their purchasing decisions, and eventually contribute as opinion makers to attract new consumers to the brands, it is important to point out that there has been a real increase of price-conscious customers in Brazil.

Large retail chains have been decisive in stimulating this consumer behavior, through an aggressive implementation of discount format stores and by expanding the portfolio of private label products.

RETAIL AND CONSUMER CHALLENGES, OPPORTUNITIES AND EMERGING TRENDS

Challenges

Rising Competition

As a result of the concentration process, large international retailers have strengthened their market-shares. Organically expanding through the opening of new stores or the acquisition of other retailer chains, the fact is that an intense development in retail activity is expected in future years, including medium-sized players challenged to enhance efficiency.

Most of the major retailers have announced relevant investment plans which include, in addition to the expansion, investments on existing stores, the introduction of new technologies on supply management, marketing and targeting of selected groups of customers.

Opportunities

Increasing Purchasing Power

The perspective of a purchasing power increase based on sustainable economic growth will certainly boost the Brazilian retail and consumer industry. A very significant part of the population which is currently considered to be on the border of the consumption market would have a strong impact on the demand and production levels when it enters this market.

The expansion of credit and the decrease of interest rates are both fuels for the consumption market. In terms of volume, the Brazilian consumer credit market is still small in comparison with developed countries. Credit penetration have increased since financial institutions began entering operational agreements or joint ventures with retailers.

Steady Growth of Shopping Centres

Shopping centres have long been a part of the retail landscape in Brazil. Customised to attend to the needs of more or less sophisticated customers, these places normally offer many options of leisure and convenience activities such as cinemas, restaurants etc.

Some expansion projects are currently in progress in the main cities and new investments are expected to be made in the second and third tier cities, as a consequence of the growth potential consumption.

According to ABRASCE, Brazil has 263 malls, most of them in the main metropolitan areas, with more than 6 million square metres of retail space and 42,363 stores. Sao Paulo and Rio de Janeiro states account for 134 shopping centres.

Emerging Trends

Consolidation in the Retail and Consumer Sectors

Consolidation in the Brazilian retail market is expected to continue, although at a lower intensity in food retail, where the share of the top-five retailers is estimated at around 60%. Acquisitions and further concentration is likely to be seen in non-food retail, where large regional domestic players are intensifying the competition and expanding their activities to other regions. The ability to integrate the acquired operations will determine the level of consolidation and how strong these current players will be.

Increase in Private Labels

In many cases, private labels have been recognized by customers as an effective way of assuring quality. This perception is a remarkable achievement of retailers, since private label products normally offer better levels of profitability.

Private labels in the segments of apparel and accessories have also been a good opportunity to enhance margins, since these categories of products already offer a higher level of profits when compared with food and beverage products.

Multiplying Retail Formats

Retailers in Brazil should be prepared to operate in different or even multiple retail formats as a consequence of the various types of consumers or group of consumers. In addition, the intrinsic concepts of each format should not be considered to be immutable, but instead dynamic, in a constant transforming process, because consumer needs and behavior are dramatically changing.

Examples are hypermarkets which have expanded non-food products space to the detriment of food categories, and department stores which have expanded or formed grocery area, reducing apparel or footwear slots.

Convenience, more than a retail format definition, is in fact a synonym of a new pattern of consumers which has been moulded and influenced by big urban centres. Understanding this consumption pattern is likely to lead to the incorporation of the principles of convenience into most of the existing retail formats.

CONCLUSION

Major global retailers and consumer product manufacturers have entered and expanded their operations in the Brazilian market, mainly through acquisitions, followed by organic growth by opening new stores, logistics parks, or industrial plants.

So while the economies of the west continue to endure the impact of the global financial crisis and consumer spending remains depressed, the emerging markets like India and Brazil have evolved to go on growing and evolving at healthy rates.

Recent years have seen a surge in both commercial and cultural change. There has been a rise in the number of affluent middle class consumers whose disposable income has helped drive demand for products and services, and cultural shifts have seen them demand must-have western consumer goods. The message is clear – global companies previously used to operating in more mature western markets now have access to a whole new generation of increasingly demanding and wealthy customers. Where previously the traditional outsourcing and manufacturing nations like China provided a source of cheap labor for smartphone production, today they and their aspired consumers are leading the way in smartphone adoption.

Throughout the next decade, it is estimated that 75% of additional consumer spend will be provided by Turkey, South Africa, Indonesia, Vietnam and the BRIC nations. This evolution of both consumer and supplier in emerging economies presents both significant challenges and major opportunities for global companies seeking to expand into them.

Companies have to acknowledge that not only are these markets home to new customers, but that they have also given birth to their next generation of competitors. Major technology companies and banking organizations have surfaced from within emerging markets and now enjoy significant success and influence on a global scale.

Forward-thinking companies must look towards the continuing evolution of emerging economies as opportunities and tailor strategies appropriately. To succeed, it is important to be both smart and adaptable, since most emerging nations retain a balance between policies of protectionism and promotion. First-mover advantage is key – as emerging market nations become increasingly stable politically and go on reforming business regulation, so too the openings available to their domestic providers increase. Global providers that have established presences in emerging market territories and have partnerships in place with freed-up, maturing incumbent organizations are those best positioned to prosper.

REFERENCES

[1] Annual Report, 2011, Associacao Brasileira de Supermercado

[2] Central Bank of Brazil

[3] Instituto Brasileiro de Geografia e Estatistica

[4] Database, Economist Intelligence Unit, www.eiu.com

[5] Annual Report, 2010, Associação Brasileira dos Servidores dos Conselhos de Enfermagem, ABRASCE

[6] The Brazil Business Magazine

[7] UNESCO and World Bank data from http://databank.worldbank.org

Dependence of Hotel Development on Location Criteria

Nidhi Chowdhry and J.K. Tandon

Jaipur National University, Jaipur

ABSTRACT

Location is a critical consideration because it affects hotels ability to draw customers.The hotel is an immovable fixture which has to use its skills in marketing to overcome any difficulties which may emerge after its initial location. In a true sense, the location tends to dominate all hotel operations substantially. Hotels benefit from high visibility and proximity to generators of room night demand. Different types of lodging operations have different location requirements. Location is perceived to be a unique selling proposition, particularly if the location of one property gives competitive advantage over another property. This paper explains the importance of a location as an important determining factor for a hotel by enlisting and describing the classification of hotels based on location. The paper uses strategic analysis methodology for evaluating the importance of location by undertaking an extensive review of literature on locational strategies for hotel with understanding of locational factors which influence internationalization of hotel chains.

INTRODUCTION

Hotels are an extremely valuable addition to an area. They bring leisure visitors and business people to the heart of a community. They can fill a compelling market need by accommodating visitors to area businesses and institutions. Hotels help generate sales for nearby retail and service businesses and capture tourism dollars in the community. Hotels also generate significant tax revenues while creating many new jobs for local residents.

Location is a critical consideration because if affects hotels ability to draw customers. It is important that hotel location be visible, accessible, convenient and attractive to market. Surrounding land uses are important for all types of lodging operations. Aesthetics of the area, noise, safety and other factors should be considered. By location along major highways or in business or industrial districts, hotels and motels benefit from high visibility and proximity to generators of room night demand. Local colleges, hospitals, attractions, services and entertainment are examples of "room night" demand generators.

Hotel locations are the primary decisions of guests, meeting planners, and travel agents. Differentiation advantage is the superiority over the resources and capabilities of the company and its employees. Differentiation occurs by market (e.g. setting standards, raising value/ expectations); by location (e.g. city centers or resorts); or by facilities (e.g.offering leisure facilities). These forms maintain basic price command and create barriers to enter causing non-price based competition, and therefore raising profitability and reducing loss of market share.

CATEGORIZATION OF HOTELS BASED ON LOCATION:

City center: Generally located in the heart of city within a short distance from business center, shopping arcade. Rates are normally high due to their location advantages. They have high traffic on weekdays and the occupancy is generally high.

Motels: They are located primarily on highways, they provide lodging to highway travelers and also provide ample parking space. The length of stay is usually overnight.

Suburban hotels: They are located in suburban areas, it generally have high traffic on weekend. It is ideal for budget travelers. In this type of hotel rates are moderately low.

Airport hotels: These hotels are set up near by the airport. They have transit guest who stay over between flights.

Resort hotels: They are also termed as health resort or beach hill resort and sodepending on their position and location. They cater a person who wants to relax,enjoy themselves at hill station. Most resort work to full capacity during peakseason. Sales and revenue fluctuate from season to season.

Floating hotels: As name implies these hotels are established on luxury liners or ship. It is located on river, sea or big lakes. In cruise ships, rooms are generally small and all furniture is fixed down. It has long stay guest.

Boatels: A house boat hotels is referred as boatels. The Shikaras of Kashmir and Kettuvallam of Kerala are houseboats in India which offers luxurious accommodation to travelers.

Rotels: These novel variants are hotel on wheel. Our very own "palace on wheels" and "Deccan Odessey" are trains providing a luxurious hotel atmosphere. Their interior is done like hotel room. They are normally used by small group of travelers

Various other classifications are also present such as:

- Airport, urban, suburban, highway, and resort
- Commercial Locations: By location along major highways or in business or industrial districts, hotels and motels benefit from high visibility and proximity to generators of room night demand. Local colleges, hospitals, attractions, services and entertainment are examples of "room night" demand generators.

- Resort Locations:Hotels and motels in resort areas generate most of their business form leisure travelers who see the lodging facility and surrounds area as their "destination." Access and visibility, while important, are secondary to the quality of the facility, services, amenities, and nearby attractions.
- Local Market Area: A lodging facility must be located in a market area thatattracts overnight visitors.

LITERATURE REVIEW

Hotel managers can develop ways to differentiate themselves from competitors by entering market where their rivals are not located, or by using creative marketing plans in locations where many of their rivals are located (Mathews, 2000). Chung and Kalnins (2001) applied agglomeration effect and performance of hotel industry by location and market. The results showed that small hotels do better in marketed populated than larger hotels. While medium chain affiliated hotels avoid a market with large chains, a small independent hotel would do well. Some good locations may attract many chain hotel entries; however, some independent hotels have already been established there in the first place. Some existing independent hotels received higher revenues than new chain hotel arrivals (Chung &Kalnins, 2001).

In the hotel industry, determining a certain location must be classified and alternative locations analysed basedon the precise concept and purpose of the business (Kim & Song, 2000). The standard of a production system in a company is judged by its potential profit. Among several candidate locations, each has conditions that affect whether or not a site should be selected, and it is difficult to decide which location would be most profitable (Kimes& Fitzsimmons, 1990). If the selected location has the potential for large profit, the decision-maker needs to investigate and compare potential alternatives (Robert & Ernest, 1992). Most scholars who research 'location' are often economists who research 'location theory'. Even though theories have changed over time, they are fundamentally divided into the following three categories: Least Cost Approach, Market Area Approach, and Profit MaximisationApproach (Ferreira, 1998). Location theory explains the structure of households, businesses, and public organisations in terms of their relationship with each of their own objectives and location. This theory attempts to provide a logical explanation as to why certain industries and/or business activities take place inspecific locations. Originally, location theory was used to explain the reasons for location for industrial places, but today, it also presents public facilities and tertiary industriesas important role-players (Kim & Kang, 2000). There are some traditional components in location theories.

Melvin (1956) had presented a theory aboutthe best location to maximise profit. It was proposed that location and commercial supremacy must attract local consumers. The boundaries of location and commercial supremacy depend entirely on the range of products,services offered, and the nature of goods. Additionally, attitudes and perceptions are determined depending on the consumer, preference level, and shopping behavior. Theseattitudes influence the consumer's choice of retail store(s). Ultimately, location is as important as the settlement of business and long-term nature of investing in the location. Additionally, location is a fundamental factor that can determine the maximum limit of revenue and costs (Ferreira, 1998). Selecting a location is the starting point for a successfulbusiness (Kimes& Fitzsimmons, 1990). The choice of location reflects the kind of advantages obtainable by the decision-maker. In other words, the choice of location depends on its purpose and type of business. Once the location of a business is decided, there must be specific standards regarding the business' purpose and its relationshipto profit and productivity.

It is clear that services, and often-in particular tourism, have become the major area of economic activityin developed countries (WTTC, 2001). However, there have been relatively few studies that haveattempted to apply conceptual models and paradigms to the tourism and international hotel industry.Dunning and McQueen (1982) and Kundu (1994) were two exceptions; Dunning developed the conceptof the eclectic paradigm, which has become a reference for studies in internationalisation, and applied itto the worldwide hotel industry. Beattie (1991) and Beattie and Litteljohn (1992) analysed the Europeanhotel industry using industry mapping and clustering. Concerning Eastern Central Europe in particular,there has been much academic interest in the tourism field. Researchers include Hall (1992, 1995, 1998a,1998b, 2000) who examines the general development of tourism in the region; Williams and Balaz (2001,2002), who have written in-depth studies with specific reference to the Czech and Slovak republics; andauthors such as Szivas and Riley (1999), who discuss employment in the tourism industry duringeconomic transition.

According to Walker (2008), deciding on a location is based on the results of six categories. First, are a region's demographic variables that include age, occupation, family size, education level, and average income (Medlik, 1993). Second, is the visibility of the main access route (Newell & Seabrook, 2006).Third, is the accessibility of the main access route (Egan &Nield, 2000; Brotherton, 2004). Fourth, is the number of potential customers passing the hotel. Fifth, is the distance to a major market (Medlik, 1993); and sixth, is the harmony of the hotels with the surrounding environment. It is important to determine and organise factors that involve location. Finally, it is necessary to develop a checklist of factors that impact the evaluation of information provided (Medlik, 1993).

Generally, the characteristics of land and housing deal with spatial immobility, durability, and heterogeneity (Kundu& Contractor, 1999; Egan &Nield, 2000). It is also important to consider that the environment is a factor that influences and, is influenced, in turn (Medlik, 1993). Straszheim (1975) asserted that location influenced housing characteristics and price fluctuations, which are the fundamental characteristics of the urban housing market. Accessibility, the characteristics of surrounding areas, and structural characteristics affect housing and land prices. Based on these factors, various studies have been performed. Olmo's (1995) research offers a slightly different classification where accessibility and characteristics of the surrounding area have the most relevance to location.

Looking at factors that impact the location of hotels, Joo (1999) suggests certain constituent elements regarding 'market area evaluation' and 'location evaluation'. Typically, there are measurements derived from evaluating the market in variables of population, income, housing supplies, employment, industrial activity, transportation, and purpose of touring. These variables appear differently depending on the hotel's location and its importance (Joo, 1999). Population has greater influence on the food and beverage department than the room department, in hotels located in urban areas. Local residents' purchasing power mainly affects the food and beverage areas (Kundu& Contractor, 1999; Pan, 2005). Additionally, characteristics of hotel guests can be significant information for selecting the hotel location (Jeffrey, 2002; Medlik, 1993; Urtasun& Gutierrez, 2006). First, the development of a city can be explained by evaluating trends found in the movement of demography. Second, age of a population is considered when determining the distribution of food and beverage restaurants in hotels, as they can be more attractive to the age range of 20s and 30s (Pan, 2005). Third, the longevity that a resident population has established in a particular region, family and community events, such as weddings, birthdays, etc., cause higher demands for nearby hotels.

FACTORS INFLUENCING ON HOTEL LOCATION

Locational attributes and features are obviously of fundamental importance for the development of the hotel sector. Factors that would be considered attractive for hotel chains include:

- The size and nature of the city in which the hotel is located,
- Size, growth and stage of development of the overall tourism market in the host country (including business and leisure tourism);
- Tourism facilities, communication and infrastructure;
- The perception of the region as an attractive business location or Policy of host government towards foreign direct investment in the country, and the overall significance attributed to tourism by the government;
- Number and type of tourist attractions (natural and man-made, including cultural and theme-type);
- Stability of the host government, politically and economically.
- Cultural and psychic distance between home country and host country (UN, 1993, Kundu, 1994).

The size and nature of the city in which the hotel is located are seen to be important by all categories, appearing as the most important factor for both the medium and smallest chains. The very large ones see the opportunities for business tourism as the most important factor, and rank the degree of market economy development as the third most important perception. For the large chains, the government policy to-wards FDI is seen to be the most important locational variable, with the region infrastructure appearing as number two. For medium ones, alongside the city size already mentioned, opportunities for both business and leisure tourism are second and third, respectively. The smallest hotel chains also perceive the country infrastructure to be important, and believe that there are strong possibilities for business tourism.

The highest rated sources of perceived advantage are the size and nature of the city in which the hotel is located, the importance of national infrastructure, and a perception of the region as an attractivebusiness destination. The identification of the first of these factors could be due to the various primary locations, such as Prague and Budapest, which have been singled out as of great importance forthe very large chains seeking to have a global network of properties.There are also a number of secondary and even tertiary locations whichto date have been under or unexploited (which, for example in Polandcould result in at least 20 locations for a mid-tier or budget brand such as Ibis/Comfort Inn/Courtyard by Marriott). The importance of infrastructure is more difficult to explain, but could be a result of the large

Compared to other businesses, the hotel industry is unique because it relies heavily on location, and because production and consumption happen simultaneously at a hotel (Nozar, 2001). Therefore, a successful hotel begins with assessing the value of its location both at its inception and for its future (Enrst, 2002; Pan, 2005). Once a hotel's location is determined and the hotel built, it is difficult to change due to the large capital investment (Medlik, 1993; Enrst, 2002). In order for a hotel to advance its worth, it must have material, social, and environmental value. Generally, the characteristics of a hotel's location, along with its own local conditions, must be in accord with the surrounding environment (Kimes& Fitzsimmons, 1990; Medlik, 1993). After researching a hotel's local environment and investigating its surrounding features, it must be determined whether or not the locale is suitable.

Urban planning, volume of traffic, population, income and consumption affect the decision to invest and develop a location (Kundu& Contractor, 1999). Due to issues such as government control over a changing environment, redevelopment projects, and a city's transportation system, the value of a hotel's location is constantly changing. In other words, the value of a location is not fixed because environments change (Medlik, 1993; Begin, 2000). Since large amounts of capital are required to build a new hotel, practical investigation and careful preplanning are necessary (Nozar, 2001).

Considering the unfixed nature of the business site, the quality of a hotel's services — such as transportation, tourism, general facilities, and the way a hotel is marketed — is also pertinent to its success (Jeffrey, 2002). When choosing a hotel destination, the way a customer has experienced his/her visit influences consumer behavior. Past experiences, psychological factors, and the way a customer experienced a hotel's location all affect his or her choice of a hotel.

The importance of ahotel's location is dependent upon the customer's reasonfor travel (business, leisure).Thus, depending on the occasion for travel, the customerplaces a different weight of importance and expectation on the location of the hotel (Yavas&Babakus, 2005). Additionally, the nationality of a customer was taken into consideration as a factor for measuring the way that he/she places importance on the location of a hotel (Kundu& Contractor, 1999; Chan & Wong, 2006).

The structural characteristics of the area in which hotels are located – city *vs*rural (Barros, 2005b) or seaside areas (Bernini &Guizzardi, 2010) – differently affect their efficiency. Likewise, differences in the infrastructural endowment among locations influence hotel efficiency: for example, hotels near main routes or airports are more efficient than hotels in other locations (Barros, 2005b). Agglomeration effects may also convey positive externalities (Barros, 2005b). Destination, as a complex system involving resources endowment, demand and climate conditions, and destination management (Dwyer & Kim, 2003; Crouch, 2011) also influences hotel performance (Molina-Azorin, Pereira-Moliner&Claver-Cortés, 2010). Lastly, it has been observed that higher competition reduces profits and force firms to improve efficiency (Bloom & Van Reenen, 2007; Pozzana&Zaninotto, 1988). With respect to tourism industry, location shapes the competitive environment, since hotels compete within relatively compact and well-defined geographic areas (Baum &Mezias, 1992). Consequently, the efficiency of a hotel is to a large extent influenced by its competitive position against competitors within the same destination.

IMPORTANCE OF LOCATION FOR HOTELS:

Location is a critical consideration because it impacts the ability to draw customers. It is important that the location be visible, accessible, convenient and attractive to market. Surrounding land uses are important for all types of lodging operations. High traffic volume is very important. Aesthetics of the area, noise, safety and other factors should be considered. How you evaluate the location will depend on the type of property being considered and the perceived customers.

Hotels benefit from high visibility and proximity to generators of room night demand. Local colleges, hospitals, attractions, services and entertainment are examples of "room night" demand generators. Future growth patterns should be analyzed before selecting good location.Hotels in resort areas generate most of their business from leisure travelers who see the lodging facility and surrounding area as their "destination." Access and visibility, while important, are secondary to the quality of the facility, services, amenities, and nearby attractions.

Dunning's (1993) eclectic paradigm has been rigorously tested in sectors including hotel (Dunning and Kundu 1995). The model offers a good fit with tourism and its hotel sector through the emphasis given to the importance of location as one of its three principle pillars. The paradigm is useful for explaining the extent, pattern, and growth of value-added activities undertaken by multinational firms outside their national boundaries.

The first pillar is the ownership advantages, which may be of a structural or behavioral nature. These include the size of the company and its ability to obtain economies of scale, international experience and strategic brand development, and level of technological advancement of the company.

The second is the location-specific advantages. These are the factors that make the location attractive to international hotel companies. Specific factors include the size, growth and stage of development of the overall tourismmarket in the host country, tourism facilities, the policy of the host government towards FDI in the country, the number and type of attractions, the stability of the host government, and the cultural and psychic distance between the home and host countries (Kundu 1994;UN 1993).

The third is the internalization advantages that companies derive from the modality of foreign involvement selected when goinginternational. Owing to the diversity in the tourism and the difficulties in organizing intermediary product markets, there are significant incentives for hotel companies to internalize (Go and Pine 1995).

DEPENDENCE OF INTERNATIONAL EXPANSION ON LOCATION

There have been two major trends with regard to the choice of approach by hotel companies in recent years: expanding acquisition/ merger activity and increased non-equity utilization.

Merger and acquisition activity is highly prevalent in the international hotel sector. There is evidence of a clear trend by major companies to expandthrough non-equity methods (Contractor and Kundu 1998). Thegrowth in such arrangements is due to a convergence of factors, including a "risk minimizing strategy".

Hotel operators pursuing international expansion may pursue both defensive and offensivestrategies (avoiding losing home market share, and gaining significantnew reach abroad). Furthermore, international hotel chains possess certain proprietary competitive advantages that allowthem to increase market penetration, includingeconomies of scale, a more profound knowledge of international guestrequirements, better-trained personnel, better management and reservation systems, and strong brand name (Dunning and Kundu 1995;Dunning and McQueen 1982).

In addition to such factors, the hotelsector is well suited to non-equity forms of expansion owing to certaincharacteristics, including a willingness to transfer knowhow, ease ofcodification of management systems, and the control that can be exerted over franchisees in the industry.Internalization occurs when a firm believes that internal transactioncosts are more efficient than external markets. Therefore, multinational enterprises can benefit from such advantages, but there are alsocosts associated with internalization, including increased communication and scale costs.

CONCLUSION AND IMPLICATIONS

Hotel guests' preferences of location and how hotel location factors are important to a customer satisfaction. A hotel can survive once it has a good reputation and steadfast loyalty among customers in the market. As hotels improve/maintain safety measures, they will retain the confidence and trust of customers (Enz& Taylor, 2002; Enz, 2009). Second, a hotel's location, surrounding environment, and scenery, all affect the overall satisfaction of guests. Tourism resources and facilities, along with the possibility of transportation impact the 'likelihood to revisit' category: 'Surrounding environment' and 'the hotel's scenery' influenced word-of-mouth among customers. To improve convenience, the provision of shuttle services, a well-equipped business centre, and other convenience options can be one of the solutions for five-star hotels, thereby attracting more guests and/or commanding higher premiums with relatively low investment.Safety should be considered as a common importance factor for hotel location for guests because regardless of nationality, participants responded that safety was important. Therefore, hotels should invest in setting up safety measures such as CCTV and electronic surveillance systems within the surrounding environment (provided that hotel management does not violate guests' privacy).Each hotel needs to have shuttle buses or be located near other means of transportation that connect guests easily to tourism resource destinations, entertainment facilities, and government and/or public offices.In relation to locational advantages, the most significant factors for the region were seen to be the size and nature of the city in which the hotel is located, the infrastructure within the region, and the perception of the region as an attractive business tourism destination. The location of scenery, climate and physical attractions is also of crucial concern for tourism and the hotel business. Generically, when companies decide to internationalize, preferred locations are those that offer markets of significant size and also have a close cultural proximity controlled by governments who are seen to impose minimum regulations.

REFERENCES

[1] India Hotel Business Management Guide 2009.

[2] India Tourism Market & Future Forecast, 2009–2015.

[3] Industry insight: Indian Hotel Industry, 2007.

[4] Indian Hotel Industry analysis, 2005.

[5] Kotler, Philip (1996). Marketing Management. The millennium ed. US Prentice Hall.

[6] Jones, Peter and Pizam, Abraham (1993). The International Hospital Industry. John Wiley and Sons Inc.

[7] Lovelock H. Christopher (2007). Services Marketing, 6th edition. Prentice Hall. By website: http://www.prenhall.com/lovelock/

[8] Analysing firms' failures as determinants of consumer switching intentions: The effect of moderating factors. European Journal of Marketing, 41(1/2), 135-158 Aydin, S., & Ozer, G. (2005).

[9] Ahn, K.-H., Chae, S.-I., & Cho, J.-W. (1999). *Retail management*. Seoul, Korea: Hakhyunsa Press.

[10] Arbel, A., & Pizam, A. (1977). Some determinants of urban hotel location:The tourists' inclinations. *Journal of Travel Research, 15*(3), 18–22.

[11] Baker, S., Bradley, P., &Huyton, J. (1994). *Principles of hotel front officeoperations.* London: Cassell Press.

[12] Begin, S. (2000). The geography of a tourist business: Hotel distributionand urban development in Xiamen, China. *Tourism Geographies,* 2(4),448–471.

[13] Brotherton, B. (2004). Critical success factors in UK budget hoteloperations. *International Journal of Operations & Production Management,* 24(9), 944–969.

[14] Bull, A.O. (1994). Pricing a motel's location. *International Journal ofContemporary Hospitality Management,* 6(6), 10–15.

[15] Chae, M.O. (1998). Spatial distribution of land prices and its determinantsin Seoul. *Journal of the Korean Planner Association,* 33(3), 95–114.

[16] Chan, E.S.W., & Wong, S.C.K. (2006). Hotel selection: When price is notthe issue. *Journal of Vacation Marketing, 12*(2), 142–157.

[17] Seo, K.-C., Lee, S.-H. (2001). The analysis of location value and spatialvariation of land prices. *Journal of the Korea Planner Association,* 36(1), 55–71.

[18] Urtasun, A., & Gutierrez, I. (2006). Hotel location in tourism citiesMadrid 1936–1998. *Annals of Tourism Research,* 33(2), 382–402.

[19] Newell, G., & Seabrook, R. (2006). Factors influencing hotel investmentdecision making. *Journal of Property Investment & Finance,* 24(4), 279–294.

[20] Nozar, R. (2001). Location is king, but perceived value has impact. *Hotel& Motel Management,* 216(17), 8.

[21] Pan, C-M. (2005). Market structure and profitability in the internationaltourist hotel industry. *Tourism Management,* 26, 845–850.

[22] Cheng, W. L., Li, H. & Yu, L. (2005). The analytic network process approach tolocation selection: A shopping mall illustration. *Construction Innovation*, 5, 83–97.

[23] Williams, A.M., and Balaz, V., (2000), Tourism in Transition, I.B. Tauris& Co. Ltd, London, UK.

[24] Witt, S.F., (1994), "Opening up of the Eastern Bloc countries", in Theobold, W., (ed) Global Tourism,Butterworth-Heinemann, Oxford, UK.

[25] Cantwell, J., and Narula, R.,(2001), "The Eclectic Paradigm in the Global Economy", in InternationalJournal of the Economics of Business, Vol. 8, No. 2, pp. 155-172.

[26] Clarke, J., Denman,R., Hickman, G., Slovak, J., (2001), "Rural Tourism in RonavaOkres: a Sléovak CaseStudy" in Tourism Management, 22, pp. 193-202.

[27] Gaba. V., Pan, Y. &Ungson. G. R. (2002). Timing of entry in international market: Anempirical study of U.S. fortune 500 firms in China, *Journal of InternationalBusiness Studies*, 22(1), 39-55.

[28] Han, J.K., Kim, N. & Kim, H.B. (2001). Entry Barriers: A Dull-, One-, or Two-Edgedsword for incumbents? Unraveling the paradox from a contingency perspective,*Journal of marketing*, 65, 1-14.

[29] Hill, C. & Gareth, J. (2006). Strategic Management: Cases, 8th edition. Boston:Houghton Mifflin.

[30] Hu, H.H., Huang, C.T. & Chen, P. T. (2009). Do reward programs truly build loyalty forlodging industry, *International Journal of Hospitality Management*, 29 (1), 128-135.

[31] Jin Jiang Hotel acquires US hotel group (2009, Dec 23), *China Hospitality News,*retrieved from *http://www.chinahospitalitynews.com/en/2009/12/23/14539-jinjiang*-hotels-acquires-us-hotel-group/.

[32] Lamond, D. (2008). Book Review: Globalization of Chinese enterprises, *Chinese Management Studies*, 2(3), 229-231.

[33] Li, X. L. (2000). Foreign direct investment in China: The importance of market entrytiming, *Journal of Global Marketing,* 14, 111-127.

[34] Bernini, C., &Guizzardi, A. (2010). Internal and locational factors affecting hotel industryefficiency: evidence from Italian business corporations. *Tourism Economics*, 16, 883–913.

[35] Molina-Azorin, J. F., Pereira-Moliner, J., & Claver-Cortés, E. (2010). The importance of thefirm and destination effects to explain firm performance. *Tourism Management*, 31, 22–28.

[36] Cantwell, J., and Narula, R.,(2001), "The Eclectic Paradigm in the Global Economy", in InternationalJournal of the Economics of Business, Vol. 8, No. 2, pp. 155-172.

[37] Dunning, J.H., and Kundu, S.K., "The Internationalization of the Hotel Industry - Some New Findings froma Field Study", in Management International Review, Vol 35, 1995/2, pp. 101-133.

[38] Lundan, S., and Hagedoorn, J., (2001) "Alliances, Acquisitions and Multinational Advantage" inInternational Journal of the Economics of Business, Vol. 8, No. 2, pp. 229-242.

[39] Sánchez, E., Pla, J. and Herbert, L. (2007). Strategic Variables Influencing the Entry Mode Choice, *Journal International Marketing*, Vol, 15, No1, pp. 67–91.

[40] Cheng, W. L., Li, H. & Yu, L. (2005). The analytic network process approach to location selection: A shopping mall illustration. *Construction Innovation*, 5, 83–97.

Destination Image: Insights for Indian Tourism

Abhilasha Chauhan, Anupriya Kaur and Yajulu Medury

Department of Humanities and Social Sciences, Jaypee University of Information Technology, Solan, Himachal Pradesh

ABSTRACT

Tourism industry in India can promise a better revenue, growth and employment than its current offerings. Although, the total contribution of travel & tourism to GDP was INR 5,651.0 bn(6.4% of GDP) in 2011, and is forecast to rise by 7.3% in 2012, and to rise by 7.8% pa to INR12,891.2 bn in 2022; international and domestic tourism can be accelerated with sharper marketing strategies and marketing mix specifically tailored for the relevant market segments. Tourism marketers and allied agencies (such as private/government associations and bodies) need to identify the unaddressed gaps and opportunities for a better response from their target groups. In this context assessing, developing and promoting the 'destination image' is absolutely essential. In the west the evaluation and analysis of destination image has been the subject of much attention in related academic literature, however it is conspicuous by absence in Indian academic literature. This paper seeks to address such a gap. The paper presents a conceptual framework on destination branding, destination image and its dimensions thereof. Discerning the dimensions for destination image, then, offers direction for the key operational areas such as urban planning, employment, retailing, foreign direct investments, market segmentation, education, political and international affairs. It is expected that this paper would provide meaningful insights and direction to academicians, practitioners and policy makers engaged with tourism marketing and development.

INTRODUCTION

In India evolution of tourism marketing started in 1950 since then it has advanced through boosterism, economic planning, physical & spatial, community and sustainable approach (Chaudhary, 2010).In India the contribution of tourismindustryin providing jobs in 2011 was 7.8% of total employment (39,352,000 jobs). This is expected to rise by 2.8% in 2012 to 40,450,500 jobs and rise by 1.7% pa to 47,911,000 jobs in 2022 (8.0% of total)"(WTTC, 2012). "Tourism is a business activity connected with providing accommodation, services, and entertainment for people who are visiting a place for pleasure, recreation, leisure, business and so on"(Chaudhary, 2010)."Incredible !ndia" campaign in 2002 was the stepping stone to tourism marketing initiatives in India. There is steady revenue from tourism; India still struggles to be at par with other nations such as Thailand, Malaysia etc; which are less attractive culturally and geographically.Across the globe tourism industry has never faced such an aggressive marketing and branding as it is facing today. Destination branding is an emergingconcept that is originated from tourism marketing (Pike, 2005). The shift from tourism marketing to tourism branding initiated a tough competition among destinations worldwide. India is also competing with various global competitors. In existing markets destinations are competing on some similar parameters and destination image has gained much importance.In travel behavior, destination image is an important factor that is considered for decision making. "Marketers are interested in the concept of tourist destination image mainly because it relates to decision-making and sales of tourist products and services" (Jenkins, 1999). This leads tourism marketers to think of market segmentation as per the motives of tourists. In tourism marketing destination image is significant to create identity in the visitor's mind to generate positive outcomes.The topic of destination image has arguably been the most prevalent in the tourism literature (Pike, 2008).

The aim of this study is to discuss destination image on the basis of cognitive and affectiveattributes. This study also focuses to identify gaps in tourism marketing strategy. The study presents a synoptic view on destination image highlighting the cognitive and affective attributes. The impact of the image of a destination can be seen in various other areas also. So, it leads to discuss unaddressed gaps in Indian tourism marketing and suggest implications of destination image in various areas.

DESTINATION BRANDING

Destination branding is the process of developing a unique identity or personality for a tourist (or investment) destination, and communicating the same to visitors (Harish, 2010). Branding in tourism involves creation of brands for diverse products such as hotels, agencies, airlines, tourist trains, destinations, etc (Chaudhary, 2010).

When various countries started their destination branding, the results were highly motivating, whether the counties were struggling with their country, regional or city level image.As was seen in the case of small countries like Spain & New Zealand they had repositioned their touristic image through destination branding and yielding high revenues. The active participation of various stakeholders leads these countries to position themselves as powerful brands (Gilmore, 2002; Morgan et al., 2003). At city level many countries has opted for branding and succeeded to position new image in the mind of visitors as well as resident's.Hersteinand Jaffe (2007)in their study demonstrate how a city image can be managed throughout the planning stage - from diagnosing a current image to implementation of a new image. This particular study shows that the Israeli city Holon was able to create a new image with the help of five stages: Diagnosis, vision, image, assimilation and control. Although such branding policies aretime driven but they are result oriented.

Various states of India havealso started promoting themselves as different brands under the umbrella brand "Incredible India". Starting from Kerala's"God's Own Country" to Rajasthan's "The Incredible State of India", Punjab's "India begins here" and Himachal's "Unforgettful Himachal" with such promotional campaigns they are trying to attract the prospective visitors. Efforts are at preliminary stage and lots of work is required in branding states and cities.Although India has a vast geographical area and is rich in heritage, culture, languages, festivals etc but it has not promoted itself as other Asian competitors are promoting themselves like Malaysia and Dubai. Malaysia's "Malaysia, Truly Asia" tagline seems successful to attract larger number of visitors than India (WTTC, 2012). Dubai is anexample where within 10 years this destination has managed to change from a desert to dreamland (Vardhan, 2008). These examples show that in both the cases the marketers are successful in branding these destinations and sending positive signals about destination image. Destination image is widely researched more in European context. The next section will present a conceptual framework of destination image.

DESTINATION IMAGE

Image isa "Sum of beliefs, ideas and impressions thata person has of a destination" (Crompton, 1979; Etchner and Ritchie, 2003).A destination image is the expression of all objective knowledge, impressions, prejudice, imaginations, and emotional thoughts an individual or group might have of a particular place' (Lawson and Baud Bovy, 1977; Jenkins, 1999). Destination images influence atourist's travel decision-making, cognitionand behavior at a destination as well assatisfaction levels and recollection of theexperience (Jenkins, 1999). "Images are more important than tangible resources all because perceptions motivate consumers "to act or not act" (Guthrie and Gale, 1991; Gallarza and Garcýa, 2002).As image plays a vital role in case of normal products and brands similarly, "Destination image is related to tourist attitude as a determinant of behavioral intentions" (Phillips and Jang, 2008; Byon and Zhang, 2010).Strong and distinctive destination image should not only be a goal of branding practices in capturing consumers minds but also as a mediator to influence consumer behaviors, directly related to the success of the tourist destinations (Hanzaee and Saeedi, 2011).Other than travel behavior, destination image is directly or indirectly related to domestic & foreign investments (Warnaby and Davies, 1997; Riviezzo et al., 2009), attracting new residents, employees, (Hankinson, 2005),urbanization (Hankinson, 2004) maintaining political and international affairs (Tan Alex J.S., 2008) and education. Contemporary events as well as the relations with the other nations create a different image in tourist's mind.

In past two decades destination image has been measured on the basis of cognitive – affective, symbolic-functional, primary-secondary and organic-induced dimensions. Out of these cognitive and affective dimensions are majorly studied by researchers and are the focuses of this paper.

Cognitive Image

"Itis the sum of what is known or believed about a destination, and might be organic or induced. This knowledge may or may not have been derived from a previous visit" (Fishbein, 1967; Pike 2008). In various studies researchers support that cognitive image is linked to the individual's knowledge(Baloglu and Brinberg 1997; Baloglu and McCleary 1999a, 1999b; Gartner 1993; Walmsley and Young,1998; Beerli and Martýn, 2004).Hanyu states that perceptual/cognitive quality refers to theappraisal of physical features of environments (Baloglu and McCleary, 1999).

Cognitive attributes are linked to physical and experiential factors such as: Natural Attractions, Climate, Culture, Tourist Sites, Nightlife & Entertainment, Infrastructure, Accommodation, Shopping facilities, Cleanliness, Safety and Costs/price level.These factors are mostly used by the following researchers in their studies at various destinations as shown below in the Table 1.

Table 1. Cognitive Image Studies & Key Findings

Author	*Destination*	*Key Findings*
Echtner and Ritchie , 1993	Jamaica, Japan, Kenya and Switzerland	Destination image is important for positioning and promotional strategies.
Konecnik, 1993	Slovenia	Familiarity withthe perceptual/cognitive components of destination affects the image perception of tourists.
Balogluand MCleary,1999	Turkey, Greece, Italy, and Egypt	Information sources, type of information sources, age, and education influenceperceptual/cognitive evaluations.
Beerli and Martın,2004	Lanzarote	Travel agency staff, guidebooksand word of mouth influences the cognitive image.
Konecnik and Gartner,2007	Germany and Croatia	Empirically verified the theoretical model of the CBBETD.
Alcaniz et al., 2009	Peniscola	Overall image (Functional&psychological) influences the future behavioral intentions.
Prayag, 2010	Cape Town	Emphasized on brand knowledge, image, differentiating attributes and choice factors.
Byon and Zhang, 2010		This paper develops an original multi-dimensional 18-item scale measuringdestination image from the perspective of tourists.
Çoban, 2012	Cappadocia	Cognitive and emotional image affects satisfaction and satisfaction has a significant effect on loyalty.

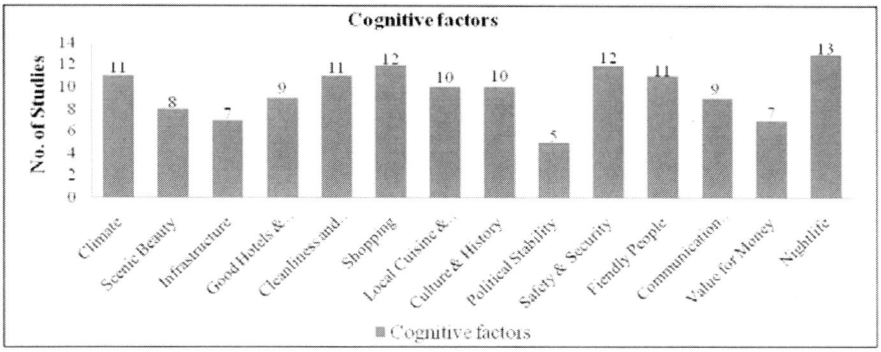

Fig. 1. Number of Studies Done on Different Cognitive Factors

As Figure 1 depicts the key cognitive factors which have been focus of past literature. Climate, cleanliness, shopping, local cuisine & food,culture & history, safety & security,friendly people and nightlife are the most studied factors by various authors.

Affective Image

Itrepresents an individual's feelings about an object, which may be favorable, unfavorable, or neutral. (Fishbein, 1967; Pike, 2008;Beerli and Martin, 2004).Hanyu suggested that "Affective meaning refers to the appraisal of the affective quality ofenvironments" (Baloglu and McCleary, 1999).The four bipolar affective images scale of Russell et al., (1981) havingUnpleasant-pleasant, Sleepy-arousing, Distressing- relaxing and Gloomy- exciting factors was used by most of the researchers and are shown in the Table 2 (Konecnik,1993).

Table 2. Affective Image Studies & Key Findings

Author	*Destination*	*Key Findings*
Konecnik,1993	Slovenia	Familiarity with the perceptual/cognitive components of destination affects the image perception of tourists.
Prayag,2010*	Capetown	Emphasized on brand knowledge, image, differentiating attributes and choice factors.
Byon, and Zhang, 2010*		This paper develops an original multi-dimensional 18-item scale measuring destination image from the perspective of tourists.
Moon et al., 2011*	South Korea	The results suggest that event quality perceptions, particularly intangible factors, positively influence the destination image

* Modified scale of Russell at et al. (1981)

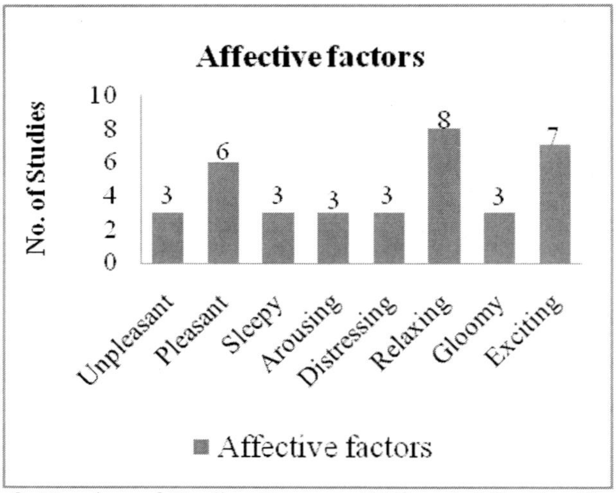

Fig. 2. Number of Studies Done on Different Affective Factors

As Figure 2 depicts that pleasant, relaxing and exciting factors are taken into consideration to know about the affective image of the destination by various authors.

Imagery is a particularly effective tool in advertising (Etchner and Ritchie, 1993). Perceptual/cognitive and affective evaluationshave a direct influence on the overall image, and also that the former,through the latter, has an indirect influence on that image (Baloglu and McCleary, 1999a, 1999b; Stern and Krakover, 1993; Beerli and Martý´n, 2004). Coban, (2012) has linked perceived image with satisfaction and loyalty. Cognitive image has a positive relationship and emotional image has negative orientation with satisfaction. There is a positively oriented relationship among touristy attractions, basic facilities, cultural attractions, touristy substructure and access possibilities and emotional image with loyalty (Coban,2012).This shows cognitive and affective attributes have an impact on overall destination image. But research on affective image is less "Affect has generally been overlooked by destination image researchers: only six out of 142 studies surveyed by Pike, 2002studied affective images" (Stepchenkova and Morrison, 2008).

INDIAN LITERATURE AND UNADDRESSED GAPS

If we link cognitive and affective dimensions of destination image to Indian context, it is difficult to find an efficient scale that can be used to measure destination image. Most of the studies are related to conceptualization of destination image of India and mainly Goa.

Conceptual Studies

Dwivedi et al. (2009) has explored the onlinedestination image of Goa, an important tourist destination in India and draw lessons for successful image management in the age of the internet.

Jauhari (2009) discussed how hospitality and tourism are contributing towards the sustainable economic growth in India.Kamat(2010) has emphasized on Goa's beach centric tourism with relation to destination life cycle model. Harish (2010) has suggested a brand architecture model for promoting India as a tourism destination brand with its diversified tourism products and vast geographical dimensions.Venkatachalam and Venkateswaran (2010) discussed that Indian tourism is facing uncertain environment but still strategies can be implement to have competitive advantage.Phukan et al.(2012)has discussed the scope of spiritual tourism in India. These conceptual studies are unable to build up a common standard that how can destination image be measured.

Empirical Studies Based on Cognitive Dimensions

Chaudhary, (2000) has determined pre and post-trip perceptions of foreign tourists through a gap analysis between expectations and satisfaction levels. Elaborated scale of Narayan et al., (2008) has included the major cognitive dimensions to measure the service quality in tourism industry. 14 cognitive dimensions has been used in this study i.e. core-tourism experience, culture Information centers, personal information, hospitality, fairness of price,hygiene, distractions, amenities,pubs value for money, logistics, food and security. Narayan et al., (2008) has implicated future directions to include motivation to travel. Agrawal et al., (2010) talked of Buddhist tourism in India and suggested implications to promote India as buddhist destination. Gupta and Gulla, (2010) studied the importance of use of internet by pilgrims to have information in Vaishno Devi shrine. Another study has taken Golden temple, Amritsar as a potential religious and spiritual destination for the tourists (Tripathi et al., 2010). In recent study, Madhavan and Rastogi, (2011) has takennineteen dimensions related to social, travel, destination and miscellaneousaspects to identify their influence on leisure destinationchoices in Hyderabad and Tirupati. This study has been done for domestic tourists in India.Nasreen and Thang,(2011)has Compared India and Malaysia on the basis of infrastructural facilities they are providing and put suggestions to improve the weak areas.

These various studies included cognitive dimensions and common attributes can be found but, till now cognitive-affective dimensions based studies are scant. As empirical studies had done by various authors have cognitive attributes but affective attributes are not considered as important factors for travel behavior.There is a need to build a scale enriched with cognitive and affective dimensions so, that physical attraction of a destination and feelings and motivation to visit can be well justified.

As India promotes international and domestic tourism, for international tourists they can enjoy diverse culture and different tourist places similarly domestic tourists are more urged to see different destination with different geographic terrain and climate in comparison to their own living destination.It is very important for tourism marketers to know that how tourists feel about the particular destination as it will be helpful in market segmentation. Hence affective dimension is significant. Perceptual mapping on the basis of cognitive and affective dimension will bring out better results for Indian tourism that which destination is more appealing for which segment of tourists? Therecent research work has shown religious, spiritual dimensions as a potential area of research in Indian tourism and it is needed to well explore in other area like medical, adventure, offbeat tourism etc. The other important issue related to Indian tourism is that India is promoting itself under monolithic brand "Incredible!ndia" and following branded house strategy (Harish, 2010) as he stated "it will be more beneficial if India will move to house of brands strategy". This suggestion has made in consideration to geographical and diversified dimensions of the country. The fact is supported by the author because India has potential to provide various tourism products as it has advantageous position in having mountains, deserts, beaches and plains.

"Incredible India" marketing campaign depicts India's sound image on the basis of culture, adventure, historical monuments, religion and festivals. But it is observed that a gap exists between the depiction and actual perception of the tourists (Jauhari, 2009). A little work has been done to analyze the destination image of India and/or its major cities. (Chaudhary, 2000; Das et al., 2007; Dwivedi, 2007; Dwivedi et al., 2009). "The image of India is something that cannot be imposed on tourist by only advertisement campaign (one way communication)" (Venkatachalam and Venkateswaran, 2010). For India, the vast potential of tourism as an employment creator and wealth distributor still remains untapped (Kant, 2009; Agrawal et al.,2010).

Considerable research in context of India shows that poor condition of roads and transport facilities is the main factor that hinders the tourist arrivals. (Travel & Tourism Competitiveness Report, 2007; Chaudhary, 2000; Ministry of Tourism, India, 2010). In addition, India lacks positive image because of hygiene and safety security problems faced by the tourists(Chaudhary, 2000; Ministry of Tourism India, 2010). This shows that India is able to portray sound symbolic images but unable to match these on experiential levels. Destination image is not important from the tourism point of view but it has significant connection to other various fields as discussed in the following section.

DESTINATION IMAGE: INSIGHTSAND DIRECTIONS

Destination image does not work in isolation; it is interconnected with other perspectives like urban planning, employment, retailing, foreign direct investments, markets segmentation, educationand political and international affairs. These implications are put forward by the author after reviewing the previous literature and relating them to Indian context.

Urban Planning

A collaborative approach is required to achieve the goals of tourism and urban planning simultaneously to uplift a place on economical dimensions. The urban planning literature focuses on the nature of the place product, its historical development and the marketing implications of its distinctive features (Hankinson, 2004). Positive destination image develops on the basis of better accommodations, roads (Echtner and Ritchie,1993), sport centers, theme parks (Tsiotsou and Ratten, 2010), cleanliness and pollution free environment etc. This implicates that all the above factors should be considered in planning stage of destinations.

Retailing

Retailing has a wider aspect in tourism marketing not only for tourists but for local residents; it will be helpful in attracting domestic and international tourists (Wong et al., 2006; Rangan et al., 2006; Balakrishnan, 2009). Retail sector is a growing sector (Hankinson, 2004) that can be seen as one of the adjacent support for tourism marketing and economic development. Balakrishnan, (2009) stated that shopping is highly preferred by the visitors in comparison to other leisure activities. Other retail oriented facilities that tourists' needs are adventures sites, parks & zoos, nightlife and Local cuisine food outlets. So, retailing facilities provided to the tourists will help in building positive perception towards the destination which results in positive destination image.

Market Segmentation

Various segments on the basis of age, culture, gender, personalityetc have different perception and image of the one same destination. For market planning purposes, a destination'sproduct mix can be described in terms of its width and length (Morrison 2002; Seaton and Bennett 1996; Lehto et al, 2004).So, it is important to make destination image significant for each segment. Segmentation has focused on identifying homogenous groups of customers that have similar attributes but future approaches should look not at the similarities but the differences that people have and plan market strategies accordingly (Tsiotsou and Ratten, 2010).

Employment

Tourism is directly related with generating employment oppotunities (Balakrishnan, 2009; Ardahaey, 2011) to its citizens and destination image of the destination affects the outsourcing of manpower from outside. It is necessary to build positive image of destination to attract employees internationally, because negative destination image have an effect on decision making of potential employees.

Foreign direct Investments

"Tourism and hospitality are significant in attracting foreign direct investment and more business and leisure travel" (Jauhari, 2009). Foreign investorsare interested to invest their money in thosedestinations whose destination image and other conditions are favorable. According to Lim (2005) in (Metaxas, 2010) the host country (place) policy framework for FDI attractionrefers to the following: the degree of social/political stability, rules regarding entry and operations, fair competition between foreignand domestic investors, privatization policy, international agreements on FDI and the host government's attitude towards foreign corporations. This shows destination image is directly or indirectly related to various economic activities other than tourism.

Political and International Affairs

Sustained terrorism, war or political instability and the consequent negative media coverage can cause long-term damage to a destination's image (Hopper,2002; Venkatachalam and Venkateswaran, 2010). Politicians in authority warn their citizens from traveling to other designated countries due to political instability or possibility of war (Alsarayreh et al.2010).Due to 2008 terrorists attacks on India a drop of 12% in tourists arrivals was shown in India's Ministry of Tourism records (Venkatachalam and Venkateswaran, 2010). Tourists pay attention towards the safety and security, crime rate when they are planning their visits. A positive destination image is helpful in making strong political and international affairs.

Education

Worldwide destinations attract students and basis for that is positive value associated with that particular destination. Indian and other students faced violence in 2011 due to that as earlier "Australia's international student numbers continue to plummet with Indian students' enrolments dropping by over 24 per cent during January-June 2012 as compared to previous year, according to government figures. Australian education providers saw a drop of 8.5 per cent in enrolments during January to June 2012,as compared with the last year (*The Economic Times*, Aug 2012). This shows destination image is widely important in various areas. Such happenings affects destination image of the place therefore it is necessary to build strong & positive images so that positive WOM can be spread throughout the world.

Domestic and International Tourism

Positive destination image is important not only to attract international tourists but it is equally important to have domestic tourists. Domestic travel spending generated 82.2% of direct Travel & Tourism GDP in 2011 compared with 17.8% for Visitor exports (foreign visitor spending or international tourism receipts).Domestic travel spending is expected to grow by 8.3% in 2012 to INR 4,009.9 bn, and rise by 8.1% pa to INR8, 710.3bn in 2022.Visitor exports are expected togrow by 3.5% in 2012 to INR 829.2bn, and rise by 5.2% pa toINR1, 382.6bn in 2022 (WTTC, 2012).This projection of WTTC shows that domestic and international segments are equally important to have large revenues in tourism industry. To build positive images of a destination both international and domestic segments should be focused.

DISCUSSION & CONCLUSION

"There was no synergy, no uniformity, nobrilliance in creativity, no convergence of media, and above all, a lack of positioning andbranding of India as a tourism destination" (Kant, 2009; Harish, 2010). Now there is need to implement destination branding policies taking under consideration India's strengths and weaknesses. Potential areas like medical tourism, religious tourism and offbeat tourism should be focused to have maximum revenues. A competitive strategy is needed to gain maximum market sharein tourism industry. In India, future of destination branding depends upon right kind of image positioning in visitor's mind. It can be only possible when government, private bodies, other stake holders and local people will join their hands.Theoretically the paper suggests building a scale that can measure effectively the destination images in Indian context. Positive images are key to behavioral intentions so cognitive and affective images should be well understood in Indian context.Furthermore an emphasis has been put on affective images as they are also important for market segmentation. As discussed in this paper destination image is closely relatedto other areas like urban planning, retailing, etc; that works for the development of the destination and in building positive image. City branding is a great idea for India as it has a vast geographical area. India has a great potential to be a successful destination in Asia and worldwide, if the scattered tourism stakeholders will work unidirectional to achieve best out of it.

REFERENCES

[1] Agrawal, M., Choudhary, H., & Tripathi, G. (2010). "Enhancing Buddhist tourism in India: an exploratory study. *Worldwide Hospitality and Tourism Themes, 2* (5), 477 – 493.

[2] Alcaniz, E. B., Garcýa, I. S., & Blas, S. S. (2009). The functional-psychological continuum in the cognitive image of a destination: A confirmatory analysis. *Tourism Management* , 715–723.

[3] Alsarayreh, M. N., Jawabreh, O. A., & Helalat, M. S. (2010). The Influence of Terrorism on the International Tourism Activities. *European Journal of Social Sciences, 13* (1).

[4] Ardahaey, F. T. (2011). Economic Impacts of Tourism Industry. *International Journal of Business and Management, 6* (8).

[5] Balakrishnan,M.S.(2009). Strategic branding of destinations: a framework.*European Journal of marketing*,43(5),611-629.

[6] Baloglu, S., & McCleary, K. W. (1999). A Model of Destination Image Formation. *Annals of Tourism Research, 26* (4), 868-897.

[7] Beerli, A., & Martý´n, J. D. (2004). Factors Influencing Destination image. *Annals of Tourism Research, 31* (3), 657–681.

[8] Byon, K. K., & Zhang, J. J. (2010). Development of a scale measuring destination image. *Marketing Intelligence & Planning,, 28* (4), 508 – 532.

[9] Çoban, S. (2012). The Effects of the Image of Destination on Tourist Satisfaction and Loyalty: The Case of Cappadocia. *European Journal of Social Sciences , 29* (2), 222-232.

[10] Chaudhary, M. (2000). India's image as a tourist destination - a perspective of foreign Tourists. *Tourism Management* , 293- 297.

[11] Dwivedi, M., Yadav, A., & Patel, V. R. (2009). The online destination image of Goa. *Worldwide Hospitality and Tourism Themes, 1* (1), 25 - 39.

[12] Echtner, C. M., & Ritchie, J. B. (1993). The Measurement of Destination Image: An Empirical Assessment. *Journal of Travel Research* .

[13] Echtner, C. M., & Ritchie, J. B. (2003). The Meaning and Measurement of Destination Image. *The Journal of Tourism Studies, 14* (1).

[14] Gallarza, M. G., Saura, I. G., & Garcý´a, H. C. (2002). Destination image Towards a Conceptual Framework. *Annals of Tourism Research,, 29 pp.* (1), 56-78.

[15] Gilmore, F. (2002). A country - can it be repositioned? Spain - the success story of country branding. *Journal of Brand Management* .

[16] Gupta, K., & Gulla, A. (2010). Internet deployment in the spiritual tourism industry: the case of Vaishno Devi Shrine. *Worldwide Hospitality and Tourism Themes, 2* (5), 507 - 519.

[17] Hankinson, G. (2005). Destination brand images: a business tourism Perspective,. *Journal of Services Marketing* , 24–32q.

[18] Hankinson, G. (2004). Relational network brands: Towards a conceptual model of place brands. *Journal of Vacation Marketing, 10* (2), 109–121.

[19] Hanzaee, K. H., & Saeedi, H. (2011). A Model of Destination Branding For Isfahan City: Integrating the Concepts of the Branding and Destination Image. *Interdisciplinary Journal of Research in Business, 1* (4).

[20] Harish, R. (2010). Brand architecture in tourism branding: the way forward for India . *Journal of Indian Business Research, 2* (3), 153-165q .

[21] Herstein, R., & Jaffe, E. D. (2008). The children ' s city The transition from a negative to a positive city image. *Place Branding and Public Diplomacy, 4*, 76–84.

[22] ORG. MARG, A. M. (2007). *Competitiveness of Tourism Sector in India with Selected Countries of World.*(Govt. of India).

[23] Indian students' enrolments drop by 24% in Australia during January-June 2012: Government. (2012). The Economic Times.

[24] Jauhari, V. (2009). The hospitality and tourism industry in India: conclusions and solutions. *Worldwide Hospitality and Tourism Themes, 1* (1), 75-80q.

[25] Jenkins, O. H. (1999). Understanding and Measuring Tourist Destination Images. *International Journal of Tourism* .

[26] JS, T. A. (2008). Destination Branding: Creating a Destination of Choice. *Perspectives in Asian Leisure and Tourism, 1* (1).

[27] Kamat, S. B. (2010). Destination Life Cycle and Assessment - A Study of Goa Tourism Industry. *South Asian Journal of Tourism and Heritage, 3* (2).

[28] Konecnik, M.(1993). The image as a possible source of competitive advantage of the destination The case of Slovenia. *Tourism Review, 57* (1), 6 – 12.

[29] Konecnik, M., & Gartner, W. C. (2007). Customer – based brand equity for a destination. *Annals of Tourism Research, 34* (2), 400–421.

[30] Lehto, X. Y., O'Leary, J. T., & Morrison, A. M. (2004). The effect of prior experience on vacation behavior. *Annals of Tourism Research, 31* (4), 801–818.

[31] Madhavan, H., & Rastogi, R. (2011). Social and psychological factors influencing destination preferences of domestic tourists in India. *Leisure Studies.*

[32] Metaxes,T. (2010). Place marketing, place branding and foreign direct investments: Defining their relationship in the frame of local economic development process.*Place Branding and Public Diplomacy, 6* (3), 228–243.

[33] Ministry of Tourism (Govt. of India), I. I. (2010). *Analyzing the Factors Responsible for Slow-down in Tourist Arrivals in India Report* .

[34] Moon, K. S., Kim, M., Ko, Y. J., Connaughton, D. P., & Lee, J. H. (2011). The influence of consumer's event quality perception on destination image. *Managing Service Quality, 21* (3), 287 – 303.

[35] Morgan, N. J., Pritchard, A., & Piggo, R. (2003). Destination branding and the role of stakeholders:The case of new Zealand. *Journal of vacation marketing* .

[36] Narayan, B., Rajendran, C., & Sai, L. P. (2008). "Scales to measure and benchmark service quality in tourism industry: A second-order factor approach", *Benchmarking:An International Journal., 15* (4), 469 – 493.

[37] Nasreen, R., & Thang, N. T. (2011). Marketing Of Asian Countries as Tourist Destination-Comparative Study of India and Malaysia. *International Journal of Scientific & Engineering Research, 2* (4).

[38] Phukan, H., Rahman, Z., & Devdutt, P. (2012). Emergence of Spiritual Tourism in India. *International Journal of Marketing and Technology, 2* (4).

[39] Pike, S. (2008). *Destination Marketing An Integrated Marketing Communication Approach.*

[40] Pike, S. (2005). Tourism destination branding complexity. *Journal of Product & Brand Management, 14* (4), 258 - 259.

[41] Prayag, G. (2010). Brand image assessment: international visitors' perceptions of Cape Town. *Marketing Intelligence & Planning, 28* (4), 462 – 485.

[42] Riviezzo, A., Nisco, A. d., & Napolitano, M. R. (2009). Importance-performance analysis as a tool in evaluating town centre management effectiveness". *International Journal of Retail & Distribution Management, 37* (9), 748 - 764.

[43] Stepchenkova, & Morrison, A. M. (2008). Russia's destination image among American pleasure travelers: Revisiting Echtner and Ritchie. *Tourism Management* , 548–560.

[44] Tripathi, G., Choudhary, H., & Agrawal, M. (2010). What do the tourists want? The case of the Golden Temple, Amritsar. *Worldwide Hospitality and Tourism Themes, 2* (5), 494 – 506.

[45] Tsiotsou, R., & Ratten, V. (2010). Future research directions in tourism marketing. *Marketing Intelligence & Planning, 28* (4), 533 - 544.

[46] Vardhan, J. (15-17 May 2008). From a Desert to a Dreamland- the case of Successful Destination Marketing of Dubai and lessons for India. *Conference on Tourism in India – Challenges Ahead.* Kozhikode.

[47] Venkatachalam, V. B., & Venkateswaran, R. N. (2010). Destination Branding: Making India Relevant and Competitive in Uncertain Environment. *South Asian Journal of Tourism and Heritage, 3* (1).

[48] WTTC.(2012).*Travel and Tourism Economic Impact,India.*

[49] http://incredibleindiacampaign.com/

Effect of Government Policies on the Higher Education Framework and Structure in Indonesia

Sandeep Puri and Divakar Narayan Singh

IMT, Ghaziabad

ABSTRACT

Indonesia is a growing country and has often being counted among other nations like Brazil, India, and China, yet it fails to show expected significant growth. The education sector in Indonesia is completely different from most other developing nations, and presents its own unique issues. At first glance, the very high literacy rate almost gives us a false idea of a healthy education system existing in Indonesia. But when one looks closely, there are serious flaws in the system, which are adversely affecting Indonesia.

In this research, I attempt to find out the effect of government policies and strategies on higher education. I take a critical look at Indonesia's education strategy, which gave her a few benefits initially, but in today's volatile scenario when the demand for higher qualifications has increased, the strategy seems ineffective and the needs to change urgently.

My research shows that due to the initial strategy of strengthening primary education, higher education was completely ignored, due to which Indonesia today lacks good infrastructure, human capital and other facilities for higher education. The lack of government expenditure on tertiary education to almost non-existent financing facilities and everything else has affected higher education. It reflects on Indonesia's labor force as well, in the form of leaks in the system that needs to be plugged.

Several steps can be taken to solve this issue, in the form of concrete steps towards the recovery of higher education. These have been elucidated at the end of the paper.

INTRODUCTION

Indonesia, which has gone through several radical political changes, from dictatorship to a democracy, and from a Muslim-majority to being somewhat secular, has continued to show a robust growth of above 6%. Indonesia is a country of several islands, which makes it unique in its own way. Majority of the population (86%) is Muslim by religion, besides other religions like Christianity and Hinduism. By ethnicity, Indonesia mainly consists of native Indonesians and Chinese people. The literacy level is very high in Indonesia and it touches the 90% mark consistently. The unemployment rate is correspondingly low, at 8% approximately.

The labour force consists mostly of people who have graduated from high school; people having tertiary education comprise only 8% of the overall labor force, while in the neighboring countries it is more than 25% (Singapore) and more than 22% (Malaysia).

This describes the lack of education, despite the fact that the literacy level in Indonesia has touched the 90% mark consistently since the beginning. This takes us to the point where it is obvious that there is a barrier between primary/basic education and higher education. This lagging nature of higher education can be understood properly if we look at the government policies which help in shaping the education scenario of any country.

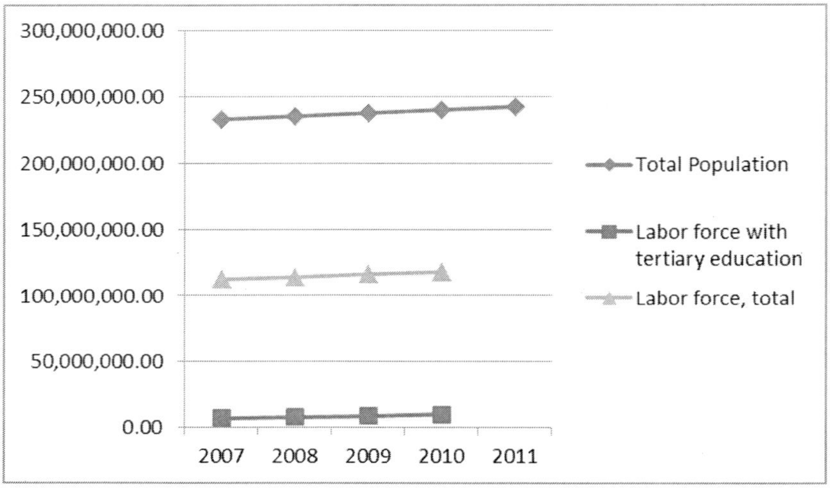

Fig. 1. Labor Force Scenario of Indonesia

EDUCATION SYSTEM IN INDONESIA

The education system in Indonesia is complex because of three reasons: the sparse distribution of population, ethnicity and social structures. These factors become challenges in the improvement of quality of education as well as its expansion. Currently, the following structure (refer to Table 1) is adopted by the government as the framework of the education system in Indonesia.

The table on the following page shows that the formal education tract consists of General schools and Islamic schools; the General schools come under the purview of Ministry of Education (MoE), while in Islamic schools the emphasis is more on religious teachings, hence they are managed by Ministry of Religious Affairs. Despite the different emphasis as regards the curriculum, for academic disciplines such as English, Mathematics, and Science, the same pedagogy is deployed at both types of schools. It helps in maintaining consistency amongst all the students, which helps in a uniform evaluation criteria for all students.

Based on higher education, Higher Educational Institutes (HEIs) can be differentiated in terms of public and private. Public HEIs act as the foundation for higher education because they are perceived to be better-equipped with a superior education quality. The other factor for their popularity is the low cost of education and the greater number of scholarships available as compared to private HEIs. Private HEIs are far greater in number, but the cost of education is very high when compared to the cost of education in other countries like India and China. To attract more students, private HEIs also have to provide scholarships, and other facilities for easy fee payment.

Table 1. Feature of Indonesia's Education System

Level	*Track*	*School*	*Age of Schooling*
Basic	Formal	1. Primary Schools 2. Islamic Primary Schools (*Madrasah Ibtidaiyah*)	7-12 Years
		1. Junior Secondary School 2. Islamic Junior Secondary School (*Madrasah Ibtidaiyah*)	13-15 Years
	Non Formal	Package A	7-12 Years
		Package B	13-15 Years
Secondary Education	Formal	1. Senior Secondary School 2. Vocational Secondary School 3. Islamic Senior Secondary School (*Madrasah Aliya)*	16-18 Years
	Non Formal	Package C	
Higher Education		Universities/Institute offers the following programs - 1. Non Degree Program 2. Degree Program 3. Professional Programs equals to Master and Doctorate	19-29 Years

As mentioned before, Indonesia has maintained a very high level of literacy, especially if we consider the fact that she recently attained middle-class income country status. It was seen in Indonesia that government spending on primary and secondary education was higher than the total expenditure on tertiary/higher education. Figure 2 helps in comparing the expenditure on primary, secondary and tertiary education as a percentage of total expenditure on education.

There are many conclusions which can be drawn based on the graph below –

- The government focused on the strategy of strengthening the primary education sector and hence invested heavily in that segment. It explains the high literacy rate maintained by Indonesia.
- Indonesia suffers from a serious lack of focus on secondary and higher education, which has resulted in a serious lack of labor having tertiary education, which can be seen as one of the reasons why Indonesia maintained a steady growth rate of 6% over the last few years, but never grew at a rate close to nations like China and India.
- If we look at the pattern, it can be easily discerned that the government has now started to shift its focus from primary education and started spending on tertiary education.

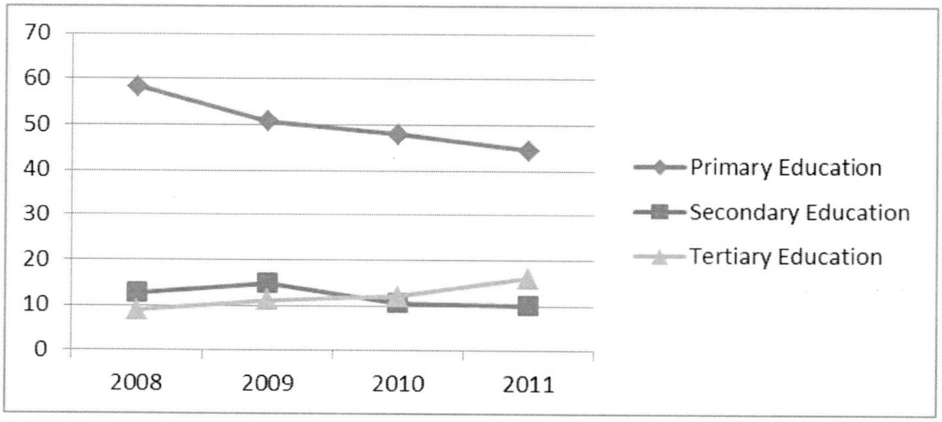

Fig. 2. Educational Expenditure as %age of Total Educational Expenditure

EFFECT OF FOCUS ON PRIMARY EDUCATION

The good effects can be seen throughout the country, but somewhere the policy of skewed concentration on primary education has hurt Indonesia. The country lacks quality education institutions, and even the government universities are not fully equipped to impart quality education. Teaching quality is another measure which indicates that tertiary education lacks the momentum to drive the nation towards growth. The most tangible effect of this policy can be seen in the gross enrollment ratio (Figure 3) in different levels of education namely, secondary, upper secondary, and tertiary.

As we can see in the figure above, increase in the level of education leads to a decline in enrollment, and the most severely hit enrollment rate exists for tertiary education. This has led to many serious complications for Indonesia. The most adversely affected by it are the poor people, because the enrollment ratio for higher education amongst poor families is the lowest, hovering around 2%. This shows that the power gap is huge in Indonesia, and due to a lack of proper reforms, it has increased manifold, even as we read this article. This issue will be addressed in detail when we cover education financing later.

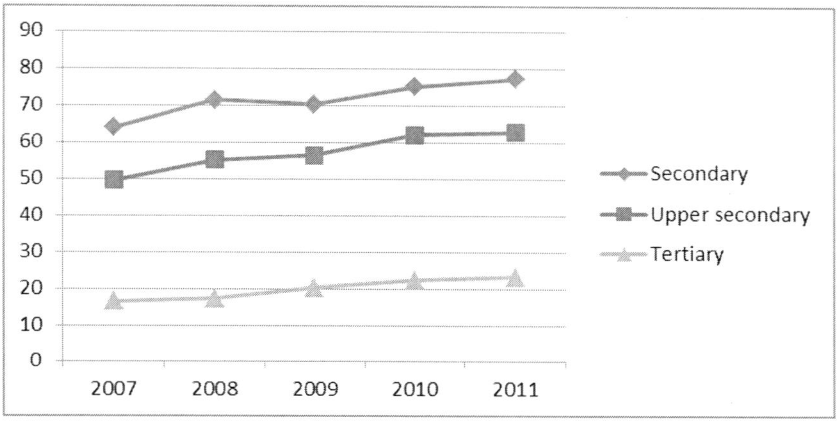

Fig. 3: Gross Enrollment Ratio (%age) at Different Education Levels

We can also compare different nations on the basis of teachers available for higher education, and to nullify the population effect, we use an appropriate ratio comparison. This ratio is the number of teachers in tertiary education segment divided by the number of teachers in primary education. Figure 4 clearly shows that Indonesia not only lacks the physical infrastructure but also the human capital needed to improve tertiary education. It also shows that this ratio continues to decline for Indonesia, while for other countries it is growing, and in this race Indonesia's neighbor Malaysia has displayed a significant improvement since 2008.

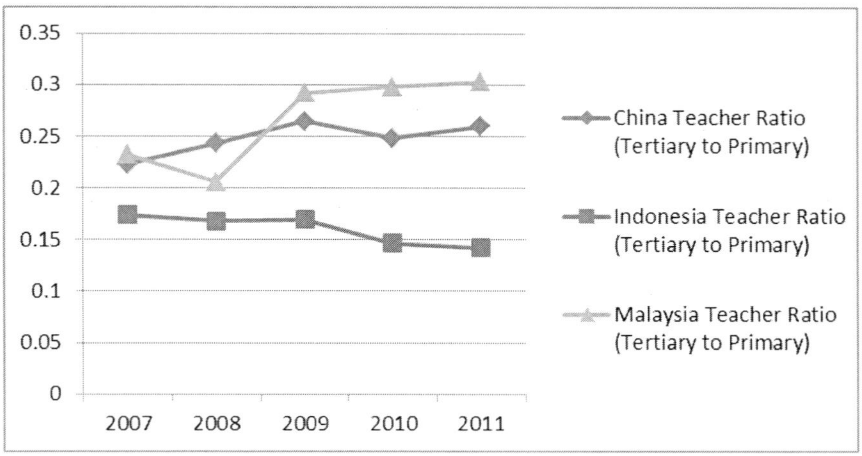

Fig. 4. Tertiary Teacher to Primary Teacher Ratio for Three Countries

These are few of the indicators that clearly indicate that all is not well with the country's education segment, and the holistic growth of the nation is not possible unless the education sector is correctly balanced. The government has recognized these issues off late, but there are bigger loop holes, which still need to be plugged to improve higher education and secure the nation's future.

HIGHER EDUCATION ENVIRONMENT

After the endorsement of the very first Education Act in 1961, Indonesia's higher education has continuously experienced rapid expansion. Moreover, the development of higher education became faster between the 1970s and 1990s, when Indonesia experienced strong economic growth, fuelled by an oil-price boom and solid non-oil and gas export performance.

It was recorded that the student population in HEIs increased from just around 200,000 students in 1975 to 2.5 million students in 1995. By 2005, there were about 2,300 higher education institutions, consisting of 86 public HEIs and about 2,200 private HEIs, with a total strength of more than 3.5 million students.

This rapid expansion can be credited to many factors, most important being growth of the economy leading to increased demand for skilled workers. There were several steps taken by the government in order to improve higher education, like enactment of the first education law, Law No. 15 of 1961, which also laid the structure for higher education.

Under this law, universities have been standardized with respect to the division of faculty and governance structure (senates and president of the universities) (Buchori and Malik 2004). It also spells out the mission of HEIs or the so-called Tri Dharma Perguruan Tinggi (Three Pillars of national higher education), namely, learning, research and community service.

By 1975, the MoE, through the Directorate General of Higher Education (DGHE), established for the first time the basic development framework for higher education. A dual system, academic and professional/ vocational was also initiated during the same period. According to the framework, academic programs consist of four-year undergraduate degree programs (strata 1-S1), two-year masters (strata 2-S2) and three-year doctorate program (Strata 3-S3). Meanwhile, the professional/ vocational programs offer one-to-four year non degree trainings. There was a significant increase in tertiary education provided by the government.

The government spends more than 11% of its overall education budget on tertiary education. This fully describes the importance attached to the tertiary segment, which is different from earlier trends that implied more focus on the 9 years of compulsory education, and corresponding investment in that area.

Table 2. Evolution of Higher Education Long Term Strategy (HELTS)

	Period Covered	*Focus*	*Key Policy Reforms*
1st HELTS	1975-1985	Emphasized on the aspect of relevance by taking into account the need of strong linkages between higher education and the development programs in the region or nationwide	Academic and professional streams; diploma, degree, and graduate programs; Credit system and standard.
2nd HELTS	1986-1995	Focused on consolidating previous achievement and improvement of quality	National Accreditation Board (Badan Akreditasi National, BAN) established in 1994 under Ministerial Decree No. 0326/U/1994.
3rd HELTS	1996-2005	Focused on three core programs, i.e. implementation of the new paradigm in higher education management, improvement of relevance and quality, and promotion of geographical and social equity	"New paradigm" redefining the roles of the center, and of the individual institutions of higher education; Board of Higher Education (Dewan Pendidikan Tinggi, DPT) was established by Ministerial Decree No. 0121/U/1996; Four public universities granted autonomy; Performance-based resource allocation proposed.
4th HELTS	2003-2010	Focused on the nation's competitiveness, promotion of decentralization and autonomy and improvement of organizational health	Institutional autonomy is greatly promoted; Three more public universities became autonomous; competitive grant and performance grant launched to public and private institutions

The growth in investment in tertiary education has been far more than 50% in recent times. The following figures (Figures 5 and 6) substantiate this investment and growth.

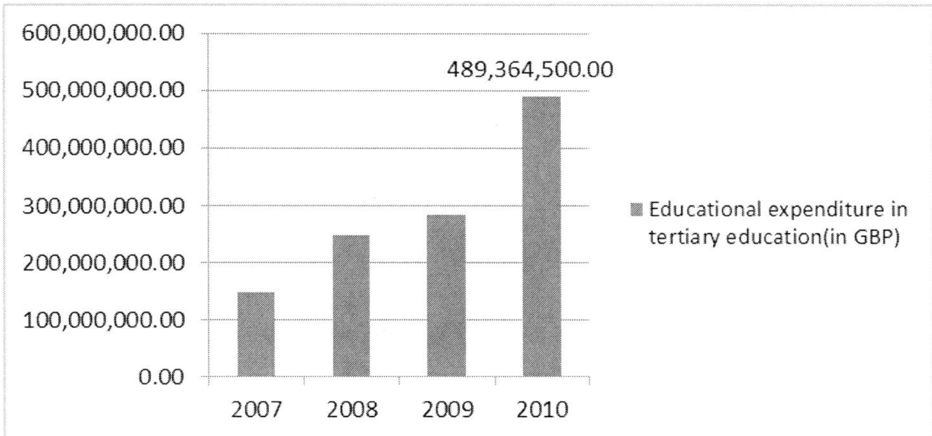

Fig. 5. Education Expenditure on Tertiary Education

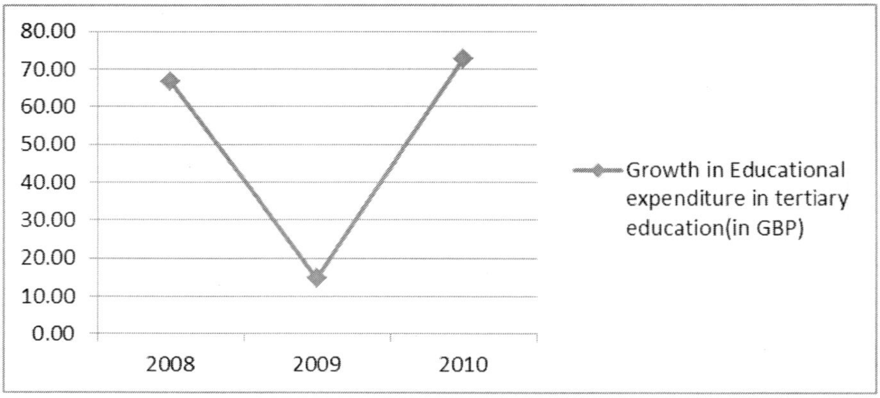

Fig. 6. YOY Growth %age in Investment in Tertiary Kducation

But despite all these efforts, gross enrollment in tertiary education remains low and currently lingers around 12%, clearly depicting that there are several issues in the education system that are hindering the growth of higher education in Indonesia.

Apart from what has already been discussed, there is one more factor which adversely affects higher education in Indonesia, the lack of financing of higher education. This issue needs to be addressed properly if Indonesia wants to be a self-dependent high growth nation.

We all agree that if a nation has to develop its higher education, it has to give its citizens proper channels through which they are able to finance their studies. The most common channel is education loans provided by banks and other financial institutions. In general, it is seen that the government imposes some regulations regarding education loans so that students can afford to pursue higher education, that too at slightly lower interest rates.

In Indonesia, such loans do not exist even on paper, and in the absence of such a noble facility, students are heavily dependent on various scholarships. These scholarships are given by government and private colleges/universities.

A large proportion of the DGHE budget goes to public institutions. The 2009 government budget for higher education is Rp 18.5 trillion, or US$ 1.8 billion. Roughly 85% of the budget is to support tertiary education institutions: 69% is allocated to 76 non-autonomous public HEIs, 11% to seven autonomous institutions, and 6% to subsidize private institutions.

Regional disparities have been narrowing, owing to the government's continuous investment in higher education in disadvantaged areas; however there is still a significant disparity in the ability of the rich and the poor to access tertiary education opportunities. Less than 2% of youth aged 19-22 years from households of the lowest wealth quintile is enrolled in HEIs (Figure 7), compared to over 60% enrolled from the wealthiest households.

This biased enrolment favoring the relatively rich leads to the highly regressive pattern of public spending on tertiary education in Indonesia (Figure 8): over 80% of public spending on tertiary education benefits the better-off 40% of the households (Q2, Q3 and Q4), further over 60% benefits the richest 20%.

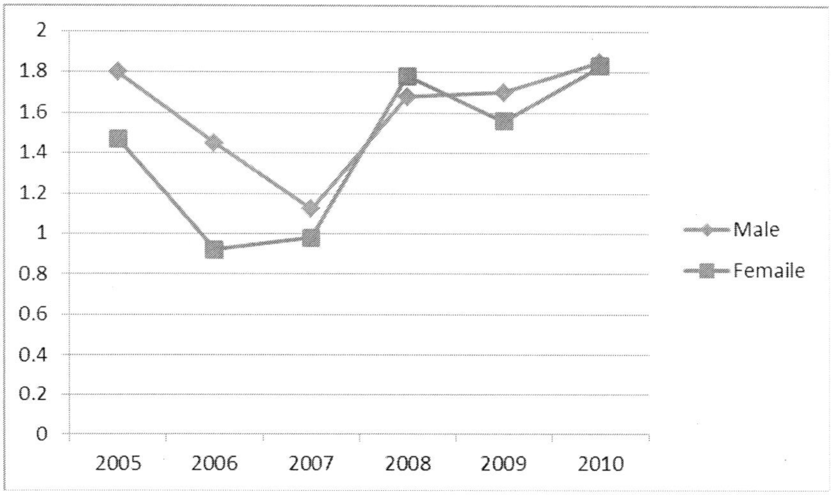

Fig. 7. Gross Enrollment Rate for Tertiary Education of the Low Income Student

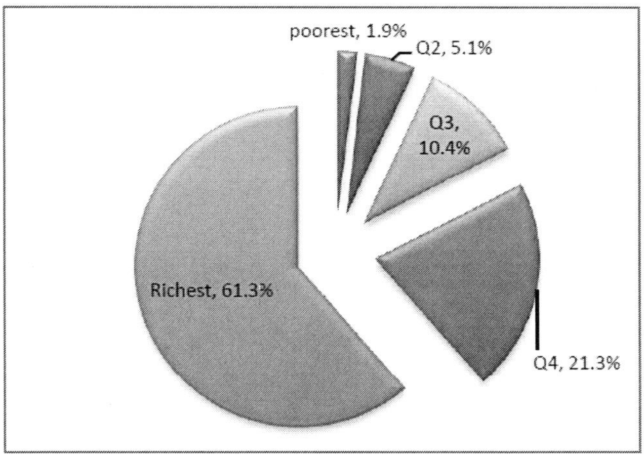

Fig. 8. Benefit Shares of Public Spending on Tertiary Education

The National Socioeconomic Household Survey (SUSENAS) data shows that among these scholarship recipients, over 60% are enrolled in public institutions. If public and private HEIs are examined separately, the scholarship coverage is 2.7% in public HEIs, three times as much as the 0.9% in private HEIs. (Figure 9)

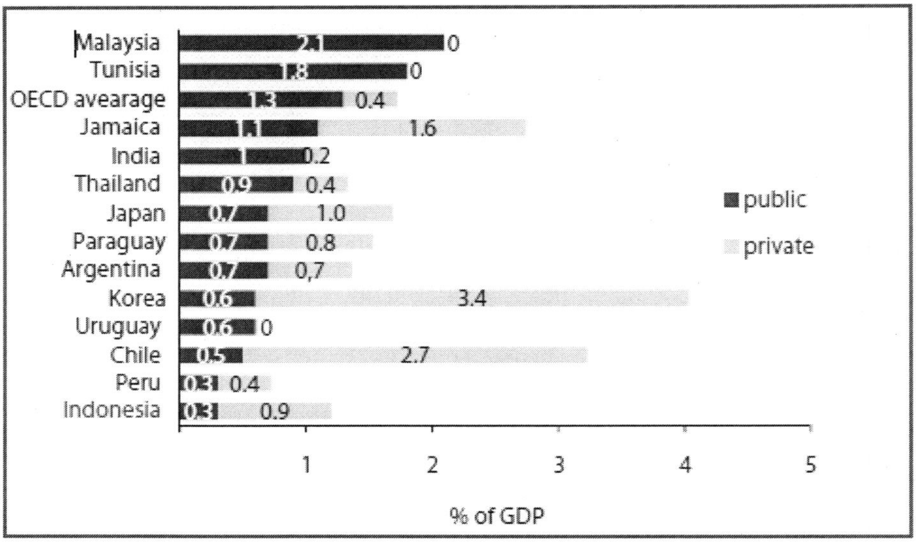

Fig. 9. Public and Private Spending on Tertiary Education as a %age of Total GDP
UNESCO: World Education Indicators (WEI, '07). The figures reflect estimates for '04-'05. The Indonesian figure is from the '09 budget.

Non-government sources provide a significant number of scholarships at HEIs. It is estimated that approximately half of the scholarships at public HEIs, and over 85% of the scholarships at private HEIs are provided by private sources.

Since most children from the poorest households drop out of the education system before they even reach the stage of higher education, and most of the relevant scholarships are awarded after a student has enrolled, there is little chance that the children from the poorest households can benefit. Scholarship schemes for financially disadvantaged high school leavers who want to pursue a higher education are very rare. This inevitably limits the opportunity for them to pursue a higher education.

RECOMMENDATIONS

Looking ahead, rationalizing public expenditure at HEIs and increasing the level of public funding will be key to strengthening Indonesia's higher education sector. Benchmarking efficiency using service standards and unit costs will be a useful tool for institutions to reflect on their internal management issues. Strengthened integrated and innovative support to private HEIs would also play a decisive role in laying the path for higher education.

The inequity in access to tertiary education can only be reduced by bridging the 'wealth divide'. Financial aid also needs to be increased and the balance between institutional and individual funding to be adjusted. One feasible start is to change the government financing channel to public HEIs. Instead of giving public HEIs a budget allocation inclusive of scholarships, part of the budget could be allocated as direct student financial aid. Some of this direct aid should be allocated to promising secondary school graduates.

The institutions would then obtain the funding indirectly through cost recovery from these students. This change would improve equity and create a culture of competition between private and public institutions. Indonesia will need to explore what type of institutions should be supported and relied on to expand coverage. Indonesia already has an open university with a large enrollment; whether more could be established can be further explored. "Community colleges" can also be considered.

There is a lot that needs to be done. It will require highly dedicated attempts from the government to revive higher education, and the shift will have to be planned gradually.

REFERENCES

[1] Bloomberg Publications (2012), *Regulatory Framework: Indonesia.*

[2} Buchori and Malik (2003), *The Evolution of Higher Education in Indonesia in Asian Universities: Historical Perspective and Contemporary Challenges.*

[3] F. Javier Arze del Granado, Wolfgang Fengler, Andy Ragatz, and Elif Yavuz (2007), *Investing in Indonesia's Education: Allocation, Equity, and Efficiency of Public Expenditure.*

[4] Gropello, Kruse, and Tandon (2011), *Skills for the Labor Market in Indonesia.*

[5] International Labour Organization, Key Indicators of the Labour Market database.

[6] Ministry of Education, Indonesia (2010), *Indonesia: Higher Education Financing Policy Brief.*

[7] Teguh Yudo and Deni Friawan (2008), *Recent Developments of Higher education in Indonesia : Issues and Challenges.*

[8] World Bank East Asia and Pacific Regional Report (2011), *Putting Higher Education to Work.*

[9] World Bank National Accounts data.

[10] OECD National Accounts data files.

[11] UNESCO and World Bank data from *http://databank.worldbank.org.*

Enhancing and Optimizing Efficiency in Aircraft Manufacturing: Airbus Information Systems

Rakesh Chopra and Samarth Gupta

Institute of Management Technology, Ghaziabad

ABSTRACT

The aircraft manufacturing industry has seen the largest quantum of advancement. Today, this industry is one of the biggest capital and technology intensive industries. What makes it unique is its scale of operations and the need for efficiency and workflow arising thereof. In the aircraft manufacturing industry, there are numerous stakeholders; suppliers, customers and partners, who are distributed by geography and even time-zones, Management Information Systems (MIS) and Enterprise Resource Planning (ERP) cannot be only considered as supporting functions but also as participants in strategic management of the organizations. In certain cases it has been observed that MIS and ERP act as key policy implementers of the manufacturing organization, while in some cases they also act as a tool to improve the efficiency and cost-effectiveness of a particular operational process. In this paper, we attempt to study and analyze the various MIS and ERP systems implemented at Airbus and their implications on their business of manufacturing aircrafts. We will also discuss how Airbus made its operations completely transparent and reduced Aircraft delivery time for its customers with the help of Customer Back Office support units while ensuring complete maintenance support to them.

INTRODUCTION

Aircraft Manufacturing is a highly complex and capital-intensive operation that requires specific capabilities and global connectivity and mobility among various stakeholders. This is the reason why not many players have been able to gain a market leader position in this industry. The amount of inter-dependence between the aircraft manufacturers and their suppliers and vendors is another important factor that determines the dynamics of this industry. In such an industry where one wrong move can lead to a disaster, aircraft manufacturers cannot afford to become complacent. The amount of price and delivery pressures being put by clients is immense and the aircraft manufacturers face a challenge to improve their own efficiency while maintaining relations with existing suppliers and vendors. Dietrich and Cudney [1], presented how experience level of the supplier in adopting new technology is as critical as deploying it within the aerospace company. In such a scenario, the proper implementation and efficient utilization of ERP software becomes highly critical. ICT and MIS are not only the need of the hour but also a strategic and tactical tool for these organizations. This paper shows how emerging Information Systems and processes are being implemented by a leading aerospace manufacturing organization like Airbus and how it has benefitted from such advanced software.

BUSINESS DYNAMICS OF THE AIRCRAFT MANUFACTURING

Aircraft manufacturing is one of the most oligopolistic industries in the world. Only few players have been able to sustain themselves in the business. The main manufacturers of wide-body and narrow-body jet airliners are Airbus, Boeing and Tupoloev while Bombardier and Embraer are more focussed on regional airlines. Ceci et al [2] suggested that because a large number of parts are needed in order to make an aircraft, the manufacturers have to outsource these parts from a large network of specialized suppliers throughout the world thereby leading to synergies between the various stakeholders. That is why aircraft manufacturing organizations need to be truly global requiring large amount of capital and labour investment- the major reason why only a few players have been able to sustain themselves in business. There are five major manufacturers of civil transport aircraft at present:

1. **Airbus:** Airbus is one of the biggest aircraft manufacturers of the world. It was created in late 1970's and since then the company has touched new heights of growth and development. It is one of the leading manufacturers of commercial jetliners and military airlifters. Airbus is also a big employer with employee strength of 55,000 people spread across 16 sites in Europe. Airbus is based in Europe and has three subsidiaries in USA, Japan and China. Airbus is an undisputed world leader in the civil air transport market with over 7000 aircrafts being ordered by international customers. Airbus is headquartered in France which houses Airbus Central Entity (ACE) in Toulouse and links it to a global network of over 200 customers and 1500 suppliers worldwide. (Source- www.airbus.com [3])
2. **Boeing:** Boeing is one of the other main aerospace companies. It was founded in 1916 and its headquarters are currently located in Chicago, USA. It is one of the largest manufacturers of commercial jetliners and military aircrafts. They are also into designing and manufacturing of rotorcraft, electronic and defence systems, missiles, satellites, launch vehicles and advanced information and communication systems. A recent report by Boeing [4] acknowledges that Boeing has contracts with over 26,000 suppliers and partners globally with total revenue of $68.7 billion in 2011. The report also shares that Boeing has around 1,70,000 employees in 50 states and 70 countries.
3. **Bombardier:** Bombardier is a global transportation company with presence in over 60 countries with 76 production and engineering sites among them. Bombardier is the world's only manufacturer of both planes and trains. Bombardier is headquartered in Montreal,

Canada and has a workforce of over 70,000 employees. It operates two businesses: Aerospace and Rail Transportation. Bombardier Aerospace manufactures business, commercial, specialized and amphibious aircrafts. Some of the well know aircrafts of Bombardier include Learjet, Challenger, Flexjet, etc. (Source- *www.bombardier.com* [5])

4. **Embraer:** Embraer is also a minor yet important player in the aircraft manufacturing industry. It mainly focuses on specific market segments with high growth potential in commercial, defense and executive aviation. Embraer employs over 17,000 people with net revenue of US $4278 million in 2012. Embraer is based in São José dos Campos, Brazil. Embraer mainly focuses on three markets- commercial aviation, defense systems and executive aviation. Embraer is a highly innovative company with regional and commercial jet product lines. Some of the well known aircrafts of Embraer include EMB 120, ERJ 120, EMBRAER 170, Super Tucano, Phantom 100, etc. (Source www.embraer.com [6])
5. **Tupolev:** Tupolev is a Russian aerospace and defence company involved in development and manufacturing of both civil and military aerospace aircrafts and weapon systems. Tupolev has a work force of over 17,000 employees and is headquartered in Moscow, Russia. Tupolev is also actively involved in the development of missile and naval aviation technologies. They have delivered more than 18000 aircrafts for USSR and Eastern Bloc countries. Tupolev has also been developing many experimental airplanes, bombers and interceptors. (Source www.tupolev.ru [7])

AIRBUS: THE NEW MARKET LEADER

Since its creation in 1970, Airbus has sold around 11,500 and delivered around 7000 aircrafts. According to the recent report published by Airbus Press Centre [8], more than 6600 Airbus aircrafts are in operation at present with more than 460 customers and operators. Such is the amount of impact, that today an Airbus aircraft takes-off every 2.3 seconds. The report also claims that Airbus has now become the market leader in commercial and military aircraft manufacturing industry with backlog of 7-8 years of production. The key factors which have made Airbus the market leader are its advanced systems and a truly global approach. Its network of 200 customers and around 1500 suppliers worldwide share both resources and risks with Airbus by synergizing with its own manufacturing capabilities. That is why Airbus has been able to achieve its objectives and has been able to improve its financial performance and physical presence.

Market Share of Airbus and its Geographical Presence

Airbus has proved itself to be a truly global company and has become a market leader in the military transport, tanker and surveillance aircraft manufacturing industry. However, in the civil aircraft market, Airbus and Boeing have been involved in a neck-to-neck competition with each other (Fitzgerald et. al. [9]). Though Boeing has been in the market for a long time, Airbus has well caught-up with its American competitor and has captured about half of the commercial airline orders and has been increasing production for past ten years. Figure-1 shows the number of orders that Airbus has received from various geographical regions all around the world.

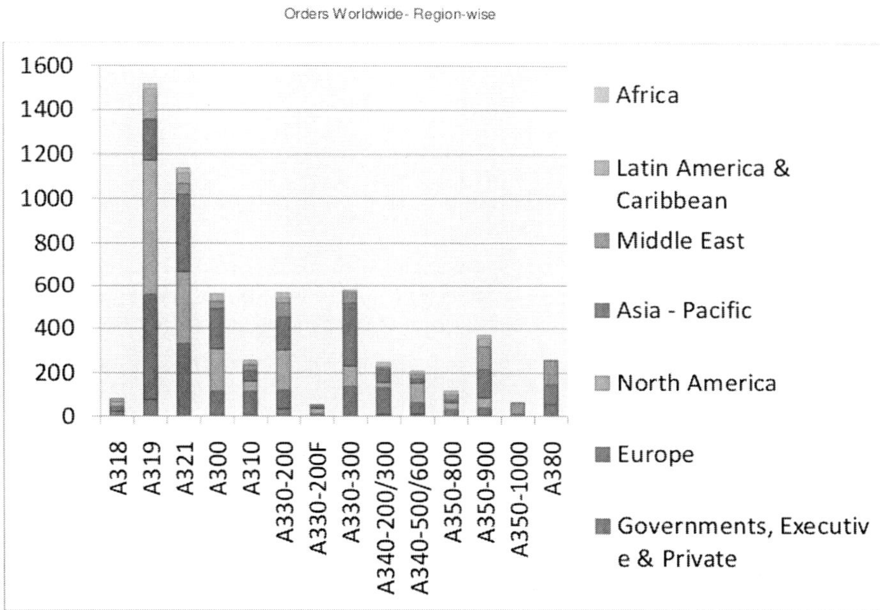

Fig. 1. Number of Aircraft Orders-region wise Received by Airbus (adapted from data provided by Airbus Press Centre [10])

The Airbus Company: SWOT Analysis

The major strengths, weaknesses, opportunities and threats of the company as identified by a Data monitor report [11] are:

1. **Strengths**
   1. Leading market position
   2. Strong support from parent EADS
2. **Weaknesses**
   1. Delays in A380 deliveries
3. **Opportunities**
   1. Expanding commercial jetliner market

   2. Growing demand for air travel in China and India
   3. Anticipated increase in passenger and freight traffic
4. **Threats**
   1. Increasing prices of titanium and aluminium
   2. US appeal against subsidies

Orders with Airbus and Future Strategy

The fierce competition between the two main players in the aircraft manufacturing industry has forced them to find methods of decreasing their costs and increasing efficiency. Only then can either of them establish a competitive advantage over other. The kind of expansion in production that Airbus has carried out in the past few years is quite substantial but in order to continue with such plans it has to develop a sustainable and advanced approach to future aircraft deliveries and orders. Figure-2 shows the number of orders received by Airbus for each of its aircrafts worldwide which is enough to give the reader a fair idea of how much capital and labor investment such deliveries are going to require.

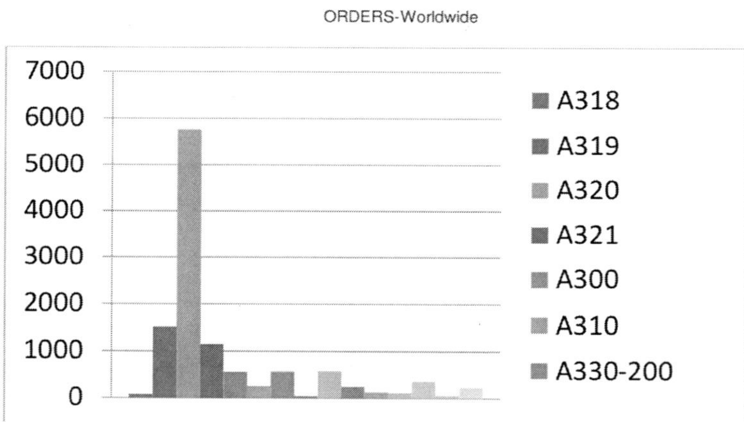

Fig. 2. Number of Orders-worldwide Recieved by Airbus by type (adapted from data provided by Airbus Press Centre [10])

The future strategy for such big expansion must comprise of due importance given to Information Systems. Airbus has quite efficiently and pro-actively used advanced Information Systems for gaining a strategic and tactical advantage over its competitors. In this pursuit, various ERP/MIS systems have been developed and deployed at all locations of Airbus manufacturing facilities. Airbus has also gone to the extent of ensuring that its suppliers and customers are also using similar systems for better integration and quality of service. The following section shows how Airbus has implemented Information Systems to not only increase its operational efficiency of manufacturing and production but also as a strategic move. The study also presents some key gaps and provides recommendations for filling up those gaps in the efficient implementation of ERP/MIS systems at Airbus.

MIS/ERP IMPLEMENTATION AT AIRBUS

Various Information Systems are being implemented at Airbus for its Customer Back Office and Manufacturing Operations. As it is a completely global organization, it is important to study how Airbus deals with its various customers and suppliers through optimum use of resources and technology. In this section we try to identify the problems that Airbus faced during its operations and how these were resolved with the help of high quality Management Information Systems. Investments in Information Systems are not only done from an operational point of view but also from a business perspective (MacDonnel et al [12]). Airbus made its operations completely transparent and reduced aircraft delivery time for its customers with the help of a Customer Back Office support team that was mainly responsible for implementing MIS in Aircraft Manufacturing, operation and maintenance systems. Airbus provides operators around the world with easy access to the latest information and to help them reduce their costs. However, Wagner et al [13] showed that in order to align the investments in Information Systems with business goals, it is imperative that the implementations of these systems are well-planned and well co-ordinated. Airbus uses various Knowledge Management Tools (like RISE and ExTra) to secure its knowledge base and to keep itself ahead of its competitors.

Airbus SAP-APO Supply Chain Management

Airbus uses SAP Advanced Planning and Optimization (APO) component for supply chain management. It is called as API- Advanced and Integrated Planning Project which has lead Airbus to new heights of supply chain management [14]. SAP-APO has helped Airbus to increase planning, accuracy and efficiency of spare parts for its worldwide fleet at various customer locations. Airbus spares uses APO functionalities for planning its requirements and supply chain networks and for supporting tactical, strategic and operational planning of spare parts. It allows the stocks to be adjusted continuously so as to reflect the actual requirements and hence reducing delivery times. It helps Airbus offer a unique Airbus-managed inventory service to its clients where Airbus handles the inventory of its clients. All the data and forecasting relating to the requirements of spare parts in future is done by Airbus and hence ensures just-in-time delivery of parts to the customers. The stock levels are fine-tuned and consumption-based planning is achieved for procurement, sales and distribution of stock levels.

Airbus Managed Inventory – Customer's Inventory Management [15]

Airbus manages inventories for its customers using a unique software service known as AMI-Airbus Managed Inventory. Using the AMI the customer materials and stocks are automatically replenished as and when required as per the agreed inventory levels. AMI automates the procurement procedure thus requiring minimal customer intervention. The AMI is a customised version of the Vendor Managed Inventory service that takes into account the nitty-gritty of the aircraft manufacturing industry. Efficient material replenishment on a regular and automated basis significantly reduces the cost of ordering Airbus material. Airbus Managed Inventory uses the latest communication standards to transform customers' material consumption data into physical replenishment shipment and hence optimizes inventory levels and cash flow. AMI can be fully customized to the customers' maintenance needs, such as on a part number, scope and service level allowing the customers to achieve the optimum balance between cost and material availability, while being adaptable to their fleet development.

Knowledge Management at Airbus

Airbus uses highly efficient Knowledge Management (KM) Systems that help in enhancing business processes through an improved use of existing knowledge and learning by people (Weber et al [16]). Airbus uses RISE (Re-use, Improve & Share Experience) Knowledge Management System to facilitate proper sharing of knowledge and experiences among various employees. This ensures that whatever learning has been made either in success or in failure have been recorded. RISE has helped Airbus save a lot of money and resources due to prior information about certain processes and decisions. All the improvements in the systems are measurable and quantifiable, making RISE not only a support tool but also helping Airbus use it for strategic advantage. Apart from that, Airbus has also implemented ExTra (Expertise Transfer) for transfer of knowledge and experiences.

Fig. 3. Key Features of Knowledge Management System at Airbus
Adapted from Weber et al [16]

e-Solutions for Maintenance & Engineering

Airbus develops innovative solutions that help to deliver cost-effective and customer-tailored services to the operators. Airbus offers a complete suite of web-enabled services to its customers through its website-"AirbusWorld" [17]. This helps in minimizing costs for the customers while enabling smooth and hassle-free ground operations. Various problems related to fleet management, operations engineering, safety and maintenance are handled on this portal only, allowing the customers to look for solutions from anywhere in the world. All these services are possible only because of the presence of effective Information Systems at the back-end of this portal. Some of the major e-solutions provided by Airbus include [18]:

Solutions	*Key features*
Airnav	1. Advanced consultation tool for maintenance and engineering technical data. 2. Provides interface between technical manuals and aircraft systems. 3. Displays virtual reality clips and 3-D models of aircrafts.
Airtac	1. Consists of a team of highly qualified structures and systems support engineers. 2. Work 24*7 and all round the year to provide support to customers. 3. Latest improvement is AirTHM developed by Airtac team.
AirTHM	1. Airbus Real time Health Monitoring System provides monitoring of aircraft's performance on basis of a number of parameters. 2. Helps in anticipating real-time trouble-shooting and guidance for the customers. 3. Improves operational reliability and maintenance scheduling of aircraft.
ADOC	1. Provides documentation support for aircrafts. 2. Customization, revision management and publication facilities are provided.
AIRMAN	1. For real time health monitoring and trouble-shooting.
Repair Manager	1. Helps in online structural damage management.
E-Logbook	1. Provides efficient management of pilot and maintenance actions. 2. Helps to optimize aircraft technical status.

Flight Efficiency Management and Information System (FEMIS)

FEMIS is one of the most efficient Information Systems that helps in tracking operations efficiently and accurately. This product has been jointly developed by Airbus and Teledyne Controls for collection, storage and analysis of operational flight data through a web based interface. FEMIS has been instrumental in enabling extensive analysis of flight performance, payload predictions, fuel data and cost variations during real-time flight operations. This allows a better and informed decision making for the customers with regards to flight scheduling, ATC negotiations and fuel usage thus leading to reduction of cost and improvement of efficiency of customers of Airbus. This software system has been instrumental in providing that strategic edge over its competitors which has made it the market leader in commercial aircraft segment. Some of the main features of FEMIS are [19]:

Feature	*Benefits*
Flight Comparison and Analysis	1. Provides access to in-depth operational information which helps to identify deviations and possible causes. 2. Improvises in flight safety and operational efficiency. 3. Helps in easy comparison of flight plan resoles in areas of operational, technical, ATC and environmental deviations.
Flight planning management	1. Data from variety of sources is gathered in a central database and useful information is extracted. 2. Helps in easy monitoring of flight schedules, predictions about payloads, estimating fuel consumption and adjusting for taxi procedures.
Reduced fuel consumption	1. Highly important in today's context when oil prices are highly volatile. 2. Increases profitability of airline operators and hence more orders for Airbus. 3. Provides fuel-burn information for monitoring block fuel, alternate fuel, taxi fuel time, and fuel waste due to departure and arrival delays.
Data transfer and analysis	1. Allows wireless and automatic transfer of data to the airline's ground facility for immediate processing. 2. Helps operators to quickly identify and adjust deviations and improve their flight planning system.

Fig. 4. Flow of information in FEMIS adapted from [19]

VIRTUAL AIRCRAFT

Digital Mock-up (DMU) are becoming useful in providing the customer a feel of what the actual product is going to look like even before the actual designs are made. A DMU is generally backed by CAD/CAM software and is managed by a Product Management System (PDM) that helps in configuration management and virtual development of the aircraft model. Airbus uses ENHANCE (Enhanced Aeronautical Concurrent Engineering) and VIVACE (Value Improvement through Virtual Aeronautical Collaborative Enterprise) for developing such DMU's for its customers which help Airbus to deliver its customers a virtual aircraft even before the actual aircraft is manufactured as well as in concurrent verification of their product by its customers. Pardessus [20] presented how Airbus used Concurrent engineering and design practices for aircraft design.

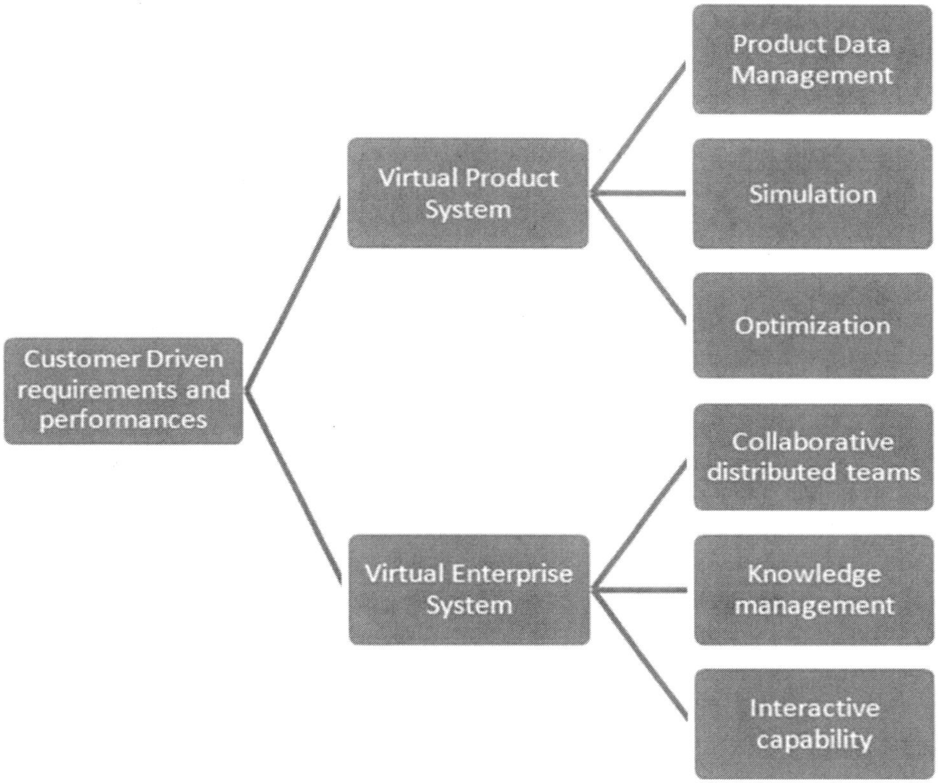

Fig. 5. Major Components of Airbus Virtual Aircraft Adapted from Pardessus [20]

HUMAN RESOURCE INFORMATION SYSTEMS AT AIRBUS

Airbus has incorporated a specialized HR information system (HRIS) for proper management of personnel in a cost-effective and efficiency-creating way. HRIS has helped Airbus to manage its 55,000 strong workforce and present to them a unique HR solution which they can use to effectively handle their HR related issues by reducing administration overheads and speeding up HR-related transactions. Employees are allowed to book holidays and shift changes and manage their own personal data by the means of Employee Self Service. Carrington [21] noted how HRIS benefitted not only the employees but also their team leaders and managers who were now more accurately able to predict the number of personnel with proper skill set required for a particular operation. This not only ensured efficient utilization of workforce but also reduction in personnel costs and administration expenses.

FUTURE AHEAD

Though Airbus has managed to gain the market leader position in the aircraft manufacturing industry, it needs to keep up to the expectations of its clients in order to sustain and survive in business. There are lessons which need to be learnt from the past failures that will keep Airbus abreast in competition with its nearest competitor- Boeing. Some of the key findings of the study are:

1. ERP implementation does not just require a process-oriented approach but it requires a people-oriented approach [22]. In order to make the implementation acceptable to the end-users, requisite level of training should be given to employees. This training will allow the employees become familiar with new roles, revised processes and other control mechanisms.
2. Proper feedback should be obtained from the employees, suppliers, vendors and clients regarding the advantages and disadvantages of the ERP/MIS implementation. This will help in strengthening the reports and query processes of the system. Lack of proper knowledge of the objectives of such systems has been noted as one of the key factors in the failure of implementation of ERP/MIS systems [23].
3. Financial risks can be reduced by ensuring that engineering department is able to predict quite accurately about the part numbers that are expected to be required when the airplanes are overhauled. Airbus materials management system needs to be strengthened so as to help the engineers be more accurate with such analysis [24].
4. Updations and improvements in the SAP ERP system should be communicated to the process owners at a regular basis so that the expertise and knowledge is not lost at any level of the organization [25].

CONCLUSION

Aircraft manufacturing industry is one of the most global industries in the world. Airbus manufacturing systems show how parts of the aircrafts are manufactured all across the globe and assembled at facility in France. In such a scenario, integration of the systems is of utmost concern to the operational engineers. This is only possible through proper communication of engineering standards to the various vendors and suppliers involved in the manufacturing process. Understanding of the SAP ERP process helps in knowledge sharing and decision making. It also increases the customer satisfaction because of quicker response and faster delivery of services. An ERP implementation is not simply a large IT implementation project- it is a sizable organizational project. Organizational benefits will not be achieved if the enterprise focuses on the technical aspects only. Information technologies cannot by itself influence the productivity of a company. The main efficiency factor lies in the way people use these technologies. Many information strategies fail for ignoring this issue.

REFERENCES

[1] Dietrich, David M., and Elizabeth A. Cudney. "Methods and considerations for the development of emerging manufacturing technologies into a global aerospace supply chain." *International Journal of Production Research* 49.10 (2011): 2819-2831.

[2] Lazoi M, Ceci F, Corallo A, Secundo G, "Collaboration in an Aerospace SME's Cluster: Innovation and ICT Dynamics" Journal of Innovation and Technology Management Vol. 8, No. 3 (2011) 393414.

[3] http://www.airbus.com/

[4] "The Boeing Company-Overview" available at http://www.boeing.com/

[5] http://www.bombardier.com/

[6] http://www.embraer.com/

[7] http://www.tupolev.ru/

[8] "Airbus_Corporate_Facts_and_Figures_Jan_2012" available at http://www.airbus.com/presscentre/corporate-information/key-documents/

[9] Fitzgerald, Tim, Noureddine Baiche, Mike Brewer, Al Collins, Kathy Knapp, Marilyn Kott, Duncan McGill, Dunstan Mensah, Mark Neighbors, and Dee Reardon. Industry Study Paper : *"The Aircraft Industry"*. Industrial College of the Armed Forces, Washington DC, 2005.

[10] "Airbus_June_2012_orders_and_deliveries" available at http://www.airbus.com/presscentre/corporate-information/key-documents/

[11] "Airbus S.A.S: Company Profile" in January 2007 by DataMonitor at www.datamonitor.com, refcode: 16510.

[12] MacDonnell, Michael, and Ben T. Clegg. "Managing IT investment for aircraft sustainment." *Symposium on Systems Engineering*. 2004.

[13] Heinz-Theo Wagner, Tim Weitzel. "How to Achieve Operational Business-IT Alignment: Insights from a Global Aerospace Firm". MIS Quarterly Executive Vol. 11 No. 1, Mar 2012.

[14] "SAP Customer Success Story Aerospace and Defense Maintenance, Repair, and Overhaul" available at www.sap.com

[15] http://www.airbus.com/support/material-logistics/inventory/

[16] Weber, Frithjof, Eva Dauphin, Renata Fuschini, Julia Haarmann, Alexander Katzung, and Michael Wunram. "Expertise transfer: A case study about knowledge retention at Airbus." *ICE 2007 Proceedings, June* (2007): 4-6.

[17] http://www.airbus.com/tools/airbusfor/customers/

[18] Airbus-017-Airbus-Customer-Services-E-June2012 by Airbus Press Office.

[19] http://www.teledynecontrols.com/productsolution/femis/benefits&features.asp

[20] Pardessus, Thierry. "Concurrent engineering development and practices for aircraft design at Airbus." *Proceedings of the 24th ICAS Conf., Yokohama, Japan.* 2004.

[21] Lucie Carrington "A breath of fresh air" in People Management Magazine June(2007) available at www.peoplemanagement.co.uk

[22] Kleiner, Morris M., Jonathan S. Leonard, and Adam M. Pilarski. "How industrial relations affects plant performance: the case of commercial aircraft manufacturing." *Indus. & Lab. Rel. Rev.* 55 (2001): 195.

[23] Sumner, Mary. "Risk factors in enterprise-wide/ERP projects." *Journal of information technology* 15.4 (2000): 317-327.

[24] Flight Airworthiness Support Technology (FAST 50), Airbus Technical Magazine by Airbus S.A.S., August 2012 edition available at http://www.airbus.com/support/publications

[25] Pabedinskait, Arnoldina. "Factors of successful implementation of ERP systems." *Economics & Management* 15 (2010): 691-697.

Evolution of India and the European Union Trade Relations: A Realistic Approach Towards Cooperation

Pradeep Kumar

Vistula University, Ul. Stokłosy 3, Warsaw, Poland

ABSTRACT

The relations between India and the European Union are very significant in all its political, economic and social aspects. The bilateral relations between the Republic of India and the European Union can be traced back to the period of 1960s when the Republic of India was among the first nations to create working relations with what is now known as the European Union. India and the European Union signed a bilateral agreement in the year 1973; this was the time when the United Kingdom also joined. Both in 1994 signed the most recent cooperation pact and an action plan was drawn and finally signed in 2005. Besides, it is stated that by 2007 the two entities were pursuing a free trade area pact. Many studies and investigations have been done with regard to India's international relations. However, these studies have not paid much attention to develop trade relations between India and the European Union.

This research study was undertaken to investigate the evolution of trade relations between India and the European Union, especially with regard to both Europe and the Asian continent. It looked into the events that led the two entities to cooperate with each other. This would help bridge the gaps that were already left by the previous studies that had attempted to study relationship between India and the international community or foreign states.

INTRODUCTION

The main purpose of the study was to establish the evolution of India and the European Union trade relations and to determine the kind of obstacles for both the European Union and India faced during the process of their relations. The study was significant in the sense that it would provide more information to various stakeholders concerned with the relations between India and the European Union. The first importance of the study was that it would provide a clear understanding of how the relation between India and the European Union evolved right from the time India was colonized. It would provide knowledge with regard to the factors that strengthened the relations between the two entities. This would be crucial to other international community members who would be willing to establish some forms of relationships with the European Union.

The study was done qualitatively by utilizing a historical case-study approach to research. The method used in data collection and analysis was textual reviews, comparison and establishments of facts and implications. The findings of the study included; (1) The relations between India and Europe began during the pre-colonial period when Europeans started arriving in India for trade purposes; (2) India was colonized by the British. The British greatly influenced the lifestyle governance in the subcontinent India; (3) The relations between India and the European Union are majorly related to trade, economy and commerce with little cooperation in the area of security; (4) There are substantial obstacles to effective relations between the European Union and India and (5) The European Union and India have substantial grounds to cooperation in the global economy and politics.

THE RELATIONS BETWEEN EUROPE AND INDIA (COLONIAL SUBCONTINENT INDIA)

Historically, the relations between Europe and the sub-continental India can be discussed within the framework of two successive eras. The first era is the colonial period that ended with the declaration of India's independence in 1947. The second era is the period following India's independence. The findings indicated that the relations between European and India began during the period between 327 and 326 BC; this was the period during which India first came into contact with the Europe. This happened when the army of Alexander the Great first came to India during the period, and later followed by various other European nations who arrived in India for various purposes, especially to conduct trade with Indians. The relationship between the European Union and India was fundamentally based on trade and commerce; this was the case even during the colonial-India subcontinent. Therefore, the commercial and trade ties between the European Union and India did not just commenced from after India's independence in 1947, but was a heritage that had moved on right from the first time Europeans got into contact with the Indian people.

The first trade contact between the European Union and India involved trade in spices. It was the trade between the two entities that had to open the way for the colonization of the sub-continental India. The colonial Indian subcontinent commenced in 1502, when the Portuguese Empire created its first European commercial center at a place known as Kollam.

The relations between the European Union and India was facilitated by the British East India Company. It was the company that actually facilitated the presence of British imperial rule in India. The company arrived in India for trading purposes but later was turned into a political tool by which the imperial British government representatives took full control of the sub-continental India. Later, the company was to be dissolved and the British take full control of the territory.

THE RELATIONS BETWEEN THE EUROPEAN AND POST-INDEPENDENT INDIA

The official relations between the European Union and the post-colonial India had evolved over a long period of time, beginning from 1963. The relations were have been established with the EEC (European Economic Community). The European Economic Community had since transformed into the current European Union (from 6 members to 27 member states) from the year 1992.

It was realized that the European Economic Community and India signed a cooperation agreement in 1973 in improve enhance the trade links between them. This might have been the first officially signed cooperation agreement between the two entities since the beginning period of the independent India. The agreement of 1973 was later advanced in 1981 to include economic cooperation. The study was able to establish that the first summit between the European Union and India was held on June 28, 2000 in Lisbon. The summit marked a turning point in the relations between the European Union and India as the two entities declared that both of them would establish a new strategic partnership grounded on shared values and ambitions and characterized by improved and complex cooperation. Comparing the progress of economic and political relations, both entities have achieved more in trade and economic cooperation than what they have achieved in political cooperation. The European Union and India did not achieve much because the European Union might have viewed India, as an entity did not have much ability to influence the politics of the world. In this case, India had to prove to the European Union the reasons it was a significant political player in the world.

TRADE BETWEEN THE EUROPEAN UNION AN INDIA

The European Union had been a major trading partner to India. India was both exporting and importing goods from the European Union countries. According to statistics obtained, the European Union was accounted 25 per cent all India's international and global trade. The bulk of products exported by India to the European Union were mainly composed of semi-manufactured and manufactured products in the segments of leather products, textile concentrated with the United Kingdom, Germany and Belgium. The study also investigated how India traded with accession nations; it found out that India's exports to accession countries were concentrated within Poland and the Czech Republic. However, it was established that the amount of India's exports to other accession nations was very limited. It was observed that, among the accession nations, India's imports majorly came from the Czech Republic at 37 per cent. Generally, it was observed that India had insufficient trade and commercial arrangements with the accession nations thereby making their cooperation in trade and commerce to remain potentially low. The figure below shows the trade between India and the European Union nations of the period of 2002-2003.

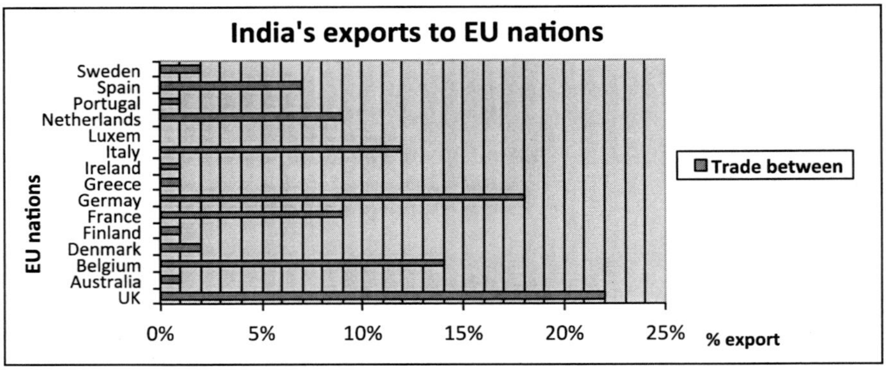

Fig. 1. Exports from India to EU in 2002-2003

Source: Jean-Joseph Boillot, *Europe After Enlargement: Economic Challenges for EU And India* (New Delhi: Academic Foundation, 2006), 154.[1]

In relation to India's imports from the European Union nations during the same period, the following Figure 2 shows the distributions among the nations.

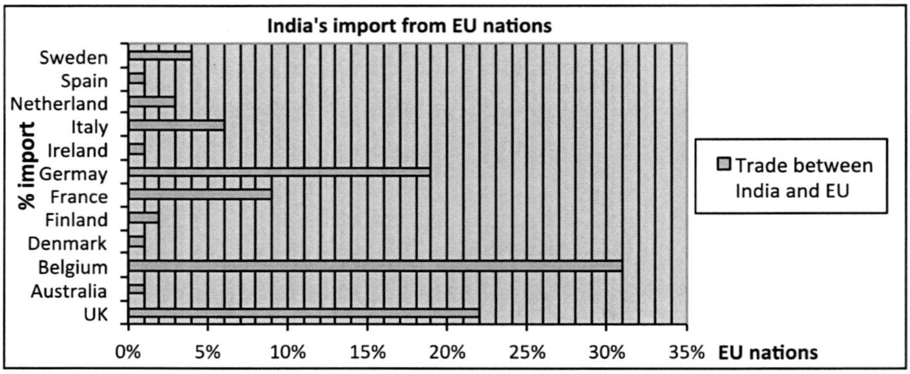

Fig. 2. India's Imports from the EU Distributions for the Period 2002-2003

Source: Jean-Joseph Boillot, *Europe After Enlargement: Economic Challenges for EU and India* (New Delhi: Academic Foundation, 2006), 154.[2]

The European Union had progressed as a major destination for agricultural products from

1 Jean-Joseph Boillot, Europe After Enlargement: Economic Challenges for EU And India (UK: Academic Foundation, 2006), 154.

2 Jean-Joseph Boillot, Europe After Enlargement: Economic Challenges for EU and India (New Delhi: Academic Foundation, 2006), 154.

India, the total India's agricultural exports to the European Union amounted to approximately $255 million in the period of 2002-2003 while a similar amount of exports to the United States was approximated at $200 million. The trade in goods between the European Union and India was found to have reached a peak in the year of 2010. This came after the trade had recorded a reduction in 2009, which was an interruption of steady growth since the beginning of 2001. It was further noted that exports from the European Union nations to India reduced from 31.3 billion units in 2008 to 27.4 billion units in 2009 then rose to 34.8 billion units in 2010. Moreover, imports reduced from approximately 29.5 billion units in 2008 to approximately 25.4 billion units in 2009. In 2010 the units increased to 33.2 billion. This scenario is captured in the graph below:

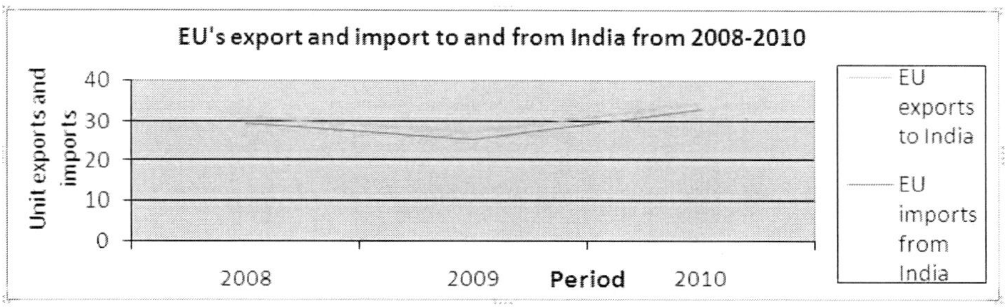

Fig. 3. EU's Trade with India

Source: Eurostat News Release, *EU-India Summit* (EU: Eurostat Press Office, 2011), 1-4.[3]

More statistics from 2011 revealed that the largest surpluses realized in the European Union's trade with India were realized in Germany and Belgium while the highest levels of deficits were realized in Italy, Spain and the Netherland. The figure below gives a summary of these scenarios;

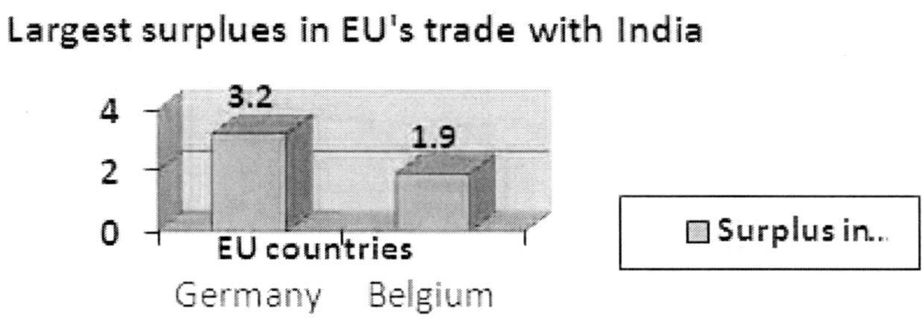

Fig. 4: Surplus Realized in Trade between EU and India

Source: Eurostat News Release, *EU-India Summit* (EU: Eurostat Press Office, 2011), 1-4.[4]

[3] Eurostat News Release, EU-India Summit (EU: Eurostat Press Office, 2011), 1-4.
[4] Eurostat News Release, EU-India Summit (EU: Eurostat Press Office, 2011), 1-4.

The following graph provides a summary of deficits realized during the same period;

Fig. 5. Largest Deficits Arising from EU's Trade with India

Source: Eurostat News Release, *EU-India Summit* (EU: Eurostat Press Office, 2011), 1-4.[5]

During the same period, machinery and motor vehicles plus other manufactured goods were found to have accounted for approximately 80 per cent of European Union's exports to India. This was recorded in the first ten months of the year 2011. Nonetheless, other manufactured goods were found to have represented about 50% of the imports. Overall, the study analyzed various statistics arising from trading activities between the European Union

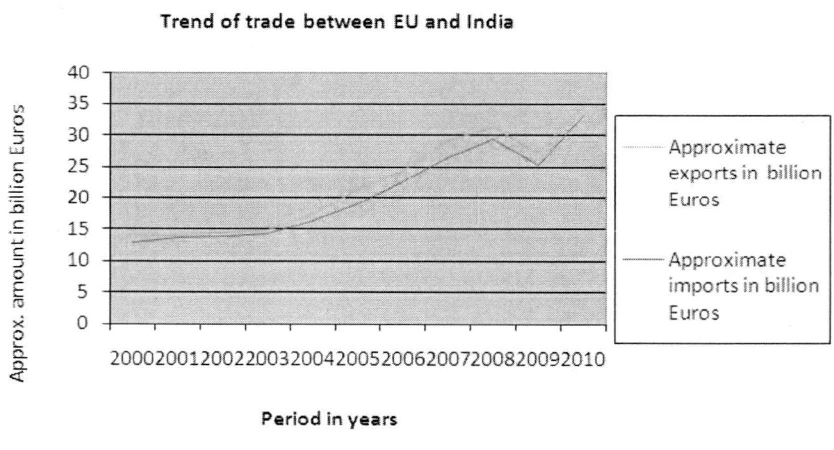

Fig. 6. Approximate India's Export and Import Values to and from EU 4.[6]

Source: Eurostat News Release, *EU-India Summit* (EU: Eurostat Press Office, 2011),

[5] Eurostat News Release, EU-India Summit (EU: Eurostat Press Office, 2011), 1-4

[6] Eurostat News Release, EU-India Summit (EU: Eurostat Press Office, 2011), 4

and India. The results were aggregated in the form of exports and imports trades from 2000 to 2010. The following figure gives statistical summaries of how the European Union and India had traded with each other right from the 2000 to 2010. These statistics were selected because the represented the most current figures showing the true picture of the level and trend of trade between the European Union and India. It is important to note that the statistics included India's trade with twenty seven member states of the European Union.

Looking at the results in the figure above, it is evident that the export to the European Union declined together its imports from the same region in 2009 before taking an upward trend in 2010. These statistics show that the India's trade with the European Union from 2000 had been on an increasing trend up to the year 2010. However, due to the scope of the study, the factors that led to the decline could not be established. The statistics were obtained from Eurostat news release.

Other statistics also showed that the European Union's Foreign Direct Investment flows in India reduced from 4.2 billion Euros in 2007 to 3.4 billion Euros in the year 2008. The statistics further indicated that the flow remained relatively constant in the year 2009 before increasing 4.7 billion Euros in the year 2010. Otherwise, India's Foreign Direct Investments into the European Union nations reduced sharply from about 10.1 billion Euros in the year 2007 to 2.6 billion Euros in 2008 and continued to decrease to 0.9 billion Euros in 2009 and finally to 0.5 billion Euros in 2010. These statistics were summarized as follows

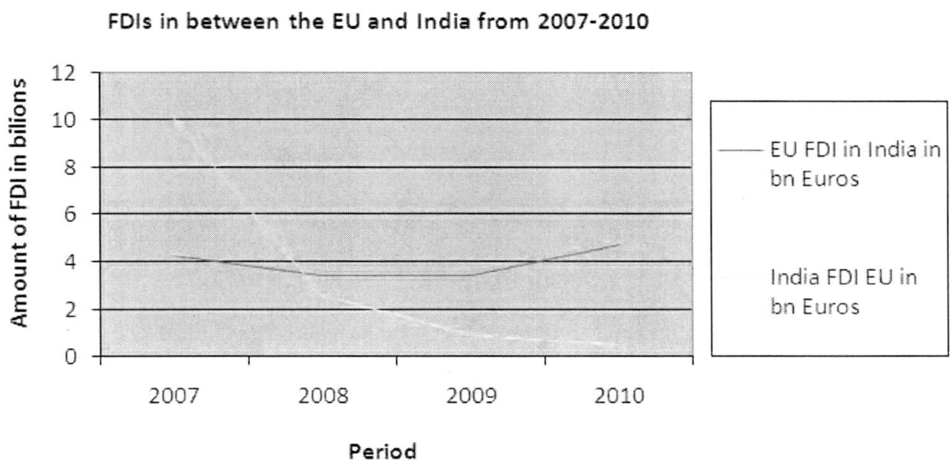

Fig. 7. FDIs between the European Union and India

Source: Eurostat News Release, EU-India Summit (EU: Eurostat Press Office, 2011), 3.[7]

[7] Eurostat News Release, EU-India Summit (EU: Eurostat Press Office, 2011), 3.

The FDIs between the European Union and India tended to favor only the European Union nations. Comparing the two, India seemed to have benefitted much from the European Union nations in terms of foreign direct investments; however, it is also important to note that even though the European Union's FDIs in India tended to rise, the investments rose at a slow rate. Once again, the scope of the study could not establish the causes of the trend.

In terms of tariffs, it was found out that tariff rates in India are higher than those in the European Union. According to statistics of 2007 comparing, Indian tariffs on beverages and tobacco sector was the highest at 88.0 per cent and lowest in the mineral fuel and lubricant sector at 11.9 per cent. In the European Union's corresponding sector, the tariff in the beverage and tobacco sector was the highest at 15.2% and lowest in the raw materials sector at 0.7%.

However, it was realized that, in all the selected sectors, India had higher tariffs that those of the European Union. This was shown by 2007 statistics on some representative sectors as follows:

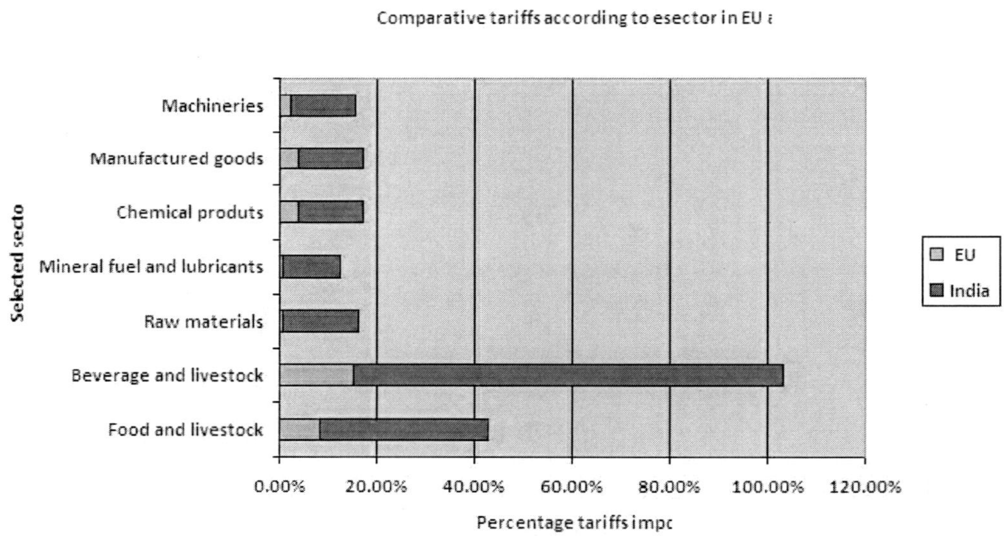

Fig. 8. Comparison between 2007 tariff statistics in EU and India

Source: Trade Hot Topics. "An EU-India Free Trade Agreement: Reflections on the Implications for Excluded Countries" *Commonwealth*, no. 54 (2008): 3.

EUROPEAN UNION-INDIA FREE TRADE AREA

The search for a Free Trade Area between the European Union and India began in 2007. However, due to hard issues, the agreement has taken longer than it was expected to materialize. The relations between the European Union and India were set to go a notch higher after the meeting that took place in New Delhi in February 2012. A free trade pact between the European

Union and India was expected enhance the bilateral trade relations between the two entities. The pact was also to enhance, between the two entities, economic and investment cooperation and was also expected to set the momentum for growth of the two entities.

Even though the ambitious Free Trade Area planned agreement had been pursued for five years between the European Union and India, it was evident that there were some significant obstacles. That threatened its materialization. It was noted that India still had imposed high tariffs in some sectors of its economy while at the same time demanded more access to the European market for its goods and services. This was viewed by the European Union representatives as being unfair to economic and commercial cooperation the two entities. Besides, there was the issue of the European Union demanding that India reduce tariffs on products such as wine, motor vehicles and milk and dairy products. According to the views of scholars and students of economics, the products from the European Union region were heavily subsidized and hence would sell cheaper in India than the local similar products. The potential consequence was found to be a possible "death" to the local industry producing similar products, especially dairy sector.

It was also noted that all car manufacturers in India were also found to be concerned about reduction of tariff being implemented on finished automobiles otherwise referred to as Completely Built Units. The study exposed the fact that there was a significant concern that lowering tariffs on Completely Build Units would harm the local industry of car manufacturers. Further possible consequences noted with respect to lowering of tariffs on such cars included reduced investment in automobile industry by the local Indians and loss of employment opportunities. Moreover, India would increasing become dependent on foreign manufactured cars from the European Union countries. It is important to note that if the reduction in tariffs on imported cars would not be managed appropriately, it could result in the reduction in domestic output, massive loss of jobs, substantial revenue tariffs and negative implications on trade balance.

Another issue that would contribute as an obstacle was related to opening up of the Indian banking sector; according to the finding of the study, the European Union wanted India to do away with restriction on its banking licenses and foreign ownership of financial institutions as part of the Free Trade Area deal. The European Union had also requested India to do away with priority sector lending on locally incorporated European Union-based banks and other financial institutions. All these requests were viewed as suspicious by India.

FACTORS ENHANCING COOPERATION BETWEEN THE EUROPEAN UNION AND INDIA

The study was eager to find out the factors that contributed to successful cooperation between the European Union and India. On economic front, the study found out that immediately after independence, India pursued a socialist model of economy. In that case, it was not easy for the European Union to pursue substantial economic cooperation between it and India. However, the study found out that most scholars were in a common agreement that India had increasingly come up with liberal policies for its economy. The liberal economic policies were viewed to be some of the factors that were facilitating economic cooperation between the European Union and India.

Another area in which it was easy for the European Union to easily establish cooperation with India was India's increasing democratic space. Even though India experienced internal civil strife, it was clear that it respected human rights and also upheld a democracy. This was a significant factor in enhancing the relationship between the two entities.

Again, numerous scholars were found to have agreed on the fact that there were strategic and geographical issues that contributed to the relations between the European Union and India. On political grounds, the European Union and India were found to have a common interest in realizing a democratic, multicultural and a multi-polar world order.

CONCLUSION

This study took the approach of a case study and was conducted by utilizing historical content analysis to establish the evolution and status of the relations between the European Union and India. In conducting this study, various literature texts were sampled to provide the data and information that were analyzed during the study process. The texts that were analyzed were selected from among the scholarly materials, journals and peer reviewed textual materials. Besides, the study utilized texts that were mostly produced from 200 to 2012. The choice for these texts was informed by the fact that the relations between the European Union and India was a continuing process and only the most recent texts would provide appropriate most current data that could provide a true picture of the evolution and status of trade relations between the European Union and India.

REFERENCES

[1] Anant, Vi Kirusna. *India Since Independence: Making Sense of Indian Politics.* New Delhi: Pearson Education India, 2010.

[2] Antonio, Di Vittorio, *and An Economic History of Europe: From Expansion to Development.* New Jersey: Taylor & Francis, 2006.

[3] Archer, Clive. *The European Union.* New York: Taylor & Francis, 2008.

[4] Bell, Holly. *Status of the BRIC: An Analysis of Growth Factors.* Alaska: Eurojournals Publishing, Inc., 2011.

[5] Boillot, Jean-Joseph. *Europe After Enlargement: Economic Challenges for EU And India.* London: Academic Foundation, 2006.

[6] Carmin, Joann and VanDeVeer, Stacy. *Eu Enlargement and the Environment: Institutional Change and Environmental Policy in Central and Eastern Europe.* London: Routledge, 2005.

[7] Chunda Romesh, *The Economic History Of India Under Early British Rule.* London: Routledge, 2001.

[8] Dedman, Martin. *The Origins and Development of the European Union 1945-2008: A History of European Integration.* London: Taylor & Francis, 2010.

[9] Dunkerley, David. *Changing Europe: Identities, Nations and Citizens.* London: Routledge, 2002.

[10] Eurostat News Release, *EU-India Summit* EU: Eurostat Press Office, 2011.

[11] Ghate, Chetan. *The Oxford Handbook of the Indian Economy.* Oxford: Oxford University Press, 2012.

[12] Ghosh, Anjali. *India's Foreign Policy.* New Delhi: Pearson Education India, 2009.

[13] McGilvary, George. *Guardian of the East India Company: The Life of Laurence Sulivan.* New York, 2002).

[14] Ombir, Singh. *Long Run Prospects for GDP Growth in India.* India: Gautam Buddha University, 2010.

[15] Page, Melvin. *Colonialism: An International Social, Cultural, and Political Encyclopedia.* London: ABC-CLIO, 2003.

[16] Riddick, John. *The History of British India: A Chronology.* London: Greenwood Publishing Group, 2006.

[17] Trade Hot Topics. "An EU-India Free Trade Agreement: Reflections on the Implications for Excluded Countries" *Commonwealth*, no. 54 (2008): 2-4.

[18] Upinder Singh, Radhakumud. *A History of Ancient and Early Medieval India: From the Stone Age to the 12th Century.* New Delhi, Pearson Education India, 2008.

[19] Weatherill, Stephen. *Cases and Materials on EU Law.* London: Oxford University Press, 2007.

[20] Wylbers, Shazia and Wulbers, Shazia. *The Paradox of EU-India Relations: Missed Opportunities in Politics, Economics, Development Cooperation, and Culture.* Plymouth: Lexington Books, 2010.

Export Led Growth Strategy: Retrospect and Prospect

Shri Prakash and Sonia Anand

Birla Institute of Management Technology, Greater Noida

ABSTRACT

The paper evaluates the empirical validity of export led growth hypothesis for Indian economy. The study uses multiple methods and models for analyzing data for empirical testing of the ELG hypothesis in order to exclude the probable results specific to particular method or model. The study uses data covering a period of 30 years from 1980-81 to 2010-11. On the whole, the findings of the paper do not lend credence to the empirical validity of ELG hypothesis. The long run sustainability and viability of the strategy is also examined.

INTRODUCTION

This paper focuses on analyzing the scope of export led growth strategy for Indian economy with reference to itslong run feasibility and viability. Though free trade has been recognized as an engine of growth for long,yet export led growth (ELG) hypothesis has recentlyattracted attention of large number of scholars globally (See Giles, Judith A. and Williams, Cara L.[1], 2000,Sarkar, A.,2006, Kaushik, K.K., Klein, Kurt,K. and Arbenser, Lawrence, 2006,Saleh, S. Tabrizy andTrofimenko, Natalia, 2010, Palley, T.I., 2011).Only some of these studies substantiated ELG hypothesis empirically. No study, to the best of authors' knowledge, has examined long run feasibility and viability aspect of ELG policy for a dynamically growing large economy like the Indian one. This study is designed to fill up this knowledge gap and vacuum in literature.

ELG hypothesis as a general paradigm of trade and growth runs counter to the theory of international trade, which postulates a country to specialize in the export of only such goods as conform to its factor endowment. But factor endowments of any country suit only a few goods for export production; most of the goods, including non-tradable ones, are produced for domestic market. Almost all countries of the world specialize in the production of few goods for export.For example, Japanese and South Korean electronic goods and automobiles, USA's burger (McDonald's, KFC), razors (Gillette), film rolls (Kodak), airplanes (Boeing), hardware and software (Apple, Microsoft), Finland's mobile phones (Nokia), Indian basmati rice bop services, and France's Champaign and air-bus dominate the export trade of these countries world-wide. Quantities in excess of domestic demand only are exported by a country, unless a good is produced exclusively for export markets. Consequently, international trade of most of the countries, including India, constitutes a small proportion of GDP. However,ELG hypothesis has not lost its sheen and appeal to policy makers despite its weak empirical and theoretical base.

The paper evaluates growth of Indian exports relative to the growth of GDP since 1981 till 2011-12 and the growth effect of exports in Indian economy so far. The impact of policy change on growth of output and its future prospects are also examined with special reference to limits to growth of output of selected export goods, and growth requirements oflabor, capital, and natural resources.**Viability**' and '**feasibility**' related implications of '**Export Led Growth**' are explored empirically.

SCOPE

The studyseekstheoretical and empirical answers to following research questions, which also define the scope of this study:

(i) What has been the share of export earnings in GDP of India and how much has it changed over the years? Answer to this question will shed light on the role of export trade in growth of Indian economy during the period of study; it may also highlight the impact of new policy on growth;

(ii) What has been the proportionate share of growth of exports in the growth of GDP and to what extent has it increased inter-temporally? Answer to this question will highlight the pivotal or non-pivotal nature and role of exports in the growth of Indian economy;

(iii) What are the limits to growth of output of selected export goods in Indian economy?Growth of output of mining products and goods which use such goods as intermediate inputs is limited by known reserves; while growth of exports of agricultural products in Indian export basket is limited by (i) current and expected growth of population; (ii) rise in domestic demand due to rising standards of living; (iii) impact of reduction in poverty on domestic demand; and (iv) statutory provisions under such Acts as*'Food Security for All*';

(iv) What has been the output effect of exports on different sectors of the Indian economy and to what extent has the output effect of exports changed over the years in the course of development? Answer to this question will require sector wise analysis of change in output of various sectors due to change in final demand for exports.

SHIFT IN POLICY AS BACKGROUND

New Economic Policy of 1990-91, enveloping export led growth, replaced the erstwhile policy of import substitution. Earlier policy sought to develop basic and heavy goods industries for long termself-sustained and self-reliant growth of manufacturing as the leading sector of economy and trade. This entailed structural transformation, requiring reduction in dominance of primary by increasingsecondary production.New Economic Policy, entailing export led growth strategy, opened up the Indian economy to international competition for domestic producers with a view to attain efficiency, competitive prices, improved quality of products, and access of Indian consumers to world class products on the one hand, and attract foreign investors and new technology to accelerate growth on the other. This policy implies that earlier goals of long termself-reliance and self-sufficiency in growth are no longer a part of vision of growth. It also implies that overall rapid growth of economy/GDP rather than rapid growth of manufacturing in general and heavy and basic goods industriesin particular are the goals of policy. One should, therefore, not be surprised to find the post reforms Indian growth being driven by growth of services rather than manufacturing. *It radically contrasts with China, whom we often compareIndia with and whom we wish to match, since has emerged as the global factory of manufactures.*India is not an international hub of services despite business outsourcing and opening up of Indian services to international investors, whose business focusis on Indian market rather than India's or their ownexport markets.Logicallytertiary dominated growth of Indian economy warrants the export led growth strategy to focus on service exports which is not evenly remotely in sight.*Is it not paradoxical to acquire super specialization in production of services but base the strategy of growth of exports of goods on narrow commodity production base*?

Antecedents of Policy

Independent India opted for planned economic development based on industrialization that revolved round basic and heavy goodsindustries.Rationale of the policy was derived the economic thrust of non-cooperation freedom movement, which involved boycott of imported goods and promotion of Khadi as a Symbol of Self-Reliance. On the eve of independence,economic development of India was constrainedby immediate as well as long run problems inherited from the colonial rule and which related toscarcity of (1) food; (2) capital; (3) foreign exchange; (4) replacement of obsolete by modern technology; (5) enhancement of very low skill and low education profile of manpower, dominated largely by illiterate workers; (6) transformation of economic structure; (7) removal of regional inequalities of development as highlighted by existence of a few enclaves of development surrounded by backwaters of under- development; and (8) extreme paucity of technical and professional manpower; and (9) cultural and customs' traps of orthodoxy to constrain rational thinking and will to change. This requires transformation of mind-set of people and their thought processes.

Development strategy focused on heavy and basic goods centric industrialization with a view to (i) close the gaps between Indian and developed countries' economic structure, and (ii) attain long run self-sustained and self-reliant growth which necessitated obviating the need for import of pricey capital goods for development. The development strategy emphasized promotion of exports on the one hand, and substitution of imports by domestic production of machinery, equipment, and other basic goods, and imposition of restriction on import of non-essential consumer goods on the other. This was necessitated by scarcity of foreign exchanging and rising import requirement of a variety of goods and machinery for growth.Besides, strategy of growth overlooked neither social aspects of development nor the inequalities of development, which prompted planners to accord high priority to such social sectors as education and health, physical and economic infrastructure and its dispersal over a wide geographical area (For rationale of selectivity approach to growth, See, Prakash and Mohapatra, 1981).

Indian Export Industries and their Changing Status

Exports comprised largely primary goods and a few simple manufactures like textiles and some chemicals in early stages of planned development. Consequently, scope for foreign exchange earnings was limited, while import payments were high on account of imports of more costly machinery and equipment, *especially machines to produce machinesto produce machines*. The policy also emphasized promotion of savingsalongwith improvement in standard of living,though promotion of savings got more emphasis in policy instruments. Implementation of ambitious programs of industrialization led to balance of payments crisis in 1956, which recurred in 1966-67 and 1990-91. Devaluation in 1966 did not help much. Indian rupee was again devalued in two installments by approximately 36 per cent in 1991.

New Economic Policy of 1991 of liberalization, privatization and globalization of Indian economy involved overhauling of trade and fiscal policies. New trade policy embodied replacement of import substitution byexport led growth strategy of development, and more importantly,liberalization of international trade. The shift in policy resulted in the rapid growth of export earnings partly because of low base effect,though imports grew even more rapidly than exports, resulting in *accentuation of perpetual adverse balance of trade.*

SCOPE OF EXPORT LED GROWTH STRATEGY FOR INDIAN ECONOMY

South Korea, Indonesia, Malaysia, Taiwan, Singapore and Vietnam, dubbed as Asian tigers, followed liberal economic policy, which differed significantly from Indian policy of controls and licenses/permits. Their economies grew much more rapidly than Indian economy. Indian planners and policy makers also opted for a similar policyunder NEP of 1991. India exported only a few manufactures upto 1980s, change in economic policy has resulted in diversification of export basket. Textiles, tea, coffee, leather & leather products, rubber products, minerals and other primary products are no longer the leading foreign exchange earners. Pharmaceutical products, gems and jewelry, ready-made garments, processed food, auto-parts and accessories, etc have emerged as important contributors to foreign exchange earnings. Export of such services as project management, consultancy, medical transcription, education, health care, and business outsourcing from abroad etc. have also entered in export basket in a small way. Butliberalization of imports has resulted in theentry of many consumer goods, including consumer durables, in import bills. Except a few goods, Indian exports are generally low priced and imports are high priced.*Theseprice differentials have to be made good by quantitative expansion and diversification of composition and direction of trade.* This is also warranted by decoupling Indian economy from disturbing trends like recession in USA and European economies. Other problem is cyclical fluctuations in demand in international markets and increasing competition from countries like China, Brazil, Russia, and South Africa. It is worth noting that despite rapid growth of export earnings, balance of trade remains adverse due mainly to more rapid growth of imports than exports. Foreign investment has however, kept balance of payments stable, though this is a poor consolation. Policy has to focus on attainment of favourable balance of trade for long term stability. Growth of exports has failed to achieve this objective. This reflects poorly on export led growth strategy.

FEASIBILITY AND VIABILITY OF EXPORT LED GROWTH STRATEGY

Technical feasibility and economic viability of export led growth strategy depends on availability of (i) technology, (ii) manpower with skill and knowledge profile needed for the use of requisite technology to produce export goods and services, and (iii) adequate capital, natural and other resources for exports, which are currently in demand and likely to be demanded in international markets during next two decades or so, (iv) productive capacity of the economy to produce exportable surpluses to meet the needs of export led growth. An important question is whether the type of goods, their quality and quantities currently produced and exported, will remain in demand in future at the current level of their growth during last two decades. If exports remain tied to natural resource based andlow pricedcommodities such as finished food items, textiles, tea, coffee, leather, ironore and other minerals, for how long will the reserves of natural resources sustain growth of exports warranted by economic growth at rates between 9-12 percent per annum? Challenge becomes even more formidable in view of the fact that demand for such exports is price inelastic; while there is an upper limit to their consumption both in India and abroad. Besides, rising living standards escalate domestic demand for many export products.

Petroleum and its products are the highest charge on import payments. Rising import of petroleum and other goods are now also an important source of inflation percolating into Indian economy from abroad.Incessantly rising prices of petroleum and its products has a cascading effect on prices of almost all sectors of the economy. Above discussion furnishes the base for empirical analysis.

REVIEW OF LITERATURE-CONTEXTUAL FRAMEWORK OF STUDY

Authors found *no study of sustainability of export led growth* (ELG) in any country in a detailed review of 110 studies pertaining to different aspects of international trade.However, there are some studies, which have examined *conceptual or theoretical framework of export led growth* and one study focuses on the stability of demand function for Indian exports, which also does not directly examine the sustainability aspect. Therefore, this study is designed to fill up an extremely important knowledge gap in literature.[1]Notwithstanding the above, selected studies are very briefly reviewed or just stated for highlighting the vacuum and knowledge gap that inspired this study.

Judith A. Giles and Cara L.Williams (2000) conducted an extensive survey of 150 studies of ELG hypothesis. Most of these studies show that 'ELG results, based on standard causality techniques, *are not typically robust to specification or method.*Findings of this survey suggest that interpretation of empirical results on ELG hypothesis requires extreme care and caution to be exercised.' No conclusive evidence on causal relation between growth of exports and economic growth is furnished by studies based on sophisticated methods or models of data analysis.

T. I. Palley (2011) studied the rising popularity of ELG and its wane as a development paradigm. Jie Yang designates ELG as 'so called growth strategy'. The study highlights that sectors, *producing non-tradable goods* are often the drivers of growth. In our view, international trade constitutes a very negligible proportion of their GDP of most of the third world economies. How can trade, especially export trade, lead the growth of entire economy?

Saleh S. Tabrizy and Natalia Trofimenko (2010),used Levinsohn-Petrin measure of total factor productivity and proxy variable for labor productivity. They find significant differences in productivity of export and non-export sectors, though they found no evidence for the impact ofexport led policy on productivity for export sectors. In our view, only such companies enter into export trade as produce goods with higher demand and greater prices in international than national markets; and hence, they earn higher profit than national average. This also reflects in the productivity. But developing countries have only few such goods and even fewer companies to produce such export goods. Market seems to be oligarchic nationally.Authors of the paper conclude that, even in the large emerging Indian economy with strong absorptive capacity and significant potential to catch-up with the leaders, effects of learning-by-exporting are not evident.

Krishan K. KaushikKurt K. Klein and Lawrence Arbenser (2010)used econometric model to investigate the relation of exports with economic growth in India for the period from 1971 to 2005. They find a unique long-run relationship between exports, instability of exports, imports, investment, terms of trade and gross domestic product.Besides, the authors find hardly any evidence for short-run causality, which flows from growth of exports to economic growth. Thus the findings do not highlight unequivocal role of export led growth as such. However, authors conclude that empirical evidence on export-led growth hypothesis is mixed but not conclusive.

Sarkar, Amal (2006) analyzed the stability of demand function of Indian exports in world market for the period from 1970 to 2003. The author finds the demand function to be stable, which prompts him to infer that the same function may be used for demand forecasting and policy simulation. It may, however, be noted that the structure of the economy and exports have changed quite a bit in post reforms period. Aggregate demand function may not be relied upon too much for forecasting in a dynamically changing world economy.Sarkar also estimated elasticity of exports with respect to price and imports. He finds the demand for Indian exports to be both import and price elastic. It means that rising imports put pressure to raise exports, whereas rising prices in international markets will reduce demand for Indian exports. This study, however, does not focus on contribution of exports to growth of GDP.

Akamal, Muhammad Shahbaz, Ahmad, Khalil and Ali, Muhammad analysed 'Exports-Led Growth Hypothesis for Pakistan.Authors used Toda and Yamamoto (1995) co-integration and multivariate Granger Causality tests. The study covered a period of 44 year from 1960 to 2003. Authors adduce some evidence of feedback effect of imports on growth of output, though causality is simply unidirectional from growth of exports to growth of output. However, authorsfind no significant causality between growth of import and growth of exports. We may point out that growth of imports follows the growth of output; so growth of imports is caused by rising import requirements of growth. But growth of output throws up more exportable surpluses. If this is so, then, growth of both imports and exports emanates from growth of output. Thus, authors inference that imports accelerate economic growth, and exports also stimulate economic growth but there is no relation between imports and exports runs counter to logic. Logically, causality in the paper to flows as follows: **Growth of Exports→Growth of Output→Growth of Imports**. Thus, authors' conclusions appear paradoxical.

Sami Taban and Ýsmail Aktar used quarterly time series data from 1980-1 to 2001-02 for Turkey to test ELG hypothesis by co-integration and error correction methods. They marshaled some evidence to support the hypothesis that there is a long-run and short-run bi-directional causality relationship between export growth and growth of real GDP in Turkey. However, the inference does not lend credence to the thesis that exports lead economic growth; they aver that growth leads growth of exports as much as exports lead economic growth.

Shiok Ye Lim, Ricky Chee-Jiun Chia, and Chong Mun Ho examined thelong-run validity of export-led growth thesis by linear and nonlinear co-integration test,' They claim to uncover long-run co-integration relationship for Singapore and South Korea, they used Breitung (2001) rank test. Breitung (2001) rank test can detect both linear and nonlinear co-integration relationships. Their finding is important as they furnished strong evidence of nonlinear co-integration of growth of GDP and growth of exports. Their finding highlights the sensitivity of empirical results to specification of model and method of data analysis.

Above brief review of literature indicates that there is hardly any study relating to sustainability of export led growth over a long period of time. This study implicitly assumes that, even if the export led growth paradigm is empirically valid in the short run, it is not possible to sustain growth of a diversified and large economy like the Indian one by growth of exports of mining and agriculture based products alone.

SOURCES DATA

All data used in analysis are secondary. Data are taken from Economic Survey, Government of India, Ministry of Finance, New Delhi, and CSO, Planning Commission, Government of India. Data relating to reserves of minerals are taken from the web-site of Ministry of Mines, Government of India.Data relating to employment are taken from the Ph.D. thesis of Dr Amit Sharma.

METHODS AND MODELS

The paper does not use one single method or model of data analysis, since attime otiose type results emanate from specific models/methods. The paper uses descriptive statistics, which issupplemented by econometric and input-output models and methods.

Random Walk Model is used to highlight the stationary property of time series data. Use ofDistributive Lag Model is prompted by considerations of inertia, ignorance, want of information and other factors that make instantaneous adjustment of dependent variable to change in independent variable difficult.Both these are preferred methodological approaches in econometrics of time series. Dummy variable is used in regression model as a proxy of change in policy. Input Output model is used to estimatetotal (both direct and indirect) capital, labour and natural resource requirements of export production. Leontief's static I-O model is used to determine direct and indirect output effect of demand for Indian exports in world market. Leontief Inverse of I-O model is the most power tool of capturing direct and indirect, visible and non-visible effects of smallest exogenous change on the economic/business system; that is why the model is also known as economic system's model. These models are outlined below:

Random Walk Model (RWM)

The following is RWM without drift:

$$\Delta Y_{jt}=\delta Y_{jt-1}+U_t \qquad \dots (1)$$

RWM with drift is given below:

$$\Delta Y_{jt}= \alpha_0 + \delta Y_{jt-1}+U_t \qquad \dots (2)$$

RWM with drift and stochastic trend is outlined hereunder:

$$\Delta Y_{jt}= \alpha_0 + \delta Y_{jt-1}+ \alpha_1 T+U_t \qquad \dots (3)$$

Y_{jt} is the variable under consideration and it refers to GDP/Growth of GDP, and Exports/ Growth of exports. T refers to time measured in calendar years, subscript t also refers to time to which the value of the variable relates. $\delta = \rho$-1, where ñ is defined as the root of equations from 1 to 3. If $\delta = 0$, $\rho = 1$, and the series of data will be non-stationary. If $\delta > 0$, series will be explosively non-stationary. In both these case, regression models shall furnish spurious results (Yule, 1927). If, however, $\delta < 0$, root shall be less than unit and series of data are appropriate for regression modeling. This aspect is examined by Dickey-Fuller unit root test and/or Engel-Granger unit root test of the residuals of chosen regression model.

Distributed Lag Model

Following distributed lag model is used in the study:

$$GDP_t = \beta_0 + \beta_1 GDP_{t-1} + \beta_1 EXPRT_t + \beta_2 D_t + U_t \quad \dots (4)$$

$$G_{gdpt} = \gamma_0 + \gamma_1 G_{gdpt-1} + \gamma_2 G_{exprTt} + \gamma_3 D_t + U_t \quad \dots (5)$$

Log-linear versions of models 4 and 5 are tested.

GDP_t refers to gross domestic product at factor cost, EXPRT stands for exports, D is dummy variable for policy change, and subscript t denotes year t. In relation 5, G stands for year on year growth rate of variables attached as subscripts to G. The dummy variable, D is assigned a value zero for all years from 1980-81 to 1989-90 and value 1 thereafter. The year 1990-91 is the water-shed when India replaced license permit raj by market oriented economy.

Input Output Models

The pivotal aspect of this research study is the evaluation of the scope of export bade growth of Indian economy with respect to known supplies of capital, human and material resources for export production. The following models deal with the total labour, capital and material resource requirement of growing export production:

$$L_t = A_0(I-A_t)^{-1} \quad \dots (6)$$

$$K_t = B(I-A_t)^{-1} \quad \dots (7)$$

$$R_t = Y(I-A_t)^{-1} \quad \dots (8)$$

L, K and R denote vectors of total labour, capital, and natural resources required directly as well as indirectly to produce export goods per unit of final demand, A and B are technology and capital coefficients matrices, $(I-A_t)^{-1}$ is LeontiefInverseand A is matrix of coefficients of intermediate inputs per unit of output.

Output effect of final demand for exports is estimated by the following model:

$$X_t\hat{} = (I-A_t)^{-1}F \quad \dots (9)$$

X_t^ is the estimated output vector and F is item-wise demand for Indian exports in world market.

t-testis used to evaluate the significance of inter-temporal and inter-sectoral differences of average output effectfor 1993-94, 1998-99, 2003-04 and 2006-07,four latest years for which CSO's I-O tables of 115×115 and 130×130 sectors are available.

Growth Estimates

Finally, following growth curve is used to estimate annual compound rate of growth and the degree and direction of shift in growth function under the impact of policy or other changes:

$$\log Y_{jt} = a + bT + cD + U_t \qquad \text{... (10)}$$

c, the coefficient of policy dummy furnishes an estimate of the rate of shift in growth curve per unit of time.

ANALYSIS OF EMPIRICAL RESULTS

Results of application of different models/methods are taken up for discussion sequentially. First, results of Dickey-Fuller unit root test are discussed.

Dickey-Fuller Unit Root Test of Time Series of Year on Year Growth Rates

OLS estimate of RWM of year on year growth rates of GDP and exports are reported below:

$$\Delta G_{gdp\ t} = -0.07583\ G_{gdp\ t-1}, R^2 = 0.035,\ F = 1.0398 > F^* = 0.3175 \qquad \text{... (11)}$$

τ : (-1.02)

$$\Delta G_{gdp\ t} = 4.8555 - 0.7750 G_{gdp\ t-1},\ R^2 = 0.381,\ F = 17.21 > F^* = 0.0003 \qquad \text{... (12)}$$

τ : (3.96) (-4.15)

$$\Delta G_{exprt} = -\ 0.2156\ G_{expr-1}, R^2 = 0.0887,\ F = 2.822 > F^* = 0.104 \qquad \text{... (13)}$$

t : (-1.68)

$$\Delta G_{exprt} = 20.151 - 1.0552\ G_{expr-1}, R^2 = 0.5218,\ F = 30.56 > F^* = 6.5E\text{-}06 \qquad \text{... (14)}$$

t : (5.061) (-5.528)

All four relations have negative sign attached to the lagged growth rates of GDP and exports. But the coefficients are not statistically significant in relations 11 and 13, implying that the coefficient does not differ significantly from zero statistically. This means that the root of these equations is unit, which indicates the series to be non-stationary.

Coefficients of lagged growth rates of GDP and exports in relations12 and 14 are not only negative but statistically significant also. It means that the random walk model with drift depicts these two growth rates to be stationary. Therefore, we may proceed to use regression models for analyzing these two series together or separately.

Growth Curves of GDP and Exports

OLS estimates of growth curves of GDP and exports with policy dummy as shift parameter are reported below:

$$\ln GDP_t = 5.103 + 0.053\ T + 0.063\ DV,\ R^2 = 0.9982,\ F = 8032 > F^* = 2.33E\text{-}39 \qquad \text{... (15)}$$

t : (620.8) (67.3) (4.24)

$$\ln EXPT_t = 3.7 + 0.069\,T + 0.145\,DV,\ R^2 = 0.996,\ F = 3466 > F^* = 2.9E\text{-}34 \quad \ldots (16)$$

t : (218) (42) (4.8)

Functions 15 and 16 fit the data well on all counts. The coefficients of time T and policy dummy in both functions are statistically significant. Significant coefficient of DV indicates that the growth function shifts upwards to the right; but the growth function of exports shifts more rapidly than the growth function GDP; this result is probably explained by the low base effect of exports. Exports have shown a growth rate which is higher by 1.6 percentage points of the growth rate of GDP. This may suggest that the growth of exports has led the growth of GDP in terms of differential growth rates. This cannot, however, be taken to lend credibility to ELG hypothesis, though the probability is not ruled out.

Selected Statistical Features of Year on Year Growth Rates

Mean and median of year on year growth rates of GDP are 6.3 and 6.4 respectively which are almost equal. The distribution of year on year growth rates of GDP may not diverge much from normal distribution. Consequently, coefficients of skewness and kurtosis also have as low values as -0.14 and -0.56 respectively. Observed values of year on year growth rates vary between 1.4 and 10.2. But range of variation is 8.8 with the value of CV as high as 210%. This implies a certain degree of volatility in growth of GDP.

Statistical features of year on year growth rates of exports appear are similar to those of growth rates of GDP. Mean and median of year on year growth rates of exports are, however, almost three times the values of rates of growth of GDP. The mean and median are 18.68 and 18.53 respectively, which are almost equal. Thus, observed values of year on year growth rates of exports approximate normal distribution. The coefficients of skewness and kurtosis also have low values of -0.35 and -0.24 respectively. Year on year growth rates vary between -7.23 and 36.70 with a high range of 43.93 and value of CV equal to 110%. Though the range of variation of growth rates of exports is much greater than that of GDP yet the coefficient of variation is much lower for exports than GDP.Greater value of range of variation suggests the growth of exports to be more volatile than GDP.

Exports and Policy as Base of Growth of GDP

In multiple regression analysis, one often encounters the problem of multi-collinearity. Therefore, method of step-wise regression modeling (See Klein, 1965) is followed to detect the location and seriousness of multi-collinearity. Distributed lag model is one of the options used. Partial adjustment hypothesis is adopted for the specification of distributed lag model. Imports have also been incorporated as an explanatory variable as a substitute of policy dummy with a view to compare our results with the study of Indian economy by Sarkar, Amal (2006). OLS estimates of both linear and log-linear regression functions are reported hereunder:

$$GDP_t = 403778.7 + 6.319\ EXPT_t,\ R^2 = 0.980,\ F = 1498.79 > 1.61E\text{-}26 \quad \ldots (17)$$
t : (6.74) (38.72)

$$GDP_t = 38198.21 + 0.981GDP_{t-1} + 0.978EXPT_t,\ R^2 = 0.9997,\ F = 47752.73 > 1.23\ E\text{-}48 \quad \ldots (18)$$
t : (3.20) (41.77) (7.60)

$$GDP_t=33076.28+0.944GDP_{t-1}+1.151EXPT_t+37275.18DV_t,\ R^2=0.9998,\ F=35431.34>4.68E\text{-}47 \quad \ldots (19)$$
t : (2.85) (32.60) (7.70) (2.01)

$$GDP_t = 38168.63+0.982GDP_{t-1}+0.960EXPT_t + 0.009IMPT_t, R^2 = 0.9997, F = 30659 > 3.67E\text{-}46 \quad \ldots (20)$$
t : (3.13) (35.47) (2.56) (0.05)

A glance at functions 17 to 20 reveals that (i) Exports are a significant determinant of GDP; introduction of lagged value of GDP and policy dummy in function 19 raises explanatory power of function 17 by almost 2 per cent, which implies that these two variables also affect change in GDP significantly; coefficients attached to these variables in relations 18 and 19 are statistically significant. The coefficient of auto-correlation for preferred function 19 is -0.091 and the corresponding value of Durbin-Watson d is 1.818 which is greater than table value of d_u=1.650.

However, imports are not an important determinant of GDP in function 20 in which imports replace policy dummy. This finding runs counter to the finding of AmalSarkar (2006). This difference in findings may probably be attributed to different data base on the one hand, and difference of method/model and approach used in these two studies on the other.

Among these functions, *function 19 is most acceptable.* Engel-Granger test, applied to this function, highlights this regression model to be genuine rather than fake:

$$\Delta U_t = -0.902U_{t-1} \quad \ldots (21)$$
t : (-4.76)

Engel-Granger test shows that the linear combination of variables included in relation 19, constitutes a stationary time series. This reinforces the inference drawn from Dickey-Fuller test of unit root.

The coefficient of partial adjustment in this function is Δ = 0.056. It takes 3 years for GDP to adjust to exports up to about 32% of total desired adjustment, which leaves 68 per cent adjustment to be completed. Thus, the process of adjustment is greatly prolonged.

Above results pave the way to examine the log-linear specification of these models which furnish direct estimate of elasticity of dependent with respect to pre-determined variables of the models. Besides, log-linear specification also takes care of non-linearity, if any, in the data, which are used in empirical analysis.

Log-linear Inter-Relations

$$\ln GDP_t = 2.382 + 0.737\ln EXPT_t,\ R^2 = 0.9956,\ F = 6620.17>8.76E\text{-}36 \quad \ldots (22)$$
t : (53.05) (81.36)

$lnGDP_t$=0.482+0.8207 $lnGDP_{t-1}$+0.1305 $lnEXPT_t$,R^2=0.9996,F=38652.49> 2.14E-47 ...(23)

t : (4.24)(17.09) (3.70)

$lnGDP_t$=0.495+0.803 $lnGDP_{t-1}$+0.150 $lnEXP_t$-0.012 DV_t,R^2=0.9996,F=27762.7>1.11E-45 ...(24)

t : (4.51)(16.96) (4.20) (-1.76)

$lnGDP_t$=0.491+ 0.813$lnGDP_{t-1}$ + 0.101$lnEXP_t$+0.035$lnIMPT_t$,R^2=0.9996,F=26453.11>2.09E-45 ... (25)

t : (4.37) (17.04) (2.45) (1.31)

Function 23 among the functions22 to 25 is most satisfactory on all counts. The function explains 99.96 per cent of total change in GDP, and coefficients attached to both pre-determined variables are statistically significant.But the policy dummy in function 24 is no more significant. Similarly, coefficient of imports in function 25 is not significant. Both these functions are rejected.

Function 23 shows that partial adjustment coefficient, Δ, in this case, has a value of 0.1793. This indicates this function to be more appropriate for partial adjustment hypothesis; nearly 45% of total desired adjustment is completed in a period of 3 years. Short run elasticity of GDP with respect to exports is only 0.1305; it means that doubling of exports will lead to an increase of only 13 per cent in the growth of GDP. But the long run elasticity of growth of GDP with respect to exports is as high as 0.7278, implying that the doubling of exports will raise GDP by as much as 72.78% in the long run. *This is more a theoretical than practical proposition at this point in time for reasons that are obvious.*

Results of this analysis lend substantial evidence to support to ELG hypothesis. These results suggest that the testing of thethesis may be sensitive to the model/method used in empirical analysis. So, the thesis is subjected to more rigorous and direct empirical test in the ensuring analysis of inter-relation between growth rates.

Inter-Relations between Growth Rates

The OLS estimate of the regression function of growth of GDP on growth of exports and policy dummy is reported below:

$G_{gdp\ t}$ = 5.724 – 0.008 $G_{exp\ t}$+1.052 DV_t , R^2 = 0.052 , F = 0.769 F* = 0.473 ... (26)

t_1 : (6.197) (–0.219) (1.239)

The function does not fit the data well; the coefficient of determination is only 0.052. *Regression coefficients attached to both explanatory variables are not significant,* while the coefficient of export growth is negative also. Negative sign is an indication of the fact the the growth of exports has not varied significantly between the years with the growth of GDP.These results also re-confirm the non-significance of policy dummy; the function alsoindicates that the growth of GDP is explained by factors other than growth of exports and policy of liberalization. Does this function suffer from multi-collinearity? This possibility is examined by dropping the policy dummy to move to the function 27:

$$G_{gdp\,t} = 6.305 - 0.0012\ G_{expt}\ ,\ R^2 = 3.44E\text{-}05\ ,\ F = 0.0009,\ F^* = 0.975 \qquad \ldots (27)$$

t_1 : (7.85) (–0.0312)

The dropping of dummy as an explanatory variable in relation 27 does not indicate the presence of multi-collinearity in relation 26, so far as the sign and significance of the coefficient of growth of exports are concerned. Besides, policy dummy is revealed to be a superfluous determinant of growth of GDP.

These two functions imply that there is no credible empirical evidence to consider growth rate of GDP as a function of growth rate of exports. This makes ELG hypothesis suspect empirically, earlier results notwithstanding.

Output Effect of Exports Based on I-O Model

This section is based on results derived from the application of I-O model. The sector wise output effect for four selected years is reported in the tables in Appendix.

The following table contains the values of important statistics of output effect of exports in 1993-94, 1998-99, 2003-04 and 2006-07 for which input output tables are available from CSO for post reforms period:

Year	*total Output Effect*	*Mean*	*Median*	*Range*	*CV*	*Kurosis*	*Skewness*
1993-94	2102379911	18281564.44	6813339.18	243050520.4	183.179	21.934	4.203
1998-99	4708105526	40940048.06	12324954.99	329831250.1	162.266	6.4	2.558
2003-04	11189333265	86071794.35	31037137.61	849306580.6	172.651	12.52	3.345
2006-07	25852890482	198868388.3	58149545.48	3398548086	203.193	32.954	5.023

Source: Own Calculations

The above table reveals that (i) in all 4 years mean value of output effect many times more than the value of median. It suggests that the estimated distribution of output effect among 115/130 sectors of the Indian economy is nether normally nor evenly distributed. It suggests substantial degree of sectoral inequality and concentration of output effect of exports in few sectors of the economy. It runs counter to regional and sectoral inclusive growth; (ii) mean output effect differs significantly between the years. This is evident from the following values of t-statistics:

t_{12}	t_{13}	t_{14}	t_{23}	t_{24}	t_{34}
6.47	9.51	3.56	5.96	8.23	5.92

Source: Own Calculations

Mean differences of all four years paired systematically show that the average output effect of exports differ significantly between the years; (iii) output effect varies in the range of Rs243050520.4, Rs329831250.1, Rs 849306580.6, and3398548086. Thus, the range of variation has been consistently rising over time. This implies skewed structure of secotral growth, suggesting that export sectors will lead the growth of the economy. As has already been pointed out these sectors need not necessarily be those sectors growth of which will be desirable on social, political, welfare and equity counts; (iv) Coefficient of Kurtosis and Skewness are not only high but these have been increasing consistently and substantially over the years. As last two years have emerged different from two years of initial phase of NEP, more rapid growth of exports and GDP has resulted in greater degree of sectoral concentration and concentration. In the long run, a few sectors cannot be relied upon to pull up the growth of the entire economy *These inferences go against ELG hypothesis even if it is empirically validated.*

Sectoral Differentials of Output Effect

The differentials of output effect between sectors in the given year and differentials of output effect between the years require an explanation. Earlier studies (Prakash and Panigrahi, Prakash and Sharma, R.) suggest that technology in use and its change through time, measured by linkages, and volume of exports may be treated as the main determinants of output effect and its variation between the sectors and time. Therefore, sector wise output effect of exports for each of the 4 years are regressed on volume of exports and index of backward and forward linkages.

OLS estimatesof these multiple regression functions are reported hereunder:

tabular OLS estimates   total output effect = a0 + a1 linkage index + a2 exports

Year	α_0	α_1	α_2	R2	F	F*	t_1	t_2	t_3
1993-94	-18281564.44	2	-1.89481E-15	1.0	2.45155E+33	0	-1.899E+16	2.9106E+16	-0.296
1998-99	-40129011.81	1.975	1.217	0.9967	16944.021	9.8482E-140	-6.197E+01	1.1400E+02	0.861
2003-04	-59683680.15	1.522	38.767	0.94	996.17	2.38613E-78	-9.912E+00	1.8504E+01	4.584
2006-07	-181294901	1.91	8.077	0.9924	8314.20	2.2786E-135	-3.054E+01	4.9906E+01	2.022

Source: Own Calculations

The table reveals that (i) the multiple regression function output effect on exports and linkages fit the data well in all four years in so far as the coefficient of multiple determination is concerned.The coefficient is statistically highly significant in all four years; (ii) coefficient attached to linkages is positive and statistically highly significant. Thus, linkages influence the output effect of exports on sectors greatly and highly significantly. It implies that technology in use in sectors of Indian economy and its inter-temporal change are important determinants of output effect of exports; (iii but volume of exports emerges as statistically non-significant determinant in 1993-94 and 1998-99, though the volume of exports is the significant determinant of output/growth effect in 2003-04. This implies that the exports and their growth up to 1998-

99 was not substantive, which made its influence on growth of sectoral output not significant. The policy of export led growth seems to have gathered momentum after 1998-99, one decade after the adoption of NEP.

Output Effect of Exports as a Proportion of GDP

Incidentally, input output model, unlike regression models, captures both direct and indirect effect of exports on output of different sectors. Output of all 115/130 sectors registered positive growth under the impact of exports of export production sectors, even if the output of most of these sectors does not enter the export basket. Output effect shown by such sectors is accounted by backward and forward linkages of export production. The estimated output effect for 4 different years, 1993-94, 1998-99, 2003-04 and 2006-07, however, constitutes a negligible proportion/percentage of GDP of the corresponding years. These are shown in the table given below:

Total Output Effect of Exports as Percentage of GDP in Indian Economy

The following table depicts the output effect as a percentage of GDP of the corresponding years.

Year	*1993-94*	*1998-99*	*2003-04*	*2006-07*
Output Effect	0.0265	0.0291	0.044	0.0654

Source: Own Calculations

The above table highlights the following facets of impact of exports on growth of GDP (i) Output effect has increased consistently from one to another year; it may be attributed to increase in the magnitude and volume of export trade of India; (ii) Increase in output effect from 1993-94 to 1998-99 has been extremely low, in fact almost negligible, but from 1998-99 onwards increase in output effect of growth of exports has increased very rapidly. It may also be attributed to the momentum gained by exports in the new millennium; (iii) These results furnish empirical evidence to refute the ELG hypothesis. Thus, these results are in consonance with the results derived from the regression of growth of GDP on growth of exports. It may, therefore, be inferred that ELG does not find empirical support from rigorous testing of the hypothesis.

SUSTAINABILITY AND VIABILITY

Even if ELG hypothesis is empirically valid, it still needs consideration of long run sustainability and economic viability. Sustainability depends on the following factors: (i) Growth of capacity to produce and production for exports to match the growth of exports for leading economic growth; (ii) Availability of adequate amount of investment/capital for capacity expansion of export sectors and human capital with appropriate profile; it depends on labour and capital intensity of production of export goods; (iii) Growth of output of intermediate inputs and raw materials to match the growth of export production; it depends a great deal on the nature of the goods and current status of industry producing the same;(iv) Growth of demand for Indian exports in international markets; it also depends on the nature of the goods and growth of export absorbing economies; and (v) sustainability of comparative cost advantage of Indian exports in foreign markets.

Consideration of some of the above factors relate to the structure of Indian exports which is shown by the following table:

Percentage Share of Major Commodity Groups in Total Exports of India and Changes therein

	1998-99	*99-2000*	*2000-2001*	*2001-02*	*2002-03*	*2003-04*	*2004-05*	*2005-06*	*2006-07*	*2007-08*	*2008-09*	*2009-10*
Agriculture and allied products	18.1	15.2	13.5	13.5	12.8	12.4	10.5	10.2	10.3	11.6	9	9.9
Ores and minerals	2.7	2.5	2.6	2.9	3.8	4	6.3	5.2	4.8	5	5.5	5.5
Manufactured goods	77.7	80.7	78	76.1	76.6	76.9	73.7	72	68.6	64.4	67.2	63.6
Crude and petroleum products	0.3	0.1	4.2	4.8	4.9	5.6	8.4	11.5	15	17.8	15	17.8
Others	1.2	1.5	1.7	2.7	2	1	1	1.1	1.3	1.2	3.3	3

Source: Economic Survey, 2010-11.

The above table shows that (i) share of agricultural goods and has declined almost to half of their initial share in total exports; (ii) Share of ores and other minerals has been more than doubled; (iii) Share of exports of manufactured goods, dominated by agro and mineral based industries, has declined substantially; (iv) Shares of exports of crude, petroleum products and others in total exports has increased substantially. Table highlights that slightly more than 15 percent of total exports are accounted by primary production, another two-third share is that of agro and mining based industries products. Others comprise largely services which account for a measly share of total exports. Thus, the sustainability aspect of these broad commodity groups of exports becomes important.

Agricultural, mining goods, agro-based industries' and mining based industries growth is limited by the following factors (i) There is an increasing pressure of population on land which is further accentuated by land required for urbanization and industrialization, which is resulting in decline in net cropped area; (ii) Mineral reserves are limited and these reserves will not last for-ever. This facet is well displayed by the following table:

Table: Reserves, Current Output and Year on Year Growth

Minerals	*Unit*	*Reserves (as on 01.04.2010)*	*Total Production (2010-11)*	*Total Production (2009-10)*	*Current Growth Rate of Production*
Ball Clay	tonnes	16777842	958000	933000	2.679528403
Barytes	tonnes	31584128	2334000	2153000	8.406874129
Bauxite	000 tonnes	592938	12641	14124	-10.4998584
Chromite	000 tonnes	53970	4262	3426	24.40163456
Copper	000 tonnes	394372	137	125	9.6
Diamond	carats	1045318	19774	16891	17.0682612
Dolomite	000 tonnes	738185	5065	5912	-14.32679296
Fire clay	000 tonnes	30104	571	549	4.007285974
Garnet	tonnes	19324793	2058000	1581000	30.17077799
Gold	tonnes	110.54	2.47	2.08	18.75
Gypsum	000 tonnes	39096	4347	3370	28.99109792
Iron ore	000 tonnes	8115301	207998	218553	-4.82949216
Laterite	000 tonnes	24714	1158	1301	-10.99154497
Lead	000 tonnes	108980	145	134	8.208955224
Zinc	000 tonnes	12453.26	1420	1280	10.9375
Limestone	000 tonnes	14926392	238000	233000	2.145922747
Magnesite	000 tonnes	41950	230	301	-23.58803987
Manganese ore	000 tonnes	141977	2881	2492	15.60995185
Sillimanite	tonnes	4085052	48000	34000	41.17647059
Steatite	000 tonnes	90026	896	877	2.166476625
Wollastonite	tonnes	2487122	183000	132000	38.63636364
Mica	kg	190741448			

Source: Ministry of Mines, Govt. of India.

If the export of these goods or the goods production of which is based on these goods grows at an annual compound rate of 10% for 20-25 years , (1) reserves of some of these goods will be totally exhausted, (2) reserves of another group of goods will be depleted by 50% or more , and (3) only adequate reserves of some goods will be left for posterity. This is not warranted by equity between current and future generations, sustainability of long term growth and balance in regional and social development.

MAIN FINDINGS

The following are main findings of the paper.

I.

(i) Regression model, based on absolute values of exports and GDP, lend some support to ELG hypothesis;

(ii) New economic policy is found to have exercised significant influence on export based growth;

(iii) Adjustment ofGDP to exports is spread over several periods. Only about 45% of total desired adjustment is realized in 3 years as per results of log-linear distributed lag model;

(iv) Imports do not exercise significant influence in growth of exports. This finding runs counter to the finding of AmalSarkar.

(v) Short run elasticity of GDP with respect to exports is low, though long run elasticity is as high as 0.73. It means that doubling of exports will lead to 73% growth of GDP. In our view, this result is theoretically valid but practically it does not sound highly probable for reasons that are obvious;

(vi) Above results are affected by the size effect of absolute values of volumes of GDP and exports so far as growth rates are concerned. Results based on absolute values, therefore, furnish weak and indirect support to ELG hypothesis. So the hypothesis is subjected to more rigorous testing;

(vii) Regression of growth rate of GDP on growth rate of exports alone and exports andpolicy does not furnish any evidence to lend empirical credence to ELG hypothesis;

(viii) Estimate of growth effect of exports, derived from I-O model, also lead to the refutation of ELG hypothesis;

(ix) The ELG strategy does not appear sustainable and viable over long period of time;

(x) Finally, an interesting finding of this study is that use of one specific model for testing of nebulous hypotheses may yield otiose type of results. Besides, appropriate data used in analysis is also important. Therefore, it is advisable not to depend on the results of one single model/method. Choice of method and model and database should also be appropriate.

POLICY IMPLICATION

The policy makers have to review the undue emphasis on strategy of export led growth. This is also warranted by major proportion of GDP being used for satisfying domestic demand.

Notes

1. This survey covers 150 studies.

REFERENCES

[1] Love J, Chandra R, (2005) "Testing export-led growth in South Asia" Journal of Economic Studies, Volume: 32 Issue: 2 2005 Katircioglu S.T, Kahyalar N, Benar H, (2007) "Financial development, trade and growth triangle: the case of India" International Journal of Social Economics Volume: 34 Issue: 9

[2] Narayan PK, Narayan S, Prasad BC, Prasad A, (2007) "Export-led growth hypothesis: evidence from Papua New Guinea and Fiji" Journal of Economic Studies Volume: 34 Issue: 4 2007

[3] Kumar S, (2011), "Estimating export demand equations in selected Asian countries" Journal of Chinese Economic and Foreign Trade Studies Volume: 4 Issue: 1 2011 Saleh S. Tabrizy, Natalia Trofimenko "Scope for Export-Led Growth in a Large Emerging Economy: Is India Learning by Exporting?"Kiel institute Working Paper no 1633 (source : www.isn.ethz.ch)

[4] Thomas I. Palley, (2011) "The Rise and Fall of Export-led Growth" New America Foundation, Emerald Group Publishing Limited

[5] JieYang , (2008) "An Analysis of So-Called Export-led Growth"IMF Working Paper Finance Department

[6] Saleh S. Tabrizy and Natalia Trofimenko, (2010) "Scope for Export-Led Growth in a Large Emerging Economy: Is India Learning by Exporting?"Kiel Working Paper No. 1633

[7] Judith A. Giles and Cara L.Williams, (2000) "Export-led Growth: A Survey of the Empirical Literature and Some Noncausality Results Part 1" (source : ideas.repec.org)

[8] Akmal, Muhammad Shahbaz, Ahmad, Khalil and Ali, Muhammad, "Exports-Led Growth Hypothesis in Pakistan: Further Evidence" (NCBA&E), Lahore (source : MPRA Paper No. 16043)

[9] Kaushik K.K, Klein K.K and Arbenser L, (2006) "An econometric analysis of export-led growth in a multivariate framework: Evidence from India"Foreign Trade Review, vol. XLI October-December 2006 no. 3

[10] Sarkar A, (2006) "Structural Stability of India's Export Demand Function: An Empirical Analysis" Foreign Trade Review, Vol. XLI October-December 2006 No. 3

[11] Dilip K. Das, (2009) "Dynamic growth of the Indian economy. Is the spurt sustainable?" Journal of Indian Business Research, Vol. 1 Iss: 2/3, pp.119 – 135

[12] Rajnish Tiwari, Cornelius Herstatt, (2012) "Assessing India's lead market potential for cost-effective innovations" Journal of Indian Business Research, Vol. 4 Iss: 2, pp.97 – 115

[13] Sanford L. Moskowitz (2006), "Internationalization and Value Creation in the Global Textiles and Apparel Industry: A Comparative Analysis of Lithuania and Moldova, in Value Creation in Multinational Enterprise" International Finance Review, Volume 7, Emerald Group Publishing Limited, pp.535-564

[14] SalihTuranKatircioglu, NeslihanKahyalar, HasretBenar, (2007) "Financial development, trade and growth triangle: the case of India" International Journal of Social Economics, Vol. 34 Iss: 9, pp.586 – 598

[15] Leonidas C. Leonidou, Constantine S. Katsikeas, DayanandaPalihawadana, StavroulaSpyropoulou, (2007) "An analytical review of the factors stimulating smaller firms to export: Implications for policy-makers" International Marketing Review, Vol. 24 Iss: 6, pp.735 – 770

[16] Christian Dreger, DierkHerzer "A further examination of the export-led growth hypothesis", DIW Berlin Discussion paper no.1149 (source: papers.ssrn.com)

[17] Economic Survey of India, Ministry of Finance, Govt of India

[18] Ministry of Mines, Govt of India

[19] www.Emeraldinsite.com

[20] www.Scopus.org

Flexible Strategic Framework for KM Factors with the Perspective of Continuity and Change: Study of Supply Chain Management Practices in India

V.K. Gupta

IMT Ghaziabad

ABSTRACT

The study is aimed at identifying Knowledge Management factors and developing a flexible strategic framework for knowledge management applicable to SCM. Study of existing KM frameworks was carried out and KM areas identified on the continuum of continuity and change. The data on KM areas on which this study is based was generated through secondary research using published sources and primary research through focused discussion with industry experts and personal interviews with experts from companies selected. A case study of industries is given in this paper validating the KM framework suggested. The research identifies and validates KM areas in terms of continuity and change factors applicable to management of supply chain.

INTRODUCTION

With increasing globalization, complexity due to changing demography and high expectations of the young consumers, supply chain design and management by business firms has become a key competitive factor. Wang (2008) explores knowledge sharing within a supply chain. Terry (2010) suggests that successfully managing the supply chain to create customer value requires extensive integration between demand-focused processes and supply-focused processes that is based on a foundation of value creation through intra organizational knowledge management. Grawe (2009) concludes that there has been a limited amount of theory-based research conducted on the topic of KM in logistics management. Marino (2010) discuses the role of KM is SCM of Italian food industry. A literature survey of the supply chains of MNCs in lighting industry reveals that there have been few studies on knowledge management practices in this industry. The reason behind this could be the large complex distribution network and too many stages and partners in the supply chain. Over the last few years, the Lighting Industry has seen phenomenal growth in emerging markets such as India, up gradation in technology, products, product design and most importantly, a huge growth and diversification in application. This has been the result of a growing interest in India as a large prospective market and entry of well known multinationals and brand leaders. On the other hand, India itself is undertaking development in infrastructure - roads, railway networks and stations, airports, sports stadium are being added and upgraded to international standards. The retail sector has also seen a boom with malls and condominium complexes mushrooming in towns and metros. There is a new generation of customers who are more discerning and demanding. However the sector has traditionally been very conservative and depends on a very complex and intervened supply chain consisting of manufacturers, wholesalers, stockiest, large and small unorganized retailers spread all over India.

Study of Knowledge Management factors with perspective of continuity and change for managing supply chain has not been done earlier. Very little literature is available on Knowledge Management factors with perspective of continuity and change (Smith, 2005). This research paper represents a comprehensive approach to study the KM factors in supply chain management from strategic knowledge management viewpoint and come out with a flexible strategic framework for knowledge management from the perspective of continuity and change for guiding the industry for its survival and growth. A case study of KM factors with perspective of continuity and change in supply chain management of industry validating the framework suggested has been discussed.

Objectives

1. The main objective of the study was to understand the knowledge management areas with perspective of continuity and change in supply chain management.
2. Understanding on how the different companies are actually managing knowledge capture and its reuse in their respective supply chains to provide the competitive quality, cost and delivery to the customers
3. Identify and study the knowledge management factors affecting forces of continuity and change influencing the supply chain of the industry.

LITERATURE REVIEW

Wong (2004) carried out the review of KM implementation frameworks. According to Parker (2005), inefficiencies in supply chain arise from a number of factors such as the lack of knowledge on international openness, cultural barriers to consumption, regulations, and cartel-like behavior on the part of firms. Latent demand can be typically higher than actual sales as there are often distribution inefficiencies that reduce actual sales below the level of latent demand. Paul (2002) makes a comparison of knowledge areas on operations enablers, customer choice, and business performance metrics covering the transition period culminating in the current focused demand *chain* scenario. Shankar (2005) discusses a framework for KM implementation.

Jan (2005) presented a project where five companies representing manufacturer, wholesaler and retailer tried to establish supply chain management practices through integrating knowledge. Mohanty and Deshmukh (1993) suggested use of analytic knowledge on hierarchic process for evaluating sources of supply. Goffin (1997) studied on managing knowledge for determining the average number of suppliers used by companies in various industrial sectors, reasons for manufacturing companies' move to reduce their supply base, importance of supplier management and relationship of supplier selection and auditing. According to Lee (2008) knowledge on limited capabilities and resources available within many small and medium-sized enterprises frequently hamper an effective response to environmental pressures, which in turn hurts large buying firms. An Integrative framework emerges that provides direction for suppliers, buyers, and public agencies seeking to improve environmental performance. Grey (2009) suggests that partial outsourcing can be an optimal strategy, due to optimum use of knowledge of in-house capabilities and supplier capabilities and risks associated. Hansen (2001) states that knowledge capture, processing and use for suppliers and technology in lighting industry are in a state of flux, there is total lack of knowledge management concepts and practices, no one knows which way to go forward. Many companies are trying to develop new products based on white and color LED with little or no knowledge of the customer acceptance and commercial viability. Erhun (2008) study a model with a single supplier and a single buyer who interacts multiple times before the buyer sells their product in the end-consumer market. The study shows the end consumers benefit from multiple trading opportunities versus a one-shot procurement agreement. Thomas (2009) suggests that forecast updating and risk sharing with the contract manufacturer are in best interest of the manufacturer. Saxena (2009) discusses role of KM in SCM. According to Low and Show (2008) study showed how the successful implementation of the just-in-time (JIT) philosophy in the manufacturing industry has helped to reduce cost and time and increase quality of products in lighting industries in Singapore.

Kumar (2008) aims to analyze and identify commonalities and differences between the supermarket industry and its logistics capabilities in developed economies such as North America, the European Union and Japan, as well as the emerging Asian economy of India. The trends are expanded service requirements, mass customization, customer loyalty and private labeling, delivery options and increased challenges in diverse markets. Reverse logistics, Point Of Sale data (POS) collection and management of supply chain by third- and fourth-party logistics providers are also becoming increasingly important for the supermarket industry. Prater, Biehl and Smith (2001) state that the firms operating in an international environment face a host of uncertainties that makes it difficult to meet deadlines reliably. Parkan and Dubey (2009) review the recent events that have shaped India's economic and business landscape and argue for the urgency of a significant modernization of KM methodologies in logistics and supply chain management practices. Another study showed that out of 8 companies, about half expect the vulnerability of their supply chains to increase over next 5 years due to lack of robust KM practices. Wagner (2006) conducted an empirical investigation into supply chain vulnerability. Lau and Wang (2009) suggest that the reverse logistic drivers vary from company to company and barrier to reverse logistics are common and are mainly external. According to Gosling (2009), supply chain flexibility can be rationalized by considering two key antecedents of flexibility, sourcing and vendor flexibility. Halley (2008) studied the relationship between supply chain and knowledge management practices. The results of a study of 163 Quebec (Canada) manufacturing companies (almost 90% of which are small and medium sized enterprises) confirmed their hypothesis that the deployment of integrated supply chain management practices with both upstream and downstream partners is associated with more effective knowledge management processes. Lin (2002) carried out studies on benefits that organizations can achieve through implementation of e-commerce technologies in collaborative supply chains. Shah (2007) discussed on several knowledge areas including forecasting of human resource requirements, designing and managing bench, arriving at the right skill mix, capacity planning in globally dispersed service operations, new analytical models for human resource planning and service contracts. Spanos (2007) suggests how the increasingly important role of South and East Asian markets in the globalization era can be amplified by the use of the latest EAI technologies that facilitate the bonding of even the most diverse information systems.

Tomas (2000), conclude that organizational learning have a positive influence on customer orientation and relationship commitment in the global supply chain. Hult (2004), using data from 58 supply chains in a *Fortune* 500 firm, found that the knowledge development process explained substantial variance in cycle time. Gunasekaran (2007) makes an attempt to review the literature available on knowledge management (KM) in manufacturing with the objective of identifying the gap between theory and practice, strategies and techniques for KM systems in advanced manufacturing environments. Hoon (2008) illustrates the conditions under which knowledge transfers during off shoring may reduce a domestic firm's in-house production costs, leading to total cost savings in both the short term and the long term. Wang (2008) explores knowledge sharing within a supply chain. The model in this research would provide a practice-oriented vehicle allowing the supply chain members to share and apply their knowledge. Stephan (2006) addresses essential concepts in supply chain networks and describes the systems approach the U.S. automotive industry has implemented to augment their supply chain management initiatives. Hult (2007) found that synergies exist between a culture of competitiveness and knowledge development.

According to Gupta (2007) forces of continuity and incremental changes were not enough to decide the future strategies for the organization. The environment has become very turbulent and the need to include change in the strategic thinking and strategy management has become essential according to Mintzberg (1994). The concept of continuity and change has been discussed in various contexts such as corporate governance. Various factors have been discussed for reasons of failure of good strategies by Jackson (2005) such a difficulty to manage change process, cultural factors demanding continuity and gaps between planning and execution. One of the ways suggested by Fredrik (2000) is to control inventory while managing the continuity in retail.

Levi (2008) has focused on impact of IT in SCM design. The continuity and change aspects have been treated separately. Cannon (1996) focuses on the paradox of continuity and change, and many other tensions and dilemma has created a new strategy revolution. The traditional approach is why should we change if we are at the best. The latest thinking, Hemp (2004), is we should change when we are at the best, hence manage continuity and change. Hilletofth, Ericsson and Lumsden (2010) discuss on how New Product Development (NPD) is connected to supply chain management (SCM). Qi (2009) consider a continuous review problem for a retailer who faces random disruptions both internally and externally form its supplier and formulated a model for cost for expected inventory cost. Trkman and McCormack (2009) present preliminary research concepts regarding a new approach to the identification and prediction of supply risk. Kull and Closs (2008) state that while evaluating risk assessment in a simulation environment, exploratory findings suggests that increased inventory in a tiered supply chain can sometimes increase supply risk rather than decrease it. Zhu and Sarkis (2006) compare drivers and practices of Green Supply Chain Management in China, focusing on three typical sectors, the automobile industry, the thermal power plants and the electronic and electrical industry. Handfield and Bechtel (2002) suggest that even in cases when buyers do not have a great deal of control over their suppliers, working to build trust within the relationship can improve supplier responsiveness. Yu, Zeng and Zhao (2009) evaluate the impacts of supply disruption risks on the choice between the famous single and dual sourcing methods in a two-stage supply chain with a non-stationary and price-sensitive demand. Schenker-Wicki (2010) takes a close look at the concept of disaster from an economic and management point of view to mitigate the impact on human beings and environment. Scholz (2010) proposes a framework for investigating interfaces between manufacturing and logistics systems along global supply chains. Most of the research above focuses on continuity or change separately.

Continuity and Change Forces

Sushil (2005), Sushil and Garg (2010), Sushil (2012), Gupta (2007, 2009) have identified the following KM factors for forces of continuity and change that need to be studied in greater details to develop a flexible strategic framework for managing supply chain in an organization. The detailed methodology for arriving at the KM factors indicated below has been discussed at length in the earlier work of the author referred to above.

KM factor for Continuity Forces

1. Customer Base
2. Infrastructure

3. Technology
4. Core competence
5. Supply Chain and Distribution network
6. Culture
7. Performance

KM Factors for Change Force

1. Globalization
2. New Opportunities
3. Competition
4. Customer Needs
5. Technology
6. Mergers and Acquisitions
7. Government policy

There is a need to study KM in the real life supply chain system of an industry and study impact of KM factors with perspective of continuity forces and change forces on supply chain management and come out with a flexible strategic framework for their survival and growth in this highly competitive fast evolving customer driven era.

RESEARCH DESIGN

Research Methodology

Exploratory Research

- Collection of the Primary Data using a detail questionnaire to be filled by the people working in the field/area of the research.
- Collection of Secondary Data, by taking the reference from the previous researches in the field of supply chain and the literature.

Scope of the Study

- Study of SCM practices in sourcing, in plant as well as, distribution supply chain of selected industries.

Method of Data Collection

- From Published Secondary Data, Internet Databases, and companies websites.
- Focused discussion and interviews of executives of selected companies and their supply

chain partners in electrical and lighting Industry in India, using a well-tested structured questionnaire.

DETAILS OF THE STUDY

The study has been carried out in the Indian companies selected. The companies selected have been leaders in this industry with annual sales of US$ 1 billion and operating at all India level for over 20 years. All the companies were approached for accessing the KM factors with perspective of continuity and change in their respective supply chain. Each company suggested 10 senior executives from all areas of their supply chain for participating in the study. A focused discussion was held with some of these experts to identify the KM factors with perspective of continuity and change and structured questionnaire developed and tested in a pilot study. Subsequently, a personal meeting and an interview was held with each of the expert from the above industry and a structured well tested questionnaire was used to collect the primary data for the above study. It was agreed to keep the names of the experts confidential to ensure the responses were unbiased and independent. The replies received in response to the interviews reflected personal opinion of the experts and not that of the company. The data collected was compiled and analyzed.

FINDINGS OF THE STUDY, ANALYSIS AND LESSONS LEARNT

A survey based on focused discussions and interviews of executives of the manufacturing and distribution companies using a structured questionnaire focused on continuity and change factors and their effect on supply chain has been carried out. Key findings have been discuses below which contribute to the forces of continuity and change.

Analysis and Discussion

Flexible Strategic Framework for Knowledge Management in Supply Chain with the Perspective of Continuity and Change

In order to map the position of an industry or enterprise with respect to these forces, a Flexible Strategic Framework for Knowledge Management in Supply Chain with the perspective of Continuity and Change is developed. This matrix has KM factor average score for continuity forces on the x-axis and average score for change forces on the y-axis. The average score of either of these factors could be 'Low' or 'High'. These KM factors could be assessed independently for each category, such as customer base, infrastructure, technology and so on and aggregated as 'KM factors for continuity forces'. Similarly, the 'KM factors for change forces' can be assessed for globalization, new opportunities, change in customer needs and so on, as given in the previous section, and an aggregate score can be obtained. As per the proposed KM forces Matrix on Continuity and Change, there can be four possible combinations of the continuity and change forces, which are named according to the characteristics of that category. KM forces Matrix on Continuity and Change on a scale of 0-5 for each of the above forces, classifies the organizations into four segments – Quadrant I Stabilizers, Quadrant II Quick en-cashers, Quadrant III Change masters and Quadrant IV Synthesizers.

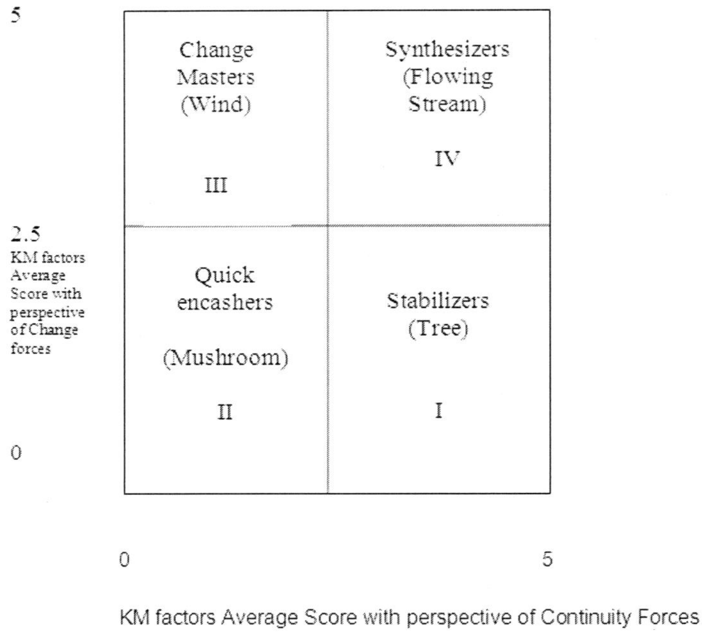

Fig. 1. KM factors Matrix on Continuity and Change for Supply Chain

All the companies' studies are the market leaders in industry globally and in India. On KM forces Matrix on Continuity and Change for all the five companies fall in segment IV "Flowing Stream". However, a detailed study of the KM factors that affect continuity forces and change forces revealed that each of the selected company has areas where it need to focus and improve, if it has to continuity to survive and grow. Losing focus these priorities, as evident from the study, could make the respective company lose its market position and competitive strength. KM forces Matrix on Continuity and Change forces developed for supply chain of lighting industry provide a flexible strategic direction to the companies in the industry to survive and grow.

Lessons Learnt, New Findings and Linkage with Literature

The above study has brought out clearly that all the five companies in the industry studied fall in High Continuity and High Change factor score and therefore fall in Flow Stream category (Sushil 2012). The companies studied in manufacturing sector fall in all the four segments of

C-C Matrix (Gupta 2009). The study of credit risks in banks in India (Service Industry) also shows that the 8 leading banks studied also fall in all the four segments of C-C Matrix (Gupta 2009). Study of four manufacturing organizations reveal that they fall in Low Continuity score and High Change score, High continuity score and a Low change score and High Continuity score and High change scores segments of C-C Matrix (Gupta 2010). This clearly reveals that the companies in electrical and lighting industry are very aggressive and continue to catch up with the competition very fast. As a result, all these companies fall in Flow Stream Segment and also are very close to one another. The benefit these companies can derive from C-C matrix and detailed analysis of KM factors for continuity and change is that now they have a framework to measure their performance and identify the factors in which they are week. This would help them to map a clear strategy to be ahead of the completion and improve its profitability substantially as compared to its peers.

CONCLUSIONS

The above research has clearly demonstrated that the flexible strategic framework for KM with perspective of continuity and change in supply chain has provided specific strategic direction to each company studied depending upon its score on each KM factor on Continuity and Change Matrix developed. Each of the company studied can take a specific flexible strategic direction for improving its supply chain depending upon the score on each KM factor for continuity and change forces. This framework can be used by a company to identify, capture, analyse and share both explicit and tacit knowledge on each KM factor with its supply chain partners for sustainable competitive advantage. This framework has been tested in a number of industries and has given very encouraging results. In this case study, where on surface all companies studies seems to be competing very closely, the companies which are able to identify week KM areas can move to clear leadership position by putting in place the KM framework suggested for aligning its strategies for completive advantage and sustained growth. The KM practitioners and researchers can apply the KM framework suggested in different sectors of their economy and validate the results. The study done so far suggests that this framework can be applied globally.

LIMITATIONS OF THE STUDY

The study was carried out in National Capital Region of India. The sample size was limited to 100 executives of five leading companies in lighting industry and their channel partners including 3 PLs. The findings of the study are suggestive and indicative. An all India study of more regional companies in lighting industry can be used to apply the framework of KM factor Matrix with perspective of Continuity and Change proposed in this study to get a deeper insight.

ACKNOWLEDGEMENT

The author would like to thank the editor and reviewers and Prof Sushil, Professor, Dept of Management Studies, IIT Dellhi, India for their valuable comments and suggestions during preparation of this research paper.

REFERENCES

[1] Cannon, T. (1996), "Welcome to the revolution, Managing Paradox in the 21st century," Pitman Publishing, London.

[2] Erhun, F., Keskinocak, P., Tayur, S. (2008),"Dynamic Procurement, Quantity Discounts, and Supply Chain Efficiency", *Production And Operations Management*, Vol. 17, No. 5, September–October, pp. 543–550.

[3] Fredrik, A. H. (2000),"Control your inventory," HBR, pp. 169-176.

[4] Goffin, K., Szwejczewski, M., New, C. (1997), "Managing suppliers: when fewer can mean more", International Journal of Physical Distributions & Logistics Management; Vol. 27 Issue 7, 15p.

[5] Gosling, J., Purvis, L, Naim, M.M. (2009), "Supply chain flexibility as a determinant of supplier selection", *International Journal of Production Economics*, Available online 9 September.

[6] Gupta, V. K. (2007), "Flexible Strategic Framework for Managing Continuity and Change in Reverse Supply Chain in the Battery Industry : Study of Lead Acid Batteries and Ni Cd batteries for Automotive, Computers Mobile Phones", Proceedings of Seventh Global Conference on Flexible Systems Management at Noida, India, pp. 471 – 492.

[7] Gupta, V.K. (2009), "Strategic Framework for Managing Forces of Continuity and Change in Risk Management of Banks in India", Global Journal of Flexible Systems Management, Vol. 10, No. 2, pp. 1-13.

[8] Gupta, V.K. (2010), "Flexible Strategic Framework for Managing Forces of Continuity and Change in Value Engineering Processes", Global *Journal of Flexible Systems Management*, Vol. 10, No. 4, pp. 43-54.

[9] Gupta, V.K. (2010), "Flexible Strategic Framework for Managing Continuity and Change - Outbound Supply Chain of Automotive Industry in India", *Int. J. Value Chain Management,* Vol. 4, No. 4, 2010 pp. 365-379.

[10] Gupta, V.K. (2011), "Flexible strategic framework for managing forces of continuity and change – study of inward supply chain of a leading automotive company in India", *Int. J. Business Excellence,* Vol. 4, No. 2, 2011pp 142-159.

[11] Gupta, V.K. (2011), Flexible Strategic Framework For Managing Forces of Continuity and Change In Retail Banking Business Process", Business Process Management Journal, accepted for publication.

[12] Gunasekaran A, and Ngai E.W., (2007), "Knowledge Management in 21st Century Manufacturing", *International Journal Of Production Research*, Vol. 45, No. 11, 1 June, pp. 2391–2418.

[13] Grawe, Scott J. (2009), "Logistics innovation: a literature-based conceptual framework", *The International Journal of Logistics Management,* Vol. 20 No. 3, pp. 360-377.

[14] Grey, J.V., Tomlin. B., Roth, A.V. (2009), "Outsourcing to a Powerful Contract Manufacturer: The effect of Learning by doing", *Production and Operations Management*, Vol. 18, No. 5, September–October, pp. 487–505.

[15] Halley Alain, Beaulieu Martin (2008), "Knowledge Management Practices in the Context of Supply Chain Integration: The Canadian Experience", *Supply Chain Forum - An International Journal,* Vol. 6 - N°1 , website : www.supplychain-forum.com

[16] Handfield, Robert B., Bechtel, C. (2002), "The role of trust and relationship structure in improving supply chain responsiveness", *Industrial Marketing Management*, Volume 31, Issue 4, July 2002, Pages 367-382.

[17] Hansen, Paul. (2001), "Suppliers, *Lighting* Technology in Flux.", *Automotive Industries*, Aug., Vol 181, Issue 8, p 20.

[18] Hemp, P., and Steward, T. A., 2004, "Leading change when business is good – Interview of Samuel J Palmisano," CEO, IBM, Harvard Business Review, pp 61-70.

[19] Hilletofth, Per , Ericsson, Dag, Lumsden, Kenth (2010), "Coordinating new product development and supply chain management", *International Journal of Value Chain Management,* Vol. 4, No.1/2 pp. 170 – 192.

[20] Hoon S. Cha, David E. Pingry, Matt E. Thatcher (2008), "Managing The Knowledge Supply Chain: An Organizational Learning Model Of Information Technology Offshore Outsourcing:, *MIS Quarterly* Vol. 32 No. 2, pp. 281-306.

[21] Hult G., David J. Ketchen, Jr., Stanley F. Slater (2004), "Information Processing, Knowledge Development, And Strategic Supply Chain Performance", *Academy Of Management Journal*, Vol. 47, No. 2, 241–253.

[22] Hult, Ketchen and Arrfelt (2007), "Strategic Supply Chain Management: Improving Performance Through A Culture Of Competitiveness and Knowledge Development", *Strategic Management Journal,* 28: 1035–1052.

[23] Jackson, G., 2005, "Continuity and change in corporate governance: Comparing Germany and Japan," Corporate Governance 13(3), pp. 351-360.

[24] Jan Ketil Arnulf, Heidi C. Dreyer And Carl Erik Grenness (2005) , "Trust and knowledge creation: how the dynamics of trust and absorptive capacity may affect supply chain management development projects" *International Journal of Logistics: Research and Applications* Vol. 8, No. 3, September, pp. 225–236.

[25] Kull, Thomas, Closs, David (2008), " The risk of second-tier supplier failures in serial supply chains: Implications for order policies and distributor autonomy", *European Journal of Operational Research*, Volume 186, Issue 3, 1 May 2008, Pages 1158-1174.

[26] Kumar, Sameer (2008) "A study of the supermarket industry and its growing logistics capabilities", *International Journal of Retail & Distribution Management*, Volume 36, Number 3, pp:192-211.

[27] Lau, K. H., Wang, Y. (2009), "Reverse Logistics in the electronics industry in China : a case study", *Supply Chain Management: An International Journal*, Vol 14, No 6, pp. 447-465.

[28] Lee, Su-Yol, Klassen, R.D. (2008), "Drivers and Enablers That Foster Environmental Management Capabilities in Small- and Medium-Sized Suppliers in Supply Chains", *Production and Operations Management*, Vol. 17, No. 6, November–December, pp. 573–586.

[29] Levi, David Shimchi, Kaminsky Philip, Shankar Ravi (2008), "Designing and Managing Supply Chain", Tata McGraw-Hill Publishing Co., India

[30] Lin C., Hung H., Wu June-Yie and Lin B. (2002), "A Knowledge Management Architecture on Collaborative Supply Chain", *Journal of Computer Information Systems*, Ebesco publishing, pp. 83-94.

[31] Lin, Chinh, Tseng, Shu-Mei (2005), " The implementation gaps for the knowledge management system", *Industrial Management & Data Systems*, Vol. 105 Issue 2, pp. 208-222.

[32] Low, S.P., Show, M Y (2008) "Facilities design incorporating just-in-time principles for ramp-up light factories in Singapore", *Facilities* Volume: 26 Issue: 7/8 pp. 321-342.

[33] Marino, Corso, Dogan, Seyhan Firdevs, Mogre, Riccardo, Perego, Alessandro (2010), "The role of knowledge management in supply chains: evidence from the Italian food industry", *International Journal of Networking & Virtual Organisations*; Vol. 7, Issue 2/3, pp. 163-183.

[34] Mintzberg, H., 1994, "The Rise, and fall of strategic planning," Free Press and Prentice International, New York.

[35] Mohanty, R.P.; Deshmukh, S.G.(1993), "Use of analytic hierarchic process for evaluating sources of supply; International Journal of Physical Distribution & Logistics Management; Vol. 23 Issue 3.

[36] Parkan, Celik , Dubey, Rameshwar (2009), "Recent Developments in the Practice of Supply Chain Management and Logistics In India", *Portuguese Journal of Management Studies*, VOL. XIV, No. 1, pp. 71-87.

[37] Parker, Philip M. (2005), "World Outlook Report 2006-2011: Non-Electric Complete Lighting Fixtures & Equipment", *Ebseco Publishing* pp. 1-188.

[38] Paul: Aitken, James; Towill, Denis R. (2002), "Analysis and design of focused demand chain", *Journal of Operations Management*, Nov, Vol. 20, Issue 6, pp. 675-689.

[39] Prater, E., Biehl, M., Smith, M.A. (2001), "International supply chain agility: Tradeoffs between flexibility and Uncertainty", *International Journal of Operations & Production Management*, Vol. 21 No. 5/6, pp. 823-839.

[40] Qi, L., Shen,Z. M., Snyder, L.V. (2009), " A continuous review inventory model with disruptions at both supplier and retailer", *Production And Operations Management*, Vol. 18, No. 5, September–October, pp. 516–532.

[41] Saxena, Avneet, Wadhwa, S. (2009), "Flexible configuration for seamless supply chains: Directions towards decision knowledge sharing", *Robotics & Computer-Integrated Manufacturing;* Aug, Vol. 25 Issue 4/5, pp. 839-852.

[42] Schenker-Wicki, Andrea, Inauen, Matthias, Olivares, Maria (2010), "Unmastered risks: From crisis to catastrophe: An economic and management insight", *Journal of Business Research*, Volume 63, Issue 4, April, pp. 337-346.

[43] Scholz-Reiter, Bernd, Frazzon, Enzo Morosini, Makuschewitz, Thomas (2010), "Integrating manufacturing and logistic systems along global supply chains", *CIRP Journal of Manufacturing Science and Technology*, Volume 2, Issue 3, pp. 216-223.

[44] Shankar, Ravi, Amol Gupta (2005), "Towards Framework for Knowledge Management Implementation: *Knowledge and Process Management*, Volume 12, Number 4, pp. 259–277.

[45] Shah Janat (2007), "Supply Chain Issues in Knowledge-based Service Industries: Discussion", *IIMB Management Review*, June, pp. 173-188.

[46] Smith, Heather A., James D. McKeen (2005), "Developments In Practice XVII:A Framework For KM Evaluation", *Communications of the Association for Information Systems* , Volume 16, pp. 233-246.

[47] Spanos A., Ponis S. and Tatsiopoulos I. (2007), "Enterprise application integration: Implications for Euro-Asian supply chains",Human Systems Management 26 (2007) pp. 257–268, IOS Press.

[48] Stephan Kudyba (2006), "Enhancing Organizational Information Flow and Knowledge Creation in Re-Engineering Supply Chain Systems: An Analysis Of The U.S. Automotive Parts and Supplies Model", *International Journal of Innovation Management.* Vol. 10, No. 2, pp. 163–173.

[49] Sushil (2005), "A flexible strategy framework for managing continuity and change", *International Journal for Global Business and Competitiveness,* Vol 1, No.1, pp. 22-32.

[50] Sushil (2012): Flowing Stream Strategy: Managing Confluence of Continuity and Change, *Journal of Enterprise Transformation*, 2:1, 26-49.

[51] Sushil and Garg (2010), "Status of continuity forces in Indian industry: a survey", *Int. J. Business Continuity and Risk Management,* Vol. 1, No. 2, pp. 166-186.

[52] Terry E., Alexender E., Theodore S., Mark M. (2010), "Demand and supply integration: a conceptual framework of value creation through knowledge management", Journal of the Academy of Marketing Science; Spring, Vol. 38 Issue 1, pp. 5-18.

[53] Thomas, D.J., Warsing, D P., Zhang, X. (2009), "Forecast Updating and Supplier Coordination for Complementary Component Purchase", *Production and Operations Management;* Mar-Apr ; 18, 2; pp. 167-184.

[54] Tomas G., Hult,Ernest L. Nichols Jr.,Larry C. Giunipero, and Robert F. Hurley (2000), "Global Organizational Learning in the Supply Chain: A Low Versus High Learning Study", *Joumal of International Marketing* Vol. 8, No. 3, pp. 61-83, ISSN 1069-031X.

[55] Trkman, P. , McCormack, K. (2009), " Supply chain risk in turbulent environments—A conceptual model for managing supply chain network risk", *International Journal of Production Economics*, Volume 119, Issue 2, June 2009, Pages 247-258.

[56] Wagner, S.N., Bode, Christoph (2006), "An empirical investigation into supply chain vulnerability", Journal of Purchasing and Supply Management, Vol 12, Issue 6, pp. 301-312.

[57] Wang C., Fergusson C., Perry D., Anthony J. (2008), "A conceptual case-based model for knowledge sharing among supply chain members", *Business Process Management Journal*; Apr, Vol. 14 Issue 2, pp. 147-165.

[58] Wong, Kuan Yew, Elaine Aspinwall (2004), "Knowledge Management Implementation Frameworks: A Review", *Knowledge and Process Management*, Volume 11, Number 2, pp. 93–104.

[59] Yu, Haisheng, Zeng, Amy Z., Zhao, Lindu (2009), " Single or dual sourcing: decision-making in the presence of supply chain disruption risks", *Omega*, Volume 37, Issue 4, August 2009, pp. 788-800.

[60] Zhu, Qinghua, Sarkis, J. (2006), "An inter-sectoral comparison of green supply chain management in China: Drivers and practices", *Journal of Cleaner Production*, Volume 14, Issue 5, 2006, pp. 472-486.

Identifying Core Competencies for an Effective Talent Management: A Study on Hindalco Industries Ltd.

Alok John and Surbhi David[1]

Xavier Institute of Management, Jabalpur
[1]*Xavier Institute of Social Service, Ranchi*

ABSTRACT

Competency is defined as a behaviour or set of behaviours that describe superior performance in a particular work context (e.g. Job, role or group of jobs, function or whole organisation). Competencies are the characteristics of a manager that lead to the demonstration of skills and abilities, which result in superior performance within an organisational area. This paper describes the various competencies required by the employees of Hindalco Industries Limited. Hindalco has developed Nine Behavioural Competencies Skills that would help its employees to deliver superior performance and build a leadership pipeline for the organization. The company uses the Competency Assessment and Development Discussion (CADD) concept for assessing the competency of an employee. It provides a platform for engagement between Manager and Employee around Competencies (functional & behavioural) required for job. The outcome of CADD discussion helps individual gain insights on his/her strengths and gap areas around Competencies which facilitates in making a Development Plan. The Manager also has the opportunity to estimate his/her team on their potential based on the Competencies displayed to help in process of Talent Segmentation. This is usually concurrently during Mid-Year.Hindalco considers people as its most critical resource. It is the differentiating factor that gives it the competitive edge. Building a leadership pipeline is the core of its Talent Management System. The process involved identifying the Talent Pool members through their competencies and assessing their potential in the present and future roles. The study relies on primary data obtained through questionnaires and observations. IT was found that the implementation of talent management increases manager's competencies. Competency Assessment provides knowledge of performance gap and it would helpful to identify the training needs.

INTRODUCTION

Core competencies are those capabilities that are critical to a business in achieving competitive advantage. The starting point for analysing core competencies is recognising that competition between businesses is as much a race for competence mastery as it is for market position and market power. Senior management cannot focus on all activities of a business and the competencies required undertaking them. So the goal is for management to focus attention on competencies that really affect competitive advantage and built up a unique talent pool.

The paper is encompassed by the following backdrop:

1. Rationale of the study
2. Review of literature
3. Research Methodology
4. Case Study of Hindalco Industries Ltd.
5. Conclusion

RATIONALE OF THE STUDY

This paper seeks to accomplish the following specific objectives:

1.1. To examine the effects of core competence on competitive advantage

1.2. To investigate the effect of core competence on Talent Management

REVIEW OF LITERATURE

Conceptualization of Core competencies

Leonard-Barton (2000) defined core competency as one which differentiates a firm from its milieu. According to Sanchez and Heene (1997), core competencies are usually the result of "collective learning" processes and are manifested in business activities and processes. The core competencies are those unique capabilities, which usually span over multiple products or markets (Hafeez et al., 2002). Prahalad and Hamel (1990) contend that "core competencies are the collective learning in the organizations, especially how to coordinate diverse production skills and integrate multiple streams of technologies." They argue that core competence is communication, involvement, and a deep commitment to working across organizational boundaries. Core competences are those competences which allow firms a superior advantage, and according to Hamel and Prahalad (1994; 1990) to be considered "core" the competence must meet three criteria:

1. Customer Value: A core competence must make a significant contribution to Customer perceived value.
2. Competitor Differentiation: Any competence across an industry cannot be defined as core unless the firm's level of competence is superior to all its competitors and should be difficult for to imitate.
3. Extendibility: The competence must be capable of being applied to new product arenas.

Conceptualisation of Talent Management

Talent Management as a concept used in the management literature which emerged in the late 1990s after the publication of the influential work "War for talent" by McKinsey consultants (Michaels et al., 2001). However, it is worth noting that Talent Management is not a new practice. There have been a variety of systems used for selecting people with exceptional performance, as well as programmes to develop their skills. Several examples of such practices can be cited. Firstly, over 3,000 years ago, the Chinese used a form of Talent Management, which came to be known by the Portuguese as the Mandarin system. The Mandarin system was a merit-based selection method for senior government officials in China, called the Mandarins, for the purpose of selecting people with exceptional performance to work in the public service. Secondly, as early as 1600, the British East India Company used competitive examinations to recruit Alpha Minds. Thirdly, Napoleon I, the Emperor of the French, (1769-1821) used a merit-based system under the Napoleonic code to select government officials. Napoleon stressed that government jobs go to the most qualified, starting from 1804. Fourthly, under Unilevers Company Management Development Scheme (UCMDS), which started in 1952, senior managers were assigned the responsibility of identifying the talent and utilising psychological tests (similar to those devised by the Army for officer selection). The psychological tests were used to test the potential of the identified talent. Fifthly, in the 1980s HR managers were urged to utilise the BCG matrix in differentiating between star, dead, solid and high potential employees and manage them differently.

RESEARCH METHODOLOGY

This is a case study about Hindalco Industries Ltd. Secondary data are used to prepare this paper. Data are collected from various periodicals, journals and websites. By objective analysis it is tried to find the actual application of Competencies in Talent Management at Hidalco Industries Ltd. The findings of the study are positive and found a holistic view of the Competencies Management.

CASE STUDY OF HINDALCO INDUSTRIES LTD. OF ADITYA BIRLA GROUP

Introduction to Hindalco Industries Ltd.

Hindalco is one of the India's largest producers of aluminium. The company was incorporated on 15th December, 1958 and commenced production in 1962. This is considered to the biggest metal powerhouse in the World with a consolidated turnover of Rs. 72,078 crore (US$ 15.85 Billion).

The company's operations are vertically integrated and include bauxite mining at Lohardaga and Samri, refining bauxite into alumina, smelting aluminia into primary aluminium, manufacturing semi-fabricated alumimuim products of extrusions, rolled products, redraw rods etc. at Renukoot, value added products of foil and wheel at Silvassa and power generation at Renusagar. The Company has sales and distribution network that covers all of India and includes five sales offices located in Mumbai, New Delhi, Bangalore, Chennai and Renukoot. Continual expansion has been the company grows into India's largest aluminium producer. Other facilities include an aluminium smelter at Hirakud (Odisha) with a captive power plant and coal mine, alumina refineries at Muri (Jharkhand), and Belgaum (Karnataka), and rolling mills at Belur (West Bengal), and Taloja, (Maharashtra), foil rolling at Kollur (Andhra Pradesh) and Silvassa (Union Territory of Dadra and Nagar Haveli) and an extrusions plant at Alupuram (Kerala). Hindalco's integrated operations and operational efficiency have enabled the company to be one of the world's lowest cost producers of aluminuim.

Competency Model at Hindalco

Competency is ability of a person to perform a job properly. In Aditya Birla Group, Hindalco the competency model is very well structured. Mainly there are two types of competencies in Hindalco. They are:

1. Functional Competency
2. Behavioural Competency

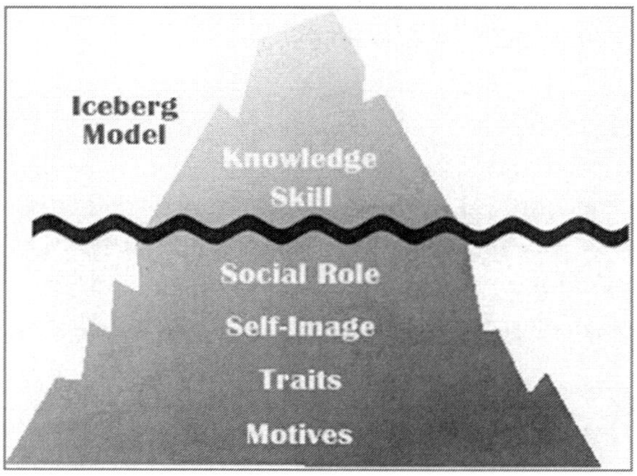

1. **Functional Competency:** A functional competency is the key knowledge and skill needed by a job holder for the effective performance of the job. They are the visible skills and knowledge.
2. **Behavioural Competency:** A behaviouralcompetency is an underlying, key characteristics needed for outstanding job performance, which leads to and predicts high performance. It describes how the job holder does a particular job. Though these behavioural components like attitude, traits, thinking styles, self-image, organizational

fit, etc., are hidden or are invisible.

Normally job related training or technical training help to build Functional Competencies, while developing competencies for the Managerial Effectiveness relate to Behavioural Competencies, i.e. team building, communication, leadership, customer focus etc.

The Aditya Birla Group along with its flagship company Hindalco has developed Nine Behavioural Competencies Skills that would help its employees to deliver superior performance and build a leadership pipeline for the organization.

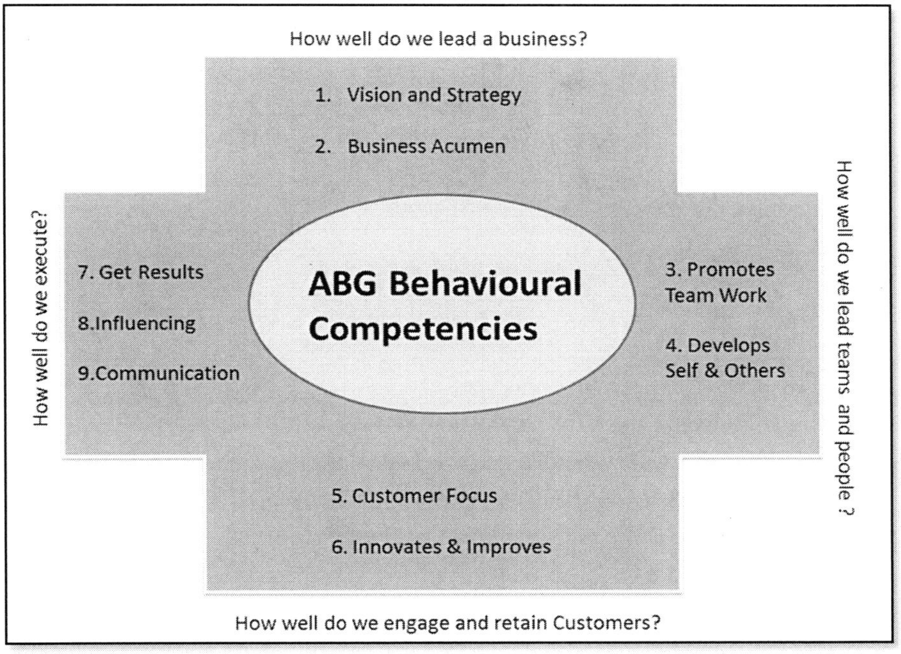

Source: Competency Development Resource Guide, Aditya Birla Group Human Resources, 2010

1. Vision and Strategy
2. Business Acumen
3. Promotes team work
4. Develop self and others
5. Customer Focus
6. Innovates and Improves
7. Get Results
8. Influencing
9. Communication

Competency Assessment and Development Discussion (CADD)

CADD is a concept for assessing the competency of an employee. It provides a platform for engagement between Manager and Employee around Competencies (functional &behavioural) required for job. The outcome of CADD discussion helps individual gain insights on his/her strengths and gap areas around Competencies which facilitates in making a Development Plan. It is subjective and basically it is by Manager's Perspective. The Manager also has the opportunity to estimate his/her team on their potential based on the Competencies displayed to help in process of Talent Segmentation. This is usually concurrently during Mid-Year.

Preparation of Skill Matrix

Following are the steps which are followed by Hindalco HR for preparing the Skill Matrix:

(a) Identifying all the skills/competencies required for a department by interviewing all the employees in the concerned departments.

(b) Matching the skills/competencies of the departments with that of the grades, thereby getting the skills/competencies of a particular job. The weightage for the skills differs according to different grades.

(c) Therefore the skills/competencies of each employee are analyzed using questionnaire and interviewing the person concerned.

(d) All the competencies need are identified in three categories namely:

- § **Technical skills:** It includes knowledge of the job related skills and expertise.
- § **Managerial skills:** It includes possession of various characteristics of a manager like decision making ability, maturity, thought process, etc.
- § **Behavioural skills:** It includes problem solving skills, social roles, awareness of inner and outer self, traits, motives, etc.

(e) Eventually a match between these competencies for a particular grade with that of the identified skills/competencies of a particular grade is done.

(f) Proper steps are taken to bridge the gap in skills/competencies identified.

Their commitment to employee learning and development at all levels is unrelenting.The training calendar is accessible to employees via AdityaDisha, the group wide intranet, and the teaching programs consist of a mix of classroom, outreach, and e-learning initiatives.

Talent Management Solutions and Processes

Talent management is the proven practice of using interconnected human resources processes to provide a simple fundamental benefit for any organization. We all know that companies with the best people can perform at a higher level. We also know that to deliver topline growth even the best people need to be engaged, developed, and rewarded. Leading organizations know that exceptional business performance is driven by superior talent that's managed with consistent processes. From Fortune 100 enterprises to small and medium businesses, companies that invest in talent management achieve significant returns. They know success is powered by the total talent quality of their workforce. Workforce cost is the largest category of spend for most organizations. Optimization of your talent management processes provides the immediate workforce visibility and insights your company needs to significantly improve your bottom line.

Recruitment, performance, compensation, learning and development, and succession management solutions tied to analytics provide the processes and information to attract, engage, reward, and develop a high performance workforce.

HR professionals and line managers need talent management insights to know more about their people and make better decisions faster. They have information that they need to know:

- How can we align individual goals to team and organizational goals?
- Who are my highest performers and what are their career paths?
- What is my best source of hire and how can I better focus my recruiting efforts?
- Who are my future leaders and how can I effectively foster their development?
- Who requires a higher merit increase to avoid turnover risk and business disruption?
- Who are my top internal and external candidates if my VP leaves?
- Who needs additional development before they can assume greater responsibility?

Talent Pool Nurturing

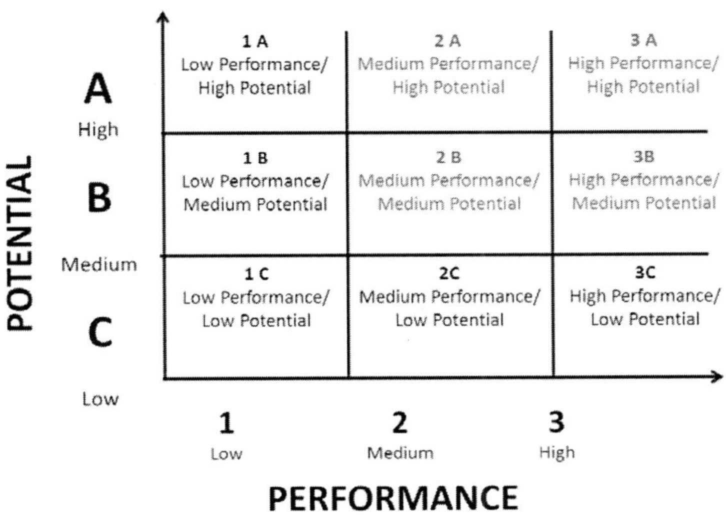

Performance Potential Matrix

The Aditya Birla Group including Hindalco considers people as its most critical resource. It is the differentiating factor that gives it the competitive edge. Building a leadership pipeline is the core of its Talent Management System. The process involved identifying the Talent Pool members through their performance and assessing their potential in the present and future roles.

The ABG Performance Potential Matrix Graph helps to access all the eligible employees in every Unit/Business for their performance and competencies. Their performance and competencies are plotted on the performance and potential axis as shown in the graph. The top four boxes (2A 3A, 2B 3B) represents the talent pool. 3A is the most preferred group of Talent Pool as it consists of employees with both High Performance and High Potential.

ABG believes in doing everything that can help its people explore their competencies and stretch their potential. It is constantly focused on fine tuning the Group's talent pool. The grooming of talent involves discussing, reviewing and working through the development plans of each of the talent pool member. Their development plans include engagement with special projects, coaching and mentoring by the top leadership team, besides attending functional and competency based behavioural programmes that open the frontiers of their mind and goad them to defy limitations. 60% of the total leadership positions were filled in from the existing talent in 2010- 11 validates the talent honing processes which have laid a robust leadership within the Group

CONCLUSION

This paper provides study of the relationship between core competencies and talent management. Core Competencies are considered to be vital determinant of talent pool nurturing. Core competencies also have a significant contribution towards the building of competitive advantage. Therefore, core competencies can improve competitive advantage and organisational performance. Hindalco Industries have successfully developed strategies that deepen competitive advantage and enhance their organisational performance. In order to remain competitive and obtain competitive advantages, the company has tried to increase organizational performance by managing each dimension of competencies.

The study shows that core competencies enabled talent management boosts the morale of the employees, upgrades their skills, improves their performance and gives them the confidence to take on challenging assignments and excel in their jobs. The finding shows that the talent management aim to bring about a positive change in behaviours and thereby contributes to the over enhancement of skill and managerial effectiveness. This might not necessarily leads to job satisfaction of employees but it can lead to increased productivity, higher quality of work, enhanced skills, knowledge, understanding and a positive attitude. Illustrative examples of this could be reduction in waste and accidents, lower absenteeism, higher motivation and collaboration among teams, better time management and prioritization of tasks, better understanding between members and so on. Thus, Identification of Core Competencies does have a positive impact on the performance of employees of different organisations.

RECOMMENDATIONS

[1] Employees should be encouraged to go for Talent Pool nurturing. This will brighten up their ideas and will enable them to know more about the recent developments in their job area.

[2] The Manger should determine the needs that would be most suitable for the achievement of individual as well as organizational goals.

[3] There should be frequent job rotation so that the employees get aware of the skills and competencies required for various jobs.

[4] There should be no communication gap between the employees and their immediate bosses, so that they can communicate with each other and managers can get proper feedback from the employees to carry out the training and development activities.

Implications of FDI in Multi Branding Retail in India

Sandeep Puri and Ujjawal Sharma

IMT Ghaziabad

ABSTRACT

Foreign Direct Investment (FDI) is considered to be the core incentive for economic and social development as far as the developing nations are concerned. Ever since the Globalisation and Liberalization of world economies have exposed to greater collectivism, inflows of foreign direct investment has greatly increased. Indian market is providing enormous opportunities for investment in both domestic as well as foreign market. With increasing growth and performance, India is welcoming the FDI (Foreign Direct Investment) in single brand and multi brands retail, which can stimulate the economic needs of the nation.

This project explores the implication of FDI in Multi branding retail in India in preview of the current resources and constraints. The paper will also focus on the benefits and effects of FDI on different segment of the business arena. The research will briefly discuss the recent trends and the market opportunities for the country, and the critical analysing of the FDI in India.

INTRODUCTION

Retail today is one of the most promising industries in the Indian economy. It contributes approximately 14% to the Indian GDP and provides 7% employment currently. This opportunity taps on the presence of a large, growing, consumption driven economy and a slowdown growth in developed markets along with a young consumer base, which is what lured the foreign retailers to invest in India.[1] This is a one in half century opportunity with a consumer base who is ready and waiting to be served.

According to the latest government figures, foreign direct investment, or FDI as it is commonly known, has risen more than fivefold over the past eight years. FDI into India during the 2011-12 fiscal year totalled almost $47bn (£29bn), up from $35bn in 2010-11 and dramatically higher than pre-2005 investment of less than $10bn per year. The biggest destinations of foreign money have been the services industry, telecommunications, computer software and hardware, as well as construction and real estate.

After analysing the facts and figures, we can estimate that there are huge gaps in the market where consumer is ready but retailers are barely available.[2]Today, there is no national multibrand consumer durable retailing chain in India, also there is no children's product retailing chain in India, opening up huge opportunities in modern retail. Hence, The Investments are undoubtedly considered as one of the biggest opportunity provider of employment in India and stands as an important value proposition. Also, it provides a new position for effectiveness and efficiency of Indian economy through integrated global Market.

Year	1999	2002	2005	2009	2010	2013(expected)
Total Retail (in billion INR)	7000	8250	10000	18450	19500	24000
Organised retail (in billion INR)	50	150	350	920	1350	2400
Share of Organised retail	0.70%	1.80%	3.50%	5.00%	7.00%	10.00%

Source: www.nielsen.com

A recent A.T. Kearney annual Global Retail Development Index (GRDI)[3] confirmed India as the most attractive market for retail investment for a third consecutive year. This led to the most awaited result of the century, the FDI inflow in the Indian retail market.

LITERATURE REVIEW

Currently, India is one of the best destinations for Investment. Investors across the globe are trying to exploit the innumerous opportunities in the country. Long after 1991, this is the time when a lot of changes and economic developments can take place.(Koshy Joseph ,Partner, Joseph and Joseph Law)

Focussing on the Retail Sector, It has been in the focus since last 10 years. There has been excitement and eagerness in the Industry with respect to the quick changes that takes place in this Industry.

A lot of reforms, policies and strategies helped in figuring out the best government policies to shape this sector.[4]

It is indeed important to know that, a huge chunk of this market comprises of unorganised players locally operating in the market. There are Mom and Pop stores, general stores, small convenience shops and pavement vendors etc. These stores are very prevalent in the Tier urban rural markets as well as the one shop point in the rural Indian Market.The Indian Council for Research on International Economic Relations (ICRIER) study (M. Joseph and N. Soundararajan, 2009) has shown that hardly 1.7 per cent of small shops have closed down due to competition from organized retail.

Also, on the other hand are the upcoming organised retail stores like Easy Day, Reliance Fresh and many more which are trying to lure the consumer with their many offerings and every day low price. These retail stores are included in a more organised trade by licensed vendors backed by huge corporate houses of the country.India stands out as an example for the late coming of modern organized retail in emerging markets and also for the kind of restrictions placed on foreign investments in retail. The arrival of modern retail in developing countries occurred in three successive waves (Reardon and Hopkins, 2006; Reardon and Berdegue, 2007).[5]

In lieu of the same Commerce ministry in its FDI notification provided that retail sales outlets may be set up only in cities with a population of more than 10 lakh as per 2011 Census. As calculated by ZRG, there are only 45 cities in the country having a population of more than 10 lakh. However, states which do not have any city above 10 lakh, population are not counted here.

The FDI enabling policy has also given full freedom to states to take a call on either allowing or rejecting foreign retailers to operate in their states.

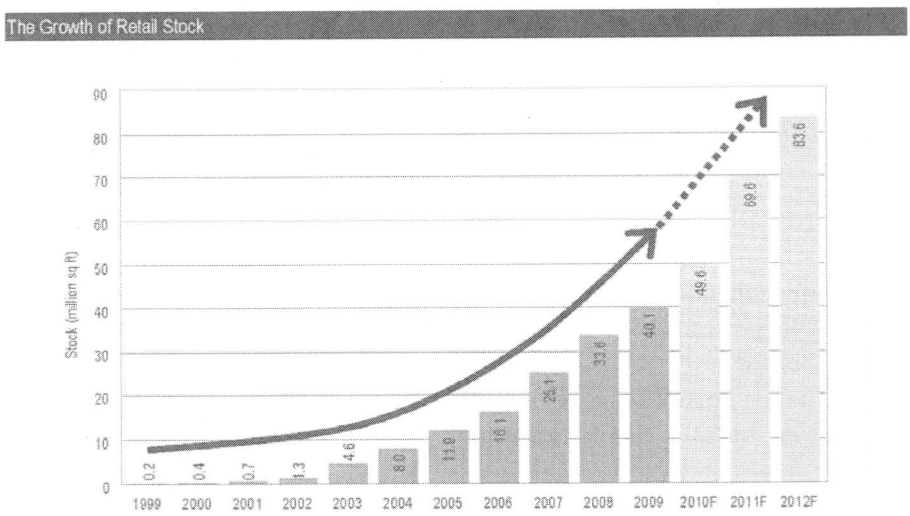

Source: http://www.edelweiss.in

Indian retailers were aware of the great market potential of the country, yet they ignored the fact that there is diversified demand culture and varying customer base in the nation. This resulted in failed organisations even when they had the best models of operation. Also, there were poor labour laws and no incentives for people working in this sector.Papola (2006) has shown that unlike the organised sector, the unorganised sector is characterised by poor working conditions and lack of social security. He suggested that policies should promote organised sector employment.

One such example is discount shopping, which is still an untapped, unorganised and fragmented market. The shopkeepers treat the whole population as one and hence lack the knowledge of customer's perceptions at various stages.Mishra (2007), The Indian market has seen vast changes in political, economic and social environment which has a great impact on consumption.

In between all this political happening, it is also important to understand what the Industry thinks about multi branding retail. Following are the views of some of the key industry experts on FDI in India.

"Opening up foreign investments will bring in funds required for expansion of the nascent modern retail sector in India. The market opportunity is large and we do not see much impact at a national level from new players. We support opening up of the sector to FDI. Most of the opposition is related to the food sector, where stakeholders are not sure of its impact on suppliers and on agriculture. Specifically for the food sector, the government may adopt a calibrated approach of opening it up to FDI."

Mr. Kishore Biyani, Managing Director, Pantaloon Retail

"To be successful in organized retail, we have to necessarily invest in backward integration of the supply chain as well as infrastructure by way of reprocessing centers, distribution centers, etc. All players in this sector need to fund growth and fund the investment in backend infrastructure. FDI can be a game changer by allowing incumbents access to lower cost funding. In my view, those who oppose FDI have not necessarily taken into account the experience in other countries, where rise in organized retail has not led to the demise of local traders, who have also grown. Rather, it has led to benefits to farmers, who get another more transparent market for their product as well as improvement in supply side infrastructure"

Mr Thomas Varghese, CEO, Aditya Birla Retail

"FDI can be a game changer. There is huge demand – the consumer wants modernization of retail. Incumbents do not have the balance sheet strength to support long-term transformational needs. There is need for more equity infusion in the sector Developing countries like India need a strong manufacturing base to fulfill demand. Retailers need to make available good quality products at reasonable prices and yet make a profit. FDI can enable increased capital allocation for the sector and enable development of a manufacturing base and a backend. Opposition to FDI is due to the perception that the big foreigner kills the small Indian; the truth is that the big Indian can also kill the small Indians. Restriction on FDI is being projected as safeguarding the jobs in small retail, but actually there is little job creation happening in small retail now. FDI should be allowed, but the sector should be opened up gradually to gauge the impact and initiate any corrective steps as we move along"

Mr. B S Nagesh, Vice Chairman, Shoppers Stop

MODERN RETAIL IN INDIA- ANALYSIS

The descriptive research methodology has been used to collect the data. To evaluate the overall position of the entry of FDI in multi brand retail in India, secondary data has been collected from various published sources and websites from the year 1999 to few assumptions for the future. Interpretation of the data is more on qualitative terms than on quantitative terms.

A lot has been said and written about what foreign direct investment can do. The arguments either lie on the side that FDI is a fortune wheel or it is a destroyer of many livelihoods. The common thread between above arguments is that they are low on facts and high on judgmental opinions. Thus, the various opinions create a lot of confusion in the market and hence somewhere affects the consumer too.

Today FDI retail has become more of a political fiasco gathering all the hype and media across the nation. In reality, there is neither a need to be too happy or too sad, as the fact states the presence of Modern FDI in India.

The government has flaunted highly on the benefits and necessity of FDI in retail, to sell the policy to the Indian population. With boastings like huge employment generation, a revolution in infrastructure and supply chain and a large share of profits to the SMEs and farmers, the government of India somehow succeeded in gaining the mind share of the consumer.

After analysing these promises, the results on the table says that a full-fledged modern retail would take approximately 5-10 years.

In most newly developed markets, modern trade accounts for only 20-25 percent of all retail. Amidst this, India is already at 8% which is a significantly large number[6], how much the new retail forms can encash this market.

IMPACT OF FDI IN DIFFERENT SEGMENTS

Small Manufacturers: There will be limited effect of FDI on the small manufacturers in India, as retailers across the world like to work with small group of selected vendors to create economies of scale. In this way, they create a huge supplier base.[7]

Kirana Stores: Again, the impact of FDI on kirana stores will be very limited for a simple reason that they operate in small towns and rural India and cater to the 66.66% of the Indian Household. Modern Retail on the other hand is targeting the top income layers in urban cities. Although, many Kirana stores will specialise and modify themselves to modernize, a lot of them will morph and consolidate with other stores. Facilities like Home delivery and quick service will set up new benchmarks for these mom and pop stores.

Infrastructure and Cold Chains: There will be very little effect of FDI on the domestic Cold chains, as each retailer will invest only for what his own business requires and hence the scope in the short run is not very convincing.

SMEs and Farmers: Modern retailers are interested in saving every bit of cost. Hence, FDI inflows are not going to make any bigger changes in the SMEs lifecycle. Big retailers are planning to have consolidated vendors for their requirements. According to the estimates a large hypermarket is likely to have no more than 2500 vendors, and apparel producers have no more than 100. So, there won't be more than 20000 SMEs with turnover of Rs 50 lakh to Rs

2 Crore doing the entire Job.

For the Farmers in the country, the situation again is not something magical. To supply everyday vegetable to the top 40 cities, 2 lakh hectares of vegetable farm will be needed. This comprises just a small fraction of the 11 million hectares of vegetable farms India has. 2 lakh hectares of vegetable need just two lakh farmers at best.

Jobs: Jobs will have the largest and the most positive effect from the FDI in retail. A new skilled category called retail jobs will be created and hence the wage rates and skill sets of the employees will improve.

Investment of $12 billion will generate direct employment of about 700000 jobs. This will include the front end and the back end support required in the retail business. Another 200000 jobs are expected in the supply chain and vendor community. These figures are not static, but will grow as the turnover of the business increases.

The only drawback expected is that most of these jobs will be contract type jobs and not employee based with full benefits. To curtail this drawback, companies are assuring a guaranteed pay check and regular income to the workers.

FINANCIAL VIABILITY

Before getting into the number crunches for the absorption of money in the FDI retail, we need to understand the target market for this segment. We need to find the consumers in areas where FDI is permitted and the one who have the money and desire to buy from these big stores. We also need to estimate the approximate breakeven time for the investors in retail market.

Close to nine types of retail formats form the pillars of modern retail. These includes cash and carry format that serves small retailers, home, fashion, deep discounters, hypermarkets, speciality, consumer durables and many more.

Following is a list of retailers with a presence in many parts of the world and would want to get into the Indian market.

Supermarket	Tesco	Walmart	SPAR	Waitrose	
Hypermarket	Walmart	Tesco	Auchan	SPAR	Carrefour
Cash & Carry	Walmart	Carrefour	Metro		
Department Stores	Target	Central(Thailand)	Lotte	Bloomingdales	Debenhams
Home	Ikea	Bed Bath & Beyond	Home Depot	Kingfisher	
Fashion	Uniqlo	Banana Republic	Aeropostale	H&M	Billabong
Consumer Durables	Best Buy	Apple	Fortress	Samsung Digital Stores	
Speciality	Watsons	Boots	Victoria's Secret		

All the above brands sustain in the world for some unique key parameters like their strategic market positioning, unique offering and the price quality range. The analysis for the entire above brand included the assessment of the consumer base for each of these specialities.

The Indian household on the basic of income is divided into three sections, Section A, B & C. The A class combines the top 10% of income earners, B combines the 33% of income earners while C makes the rest 60% of the market.

(a) Hypermarkets like Walmart, Tesco and apparel discounters like Target have the pocket to target the top 60% of urban households by income.

(b) Market players like Bed Bath and Beyond, Victoria's secret etc are able to target only top 33% of the income earners.

(c) Other Fashion and speciality stores may just cater to the top 10% of all income earners.

To cater all the demand, there is an opportunity to add $25 billion in revenues to the $45 billion that already exists. As per current estimates, retailers collectively need to invest approximately $12 billion, which includes development of real estate and infrastructure for the desired store formats.

A big thrust for the market comes from the fact that the incomes of the top 30% in urban India will double in about seven years and hence a better market is expected till the next decade.

CRITICS TO MODERN RETAIL

The real estate roadblock is one critical ingredient in delaying the set-up of modern retail stores. There are many reasons as to why investing in modern retail is not a cash cow in the short run.[8]

(a) FDI has a huge disadvantage of political rattling, and there is a threat that different states will pose different conditions on the entry and exit barriers for these retailers due to political instability in the country.

(b) There is heterogeneity in consumer preference in India, while all these big stores are known for standardization. A country where language and culture changes every 100 miles, how these big players are going to manage the demand and supply of the individual states.

(c) The gross margin return on investment per square foot in India is comparatively less as in comparison to the more developed markets because there is less money in a given area and the structure of demand is also complex.[9]

(d) Sales per square foot to the prices of real estate have a huge difference in the Indian market and hence it adds to the criticality on investment in this sector in the short run.

(e) Solution to soaring real estate prices is not very attractive, as going to outskirts is not viable because of expensive fuel and poor public transport in India.

MARKET TRENDS & OPPORTUNITIES

The highest contributor to the retail sector would be the Food and grocery segment with the contribution margin of 60% , there is minimum penetration of organized retail in this area.On the other side, penetration of modern retail is maximum with contribution margin of 23% . Apart from this retail in wellness, e-tailing, speciality and fashion are growing at a rapid pace.[10]

According to the policies and strategies by government now, Multinational companies can invest upto 51% to open stores in 10 states and UTs which have so far agreed to implement the decision. The decision to allow multibrand retailers to open stores rests with the state government.

The minimum amount to be brought by the foreign investor would be $100 million and outlets may be set up only in cities with a population of more than 10 lakhs.

The decision is a right step and will go a long way in capital infusion and is expected to strengthen the farmer's community.

Following are some key trends strengthening the presence of modern retail in India.

(a) 48% of income is spent on food and grocery, which is one of the highest in the world.

(b) Personalized services, Customisation and Urbanisation have developed huge untapped market in the Industry.

(c) Readymade clothes and western outfits are growing at 40-45% giving a boost to the apparel industry.

(d) Accessible and affordable fashion is thr new trend in the Industry,

(e) Pharmacy retailing is another big area where retailing is almost negligible as of now.

(f) The Consumer durable market is estimated to grow at a CAGR of 18% which currently operates on $ 6.5 billion.

(g) Wellness, Furnishing and speciality are leading the home furnishing market.

CONCLUSION

There is an uneven distribution of income in India. Hence, there are a lot of stress points in balancing the macro economics of the nation. The food prices in the country are increasing due to less supply and increased exports which creates deficit in the country, thus increasing inflation. There is a need for higher purchasing power of population and hence higher wages. There are constraints of resources which lead to inefficiency in making a robust economic system.[11]

A balancing act is required to maintain the various stake holders, local and global in the whole retail scenario. There is a need to maintain the credibility without putting pressure on the economic growth of the nation. Also, Feeds to the inflationary process shouldn't be fulfilled by the lower wages and disproportionate growth of the labours working in the Industries.

After the critical analysis of the modern retail, Investors and bureaucrats are thinking twice about their investments. The analysis isn't held to depress people but to help them in getting the right picture today.[12]It would be wrong to say that modern retail is not a profitable venture; the reality states that it just needs harder work and longer duration to flourish the ripened results.

Many local businessmen are trying a shot to enter in the modern retail business along with the foreign partners because of power of investing and getting into a high margin business. Over the next five to ten years, India is going to witness a revolutionary change in the industry with strong foundations, new skilled and semi-skilled jobs, more joint ventures and more consolidations.

REFERENCES

[1] Jia, Panle, 2008. "What Happens When Wal-Mart Comes to Town: An Empirical Analysis of the

[2] Discount Retailing Industry,"Econometrica, Vol. 76, No. 6, pp. 1263–1316.

[3] http://www.atkearney.com/consumer-products-retail/global-retail-development-index

[4] Chakraborty .C; Nunnenkamp .P: Economic Reforms, Foreign Direct Investmentand Its Economic Effects in India , Kiel Working Paper No. 1272 , March 2006.

[5] BaskaranKamladevi, 2012 January, FDI in India's Multibrand retail- Boon or Bane, Universal Journal of Management and Social Science. Vol 2, No 1.

[6] FDI in Retail Sector in India, Department of Consumer Affairs, Ministry of Consumer Affairs, Public and Food Department, Government of India.

[7] The New FDI policy in Retail in India: ISSN 2229 – 3795 Asian Journal of Management Research, Promises, Problems and Perceptions Chandu. K. L Research Scholar, Jawaharlal Nehru Technological University, Kakinada

[8] Sameena Khan &FayazAhamed., (2011), Foreign Direct Investment in India: Challenges and Opportunities in Multi-brand Retail Sector, International Journal Of Research In Commerce And Management, 2(1), pp 97-98.

[9] Raghunandan D. 2010, 'Fdi in Organised Retail: A Lose-Lose Game' India Current Affairs, Economy, posted on 17-07-2010.

[10] Popli, G. S. and Singh, Sima, Impact of Multi Brand Foreign Direct Investment in Retail Sector in India (May 9, 2012). Available at SSRN: http://ssrn.com/abstract=2055033

[11] Foreign Direct Investment in Indian Retail Sector – An Analysis Author: Dr. Usha. N. Patil ISSN No :2230-7850 RNI : MAHMUL/2011/38595

[12] Singhal, Arvind, 2009, Indian Retail: The road ahead, Retail biz, available at www.etretailbiz.com, last visited 14th Oct.2010.

Influence of Strategy on Firm Performance in Multinational Tech Firms

K. Vijay Kumar and R.P. Sundarraj

Department of Management Studies, IIT-Madras, Chennai

ABSTRACT

Tech firms need to constantly make seemingly contrarian strategic decisions of either pursuing innovation or cost efficiency, or at times, both. Panel studies are undertaken to investigate the impact of this strategic mix on firm performance using Porter's generic strategy framework. Firm performance is a function of the position on the Porter's grid, with outlays driving profitability and valuations, while patenting and market value exhibit tight coupling. 'Stuck-in-the-middle' firms are the best performers, contradicting Porter's postulate that such firms will underperform. The investigations span across the US, Europe and Asia, the bastions of innovation, and this heterogeneity of data lends itself to robust results.

INTRODUCTION

Tech firms incessantly pursue divergent corporate goals of pursuing short term profitability or long term market value. The strategies adopted by firms to achieve these corporate goals could be equally divergent. We investigate the impact of this strategic mix on firm performance by using Porter's generic strategy framework. A scholarly work that has received widespread attention and recognition in the Strategic Management area and beyond is Porter's (1980) typology of generic competitive strategies: Cost leadership and differentiation (Datta, 2009). The Porter (1980) model of generic strategies in terms of simplicity, accuracy, and generalizability, captures much of the complexity inherent in strategic intents (Miller and Dess, 1993). In this study, aspecific Porter's framework that is appropriate for the tech sector is developed to examine firm performance under different Porter's strategies.

One dimension of Porter's strategy framework is cost leadership measured as output (revenue) per unit direct cost and reflects the cost efficiency of the firm. For the other strategy dimension,Porter (1980) defines differentiation rather narrowly and equates it with uniqueness. One of the many forms of differentiation therefore is one founded on innovation and technology (Spanos et al., 2004). As Hambrick (1983) argued, innovation is primarily an indicator of differentiation and this differentiation of business is achieved through technologicalprotection achieved through patenting measured by patent counts (Hambrick, 1983).Several tech firms attempt to be different through innovation that is legally secure;patent counts fit the bill as a discriminating yardstick.

We have used two disparate measures consisting of profitability and market value to provide a holistic picture of firm performance. While profitability has been a very popular measure (Geroski et al., 1993; Cefis, 2003), others have used market value as a long term value measure (Anandarajan et al., 2008; Hall et al., 2005; Cockburn and Griliches, 1988). While the management would be interested in profitability, the market watchers look at the valuation of the firm.

The backdrop of this investigation is the tumultuous period of 1990-2009. It was a period that witnessed the disruptive advent of internet, an upsurge in mobile communication and a paradigm shift in personal computing. The question we are asking is which of the Porterian strategies created value and what kind of value. In order to discriminate between the Porterian strategies, we have sought answers to the following research questions:

(i) Do Porter's strategies influence firm performance?

(ii)Is the Porter's postulate that 'stuck-in-the-middle' firms underperform valid?

LITERATURE REVIEW

While the concept of generic strategies is well established, the credit for articulating and developing them into atestable typology goes to Porter (1980) (Kotha andVadlamani, 1995). We build on this much analyzed framework to investigate the impact of innovation and outlays on firm performance in the technology sector. Our choice of the Porter's model was dictated by the fact that the empirical support and the construct validity of Porter's typology have been established by several researchers (Hambrick, 1983; Dess and Davis, 1984, Miller and Friesen, 1986).Thus, the core constructs of Porter's genericstrategies seem robust (Kotha and Vadlamani, 1995).

Porter's (1980, 1985) typology of genericcompetitive strategies has essentially two dimensions-Cost leadership and Differentiation (Datta, 2009). According to Porter, cost leadership is "when the firm sets out to be the low cost producer in its industry" and differentiation strategy is "when a firm seeks to be unique in its industry along some dimensions that are widely valued by buyers" (Porter, 1985). The Cost leadership dimension has seen analyzed extensively in the literature (Kiechel, 1981; Wright, 1987; Spanos et al., 2004; Richardson, 1988; Hambrick, 1983; Mathur, 1986; Wensley, 1981). The other dimension, Differentiation, has probably seen even more interpretations in the literature (Dickson and Ginter, 1987; Dertouzos et al., 1989; Kotter 1995; Hambrick 1983; Spanos et al., 2004; Gale, 1992; Hambrick, 1983;Oskarsson & Sjoberg, 1994; Giddens-Emig, 1983). In our study, the efficiency of management of direct outlay is used as a measure of cost leadership, while patent-centric innovation captures differentiation, and this kind of differentiation is highly criticalto survive and prosper in high technology markets (Datta, 2009).

'Stuck-in-the-middle' firms are those which pursue neither or both of the strategies. Porter (1980) suggests firms attempting at combining both the strategies are likely to underperform (Miller and Dess, 1993) compared to firms which follow one of the strategies (Thornhill and White, 2007; Dess and Davis, 1984). As a part of this study, we will investigate if the original Porter's postulate about 'stuck-in-the-middle' firms is valid or not.

Literature has used different firm performance measures, but we have used two disparate measures (profitability and market value) to provide for a more robust assessment of firm performance. First, profitability has been a very popular short term measure used in the literature (Geroski et al., 1993; Cefis, 2003; Scherer, 1965; Cefis and Ciccarelli, 2005) Second, market value is extensively used as a long term value measure (Anandarajan et al., 2008; Hall et al., 2005; Cockburn and Griliches, 1988; Griliches, 1981) and is viewed as a measure of quality of management and diversity of firm's patent portfolio (Lin et al., 2006).

Our effort is to buildon the previous research efforts to seek answers to the research gaps that we have identified (table 1).

Table 1. Research Gaps

Research gaps	Proposed method to bridge the gap
RQ 1 - Firm performance under Porter's generic strategies	Estimating average firm performance for each of Porter's 4-quadrants and then performing ANOVA between the 4- quadrants
RQ 2 - Validating the Porter's original postulate of *'stuck-in-the-middle'* firms underperforming	Estimating firm performance of 'stuck-in-the-middle' firms and then performing ANOVA w.r.t to the two quadrants which pursue one of the two Porter's strategies

THEORY AND HYPOTHESES

The original Porter's model postulated in 1980 is extended and adapted to create a framework that facilitates our investigation of examining firm performance in the tech sector under different strategy mixes. Porter's (1980) typology of generic strategies seems appropriately broad (Hambrick, 1983) that allows context specific frameworks. We develop the metrics and cut offs for the Porter's framework that results in a 2×2 Porter's grid that facilitates the entire data set of 400 firms × 20 years to be marked on this grid. Firm performances in the four quadrants are estimated and significant differences between them are computed.

PORTER'S GENERIC MODEL

With efficient supply chains being business-critical, cost leadership in the tech sector takes the hue of cost efficiency. In other words, for every unit of input *direct* (labor + material) cost, we must assess the output (revenue)-how well the output is maximized for each unit direct cost. In the field of technology, differentiation largely implies unique products/services achieved through innovation (Datta, 2009) which is proxied by patent counts. Porter (1985) suggests that differentiators are more profitable than cost leaders (Hambrick 1983; Peters and Waterman, 1982). Differentiation achieved through innovation is a source of monopolistic rents and allows greater returns (Fontana and Moriniello, 2011; Kotabe et al., 2002) and these returns are greater if the innovation is protected by legal instruments like patents. One way of evaluating the returns to innovative activity is by relating it to the market value of firms' tangible and intangible assets (Hall, 1998; Toivanen, 2002).

A representation of differentiators and cost leaders of Porter's model is shown in Figure 1(a).

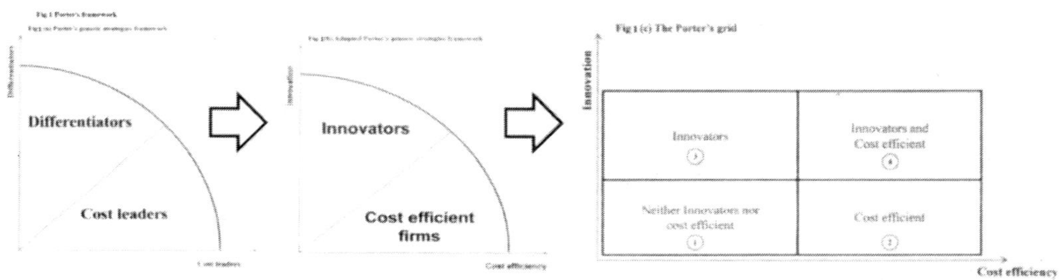

Fig. 1 Porter's Framework

With tech firms being heavily dependent on efficient supply chains, direct cost management reflectscost leadership, while patent-centric innovation (patent counts) captures the differentiation dimension. To develop the cost efficiency measure, we compute revenue generated per unit COGS (direct material cost + direct labor cost). To quote Hambrick (1983), *'The cost efficiency is the degree to which inputs per unit of output are low'*and is expressed as:

$$cost\ efficiency = \frac{revenue}{COGS}$$

The original Porter's model is transformed into as shown in Fig 1(b).The above framework needs to be expanded to provide for instances where (1) innovation and cost efficiency coexist and (2) firms which are neither innovators nor cost leaders. This enhanced Porter's model is represented as follows in Fig 1(c). Our intent is to examine firm performance in each of the quadrants to ascertain any significant difference between them. Porter (1980) suggests firms attempting at combining both the strategies will result in the firms getting stuck-in-the-middle and are likely to underperform (Miller and Dess, 1993) compared to firms which follow one of the strategies (Dess and Davis, 1984; Thornhill and White, 2007).

This leads us to formulate the following hypotheses:

Hypothesis 1: *Cost efficient firms are more profitable than innovators*

Hypothesis 2: *Innovators have higher market capitalization than cost efficient firms*

Hypothesis 3: *Stuck-in-the-middle-firms' (firms which are both innovators and cost efficient) are least profitable*

The complete research framework is provided in Fig. 2.

H1: *Cost efficient firms and innovators differ in their profitability*
H2: *Significant difference exists in the market value of cost efficient firms and innovators*
H3: *'Stuck-in-the-middle-firms' (firms which are both innovators and cost efficient) are least profitable*

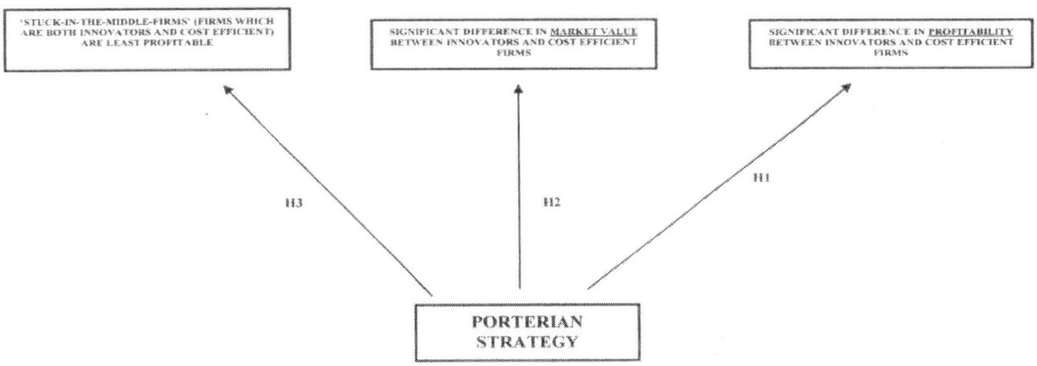

Fig. 2. Resarch Framework and Bypotheses

DATA

All the firms chosen for analysis were listed global tech companies. The companies have had their main line of business in Semiconductors, Wireless communication (excluding service providers), Electronics, Software or Computers. The investigations spanned across the US, Europe and Asia, the heartlands of innovation, and this heterogeneity of the data lent itself to robust results. Patent count data was obtained through Thompson's innovation tool, citation counts through USPTO, and financial data from Thompson Reuter's Datastream. Nearly 400 listed tech firms were chosen from 16 diverse segments to provide a well represented data set that reflected the composition of the tech sector. A panel data set was then constructed by compiling financial and patent data for these firms for a 20 year period of 1990-2009.

METHODOLOGY

Cutoffs are established for the Porter's two dimensions and a 2×2 Porter's grid was developed. The dataset involved financial and patent data of 400 tech firms for 20 years. Using the cutoffs, data is segregated into the 4 quadrants, and for each one of the data element, firm performance measures (profitability and market value) are plotted on the corresponding quadrant of the Porter's grid. Because of wide heterogeneity in both the variables (more so with patent counts), frequency distribution of both these variables was first developed and then the weighted average of these distributions was computed. The weighted averages so calculated were used as discriminating cutoff values of patent counts and cost efficiency to develop the four quadrants of the Porter's grid.

To test *hypotheses 1, 2 & 3,* the average profitability and market value of each of the quadrants is then calculated and subsequently tested using ANOVA measures to see if there is significant difference in the profitability (and market value) between the quadrants, including 'stuck-in-the-middle' firms.

RESULTS AND DISCUSSIONS

The challenge is to have a cut off to discriminate innovators and 'non-innovators' in such a manner that it reflects the distribution of patents in the tech sector. We chose to calculate the weighted average at 70% cumulative frequency (which equals 29 patents) and this cut off categorizes 30% as innovators and 70% 'non-innovators' which appears as a reasonable representation of the distribution in the tech sector.The frequency distribution of cost efficiency is fairly homogeneous as seen in the frequency distribution for which the weighted average is 2.25 and discriminates 30% as cost efficient and 70% as cost inefficient roughly in the same proportion as innovators and non-innovators.

The Porter's grid with these values is shown in Fig. 3.

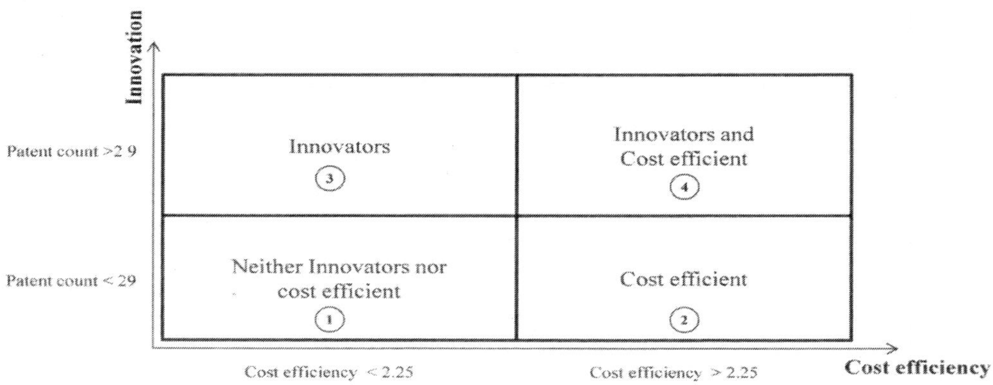

Fig. 3. Porter's Grid with Cutoff Values

Hypothesis 1 & 2

Figure 4 shows the profitability and market value of the four segments.

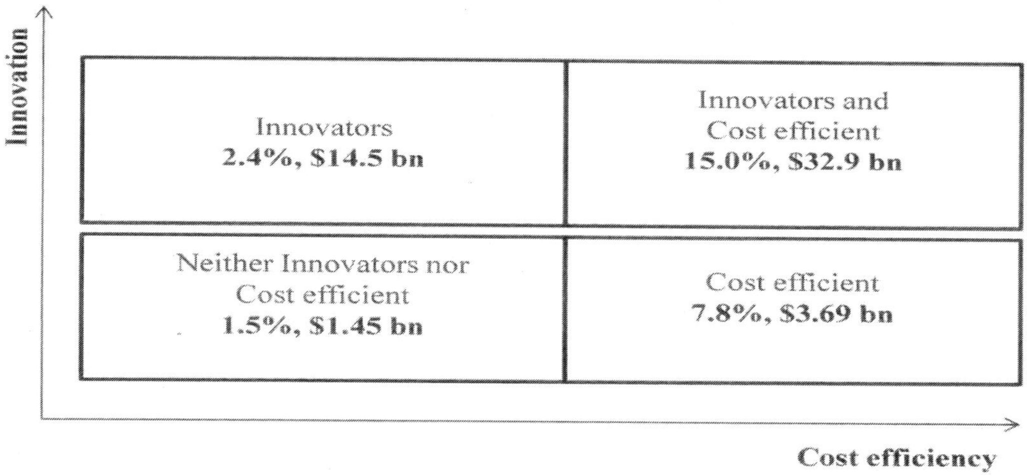

Fig. 4. Profitability and Market Value of Innovators and Cost Leaders

The ANOVA results (Table 2) yield F-values for both profitability and market value far in excess of the critical values (*p*<*0.000*) indicating that the mean profits and market values in the 4-segments differ significantly, validating hypothesis 1&2.

Table 2. Anova Results of Profitability & Market Value of Porter Quadrants

Parameter	F-value	Critical F-value	*p-value*
Profitability	118.7	2.60	*p*<*0.000*
Market value	64.1	2.60	*P*<*0.000*

It is evident that while the cost efficient firms enjoy the highest profitability, innovators enjoy the highest valuations. Cost efficiency does improve valuations, though not to the extent as innovation does.

Hypothesis 3

Figure 4 also indicate that it pays to be "stuck-in-the-middle" and in fact this segment seems to produce the best results contrary to the original Porter's hypothesis of such firms not doing well.

The relentless pursuit of innovation and the tight coupling between patent counts and market value manifests in the innovators enjoying the highest valuations over the last two decades (Fig. 5). The two upper quadrants (the innovator quadrants) enjoy consistently much higher valuations compared to the bottom two quadrants (the cost efficient quadrants) validating the hypothesis that innovation drives valuations.

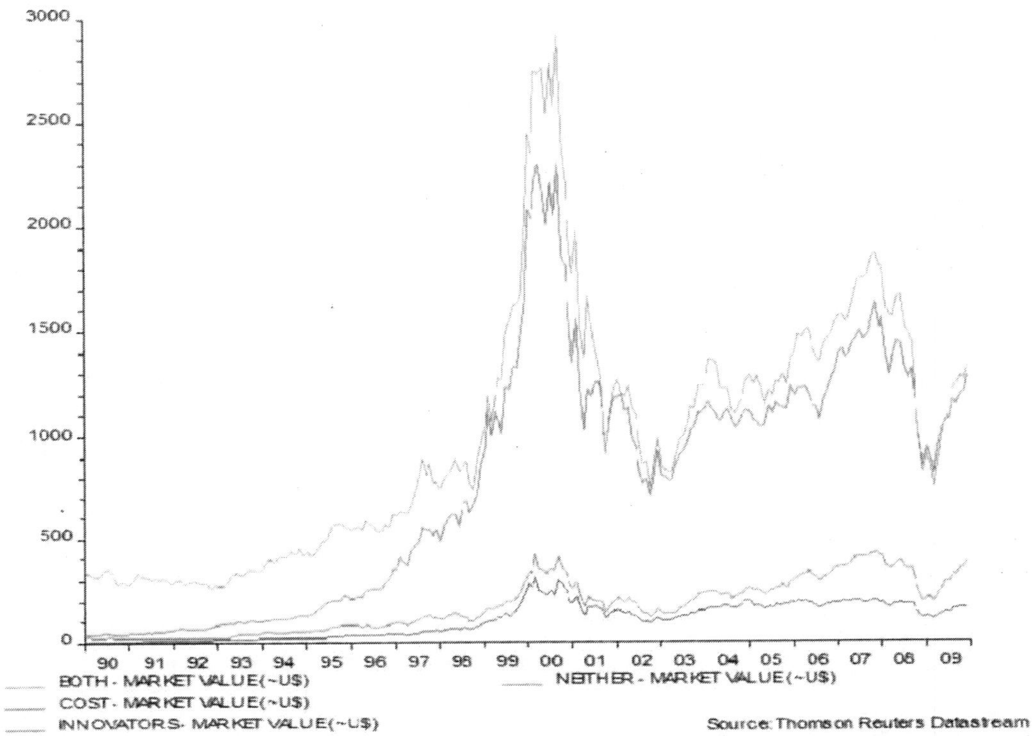

Fig. 5. Market Value of Porter's Four Quadrants

IMPLICATIONS

Table 3 summarizes the important results obtained through the various steps. Innovators (the upper 2 quadrants) enjoy higher valuations while cost efficient firms are more profitable and this has been consistently true for the last 20 years. We can conclude that while innovation is a long-term value builder, outlays determine both valuations and profitability. There are operational limits to the improvement that can be achieved in cost efficiency, while firms' have more leeway in enhancing innovative activity, limited only by the firm's ability to fund patenting endeavors. The fact that innovation leads to positive value accrual encourages managements to look at innovation-led nonlinear growth through organic and inorganic means. Since market value tightly couples with patent counts as can be seen in Fig. 6, patenting activity remains a very strong lever for firms to increase their valuations.

Table 3. Finding and Implications

Key findings	Managerial implications
Firm performance differs depending on the position on the Porter's grid	Firms' strategic mix decides which aspect of firm performance can be maximized.
Cost efficiency drives profitability *and* valuations	Improvement in cost efficiency is twofold - Profitability and valuations
Innovation drives market value	Valuations go up with increase in patenting activity
Innovators are valued *ten times* more than non-innovators; profitability of cost efficient firms is *tenfold* more than inefficient firms	Firms' choice of specific strategies lead to specific value creation
'Stuck-in-the-middle' firms are the best performers-both in profitability and market cap	The best of breed in the tech sector are both innovators and cost efficient.
Firms which pursue neither strategy are the worst performers	Firms with low value add (ex. Distributors) are the worst performers since they neither innovate nor are cost efficient. Firms with high value add usually excel in one of the strategies.
Firms emphasizing innovation with deteriorating cost efficiency in the last two decades	Differentiation through patenting has been pursued by the tech industry as the dominant strategy in the last 20-years; cost efficiency seems to have been given a goby
Firms improve profitability through a lateral movement on the Porter's grid	Firms can improve profitability by controlling costs without increasing innovation activity
Firms improve valuations through an upward movement on the Porter's grid	Firms can improve valuations by innovating more; improvements in cost efficiency further improves market values
Theoretically, there are limits to improving cost efficiency while enhancing innovative activity is boundless	Firms will face operational limits in improving cost efficiency. Enhancing innovative activity is more open ended and is limited only by the firm's wherewithal to fund the patenting endeavors
Overall, the choice of strategy has an impact on firm performance	Firms have at least two strategic levers (patenting or outlays) to improve firm performance

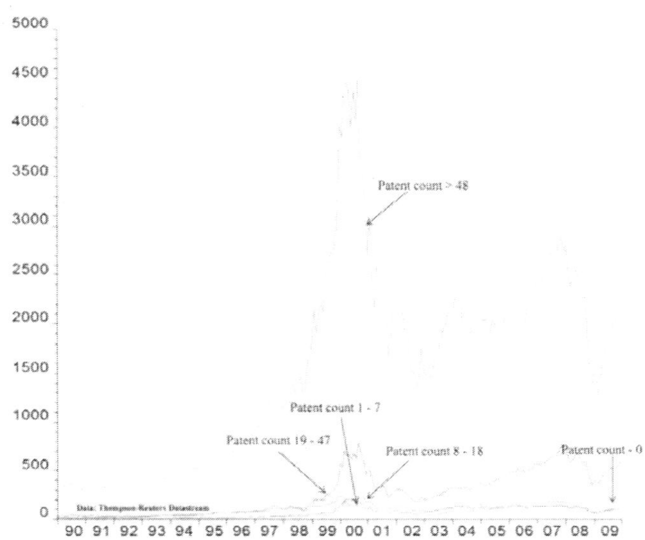

Fig. 6. Market Value (in $ bn) Driven by Patents

Firms improve profitability through a lateral movement, while valuations will improve if firms move upwards. However, it is challenging for firms in the bottom two quadrants to move up to the upper quadrants in a short span since it requires a quantum leap in the level of innovation. This also means increasing the revenue base substantially, since only mid-sized and large firms have the wherewithal to be consistent and large innovators. We also observe that the level of patenting and firm size (revenue) go together (correlation coefficient=0.83, $p<0.000$). A firm needs to have at least billion dollar sales to enter the innovation quadrant.

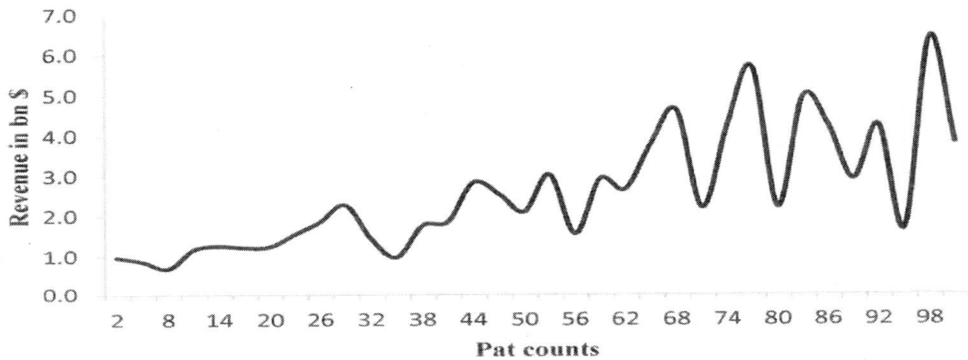

Fig. 7. Firm Size Increases with Patent Count

CONCLUSIONS

Innovation leads to higher valuation while closer monitoring of firms' outlays has a direct bearing on profitability and valuations. The best of breed firms innovate and control outlays *both*to come up with performance that is a cut above the rest. Firms have to choose their strategic moves to improve firm performance, either through a lateral movement on the Porter's grid that improves profitability or move upwards to improve valuations. The results broadly support the conclusion that high end innovation will bring higher valuations, but the activity seems to be restricted to a few large firms; a significant number of tech firms have low levels of innovative activity. Value driver in a large number of tech firms is not innovation.

REFERENCES

[1] Anandarajan, A., C. Chin, H. Chi and P. Lee (2008). 'The effect of innovative activity on firm performance:The experience of Taiwan', *Advances in Accounting, 23*, pp. 1-30.

[2] Cefis, E. (2003). 'Is there persistence in innovative activities?' *International Journal of Industrial Organization, 21*, pp. 489-515.

[3] Cefis, E. and M. Ciccarelli (2005). 'Profit differentials and innovation', *Economics of innovation and new technology, 14* (1), pp. 43-61.

[4] Cockburn, I. and Z. Griliches (1988). 'Industry effects and appropriability measures in the stock market's valuation of R&D and patents', *American Economic Review,* 78 (2), pp. 419-423.

[5] Datta, Y. (2009). 'A Critique Of Porter's Cost Leadership And Differentiation Strategies', 9th Oxford Business & Economics Conference, Oxford, England, June 22-24.

[6] Dess, G. G. and P. S. Davis (1984). 'Porter's generic strategies as determinants of strategic group membership and organizational performance', *Academy of Management Journal,* 27 (3), pp. 467-488.

[7] Fontana, R. and D. Morineillo. (2011). 'Technological leadership and innovation persistence: empirical evidence', *DIME final conference.*

[8] Gale, B. T. (1992). 'Quality comes first when hatching power brands', *Planning Review,* July-August, pp. 4-9.

[9] Geroski et al., P., S. Machin and J. V. Reenen (1993). 'The Profitability of Innovating Firms'. *The RAND Journal of Economics, 24* (2), pp. 198-211.

[10] Giddens-Emig, K. (1983). 'Portfolio planning: A concept in controversy', *Managerial Planning,* November-December, pp. 4-15.

[11] Griliches Z. (1990). 'Patent statistics as economic indicators: a survey', *Journal of economic literature*, Vol. 28, pp. 1661-1707.

[12] Hall, B. H. (1998). "Innovation and Market Value", NIESR conference on Productivity and Competitiveness, London.

[13] Hall, B. H., A. Jaffe and M. Trajtenberg (2005). 'Market value and patent citations', *The Rand journal of economics, 36* (1), pp.16-38.

[14] Hambrick, D. C. (1983). 'High Profit Strategies in Mature Capital Goods Industries: A Contingency Approach', *The Academy of Management Journal,* 26 (4), pp. 687-707.

[15] Kiechel, W. (1981). 'Three (or four, or more) ways to win', *Fortune,* October 5, pp. 139-146.

[16] Kotha, S. and B. L. Vadlamani (1995). 'Assessing generic strategies: an empirical investigation of two competing typologies in discrete manufacturing industries', *Strategic Management journal,* Vol. 16, pp.75-83.

[17] Kotabe, M, S. S. Srinivasan and P. S. Aulakh (2002). 'Multinationality and Firm Performance: The Moderating Role of R&D and Marketing Capabilities',*Journal of International Business Studies,* 33(1), pp. 79-97.

[18] Lin, B., Y. Lee, and S. Hung (2006). 'R&D intensity and commercialization orientation effects on financial performance', *Journal of Business Research*, Vol. 59, pp. 679–685.

[19] Miller A. and G. G. Dess (1993). 'Assessing Porter's (1980) model in terms of its generalizability, accuracy and simplicity', *Journal of Management studies,*30 (4), pp. 553-585.

[20] Miller, D. and P. H. Friesen (1980). 'Porter's (1980) Generic Strategies and Performance: An Empirical Examination with American Data', *Organizational studies*, Vol. 7(1), pp. 37-55.

[21] Oskarsson, O. and N. Sjoberg. (1994). 'Technology analysis and competitive strategy: The case of mobile telephones', *Technology Analysis & Strategic Management*, 6 (1), 3-19.

[22] Peters, T. and R. H. Waterman (1982). 'In search of excellence', New York: Harper & Row.

[23] Porter, M. E. (1980). 'Competitive strategy', New York: Free Press.

[24] Porter. M. E. (1985). 'Competitive advantage', New York: Free Press.

[25] Scherer, F. M. (1965). 'Firm Size, Market Structure, Opportunity, and the Output of Patented Inventions', *The American Economic Review, 55* (5), pp. 1097-1125.

[26] Spanos, Y. E., G. Zaralis and S. Lioukas. (2004). 'Strategy and industry effects on profitability:evidence from Greece', *Strategic Management Journal*, Vol. 25, pp. 139-165.

[27] Thornhill, S. and R. E. White (2007). 'Strategic purity: a multi-industry evaluation of pure vs. hybrid busness strategies', *Strategic Management journal*, Vol. 28, pp. 553-561.

[28] Toivanen, O., P. Stoneman and D. Bosworth (2002). 'Innovation and the Market Value of UK Firms, 1989-1995', *Oxford Bulletin of Economics and Statistics,* Vol. 64, pp. 39-61.

[29] Wright, P. (1987). 'A refinement of Porter's strategies', *Strategic Management Journal*, Vol. 8, pp. 93-101.

Innovative Business Model for Rural Turf: The Holy Grail for Companies of the Morrow

Amit Agrawal, Amit Kumar and Krishanveer Singh

Department of Management, GLA University, Mathura, Uttar Pradesh

> 'Rural Markets are future battle Grounds'
>
> 'Future lies with those companies who see poor as their customer.' – *C K Prahalad*
>
> 'To get rich, sell to poor'. – *Pradeep Kashyap*

ABSTRACT

The South Asian, preferably the Indian rural scenario remains largely an untapped one. Although this is bound to be changed in the times ahead keeping in view the tectonic shift one is witnessing in and around the Indian agro-business scene vis-à-vis the recent trends in FDI in the retail sector as propounded by the present government. In this context, it becomes even more significant for the companies that they should be differentiated from those lesser prepared for these developments. The winning organizations would be differentiated from the losing ones more so on the basis of their exploits of the rural turf. This holds significance owing to the fact that the saturation levels being witnessed in the urban market has compelled them to look otherwise, that is, towards greener pastures (in literal sense). This phenomenon derives its genesis from the philosophy of west versus east marketing. Further, it is to be comprehended that such strategies which have worked in the urban context won't find many takers in the rural setting because what they need instead are customized solutions for their unique requirements (say cooking oil pocket pouches). Thus, such companies which would go the extra mile vis-à-vis offering unique or out-of-the-box products (such as Godrej Chotukool cooling solution) would be hailed by the rural clientele who would be driving the next Indian consumption wave, which is set to happen with time, sooner than later. All this and much more would be finding mention in this paper where the authors would try to come up with a unique model to present an alternative approach towards capturing the potential of the rural market to the hilt thereby acting as a win-win scenario of all the stakeholders involved.

KNOWING THE INDIAN MILIEU

With more than 70 crores people living in rural areas, about two-third of Indian workforce is engaged in agriculture and related activities which contribute a rather dismal 29 percent towards India's Gross Domestic Product (GDP). The urban consumer used to be the cynosure of retailers until recent times. Not many efforts were made towards placating the rural markets. However, that has certainly changed with time. The momentum of development is accelerating in rural India which has been well supported by increase in purchasing power. Scientific agriculture, changing life style and consumption patterns have happened due to rise in education levels, improved means of transportation, social mobility, communication and mass media such as television.

CHANGES MARKING THE RURAL MARKET

Previously, only a selected few rural households preferred branded goods. Big companies used to procrastinate opening centers in rural markets but not anymore. Today, rural markets are crucial for every marketer. Earlier, marketers used to think that cinema advertorials, mobile campaigns, and wall sketches would attract rural customer but thanks to television and technical revolution, today a rural customer is quite literate in every sense.

The richest of urban Indians and the poorest of rural India are the extremes of the Indian economy. The rest are fairly comparable, showing that a meaningful scale is possible by skillful combination of urban and rural consumers. This holds true especially for well-progressive states and connected geographies. Past years of good GDP growth have significantly increased middle-income households and high-income households in rural India. Even moderate GDP growth will double the high and upper-middle income groups.

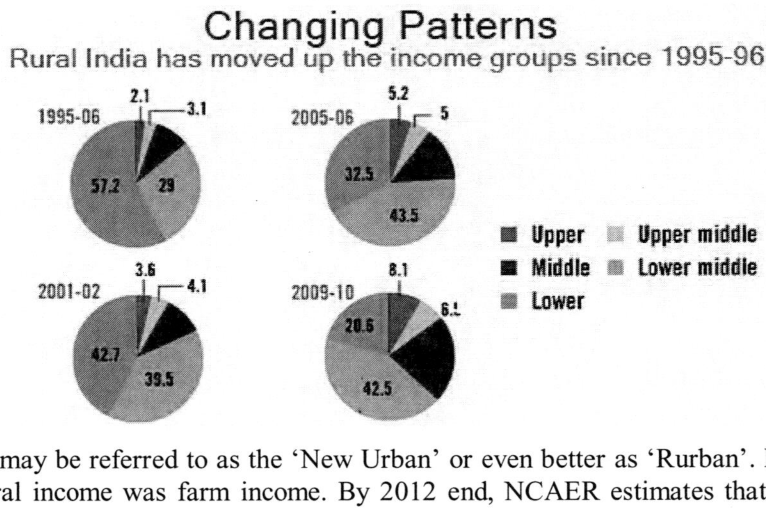

'Rural' may be referred to as the 'New Urban' or even better as 'Rurban'. In 1980, two-thirds of rural income was farm income. By 2012 end, NCAER estimates that the situation will be exactly the opposite. According to Indian Revenue Service data, colour television sets penetration improved by 7% during 2005-08 and packaged biscuits went up by 10%. Aggressive categories such as shampoo even increased by a staggering 37%. It is important to comprehend that even a meager 1% rise in rural India purchase ability means a lot. A 1% increase in refrigerator penetration, over a five-year period, means that over 1.5 million refrigerators were sold. The owners of new C TVs in the past three years are equivalent to the population of Sweden or half of Australia! So, even at this *unimpressive* rate, rural India unleashes enormous consumption power and opens new vistas. **The point worth pondering is - a small percentage of a large number is a large number. One percent of rural India is 1.4 million households, 10% is at least 10 million households.**

IMMENSE OPPORTUNITIES EMBARKING ON THE RURAL WAY

To gauge its significance, the Indian rural market is almost twice as large as the entire market of USA or Russia coupled with huge growth initial signals, exhibited by industry specific facts, as given below:

FMCG: Rural consumers spend around 13 per cent of their income, the second highest after food (35 per cent), on FMCG, as per an RMAI study. The FMCG industry in India was worth around US$ 16.03 billion in August 2008 and the rural market accounted for a robust 57 percent of the FMCG market. Moreover, according to an ASSOCHAM study, FMCG is expected to hop by 40 percent rurally as against 25 per cent in urban areas.

Retail: The rural retail market is currently estimated at US$112 billion, or around 40 per cent of the US$ 280 billion retail market. Major domestic retailers like AV Birla, ITC, Godrej, HUL, Reliance and many others have already set up impressive farm linkages.

Telecommunication: A Gartner study revealed that Indian cellular services revenue grew at a compound annual growth rate (CAGR) of 18.4 per cent to touch US$ 25.6 billion in 2011, with most of the growth being driven by rural markets. Also, a joint CII and Ernst & Young report reveals that of the next 250 million Indian wireless users, approximately 100 million (40 per cent) are likely to be from rural areas. By 2012 end, rural users will account for over 60 per cent of the total telecom subscriber base in India, an impressive number indeed.

Automobiles: Passenger car and by-wheeler auto cos. are driving on the rural road to push sales. While growth in urban markets has been mostly flat or negative, the rural markets are growing. The share of rural sales in Maruti Suzuki has increased significantly. Mahindra & Mahindra (M&M) is now selling more Scorpios in rural and semi-urban markets.

Consumer durables: A survey conducted by RMAI revealed that 59 percent durables sales come from rural markets. Thus, many leading companies are now consolidating their rural presence. A large number of corporate are excited about the potential of rural areas. The entry of corporate like HUL, Bharti, ITC, DCM, EID parry and Amul etc. is a testimony to that.

What one must never commit is the same mistake with rural India that Western MNCs did with India - assuming that it will grow with a lag. The rural consumer yearns for sophisticated new marketing strategies and paradigms, not a throw-back to old times. Thus, a fresh and innovative approach is needed to gain optimally.

HARKING BACK TO THE ERA GONE BY

What is required is to hark back to the era gone by and know your customer, understand him, give him whatever he wants in an innovative manner.

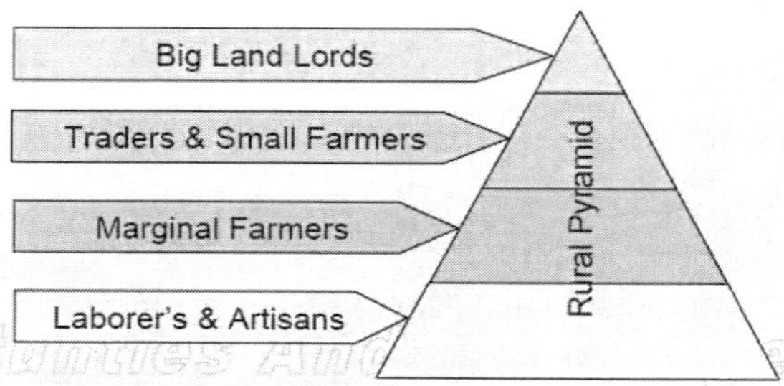

The story of urban market can't be replicated in rural market to a great extent, as they are altogether different. Therefore, before coming up with some business model for rural market, it needs to be understood. Following facts need reckoning:

- **Market which is Large & Fragmented:** Rural market in India is huge, but fragmented. Less number of shops is available.
- **Heterogeneous Market:** Various tiers exist on income-basis such as big landlords; traders, small farmers; marginal farmers, laborers, artisans. State-wise variations can be quite significant as well vis-à-vis literacy (Kerala 90%, Bihar 44%) or BPL population (Orissa 48%, Punjab 6%).
- **Agriculture-based Economy:** Although reducing, but still rural prosperity is tied with agriculture prosperity. In the case of a crop failure, the income of the rural masses is badly hit.
- **Rising Disposable Income and Standard of Living:** Gradually, disposable income of rural market is increasing owing to modern technique of agriculture, cultivation of cash crops, small scale industries, services in nearby city and various government schemes.
- **Traditional Outlook:** Change is a continuous process. Most rural people accept change gradually. However, this is changing due to literacy especially in the youth. 'Rural Youth is New Urban'.
- **Rising Literacy Levels:** It is documented that approximately 45% of rural Indians are literate. The urban people are educating themselves on the new technology around them and aspiring for a better lifestyle.

CHALLENGES WHICH PLAGUE THE THRIVING RURAL MARKET

- **Lack of Accessibility:** Almost half of the villages do not have all-weather roads. Physical movement is highly expensive. Even today most villages in the eastern parts are inaccessible during the monsoon.
- **Media for Rural Communication:** At some point of time, radio was considered to be a potential medium for rural communication. Another mass media which has emerged is television and cinemas.
- **Dispersed Market:** It is a gargantuan task to ensure availability of a brand countrywide. Seven Indian states account for almost three-fourth of the country's rural retail outlets.
- **Low Per Capita Income:** Even though about 33-35% of gross domestic product is generated in the rural areas, it is shared by 74% of the population. Hence the per capita income is low compared to the urban area, although it is improving gradually.
- **Low Levels of Literacy:** The literacy rate is on the down side. This again leads to problem of communication for promotional purposes.

Strength	*Weakness*
➢ High Target Population ➢ Rising number of middle and upper middle class ➢ Urban Life style of Rural Youth ➢ Increasing Purchasing Power ➢ Increasing consumption level across the board	➢ Large and Scattered Market ➢ Agri- based Economy and its dependency on Rainfall ➢ Poor Infrastructure ➢ Many Languages and Dialects ➢ Low Level of Literacy ➢ Low number of Retailers per village
Opportunites	*Threats*
➢ Low level of competition ➢ Government Support for Rural Development ➢ Increased Banking exposure ➢ Changing Lifestyle and Standard of Living	➢ Cheap Local Brands and Duplicity ➢ Shifting of Young Generation to Urban areas ➢ Various Laws related to Agri inputs-outputs ➢ Increasing cost of Land

THE 'FUTURE' RURAL MARKET: TERRITORY TO BE CONQUERED

Considering all the facts, it is to be understood that rural business cannot be feasible until and unless it is multi-dimensional. Most of the FMCG products are based on agri-inputs, directly or indirectly, and these agri-inputs are sourced from villages. This creates an opportunity for FMCG firms to reap the dual-side benefit by adopting the multidimensional approach for rural business.

AN ALTERNATIVE MODEL FOR RURAL MARKETING – AN ALL-ENCOMPASSING APPROACH

All possible transactions related to rural market can be summarized through the 'Re-defined Rural-Urban Matrix'.

	Rural	Urban
Rural	* Agri-input based items which can be processed at local level	* Agri-input purchased from farmers * Processed food items
Urban	* Seeds, Fertilizers, Pesticides etc. * Consumables, FMCG	

Therefore, an integrated model is needed for rural business which covers all aspects of rural business viz. Urban to Rural, Rural to Urban and Rural to Rural.

THE PRE-REQUISITES BEFORE DEVELOPING THE MODEL

- **Value for Money:** Rural consumer wants 'Value for Money', thus desiring quality at lowest possible price.
- **Way to increase their Purchasing Power:** Rural consumer earns mainly from agriculture. We need to increase their earning from other sources to increase our market size.
- Product Awareness / Demand Creation
- Lack of Accessibility

HOW TO STRATEGIZE FOR THE VALUE FOR MONEY ASPECT

- Simple product performing basic functions
- Shortening the input source chain to buy inputs at low prices

  Instead of **Farmer → Mandi → Manufacturer/Processing Center,**
- Use **Farmer à Manufacturer/Processing Center**, through own rural stores.
- Focus on shortening the Distribution chain, thus less distribution of margin overheads

  Instead of **Manufacturer → Stockist à Wholesaler → Retailer → Consumer**

  Use **Manufacturer → Rural Stores → Consumer**

  See a typical example of 'Dal', which need polishing before use,

  Instead of **Farmer → Mandi → Manufacturer/Processing Center → Wholesaler → Retailer → Consumer**

  We can use **Farmer → Manufacturer/Processing Center → Consumer**

TAKING THE RURAL EARNINGS NORTH REQUIRE

- Better Price for their product, as Mandi margin will be shared between farmer and manufacturer
- No transportation cost for farmers as well as manufacturer, as source of inputs and markets are the same.
- Contract Farming can further help farmers to earn fixed income thus helping manufacturer to have the desired product.
- Can be guided regarding increasing productivity.

HOW TO GO ABOUT PRODUCT AWARENESS / DEMAND CREATION

- A team would be required to make rural consumers aware about the products. This team would be expected to convert their wants into demand.
- Further this team will understand the rural consumers and their specific needs to serve them better products.

COUNTERING 'LACK OF ACCESSIBILITY' FACTOR STRATEGY-WISE

Inputs which can be processed locally using a small set-up, should be processed and converted into finished goods. For this processing facility, some tie-up or partnering can be done with local entrepreneurs. It will also generate employment opportunities and increase the purchasing power of local consumers.

On the basis of above strategies, a comprehensive integrated model for rural business is thus proposed covering all the aspects, to reap maximum long-term competitive gain in the rural market.

THE MARKET AND SUPPLIERS

Farmers make this rural market and rural business full of opportunities. They are buyers as well as sellers. They will buy fertilizers, seeds, pesticides and agri-inputs. They produce agri-products and sell them to Rural Processing Center. They further buy consumable items like for their consumption. Apart from the farmers other rural consumers like labourers, salaried employees, rural youth make the market for different consumables.

THE RURAL SHOP- HOW IT ALL WOULD SHAPE UP

Center point of above model will be the '**Rural Store**' – selling all the goods specifically designed for particular strata of rural market. It will include agriculture inputs along with FMCG products. This center will receive supplies from 'Rural Processing Center' and Urban warehouse.

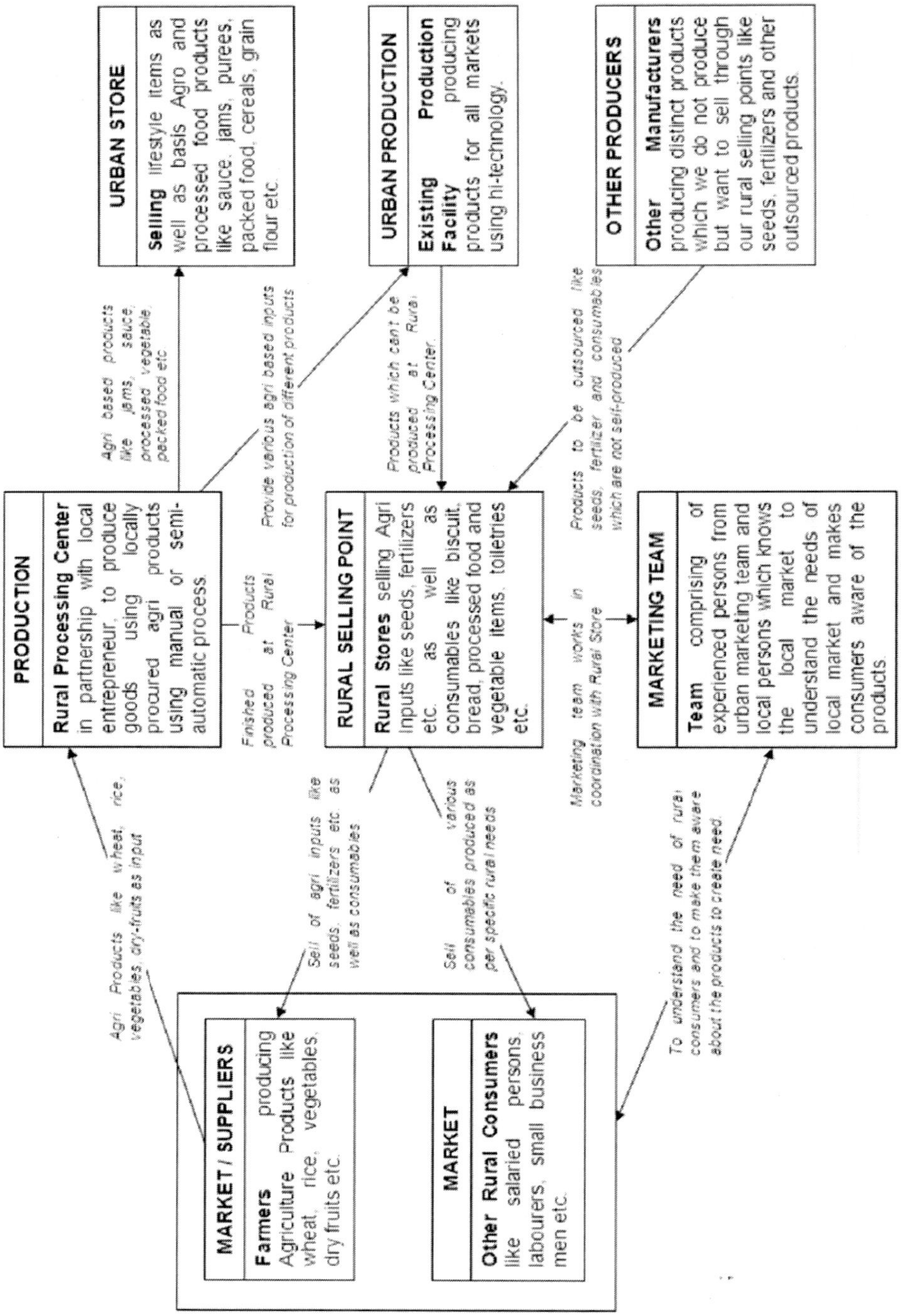
PRODUCTION
Rural Processing Center in partnership with local entrepreneur, to produce goods using locally procured agri products using manual or semi-automatic process.
URBAN STORE
Selling lifestyle items as well as basis Agro and processed food products like sauce, jams, purees, packed food, cereals, grain flour etc.
URBAN PRODUCTION
Existing Production Facility producing products for all markets using hi-technology.
OTHER PRODUCERS
Other Manufacturers producing distinct products which we do not produce but want to sell through our rural selling points like seeds, fertilizers and other outsourced products.
RURAL SELLING POINT
Rural Stores selling Agri inputs like seeds, fertilizers etc. as well as consumables like biscuit, bread, processed food and vegetable items, toiletries etc.
MARKETING TEAM
Team comprising of experienced persons from urban marketing team and local persons which knows the local market to understand the needs of local market and makes consumers aware of the products.
MARKET / SUPPLIERS
Farmers producing Agriculture Products like wheat, rice, vegetables, dry fruits etc.
MARKET
Other Rural Consumers like salaried persons, labourers, small business men etc.
Agri based products like jams, sauce, processed vegetable, packed food etc.
Provide various agri based inputs for production of different products
Products which can't be produced at Rural Processing Center.
Products to be outsourced like seeds, fertilizer and consumables which are not self-produced
Finished Products produced at Rural Processing Center
Marketing team works in coordination with Rural Store
Agri Products like wheat, rice, vegetables, dry-fruits as input
Sell of agri inputs like seeds, fertilizers etc. as well as consumables
Sell of various consumables produced as per specific rural needs
To understand the need of rural consumers and to make them aware about the products to create need.

A '**Rural Processing Center**' is a place to process the locally procured agri-products. It will be having a manual or semi-automatic processor and local labour to convert inputs to processed form. Processed item will be sent to 'Local Rural Store' for sell. It will also supply 'low-cost processed products' to urban stores along with the low cost agriculture products as raw material to further process them in hi-tech production facilities.

Rural Marketing Team would be responsible for understanding the need of the consumers and creating the demand. This team will also undertake all the promotion and awareness activities in the rural market.

TO SUMMARIZE IT...

The model presented above is just one about how to do business in an untapped-yet-potential market, in this case the rural Indian market. There can be many more models for harnessing benefits out of this segment which could be full of opportunities. Thus, what India need are ingenious solutions to begin a campaign that could fast forward villages thereby changing them into lucrative business destinations units and progressive destinations which would provide wings to the dreams of the villagers, and new vistas with the promise of a better tomorrow.

REFERENCES

[1] Velayudhan, Sanal Kumar (2007). *Rural Marketing – Targeting the Non-Urban Consumer.* New Delhi: Sage Publications India Pvt. Ltd.

[2] Gopalswamy, T. P. *Rural Marketing, Environment – Problems and Strategies*, New Delhi: Wheeler Publishing.

[3] Kashyap, Pradeep & Raut, Siddhartha (2008). *The Rural Marketing Book*, New Delhi: Biztantra Publisher.

[4] Gandhi, Mihir (2010). Redefining Rural India. *The Rural Marketing Journal*,4(2), 9.

[5] Muthukumar, K. (2009, June 20). Blurring Lines of Rural India. *Business World*,

[6] Bali, Monish (2000, August 23). The rural market likes it strong. *The Economic Times*

[7] Jha, Neeraj (2000, June 19). Gung-ho on rural marketing. *The Financial Express*

[8] ASSOCHAM reports for various years related to Rural India and Retail revolution such as 'Rise of Rural India'

[8] Various reports published by NCAER over years highlighting the changing patterns of rural consumption

[9] Study conducted by Gartner regarding the telecommunication potential of rural India

[10] Joint report on Indian telecom market conducted by CII and Ernst & Young

[11] Survey conducted by RMAI regarding the sales of consumer durables.

Integrating Logistics Cost in International Pricing Framework for Exporting Firms: A System Dynamics Approach

Ashutosh Kar and Deepankar Sinha[1]

NSHM College of Management Technology, Kolkata, West Bengal
[1]Indian Institute of Foreign Trade, Kolkata, West Bengal

ABSTRACT

In international business, logistics cost plays a significant role in pricing of goods (Kar & Sinha, 2011). Armington's trade theory (1969) and further work by Anderson and Van Wincoop (2003 & 2004) pointed out that non-trade cost play an important role in trade between two countries. They identified that these primarily include the transportation and other related cost not collected by the producer. There is a gap in the literature studied so far and the specific inclusion of logistics costs in international pricing framework and means to articulate the same has not been done. Moreover research so far has identified factors and its determinants including their weightings but have not proposed outcome of the pricing decision strategies. That is, the studies so far focused on the underpinnings of the pricing process rather than on the outcome of the process.

The purpose of this research is to suggest an international pricing framework incorporating logistics cost aligned with revenue and marketing dimensions of a business. The paper aims at identifying the impact of logistics cost at the different stages of organizational life cycle (OLC) of an international firm. In this paper, a causal model, based on principles of System Dynamics, has been proposed to understand the outcome of the pricing decisions. The System Dynamics approach identifies the loops that explain the dynamics of pricing products in global markets. Logistics cost is more significant in export-marketing firms. The logistics cost comprises freight and insurance. It is also affected by the exchange rates. The impact of logistics cost is guided by the logistics coefficient. It ranges from 0 to 1. The value is zero when the demand exceeds the threshold quantity or when the firm moves up the OLC. That is, for a global firm logistics cost may not cause a distinct impact on pricing while the reverse is true for an export-marketing firm. . It suggests that a pricing strategist should fix up the prices considering the interplay of all these variables. The effect of interplay of all these variables on the price of the product as captured in the System Dynamics model can be observed through simulation and policy experimentation. As a further scope of work the simulation model can be run by use of software such as Stella and Vensim and validated with real life cases.

INTRODUCTION

In international business, logistics cost plays a significant role in pricing of goods (Kar & Sinha, 2011). Armington's trade theory (1969) and further work by Anderson and Van Wincoop (2003 & 2004) pointed out that non-trade cost play an important role in trade between two countries. They identified that these primarily include the transportation and other related cost not collected by the producer.

The pricing of goods in international trade are referred with standard terms laid down by International Chamber of Commerce (ICC). These are called INCO (international commercial) terms. The most commonly used terms include FOB (free on board) and CIF (cost-insurance and Freight). However, there are eleven such terms. The most popular terms of trade is FOB, leaving the freight and the insurance with the buyer. The buyers' choice of transportation may lead to higher cost as (s)/he may not be adept in logistics management or does not have the economy of scale of operation to avail price advantage. In addition insurance cost when left to the buyer may vary according to the coverage which in turn is dependent on his / her perception.

Price has been considered as an important factor of the marketing mix and different studies reveal the importance of price for an exporting firm. (Chung, Wang, Huang, 2012). A review of literature on international pricing (Forman & Hunt, 2005, Theodosiou & Katsikeas, 2001) suggests that various internal and external factors affect the price of goods in global market. Studies so far have emphasised on articulating the price based on the product life cycle (PLC), environmental factors and market conditions (Zaribaf, 2008). There is no study to include the impact of OLC (organization life cycle) in global markets. The organisation involved in foreign trade matures from an exporting firm to a multi-national company and finally to a global entity. Thus the pricing along this path will also need to be reframed to capture the characteristics of various stages and remain competitive, considering the factors already proposed and in-built in pricing models.

The purpose of this research is to suggest an international pricing framework incorporating logistics cost aligned with revenue and marketing dimensions of a business. The paper aims at identifying the impact of logistics cost at the different stages of organizational life cycle (OLC) of an international firm. In this paper, a causal model, based on principles of System Dynamics, has been proposed to understand the outcome of the pricing decisions.

PROPOSITIONS

Discussions	*Supporting Literature*	*Propositions*
Logistics cost play a significant role in pricing of goods and a crude approximation suggests that the sector producers in the exporting countries do not incur 30% of the trade costs supported by consumers in importing countries.	(Kar & Sinha, 2011). (Armington, 1969) and (Anderson and Van Wincoop 2003 & 2004)	Logistics cost plays a significant role in international trade.
The pricing of goods in international trade are referred with standard terms laid down by International Chamber of Commerce (ICC). These are called INCO (international commercial) terms.	**NA**	Reflection of logistics cost in the price offered globally is ascertained from the INCO term.
Price is the reflection of the perceived value of the product offered. The complexity in translating perceived value into price arises from the fact that different customer groups perceive value differently. In addition, different customer groups show different price elasticities. This becomes complex in international market as different countries show different price sensitivity. The perceived value in domestic market thus cannot be extended to the international market owing to heightened competition, gray market activities, counter trade requirements, the cost of logistics, regional trade blocks, volatile exchange rates and entry barriers, as these factors tend to exceed the value delivered to the market	(Eckhard, 1997), (Cavusgil, 1996), (Myers 1999), (Assmus and Wiese 1995), (Cavusgil and Sikora 1988), (Weekly, 1992), (Knetter ,1994)	Logistics cost forms a distinct component in pricing of goods by an exporting and international firm.
Three basic factors determine the boundaries of the pricing decision - the price floor, or minimum price, bounded by product cost, the price ceiling or maximum price, bounded by competition and the market and the optimum price, a function of demand and the cost of supplying the product. In addition, in price setting cognizance must be taken of government tax policies, resale prices, dumping problems, transportation costs, middlemen and so on	(HTTP1, 2012)	The articulation of logistics cost may remain the only option for a exporting country as reduction of home price may attract dumping restrictions.
Pricing depends on both internal and external factors. Cost related to production, marketing and capacity utilisation are being identified as internal factors, while external factors include the price sensitivity, switching cost barriers to entry. Authors identified factor determinants as international experience, technological dimensions of products, degree of industrialisation, market share and environmental determinants as exchange rates, tariffs, inflation and government intervention.	(Monroe, 1990), (Stango, 2002), (Naumann & Lincoln, 1991). (Forman and Hunt 2005), (Noble, 1995), Noble & Gruca, 1999),	Pricing depends on internal and external factors.

Contd...

The firms today strive at maintaining a standardized cost in all markets to bring in a consistent image across markets and better coordination, control of international operations and avoid parallel trade. The findings suggest that the cost of logistics has been left out arriving at a standardized cost.	(Harvey, 1993), (Douglas and Craig, 1986), (Theodosiou & Katsikeas, 2001)	Logistics cost may serve as supply chain decision factor in a multinational or global firm. Pricing by these firms may trade off logistics cost with their value offerings as their product and supply network have been set up considering the logistics factor
In international marketing operation a firm moves from the export marketing stage to international marketing to multinational marketing and finally graduating to global marketing. At each stage the position of the firm on its life-cycle curve emphasizes the influence it will bear on the pricing decision. Logistics cost play a vital role in export-marketing which represents an entry mode for a firm. Such a firm has little or no control over the distribution and promotion functions. Therefore, price becomes the only variable that remains controllable given the product. Such a firm, therefore, uses price as its unique selling proposition. The impact of logistics cost reduces as we move up the OLC.	(Chung, Wang and Huang, 2012), (Sousa and Bradley, 2009), (Jobber and Shipley, 2012)	Pricing varies with every stage of OLC (organizational life cycle) of an international firm. The different stages include, exporting firm, international firm, multinational and global firms.
There are three factors that impact logistics cost. These are the distance, exchange rate and insurance cost. Logistics cost is proportional to distance. However the cost per unit for a given distance differs between LCL (less container load) cargos to FCL (full container load) cargo. The price per unit is higher in less container load than full container load. Then the option left is to convert the less container load cargo to full container load consignment. This can be achieved through mode shifting meaning combining more than one less container load to one full container load. However, this course of action is guided by the constraint namely response time to customer and inventory cost. The freight cost may be included in the offer by the exporter in order to have the control on it.	(Ghosal, 1987), (Miller, 1992), (Knetter, 1994), (Myers, Cavusgil, Diamantopoulos , 2002)	Logistics cost may be articulated through mode shifting, bulk shipment, hedging of exchange rates and bearing the right perception on shipment risk, i.e., taking control on the total landed cost by offering a CIF or CIP (carriage and insurance paid) price.

Contd...

Contd...

the exporter in order to have the control on it. That is, a CFR (cost and freight) price is preferred over FOB. The exchange rate fluctuations can be articulated through different hedging options such as forward contract. This course of action is constrained with the risk factor associated with it. The insurance cost has to be borne either by the shipper or importer but the coverage may range from minimum cargo insurance (Clause C) to all risk coverage (Clause "A") under Institute Clause Coverage. This choice varies with the risk perception of the insurer. Hence in order to articulate this cost the shipper may look for CIF pricing in lieu of FOB		

RESEARCH METHODOLOGY

The Methodology Includes

- Identifying the dimensions and variables of pricing of a product through literature survey
- Deducing the propositions of international pricing and establishing the causality amongst the factors and their determinants
- Developing a causal model using principles of Systems Dynamics

System Dynamics

System dynamics is a computer aided approach to theory building, policy analysis and strategic decision support emerging from an endogenous point of view. It applies to dynamic problems arising in complex, social, managerial, economic or ecological systems, literally any dynamic system characterized by interdependence, mutual interaction, information feedback and circular causality. Developed by Jay W Forrestor, identifies stocks on levels in the system and their inflow and outflow rates. It captures delays and feedback loops that determines the stabilizing and de-stabilizing behaviour of the system (Sterman, 2000)

FINDINGS AND DISCUSSIONS

The causal diagram below depicts three loops that explains the dynamics arising out of inclusion .f logistics cost and movement of the along the OLC.

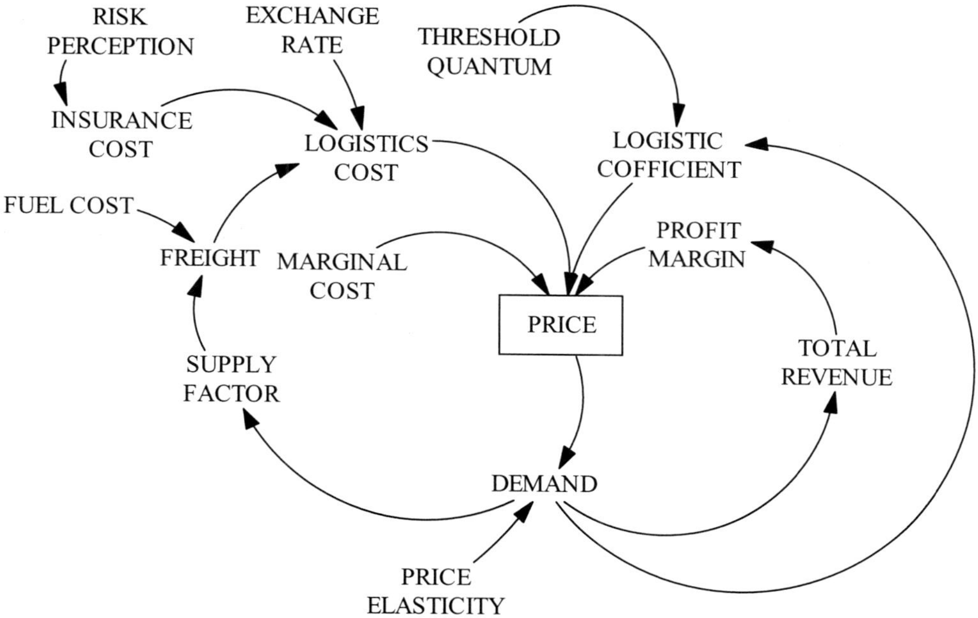

Fig. 1. Causal Model for International Pricing

It suggests that the total landed cost or the price a consumer pays should be such that it sustains the price-elasticity, else would loose the market. In the event the product is highly price elastic it may have to lower the price of the goods without attracting the dumping laws that may be in short run may not meet the revenue objectives, but in long run would increase the demand. That is, may resort to penetration pricing. Increase in demand for a good may cause the logistic cost to go up due to supply constraint. The increase in logistics cost would not have direct bearing on the price as it is effected by the logistic-coefficient. The value of coefficient ranges from 0 to 1, meaning logistics cost has no effect on price when the value is equal to zero and vice versa. This coefficient also reflects the stage of growth of the international firm, i.e., has no or very insignificant effect when the firm is global while major impact when the firm is an exporting firm. That is, the model captures the PLC and OLC of the product and the firm respectively. The logistic cost of the exporting firm may be reduced through increase in economy of scale, followed by vertical integration, as this is likely to contain the supply factor.

CONCLUSIONS AND IMPLICATIONS

The System Dynamics approach identifies the loops that explain the dynamics of pricing products in global markets. Logistics cost is more significant in export-marketing firms. The logistics cost comprises freight and insurance. It is also affected by the exchange rates. The impact of logistics cost is guided by the logistics coefficient. It ranges from 0 to 1. The value is zero when the demand exceeds the threshold quantity or when the firm moves up the OLC. That is, for a global firm logistics cost may not cause a distinct impact on pricing while the reverse is true for an export-marketing firm. It suggests that a pricing strategist should fix up the prices considering the interplay of all these variables. The effect of interplay of all these variables on the price of the product as captured in the System Dynamics model can be observed through simulation and policy experimentation.

As a further scope of work the simulation model can be run by use of software such as Stella and Vensim and validated with real life cases.

REFERENCES

[1] Anderson, J. & Van Wincoop, E. (2003), Gravity with gravitas: A solution to the border puzzle, American Economic Review, 93, 170-192.

[2] Anderson, J. & Van Wincoop, E. (2004), Trade costs, Journal of Economic Literature, 42, 691-751.

[3] Armington, P. (1969), "A Theory of Demand for Products Distinguished by Place of Production", International Monetary Fund, Staff Papers, 26,159-178.

[4] Baalbaki, Imad B. and Naresh K. Malhotra (1995), "Standardization Versus Customization in International Marketing: An Investigation Using Bridging Conjoint Analysis," Journal of the Academy of Marketing Science, 23 (3), 182-94.

[5] Carlos M.P. Sousa, Frank Bradley, (2009),"Price adaptation in export markets", European Journal of Marketing, Vol. 43 Iss: 3 pp. 438 – 458.

[6] Cavusgil, S.T (1996), "Pricing for global markets", Columbia Journal of World Business, Vol.31, Winter, pp.67-78.

[7] Cavusgil, S.T and Sikora, E.(1988), "How multinationals can counter gray-market imports", Columbia Journal of World Business, Vol.23, November/ December, pp.27-33.

[8] David Jobber, David Shipley, (2012),"Marketing-Orientated Pricing: Understanding and Applying Factors That Discriminate Between Successful High and Low Price Strategies", European Journal of Marketing, Vol. 46 Iss: 11.

[9] Douglas, Susan P. and Samuel C. Craig (1986), "Global Marketing Myopia," Journal of Marketing Management, 2 (2), 155-69.

[10] Eckhard, K, (1997), An international strategy for pricing and profits, Scrip Magazine, pp 30-32.

[11] Forman, H, Hunt, J. M, (2005), Managing the influence of internal and external determinants on international industrial pricing strategies, Industrial Marketing Management 34 (2005) 133– 146.

[12] Harvey, Michael G. (1993), "Point of View: A Model to Determine Standardization of the Advertising Process in International Marketing," Journal of Advertising Research, 33 (4), 57-64.

[13] Henry F.L. Chung, Cheng Lu Wang, Pei-how Huang, (2012),"A contingency approach to international marketing strategy and decision-making structure among exporting firms", International Marketing Review, Vol. 29 Iss: 1 pp. 54-87.

[14] HTTP1:http://www.egyankosh.ac.in/bitstream/123456789/35470/1/Unit-11.pdf, 21.05.2012

[15] Ghosal, Sumantra. (1987). Global Strategy: An organizing framework. Strategic Management Journal, 8: 425-40.

[16] Johnson, Jean L. and Aruthanes, W., (1995), "Ideal and Actual Product Adaptation in US Exporting Firms: Market Related Determinants and Impact on Performance," International Marketing Review, 12 (3), 31-46.

[17] Kar, A and Sinha, D (2011), The Impact of Cost of Logistics in Pricing of Goods for Global Markets: A Pricing Framework, Indore Management Journal, Special issue.

[18] Kent D. Miller (1992), "A Framework for Integrated Risk Management in International Business", Journal of International Business Studies, Vol.23, No.2, pp.311-331.

[19] Knetter, M.M (1994), "Is export price adjustment asymmetric? Evaluating the market share and marketing bottle neck hypothesis", Journal of International Money and Finance, Vol.13, February, pp. 13-68.

[20] Matthew B. Myers, S. Tamer Cavusgil, Adamantios Diamantopoulos, (2002),"Antecedents and actions of export pricing strategy: A conceptual framework and research propositions", European Journal of Marketing, Vol. 36 Iss: 1, pp. 159-188.

[21] Monroe, Kent D. (1990). Pricing: Making profitable decisions, New York, NY7 McGraw-Hill.13.

[22] Morris, M.H and Morris, G.(1990), market Oriented Pricing, Quorum, New York, NY.

[23] Musonera .E & Ndagijimana. U (2011), An Examination of Factors that Affect Pricing Decisions for Export Markets, Journal of Global Business Management (http://www.jgbm.org/page/22%20Etienne%20Musonera%20.pdf).

[24] Myers, M.B(1999), " Incidents of gray market activity among U.S exporters: occurrences, characteristics and consequences", Journal of International Business Studies, Vol.30 No1, pp.105-25.

[25] Naumann, Earl, & Lincoln, Douglas J. (1991). Non-tariff barriers and entry strategy alternatives: Strategic marketing implications. Journal of Small Business Management, 29(2), 60–70.

[26] Noble, Peter, Determinants of Industrial Pricing Strategies. PhD Dissertation, University of Iowa 1995.

[27] Noble, Peter, & Gruca, Thomas S. (1999). Industrial pricing: Theory and managerial practice. Marketing Science, 18(3), 435– 454.

[28] Stango, Victor (2002). Pricing with consumer switching costs: Evidence from the credit card market. Journal of Industrial Economics, 50(4), 475– 492.

[29] Sterman, J. D. (2000), Business Dynamics : Systems Thinking and Modelling for a Complex World, Irwin Mcgraw Hill

[30] Theodosiou. M, and Katsikeas. C.S.,(2001), Journal of International Marketing. Vol. 9, Iss. 3; pg. 1-18.

[31] Weekly, J.K (1992), "Pricing in foreign markets pitfalls and opportunities", Industrial Marketing Management, Vol.21 No.2, pp. 173-9.

[32] Zaribaf M., (2008), International Journal of Management Perspectives, 2(1), pp. 19-31.

Modeling Sustainable Development: India's Strategy for the Future

Rajul Singh and Roma Mitra Debnath[1]

IILM-Graduate School of Management, Uttar Pradesh
[1]*Indian Institute of Public Administration, Ghaziabad*

ABSTRACT

The main objective is to understand the relation among the various enablers of CDM to know their degree of dependence and driving power. As there has been non-agreement among the various stakeholders regarding the benefits of sustainability brought about by CDM, this paper explores the viability of sustainable development in Indian scenario.This paper discusses a model to address the issues of sustainable development in the context of CDM. An Interpretive Structural Model (ISM) has been used to model the various parameters of sustainable development in Indian context. The relevant parameters have been considered as per the existing literature review. The result shows that sustainable development is achievable if the nation emphasizes on strategic goals and mission because sustainable development is driven by the strategic parameters like 'employment creation' and 'long-term economic goals'.

INTRODUCTION

The challenges of how to respond to climate change and ensure sustainable development are currently high priority for the world's leading economies. According to model projections, developing country greenhouse gas (GHG) emissions are going to exceed industrialized country emissions sometime between 2010 and 2020 (IPCC, 2001). At the same time, developing countries are struggling with immediate development concerns. The CDM is the first type of climate change mechanism to take into account this challenge. It also explores the potential for integrating climate change and sustainable development (SD) considerations in specific projects. Projects that qualify for CDM include the following: end-use energy efficiency, supply-side energy efficiency, renewable energy, fuel switching, agriculture, industrial processes, solvent and other product use, waste management, and sinks (afforestation and reforestation).These projects also satisfy additionality and contributions to sustainable development (Pacudan, 2005).

The CDM has been subject to extensive discussion in academic literature during the last few years, and a common assessment is that the current structure of the CDM leads to a focus on cheap emissions reductions at the expense of sustainable development benefits for the host countries. According to Chung (2007) and Schatz (2008), CDM is a mechanism that does not itself reduce emissions, but offsets the increase in emissions elsewhere. In response, there have been calls to move the CDM beyond an offsetting-only approach (Schneider, 2009). Cameset *al.* (2007) and Michaelowa (2005) opined that the additionality of CDM projects is questionable, even though the degree of additionality may be different for different project types. In the view of Rosales and Pronove (2003) determining which projects contribute to sustainable development and which ones do not is context-specific and subjective as countries and even regions or communities may have different views on what is sustainable, and what is development.. Olsen (2007) concluded that left to market forces, the CDM does not significantly contribute to sustainable development. Sutter and Parreño (2007) believed that the greatest amounts of Certified Emission Reductions (CER's) are being generated by projects with the lowest or no contribution to sustainable development in the host countries. Recently, the questionable additionality of many CDM projects has become a central issue (Paulson, 2009). According to IUCN (1980) and Markandya and Halsnaes (2002) in order to achieve SD in developing countries and with CDM projects in particular, there is a need to emphasize strongly on national development priorities such as poverty reduction, local environmental health benefits, employment generation, economic growth prospects, etc. According to Daly (2002) a few principles are required to achieve sustainable development.

CDM PRACTICES IN INDIA

India is perceived as one of the most attractive Non-Annex I countries for CDM project development. Even though more than 28.18% of the total CDM projects registered by United Nations Framework Convention on Climate Change (UNFCCC) are from India, it has been highlighted that a majority of the CDM projects have purely economic orientation and are not directed towards achieving overall sustainable development (Sharma and Das, 2009). In the Indian context the goal of SD is inextricably linked to poverty, education and employment as much as to climate change and global governance response. These issues now hold the key to environmentally effective modeling that can show us the way to SD.

Since the establishment of the Indian DNA (Designated National Authority) in 2003 it has approved a significant number of projects. 420 projects have been registered by the CDM executive board, which account for close to40% of all the registered projects (as of 1 May 2009).India has registered CDM projects that include energy efficiency projects (cement, steel and etc.), fuel switch projects, hydro fluoro carbons (HFC) reduction projects and transportation projects. CDM promotion cells have been established at a state level. They conduct supportive activities such as information dissemination on CDM and coordination between local and national governments. One of the features of CDM in India is its large share of unilateral CDM projects, Therefore, the price of credits issued by unilateral projects tends to be higher than bilateral or multilateral CDM projects (Okubo, 2009).

Sustainable development may become an elusive concept unless a holistic development including social, economic and environmental development is not taken forward. To evaluate performance of countries like India, several indicators have been considered to model the social, economic and environmental aspects of development.

MODELING SUSTAINABLE DEVELOPMENT

The challenges of how to respond to climate change and ensure sustainable development are currently on the agenda of the world's leading economies. One of the aims of CDM is to achieve sustainable development in developing countries, however, uncertainty prevails as to whether the CDM is doing what it promises to do. A large number of studies have emerged on CDM, but very few assess the state of knowledge on the contribution of CDM to sustainable development.

According to the UNDP (2002), a fairly basic strategy for the fight against poverty consists of (i) Providing opportunities, i.e. the formation of human capital and (ii) Increasing the capacity of the poor to take advantage of these opportunities, i.e. making use of the acquired human capital.

Employment creation has received surprisingly little attention in the literature on environmental sustainability. There is a need for closer ties between sustainable development and employment-creating development at both the global and the national levels of planning and policy (Mehmet,1995). For India, a central challenge is to improve the quality of its education system. Microeconomic studies for numerous developing economies have found that individuals with higher levels of education tend to have relatively higher earnings (Levin and Raut, 1997). Educational investment may also contribute indirectly to economic growth by reducing fertility and improving health and life expectancy.

The concept of economic growth is the main focus for the policy strategies of most developing economies. India has started moving towards macroeconomic stability and created more stable long-term growth prospects. A consumer boom, increase in real wages, growth in exports, low inflation and transfer of jobs from the informal to the formal sector are indicative of the success of the financial structure and reforms.

Sustainable development is closely related with the provision of an environment that promotes and supports health. Understanding the different environments within a community and how they relate to health is the first step. Engaging the various stakeholders in decision making on environmental and health issues promotes the idea of sustainable development (Gupta and Asher, 1998). The principles of SD balance the population's entitlement to a healthy life with a consideration of the impact of economic growth upon the environment (Shellberger and Nordhans, 2004).Good corporate governance requires corporations to manage an organizations wider influence on society for the benefit of the society as a whole which results in good corporate citizenship. Good corporate citizenship is closely associated with the idea of sustainability. It is also synonymous with the concept of 'corporate societal responsibility'.

Sustainable development is achieved through optimizing gains from several variables. This requires government departments to work together. The richness of skills available in society must be harnessed through partnerships involving institutions in civil society, such as Non Governmental Organizations (NGO's), Community Based Organizations (CBO's), corporate (including private) bodies, academic and research institutions, trade unions, etc., which must be made an integral part of planning and implementation for sustainable development.

Climate change is one of the most important global environmental challenges facing humanity with implications for food production, natural ecosystems, freshwater supply, health, etc. The impact would be particularly severe in the tropical areas, which mainly consist of developing countries, including India (Garg, *et al.*2003).The impact of climate variability and change, climate policy responses, and associated socio-economic development will affect the ability of countries to achieve sustainable development goals (Climate Change, 2001).

India has a territory of 328 million hectares, which receives an average annual rainfall of 120 cm. This is among the highest for a comparable geographical area in the world. Despite India's vast water resources, droughts and famines are a common occurrence in many parts of country (Bobba, *et al.*1997).

The transportation sector is also expected to grow rapidly. These considerations suggest that India will be responsible for a growing share of global greenhouse gas (GHG) emissions in the future. There is therefore a strong argument, articulated by countries like the United States that India ought to actively participate in any future emissions reduction targets

To achieve the objective of sustainability it is necessary to establish a system of solid waste management, which harmonizes the technical requirements with the objectives of environmental protection and the needs and interests of different stakeholders especially the urban poor. Based on existing literature presented above, the following enablers of sustainable development have been considered in the present research, which are exhibited in Table 1.

Table 1. Enablers of Sustainable Development in India

Sr. No.	*Enablers*
1	Long-term economic growth
2	Improved Health care
3	Enhancing Education skill
4	Corporate-Government collaboration
5	Employment Creation
6	Inclusive employment growth
7	Solid waste management
8	Managing climate change
9	Natural resource management
10	Land and displacement management
11	Water resource management
12	Effective Corporate governance
13	Poverty alleviation
14	Green house Gas (GHG) Reduction

ISM: AN OVERVIEW

Interpretive structural model (ISM) offers a methodology for structuring complex issues and it is a combination of three modeling languages: words, digraphs and discrete mathematics. It differs significantly from many traditional modeling approaches, which use quantifiable variables. ISM provides a modeling approach, which permits qualitative factors to be retained as an integral part of the model.

On the other hand, ISM has advantages over other methods. ISM was proposed by Warfield in 1973 to analyze the complex socioeconomic systems. Since then ISM is often being used to understand the complex situations and to make a strategy for solving problem. Sage in 1977 defined that ISM is used for identifying the relationship between various factors, which define a specific issue or a problem. It is an interactive process, which also uses the notion of graph theory to explain the complex pattern of contextual relationship among a set of variables (Malone, 1975).

The steps of ISM have been described as a process within the present context. The process starts with the identification of the relevant elements to the problem. Group solving techniques have been used to solve this step. In the next stage, a contextually relevant subordinate relation is chosen. Based on this relation, a self-structural self-interaction matrix (SSIM) is developed. In the next step, the SSIM is converted into a reachability matrix and its transitivity is checked. Once it is done, a well-defined representation system in a form of matrix model is obtained. In the final step the partitioning of the elements and the extraction of the structural model is done to complete the ISM. Deshmukh and Mandal (1994) presented the process in the form of flow chart.

EMPIRICAL ANALYSIS

The main objectives of this paper are

(i) To explore the enablers of sustainable development.
(ii) To recommended strategies to achieve sustainable development in India.
(iii) To identify the relationship between CDM and sustainable development in India in the present scenario.

This research is based on 14 important parameters under the "enabler" category. The selection of parameters is done through the literature review and discussion with 2 experts from the academia.

METHODOLOGY

To collect the desired data, a questionnaire was developed and ISM has been used to achieve the research objectives. The methodology is being discussed in the next section. The initial step in this study is to facilitate experts in developing a relationships matrix. The survey included a structured questionnaire where the respondents are asked to indicate the importance of 14 enablers. These questions were scaled on likert scale of 1(no importance) to 5(very high importance). The variables were selected through discussion with educators and from existing literature review.

FORMULATION OF STRUCTURAL SELF-INTERACTION MATRIX (SSIM)

In this research, the experts were consulted in identifying the nature of contextual relationship among the variables of technical education system. In order to analyze the relationship among the sustainable development variables, a contextual relationship of "leads to" type is chosen. The following symbols are used to denote the direction of relationship between enablers (*i* and *j*) to analyze the enablers and barriers in developing SSIM.

1. V Enabler i will help to achieve enabler j;
2. A Enabler j will help to achieve enabler i;
3. X Enabler i and j will help to achieve each Other;
4. O Enablers i and j are unrelated.

Table 2: Structural Self-Interaction Matrix (SSIM) of the Enablers in Sustainable Development

Sr. No.	*Enablers* ⇨	*14*	*13*	*12*	*11*	*10*	*9*	*8*	*7*	*6*	*5*	*4*	*3*	*2*
1	Sustainable economic growth.	O	V	X	O	O	X	O	O	X	V	V	V	X
2	Improved Health care.	O	X	O	O	O	O	O	O	A	A	A	A	
3	Enhancing Education skill.	O	V	X	X	O	V	O	O	V	X	X		
4	Corporate-Government collaboration.	O	V	X	X	O	X	O	O	V	X			
5	Employment Creation.	A	O	O	O	O	O	O	O	X				
6	Inclusive employment growth.	O	X	O	O	O	O	O	O					
7	Solid waste management.	O	A	O	V	X	X	X						
8	Managing climate change.	A	V	O	X	X	X							
9	Natural resource management.	X	A	O	V	A								
10	Land and displacement management.	O	V	O	X									
11	Water resource management.	X	V	O										
12	Effective Corporate governance.	A	X											
13	Poverty alleviation.	V												
14	Green house Gas (GHG) Reduction.													

The following statements explain the use of symbols V, A, X and O for enablers in SSIM (Table 2):

(i) Enabler 1 helps achieve enabler 13. Enabler 1 i.e. sustainable economic growth will achieve enabler 13 i.e. poverty alleviation. Therefore 'V' describes the relation in Table 2.

(ii) Enabler 3 would help to achieve enabler 2. If proper emphasis is given on enhancing education skills (enabler 3), it would help achieve the improved health care. Hence the relation is 'A'.

(iii) Enabler 3 and 10 are unrelated. Enhancing education skill and land and dispute management does not share any relationship. Thus 'O' represents their relation in SSIM (Table 3).

(iv) Enabler 9 namely, natural resource management and enabler 14 namely, GHG emission reduction would help achieve each other. Therefore 'X' depicts the relationship.

Reachability Matrix

The SSIM is transformed into a binary matrix, called the reachability matrix by substituting V, A, X, O by 1 and 0 as per the case. The rules for the substitution of 1s and 0s are as follows:

1. If the *(i, j)* entry in the SSIM is V, then the *(i, j)* entry in the reachability matrix becomes 1 and the *(j, i)* entry becomes 0.
2. If the *(i, j)* entry in the SSIM is A, then the *(i, j)* entry in the reachability matrix becomes 0 and the *(j, i)* entry becomes 1.
3. If the *(i, j)* entry in the SSIM is X, then the *(i, j)* entry in the reachability matrix becomes 1 and the *(j, i)* entry also becomes 1.
4. If the *(i, j)* entry in the SSIM is O, then the *(i, j)* entry in the reachability matrix becomes 0 and the *(j, i)* entry also becomes 0.

Table 3. Reachability Matrix of the Enablers of Sustainable Development

Sr. No.	*Enablers* ⇨	*1*	2	3	4	5	6	7	8	9	*10*	*11*	*12*	*13*	*14*	*Driving Power*
1	Sustainable economic growth.	1	1	1	1	1	1	0	0	1	0	0	1	1	0	9
2	Improved Health care.	1	1	0	0	0	0	0	0	0	0	0	0	1	0	3
3	Enhancing Education skill.	0	1	1	1	1	1	0	0	1	0	1	1	1	0	9
4	Corporate-Government collaboration.	0	1	1	1	1	1	0	0	1	0	1	1	1	0	9
5	Employment Creation.	0	1	1	1	1	1	0	0	0	0	0	0	0	0	5
6	Inclusive employment growth.	1	1	0	0	1	1	0	0	0	0	0	0	1	0	5
7	Solid waste management.	0	0	0	0	0	0	1	1	1	1	1	0	0	0	5
8	Managing climate change.	0	0	0	0	0	0	1	1	1	1	1	0	1	0	6
9	Natural resource management.	1	0	1	1	0	0	1	1	1	0	1	0	0	1	8
10	Land and displacement management.	0	0	0	0	0	0	1	1	1	1	1	0	1	0	6
11	Water resource management.	0	0	1	1	0	0	0	1	0	1	1	0	1	1	7
12	Effective Corporate governance.	1	0	1	1	0	0	0	0	0	0	0	1	1	0	5
13	Poverty alleviation.	0	1	0	0	0	1	1	0	1	0	0	1	1	1	7
14	Green house Gas (GHG) Reduction.	0	0	0	0	1	0	0	1	1	0	1	1	0	1	6
	Dependence power	5	7	7	7	6	6	5	6	10	4	8	6	10	4	

Table 3 also shows the 'driving power' and the 'dependence' of the enablers. The driving power of a particular variable is the total number of variables (including itself), which it may help achieve while the dependence is the total number of variables, which may help achieving it. For instance, Enabler 1(sustainable economic growth), 3 (enhancing education skill) and 4 (corporate-government collaboration) having the maximum 'driving power', which has been calculated as 9. Similar justification is given for dependence too. Enabler 9 (natural resource management) and enabler 13 (poverty alleviation) are having the maximum dependence i.e. 10.

These driving power and dependencies of variables will be used in the MICMAC analysis, where the variables will be classified into four groups of autonomous, dependent, linkage and independent (driver) variables.

LEVEL PARTITIONS

The reachability and antecedent set (Warfield, 1974) for each variable are obtained from final reachability matrix. The variable for which the reachability and the intersection sets are the same is assigned as the top-level variable in the ISM hierarchy as it would not help achieve any other variable above their own level. After the identification of the top-level element, it is discarded from the list of remaining variables. Table 4 represents the level partition of the enablers of sustainable development.

Table 4: Level Partition of the Enablers of Sustainable Development

Enablers	*Description*	*Level*
1	Sustainable economic growth.	III
2	Improved Health care.	I
3	Enhancing Education skill.	III
4	Corporate-Government collaboration.	III
5	Employment Creation.	II
6	Inclusive employment growth.	II
7	Solid waste management.	IV
8	Managing climate change.	IV
9	Natural resource management.	IV
10	Land and displacement management.	IV
11	Water resource management.	IV
12	Effective Corporate governance.	I
13	Poverty alleviation.	IV
14	Green house Gas (GHG) Reduction.	III

From Table 4, it is seen that improved health care and effective corporate governance. (Variable 1 and 12) are found at level I. Thus, they would be positioned at the top of the ISM hierarchy. This iteration is repeated till the levels of each variable are found out. The identified levels aids in building the digraph and the final model of ISM.

FORMATION OF ISM-BASED MODEL

From the reachability matrix, a structural model is generated. If the relationship exists between enablers j and i, an arrow pointing from j to i shows this. This resulting graph is called digraph. The digraph without removing the transitivities as explained in the steps involved in ISM. The ISM model for the enablers of sustainable development is shown in Figure 1.

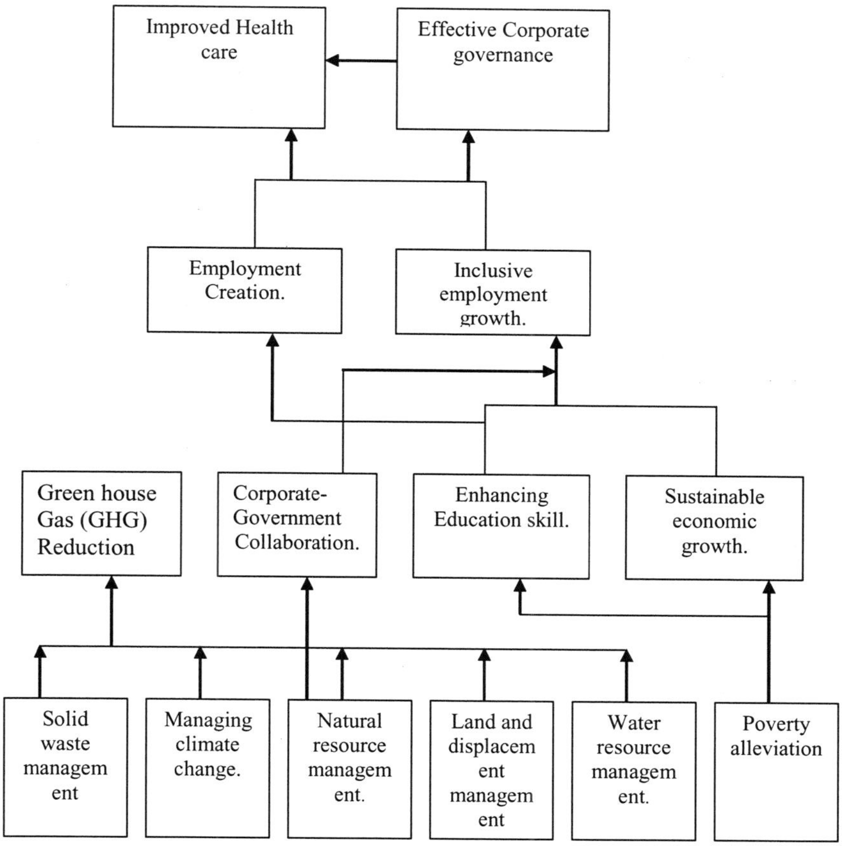

Fig. 1. ISM-based Model for the Enablers of Sustainable Development

MICMAC ANALYSIS

The objective behind this classification is to analyze the driving power and dependency of the enablers. Based on driving power and the dependence; the enablers have been classified into four categories by MICMAC analysis (Mandal and Deshmukh, 1994).

1. Autonomous enablers
2. Dependent enablers
3. Linkage enablers and
4. Independent enablers

The first cluster includes 'autonomous enablers' that have a weak driving power and weak dependence. These parameters are relatively disconnected from the system. In the present study, seven enablers are in the first quadrant and they are enablers 5, 6,7,8,10,12 and 14. These enablers have few links, which may be strong. The second cluster consists of the dependent variables that have a weak driving power but strong dependence. In the present case, enabler 2 is in the second category. The third cluster includes linkage variables that have a strong driving power and also a strong dependence. Any action on these variables will affect others and there would be a feedback effect on them. It has been found that a variable with a very strong driving power called as the key variable, falls into the category of independent or linkage variable. In the present context, there are five linkage enablers and they are 3,4,9,11,13. Finally the fourth cluster is known as independent variables with a low dependence and a high driving power. There is only one enabler that is enabler 1 in this section. Figure 2 exhibits the categories of the various enablers of sustainable development.

The dependence is plotted on X-axis and the driving power is plotted on Y-axis. As an illustration, enabler 3 has a dependence power of seven and the driving power of nine as same as enabler 4. Therefore, in Figure 2, both have been positioned in the third quadrant corresponding to high driving power and high dependence power. Similarly, enabler 10 has dependence power of 4 and driving power of 6, hence it is in the first quadrant (autonomous enabler).

RESULTS AND DISCUSSION

The term sustainable development has been used extensively by economists, policy makers and other social researchers. It has been found that there is a very close and positive relationship between environment and development. Though India is growing at a fast rate, the growth may not necessarily lead to sustainable development unless it is accompanied by environmental protection.Early attempts to model sustainable development were undertaken by Forrester(1971), Meadows *et al.*,(1975) to examine the impact of population growth, pollution and resource use on the planet. An overview of neoclassical models of sustainable development was given by Toman*et al.* (1995) and Heal (1996). A broader perspective on models for sustainable development, with special attention for integrated models, was presented by Bergh (1996). Evolutionary models addressing sustainable development issues were discussed by Clark*et al.* (1995). Faucheux*et al.* (1996) also offered a variety of formal modeling studies in the context of sustainable development. Presently, two modeling approaches namely Computable Equilibrium Modeling (CGE) and Input/Output (I/O) Analysis have emerged. CGE modeling

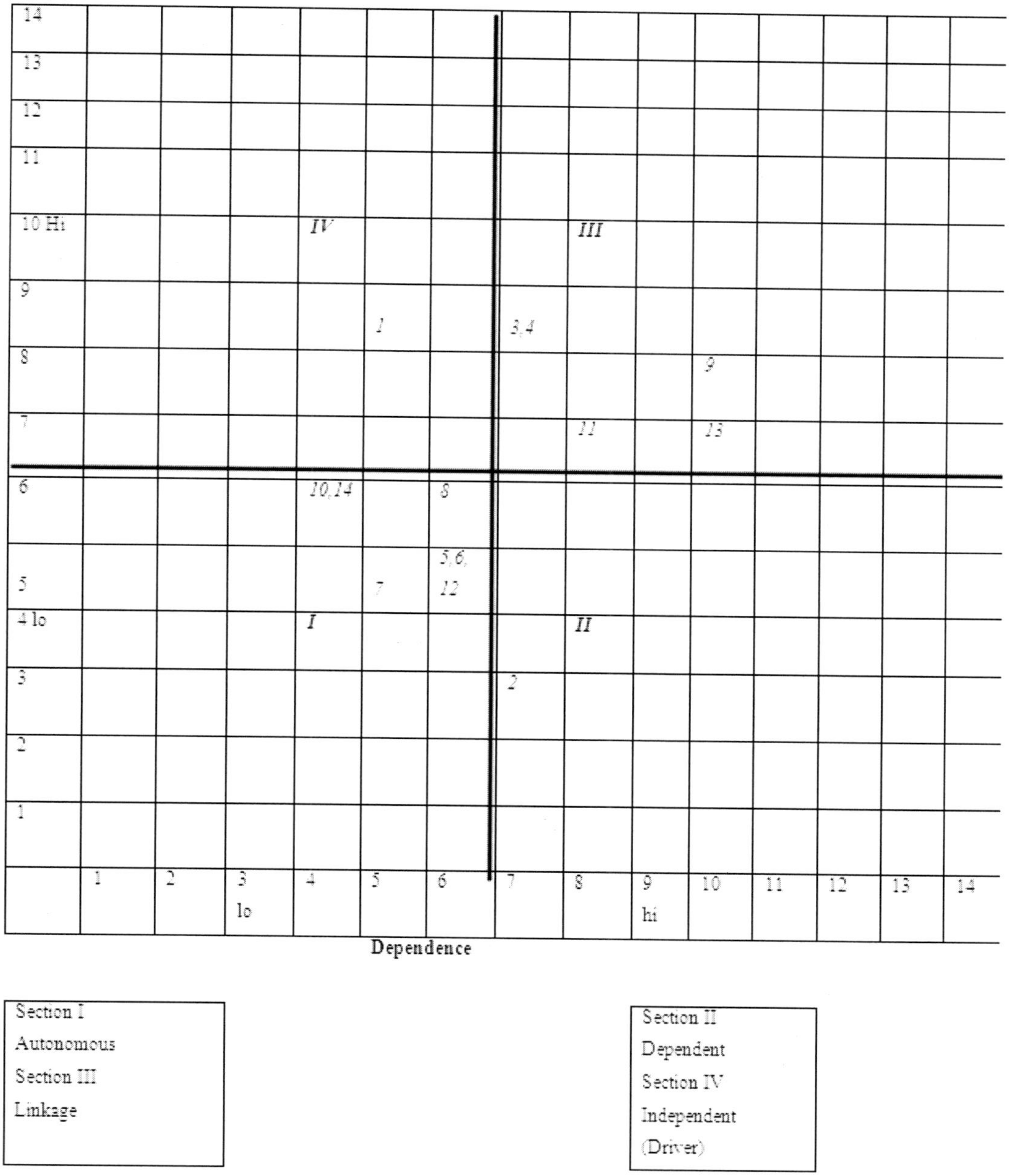

Fig. 2. Driving Power and Dependence Matrix of the Enablers of Sustainable Development

has been used intensively to study the economic implications of environmental policy (Hazilla and Kopp, 1990). I/O models have been used for pollution generation, pollution abatement (Miller and Blair, 1985), requirements for emission reductions and energy conservation sectors (Hafkamp, 1991). On examining models for sustainable development, a large number of differences are found, due to distinct theoretical starting points and, consequently linked to these, alternative demarcations of the complex problem associated with the overall objective of sustainable development.

The potential for poverty alleviation with the help of economic growth is widely accepted. Hence, to achieve the sustainable development, one of the first steps to alleviate the poverty is to be initiated. Poverty is generally considered to be a barrier to education. Poverty alleviation would cause an enhancement in education and also it would lead to economic growth.

In the second stage, parameters like corporate government collaboration, GHG reduction, enhancing education skills and sustainable economic growth are being highlighted. Industry, services and agricultural contributes around 26%, 48% and 25.6 % to the GDP of India, which is approximately $390 billion dollar. Though it occupies only 2 percent of the land's area, it supports over 16 per cent of the world's population. Although industrial growth plays a major role from an economic point of view, India has to pay a heavy price for it and the burden is on the environment.

Corporates, whether they are low or highly technical, manufacturing or agricultural, all produce wastes that are capable of polluting.Employment creation which is at third level is led by enhancing education skill and sustainable economic growth. These two parameters fully would lead to improved health care and effective corporate governance. A major concern of increased risk to health and safety has led to a significant interest in environmental management.

CONCLUSION

The present scenario suggests that a lot of focus is required by the Government of India (GOI) to attain sustainable development. India with its 1.1 billion plus population is the youngest country in the world, with a higher percentage of the population below the age of 25 than any other big nation. Out of 1 billion plus population, 43.6 per cent belongs to the labor force and 41.6 per cent are employed. For more than 50 per cent unemployed population, poverty plays a significant role in the economy. Poverty and a degraded environment are closely inter-related, especially where people depend for their livelihoods primarily on the natural resource base of their immediate environment. Restoring natural systems and improving natural resource management practices at the grassroots level are central to a strategy to eliminate poverty. As not many poverty alleviation programs have been inducted in the official policies and strategies, the result would give an important insight to the policy makers. A positive development is the gradual slowing down of the population growth and the labor force. With higher education achievement, the labor force is expected to go down further.

Health in India is directly linked to the issue of poverty plaguing a huge population especially those in rural areas and urban slums such that it affects the accessibility and quality health care services to people. The annual expenditure on health by the GOI has experienced an increase of 1 % to 2% of the GDP in XIth five year plan. Corporations are the power houses that generate employment, provide education and health care and give sustenance to the society. Good governance needs to ensure that the corporations take in to account the interests of all constituencies in which they operate. A business enterprise's corporate actions must be compatible with long term societal needs such as the quality of environment and welfare of local community.

In recent years, development planning in India has increasingly incorporated measurable goals for enhancement of human wellbeing, beyond mere expansion of production of goods and services and the consequent growth of per capita income. With the increasing pressures on land due to urbanization, rapid economic development, increasing infrastructure requirements etc., especially in a fast growing economy like India, the acquisition of land by the Government has increased.

REFERENCES

[1] Bergh, J.C., Van den,J.M. (1996),*Ecological economics and sustainable development: theory, methods and applications*, Edward Elgar, Aldershot and Vermont.

[2] Bobba, A.G., Singh, V.P., Bengtsson, L. (1997), "Sustainable development of water resources in India",*Environmental Management,*Vol. 21, No. 3, pp. 367–393.

[3] Brundtland Report (1987), *Our common future*, Report of the World Commission on Environment and Development.

[4] Cames, M., Anger, N., Böhringer, C., Harthan, R.O., and Schneider, L. (2008), "Long-term development: A Review of the Literature",*Climate Change*, Vol.84, pp. 59-73.

[5] Chung, R.K. (2007), "A CER discounting scheme could save climate change regime after 2012", *Climate Policy,* Vol. 7, pp. 171-176.

[6] Clark, N., Perez-Trejo, F. and Allen, P., (1995*), Evolutionary dynamics and sustainable development: A systems approach*, Edward Elgar, Aldershot and Vermont.

[7] Climate Change, (2001),*The scientific basis, Summary for policy makers and technical summary of the working group report*, Intergovernmental Panel on Climate Change, Geneva, Switzerland.

[8] Deshmukh, S.G. and Mandal, A. (1994), "Vendor selection using Interpretive Structural Modeling (ISM*)", International Journal of Operations and Production Management*, Vol.14, No. 6, pp. 52-59.

[9] Daly, H.E. (2002), *Sustainable development- definitions, principles, policies, Invited address*, World Bank, Washington DC (*available at www.worldbank.org*)

[10] Faucheux, S., Pearce, D.W. and Proops, J.L.R.,(1996),*Models of sustainable development*, Edward Elgar Publishers, Aldershot and Vermont.

[11] Forrester, J.W., (1971), *World dynamics*, Cambridge, MA.

[12] Garg, A., Ghosh, D. and Shukla, P. R. (2003), "Energy sector policies and mitigation of GHG emissions from India", In Climate change economicsand policy: Indian perspectives (Ed. Toman, M.), *Resources for the Future Publication*, Washington DC.

[13] Government of India (2001), *Census of India*, Office of the Registrar General, India.

[14] Government of India (2004), *India's initial national communication to the United Nations Framework Convention on Climate Change.*

[15] Gupta, A. and Asher, M. (1998*), Environment and the developing world*, John Wiley & Sons Ltd., Chichester.

[16] Hafkamp, V.(1991),Three decades of environmental economic modeling. In: Dietz, F.(Ed.). *Environmental Policy and the Economy*, Elsevier. Amsterdam.

[17] Hazilla, M. and Kopp, R.J. (1990), "Social cost of environmental quality: A general analysis", *Journal of Political Economy*, Vol. 98, No. 4, pp. 853-873.

[18] Heal, G.M. (1996), *Interpreting sustainability*, Plenary presentation, 7th annual conference of the European Association of Environmental Economists (EAERE), June 27-29, Lisboa, Portugal.

[19] IPCC (2001), Intergovernmental Panel on Climate Change, Geneva, Switzerland.

[20] IUCN (1980),*World conservation strategy: living resource conservation for sustainable development.*

[21] Jain, A.K. (2007), Sustainable development and solid waste management, International Society for Environmental Botanists Newsletter, Vol. 13, No. 1, (available on http://isebindia.com/05_08/07-01-1.html)

[22] Lall, S. (1994), *Credit to the decentralized sector: Constraints and rationalisation of delivery system,* Society for Development Studies, India.

[23] Levin, A. and Raut, L.K. (1997), "Complementarities between exports and human capital in economic growth: evidence from the semi-industrialized countries", *Economic Development and Cultural Change*, Vol. 46, No. 1, pp. 155–174.

[24] Mallick, S. (2002), "Determinants of long-term growth in India: A Keynesian Approach",*Progress inDevelopment Studies,* Vol. 2, No.4, pp. 306–324.

[25] Malone, D.W. (1975), "An introduction to the application of Interpretive Structural Modeling",*Proceedings of IEEE, Vol.* 63, pp. 397-404.

[26] Markandya, A. and Halsnaes, K. (2002), *Climate Change and Sustainable Development, Prospects for Developing Countries*, Earthscan Publications Ltd., London, UK.

[27] Meadows,D.H., Meadows, D.L., Randers, J. (1992)*Beyond the limits*, Earthscan, London.

[28] Mehmet, O. (1995), "Employment creation and green development strategy", EcologyEconomy, Vol. 15, No. 1, pp. 11-19.

[29] Michaelowa, A. (2005), CDM: *Current Status and Possibilities for Reform*, HWWI, .Hamburg: Hamburg Institute of International Economics.

[30] Miller, R.E., Blair, P.D. (1985), *Input-Output Analysis: Foundations and Extensions*, Prentice -Hall, Englewood Cliffs, NJ.

[31] Okubo, N. (2009), CDM country Fact sheet India :IGES (Institute for Global Environmental Strategies) Market Mechanism Project / Climate Change Area,(Available on http://cdmindia.nic.in/cdmindia/projectList.jsp) accessed June 2009.

[32] Olsen, K. H. (2007), *The Clean Development Mechanism's Contribution to Sustainable objectives: An evaluation of the CDM and options for improvement*, Öko-Institute, Berlin.

[33] Pacudan, R. (2005),"The clean development mechanism: new instrument in financing renewable energy technologies", in:Iacomelli, A. (Ed.), *Renewable Energies for Central Asia Countries*, Springer. Printed in the Netherlands, Economic, Environmental and Social Impacts, pp. 27–42.

[34] Paulson, E. (2009),*A review of the CDM literature: from fine-tuning to critical scrutiny? International Environmental Agreements,*Öko-Institut, Berlin.

[35] Rosales, J. and Pronove, G. *(2003), An implementation guide to the clean development mechanism*, UNCTAD Earth Council (Available online at http://r0.unctad.org/ghg/sitecurrent/download_c/publications.html)

[36] Sage, A.P. (1977), *Interpretive structural methodology for large scale systems*, McGraw-Hill, New York, NY.

[37] Schatz, A. (2008), "Discounting the clean development mechanism", *International Environmental Law Review*, Vol. 20, pp. 704-742.

[38] Schneider, L. (2009) "A clean development mechanismwith global atmospheric benefits for a post- 2012 climate regime", *International environmental agreements: Politics, Law and Economics*, Vol. 9, No. 2, pp. 95-111.

[39] Sharma, V. and Das, K. (2009), "CDM, development benefits and energy project in India: Issues and concerns" (available at http://www.environmental-expert.com/resultEachArticle.aspx) accessed on July 2009.

[40] Shellenberger, M. and Nordhans, T. (2004), "The death of environmentalism: Global warming politics in a post-environmental world", (available at www.breakthrough.org) accessed 20 February 2009.

[41] Sutter, C., and Parreño, J.C. (2007), "Does the current clean development mechanism (CDM) deliver its sustainable development claim? An analysis of officially registered CDM Projects", *Climatic Change*, Vol.84, pp.75-90.

[42] Toman, M.A., Pezzey, J. and J. Krautkraemer, J. (1995), "Neoclassical economic growth theory and sustainability", in: Bromley, D. (Ed.), *Handbook of Environmental Economics*. Blackwell, Oxford.

[43] UNDP (2002),*Linking poverty reduction and environmental management: Policy challenges and oppurtunities*, Washington, The World Bank.

[44] UNFCCC(1997), Kyoto Protocol to the United Nations Framework Convention on Climate Change (UNFCCC). FCCC/CP/1997/L.7/Add.1, Bonn.

[45] Warfield, J. (1973), *Societal Systems: Plantag, policy and complexity*, John Wiley & Sons, Inc., New York, NY.

[46] Warfield, J.W. (1974), "Developing interconnected matrices in structural modeling",*IEEE Transcript on Systems Men and Cybernetics*, Vol.4, No.1, pp. 51-81.

[47] Wisner, J.D. (2003),"A structural equation model of supply chain management strategies and firm performance", *Journal of Business Logistics*, Vol. 24, No.1, pp.1-26.

Paradigm of an Organization's DNA and its Impact in an Organization

Bharti Venkatesh

VNS Institute of Management, Bhopal

ABSTRACT

In today's fast-paced, information-rich, and quickly expanding landscape, organizations face a monumental task. Building and maintaining solid foundations to support adaptable, positive cultures is difficult in the face of a shifting economy, physically separated workplaces, and increasing diversity in the workforce. These changes in the landscape are forcing organization leaders to think about organizational sustainability in new and different ways.

The purpose of this paper is to describe the concept, processes and functionality of an organization's DNA and how organization DNA helps in developing "simple rules" as a key to establish the adaptability and flexibility that is necessary in complex organizational environments.

INTRODUCTION

Organizations struggle when trying to manage an existing business and a related new strategic experiment simultaneously. The new venture must forget much of what has helped the corporation become successful but must borrow its resources at the same time. To overcome the challenges posed by strategic innovation, organizations must adopt a dual-purpose design. In dual-purpose organizations, the core business and the new venture are distinct subunits within the corporation and have very different DNA.To create its own organizational DNA; the new business must forget the core firm's business definition and competences, as well as the predictability associated with its proven business. The new firm must also hire outsiders at the operational and management level, create its own business functions and processes, develop its own performance measures, and establish its own unique culture of experimentation and learning. Once the new firm has overcome the difficulties that accompany borrowing, it can borrow, among other things, the core enterprise's physical assets (such as manufacturing capacity), brands, expertise, and process outputs.

Now first let us understand what we mean by organization DNA, its origin and how it is considered to be important for an organization.

Organizational DNA is not simply inherited at birth. Consciously or unconsciously, the elements of DNA are selected by leaders. Organizational DNA can be changed, though not easily. DNA becomes deeply entrenched fairly early in an organization's life. It can be changed only through a diligent and time-consuming effort by the senior team. Organizational DNA consists of four elements: staff, structure, systems, and culture as depicted in the following figure:

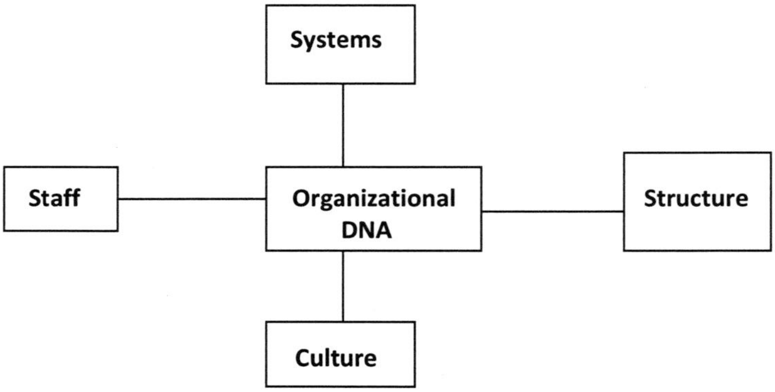

Fig. 1. Four Elements of Organizational DNA

- Staffing choices can create new areas of expertise, e.g. there are many organizations that hire talented networking engineers by acquiring small technology companies.
- Structure shapes an organization's flexibility, e.g. organization decentralized structure enables it to serve markets as diverse as credit cards and nuclear reactors.
- Systems send signals regarding dimensions of performance that are more or less valued.
- Culture establishes the values that employees aspire to, e.g. "the credo" of an organization captures the central promise that the organization makes to each of its stakeholders.

In the context of strategic innovation, DNA matters because management cannot be on call to solve every problem that organization faces. They cannot make every decision. Instead, they must shape decisions by encoding assumptions, values, and decision biases into an organization's DNA — at the time organization is created.

Staff includes attributes of leadership style, plus policies for hiring, training, and promotion. When building a new organization, senior executives must decide who should lead: Entrepreneur or corporate executive? An insider who is politically connected within the organization or an outsider who is more familiar with unique technologies? A general manager or a technical expert? A naïve young executive who cannot imagine failure, or a seasoned executive who cannot risk failing, losing everything invested toward reaching the top? Where should the remaining staff come from? It may be more convenient to transfer insiders, but only outsiders are capable of bringing in new expertise and new perspectives. Should outsiders fill management posts within the organization or just operational ones?

Structure includes the specification of formal reporting relationships, decision rights, information flows, and task flows. A key decision is who the head of an organization should report to. The functional manager within organization who can help the organization the most? A general manager of an existing business unit? Directly to the CEO? In any case, what roles should the executive to whom the organization reports are prepared to play? Should he or she simply set expectations and monitor results, or is the role more complex? What should the reporting structure inside of the organization look like? Should it mimic the structure of other core business units? How and for what purpose should organization and Core Company interact? Which should be the more powerful party in the interaction?

Systems include planning and budgeting processes, norms for evaluating business performance, selection of performance measures, and incentive systems. What expectations are reasonable for the organization? To what extent can the leader of the organization be held accountable for the results of an experiment? How frequently should the organization be evaluated? On what basis? Which performance measures are most relevant? How similar are these measures to the ones used in Core Company? How much should be invested in the organization and when? How frequently should the organization's budget be revisited? Finally, what career and compensation incentives make sense for the company's leaders? If they have the opportunity for tremendous bonuses, what commensurate risks are they exposed to?

Finally, culture includes shared notions about behaviors that are valued and embedded assumptions about what leads to success in business. Which assumptions that are deeply ingrained in Core Company may not apply to new company? Which elements of Core Company's culture might create barriers for new company, and how can this be overcome? How can risk-taking, experimental culture be created within the organization?

INTERLINKAGES BETWEEN ORGANIZATIONAL DNA AND VISION

What is the underlying purpose of the organization? Is it only to make profits? Yes, a business has to make money that is not a point of debate. It must be profitable, must make tons of money. But why? To make the shareholders happy? That would be too narrow a vision. What if we were to broaden the vision to include the customers, and all people who come in contact with the Company must leave happy? What would bring this happiness? Maybe the product or the service? The feeling of joy of experiencing the service is what brings in the sales. A satisfied customer is ultimately your best salesman! The customer is not only the person who buys the end product; it is anyone who comes in contact with the organization at any point of time. That means, it includes the employees, the share holders and myriad people such as the vendors, suppliers etc. Keeping or making everyone happy does not mean doing 'yes sir yes sir' to one and all. Making everyone happy means striving to create a win-win at every stage of the organizational process.

A Vision is all encompassing. A Vision is generally not easily attainable, while it can be realized; it cannot be reached easily or in a defined time frame. A mission is more task specific, has clear objectives to be reached & in a defined time frame. Mahatma Gandhi's vision was not just to throw the British out of India, it was the upliftment of mankind; not just the poor down trodden people. His vision encompassed the entire world. To achieve this, yes, he had to strive to throw the British out of India, he had to fight the caste system, fight social oppression etc. These became his mission criteria for realizing his vision.

Hence, vision becomes the DNA of the organization and just like the DNA it must be able to be passed on from one generation to the next without change. It cannot change with the 'change of guard' or the board of directors or a change in share holding pattern. Hence, Vision must not change with change in ownership or if the man at the helm changes. The vision remains steadfast in its place, because it is eternal. The Vision is like the super ordinate Goal – all encompassing. And in turn, it would have various missions which will synchronize and lead to the Vision.

An organization is made up of people who live, eat, and breathe their own individual visions. Individuals make up the organization and the combination of individual DNAs make up the organizational DNA and vice versa. Hence, the various DNAs need to match or align themselves to form one seamless organization, which is depicted in the following figure.

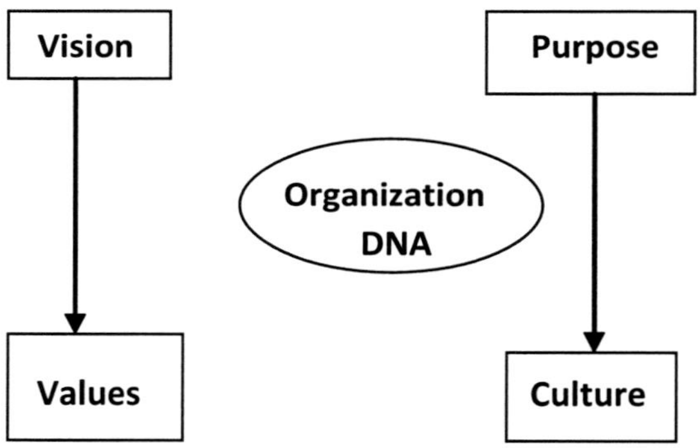

Fig. 2. Interlinkages between Organizational DNA and Vision

There are three activities involved in establishing an Organization's DNA: Identifying it, activating it, and expressing it.

Identifying DNA focuses on Purpose. This is where we set the context of the organization through its vision, mission, guiding principles, etc. Engaging with leadership is essential, as is involving and communicating with employees and other internal stakeholders (e.g., consultants, contractors, etc.).

Activating DNA requires consistent alignment of thought, word, and action throughout the organization via its people. All principles, policies, procedures, strategies, and success metrics must begin to reflect, reinforce, and renew the ideas and intentions established by purpose.

Expressing DNA embraces fully the personal, interpersonal, and public sense of place that the client conveys and people experience every day - internally and externally - through its presence. The built environment, along with the organization's culture, corporate responsibility, interpersonal behavior, public relationships, and communications via all media determine how stakeholders experience this sense of place.

BUILDING BLOCKS OF ORGANIZATION'S DNA

However, like the DNA of living organisms, the DNA of living organizations consists of four building blocks, which combine and recombine to express distinct identities, or personalities. These organizational building blocks — structure, decision rights, motivators, and information — largely determine how an organization looks and behaves, internally and externally, which is shown in the below figure.

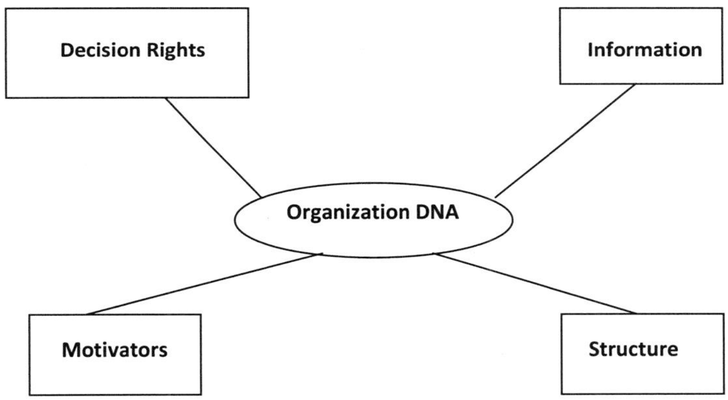

Fig. 3. Four Building Blocks of Organization's DNA

- Decision rights: Who decides, what and how?
- Information: How performance is measured? How activities are coordinated and knowledge is transferred?
- Motivators: What are the objectives, incentives and career alternatives people have?
- Structure: How overall organization model look like?

Structure: What does the organizational hierarchy look like? How are the lines and boxes in the organization chart connected? How many layers are in the hierarchy, and how many direct reports does each layer have?

Decision Rights: Who decides what? How many people are involved in a decision process? Where does one person's decision-making authority end and another's begin?

Motivators: What objectives, incentives, and career alternatives do people have? How are people rewarded, financially and non-financially, for what they achieve? What are they encouraged to care about, by whatever means, explicit or implicit?

Information: What metrics are used to measure performance? How are activities coordinated, and how is knowledge transferred? How are expectations and progress communicated? Who knows what? Who needs to know what? How is information transferred from the people who have it to the people who require it?

Structure: In principle, companies make structural choices to support a strategy (for example, the decision to organize business units around customers, products, or geography). In practice, however, a company's organizational structure and strategic intent often are mismatched. The variance can usually be exposed by, in effect, superimposing the organization chart — an efficient communicator of power and status in a firm — over a business unit's strategic plan.

INNOVATION AND ORGANIZATION DNA

There are fundamental rules that determine how organizations behave — policies and practices that have a tremendous impact on motivations, capabilities, and behavior. These rules are so powerful, and so often taken for granted, that it is entirely apt to refer to them as organizational DNA. Crucial elements of DNA include hiring and promotion practices, leadership styles, planning processes, performance measures, reporting arrangements, formal and informal power structure, how relationships between groups are defined, how individuals are rewarded, and core values.

All companies have DNA, even small ones. As soon as a company gets big enough that the founder can no longer make every decision on its own, the founder has no choice but to start creating DNA. To succeed, companies must create a DNA that fits their business model.

Organizational DNA and biological DNA have some similarities. They both are difficult to observe directly, and have powerful impacts on behavior. But there are crucial differences, too. Biological DNA is inherited at birth, and cannot be changed. Organizational DNA is created early in life, and can be changed, albeit with some effort.

Some innovation efforts fail because a company's weaknesses are simply the flip side of its strengths. An organization that is hard-wired for success in one business is highly unlikely to succeed in a much different one. Unless, that is, it creates a subunit with an entirely different DNA.

Thus, once leaders choose a set of innovative ideas to invest in, there must be two separate tracks for converting those ideas to reality - one set for implementation within the existing organization, and a second set of strategic innovations that only have a chance within a distinct subunit that is carefully constructed from the ground up.

TO SUM UP

Any attempt to address a business weakness or strategic opportunity must start with an analysis of what makes that organization tick—it's DNA. Yet so many traditional approaches to organizational transformation start with the conclusion that the problem lies in the strategy or in the culture of the company. Culture plays a key role in organizational performance, but it's an outcome of the organizational system, not an input to the system. Adjust the building blocks, and you change the system. Change the system, and you change the culture. Change the culture, and you unlock strategy by enabling execution. We call it "culture change for engineers" (and accountants) because it is predicated on specific, actionable adjustments to each of the four levers of an organization's DNA. That difference in starting point and perspective, coupled with the recognition that the task is difficult, represents an opportunity to create an enduring competitive advantage over rivals and leads to a fundamentally different way of thinking about organizational issues and strategy. The most resilient and consistently successful companies have discovered that the devil is in the details of their organization and its culture.

REFERENCES

[1] Chuck Lucier, Rob Schuyt, and Eric Spiegel, "CEO Succession 2002: Deliver or Depart," s+b, Summer 2003.

[2] Jeffrey W. Bennett, Thomas E. Pernsteiner, Paul F. Kocourek, and Steven B. Hedlund, "The Organization vs. the Strategy: Solving the Alignment Paradox," s+b, Fourth Quarter 2000.

[3] Michael C. Jensen, Foundations of Organizational Strategy (Harvard University Press, 1998)

[4] Randall Rothenberg, "Larry Bossidy: The Thought Leader Interview," s+b, Third Quarter 2002.

[5] Verschoor, C. (2005), "Organizational DNA Should Contain Ethics Component," February, *Strategic Finance*, 86(8), pp.19-21.

Product Innovation Driven Product Leadership Resulting into Competitive Advantage: Case of Micromax Mobile

Pardeep Bawa, Anirudha Bahuguna, Harneet Kaur, Sunil Kumar Verma and Amanjeet Singh

Lovely Professional University, Punjab

ABSTRACT

In order to sustain in a market where every day is a brand new day & on most of the occasions you can't take forward the advantage of what you did the last day, you have to lead as an innovative & learning organisation that is way ahead of the rest that are in the fray. Innovations that make a difference to a large set of people would take you at a position which would put you in a different league. Product leadership is an outcome of innovative culture, organisations strive for. As it is something which is very tough to do, very few organisations are there that can be quoted as an example. There is only one Google, one Intel & one Apple but there are countless companies that are into their kind of business but they aren't product leaders. Product leadership shouldn't be judged on criteria of sales numbers but the difference you make to one's life by your products but you need not always to be as Google to do that. For example Micromax Mobile filled a gap by bringing a battery in its phones that had more meat in it so that villagers in thousands of Indian villages with low power supply would need lesser battery refills. This paper examined the role of product innovation driven product leadership in achieving competitive advantage by some learning organisation. It was found that product leadership can only be achieved with an emphasis on innovation centric organisation culture but to use it as a competitive advantage you have to be far more proactive than rest & shouldn't have a competition oriented approach because in that case you are being affected by your competition.

INTRODUCTION

In a business environment of extreme volatility in terms of consumer taste, preferences & very short product life cycles, consistent emphasis on product innovation can prove as a savior. The fact that very few companies are able to develop a culture where innovation is life, proves that it is something which is not very common & an easy task. If we try to get into some real life examples we would find that companies that are product leaders aren't product leaders in all product categories they are dealing in but these companies are very rare. Most of the product leader companies involve themselves in one or very few product categories & put all their resources in them to consistently innovate. Companies involved in using their product leadership as a competitive advantage have never been seen trying to be best in everything they are into. They try to dominate one product category which they think their resources can put into best use. These types of companies take one project at one time, gets deep into it, allocate their best resources in terms of compatibility & come up with something which is new in all respects. Nobody has seen these kind of companies getting indulged into some kind of competition because they compete with something best that they themselves have created. Business is all about finding a gap in between what customers want & what is being offered to them. Product leaders would always do that & consistently filling the gap which other aren't able to see. Filling that gap sometimes doesn't need a product innovation but a slight change in some other part of value chain may bring the results. So a practical definition of innovation might be the 'process of making changes to something established by introducing something new that adds value to customers.'

INNOVATION MANAGEMENT

Process of managing innovation within an organisation can be to a great extent be termed as innovation management. This may include tasks like managing innovative ideas, defining time bound targets, improving inter department communications& coordination, prioritizing projects & motivating project teams. Innovations normally have specific life cycles aspresent innovation would become outdated in near future. From performance point of viewso as to sustain competitive advantage, companies have to consistently innovate and replace products, processes, and services just before they become outdated. And the products, services & processes replacing existing ones should have the capacity to bring a change in consumers' lives in one way or the other. A clear focus on innovation withconsistencywould acknowledge the impact that the learning has on creation of knowledge.It can be applied in developing an innovating product before others once the knowledge has been created.

INNOVATION, CUSTOMERS AND PRODUCT LEADERSHIP

From a perspective of practicability an innovation must bring value for customers but failing to do that an innovation is just knowledge that isn't making a difference to one's life. For example a drug which can cure a disease but has got considerable side effects which negate the positive effect is of no use. Instead a medicine which has a little lesser degree with which it cures but with no side effect is better. But some cases are differentfor example case of Apple & Intel. Both companies are known for bringing products with breakthrough technologies. But Intel is able to bring down the prices at a level that Apple can't match or maybe they don't want to match even in case they can. Apple is making a difference in the lives of customers that only want to buy Apple products. On other hand Intel has got different set of customers who are value for money customers & it takes something different to make a difference in their lives and that is affordable computing. And Apple & Intel aren't second to anybody & are product leaders though they make same thing.

LITERATURE REVIEW

The competition across the world, that became specificallyvery tough after mid 80's, pushed thefirms' focus on their corporate objectives, & innovations more precisely (Kuratko and Hodgetts, 1998). Due to the tough competition globally, companies and individuals start to figure out and to apply their innovation streak and business abilities with the scope of achieving competitive advantage (Drucker, 1985; Hult et al., 2003). Earlier, innovation was considered as new applications & developments, with a mean of launching newness in the business area. It can well be conceived as transforming knowledge into commercial value. Innovation always has high commercialsignificance due to its capacity for enhancing the effectiveness and the profitability of firms.In reality, the major reason for innovative approach is the zeal of companies to achieve enhancedbusiness performance & a sharp competitive edge. Companies achieve more competitive advantage & market share as per the level of importance they give to innovations, which are significant factors for firms to build a stature in the marketplace & therefore to enhance their market share. When the flow of newness& innovations dries out, firms' business structure comes down in astationary state witha limited growth.So innovation plays a vitalrole in creating the differentiation on the basis offinancial results& competition among companies, regions & even countries (Metcalfe, 1998). It is quite relevant as innovative countries had far more productivity levels & income than the lesser-innovative ones (Fagerberg et al. 2004). One of the OECD reports shown that firms thatgone for innovations in a more decisive manner& briskly, had more qualified & trained work force,paid higher compensation & shown more firm & deciding future plans for employees. In fact,the impact of innovations on performance of the firm vary in a wide array from market share, sales&productivity, profitability to effectiveness (OECD Oslo Manual, 2005).The companies' liking towardsinnovations was of vital significance in the competitive business environments so as to achieve bigger competitive advantage (McAdam and Keogh, 2004). (Geroski, 2005) studied the impact of the big innovations & patents to many business performance measures likestock market rates of return, accounting profitability & business growth. The evaluated direct impact of innovations oncompany's performance is relatively not that big & the benefits from it are indirect in most of the occasions. Innovative firms are less prone to cyclical &environmental pressures than firms that are non-innovative. Previous studies have shown that there is a very strong association in between distinctive advantage & the assessment of sales of a firm. There is a huge literature that found out about the positive association in between distinctive advantage & the performance of firms. Wang & Lo, 2003 measured the same that is organizational excellence by using the efficient organizational internal processes & found that it is true. Different resources and capacities have an impact on export business enterprise. Distinct options & the positional upgrading done in especially the export market which change export business venture's performance (Morgan, Kaleka, & Katsikeas 2004). They further examined product competency in terms of enhanced product quality, packaging, labelling, style & design. Similarly research shown that there is animportant association of services based gain on the firm'sresults. (Ismail, Rose, Abdullah et al., 2010) argued that distinct edge is a part of the institution of performance of high level. This association would be inflated by affecting variables like age & size of companies.The moderating effects of these variables provide vital information about strategic management in attainment of distinct edge & to enhance performance. In another study conducted by (Raduan et al., 2009)shown that there is a significant association in between distinct edge &firm's success. (Henderso & Cockburn, 1994) have studied that the non uniformity across firms have a substantial role in shaping difference in productivity. It shown that a spotlight on architectural or combinative capabilities as a source of durable spirited gain may provide useful information into the sources of continuing differences in firm performance. Competitive advantage has to do with the interrelation in between different types of competitive advantage, i.e., cost, and differentiation, and the scope of the firm'sactivities. Without a sustainable competitive advantage, above average performance is usually a sign of harvesting (Porter, 1985; Hamel and Prahalad, 1991; Porter1980). The basis for competitive advantage is the capacity to get knowledge & move it from onepart of the firm to another. The creation of knowledge is a volatile, dynamic & consistent process involving interactions at many levels in a firm.In a dynamic business world, only firms which are able to continuallycreate new long term assets quicker and cheaper than of their competitors would earn better returns & create strategic competitive advantage. In this process strategic competencies have a significant role toplay (Ray et al., 2004; Markides and Williamson, 1994).

OBJECTIVES

To study the relation among innovation, product leadership & competitive advantage.

RESEARCH METHODOLOGY

Case study of Micromax mobile has been taken to analyse the relation among product innovation product leadership and competitive advantage.

CASE OF MICROMAX MOBILE

Standings of 2008 were in favour of MNC companies with Nokia topping the chart with 64% market share in Indian mobile handset market. Dominance of Nokia was such that the closest rival Samsung with a market share of 10% was at second spot. Rest of the players were in between 1-6%. This was an insight for the team of four of Micromax Mobile to how to go about what they were thinking of. The safest target audience was the one residing in rural areas across India with low & interrupted power supply because there was no phone for them literally. For a startup company bringing a product at a price point lower than Nokia was something must but challenging at the same time. More challenging was to bring a mobile phone that target audience would be buying ahead of Nokia which at that time (even today as well) was considered the most user friendly mobile phone at an affordable price. Quite obviously & rightly Micromax Mobile didn't think of competing (Had they thought of competing they would haven't been existed) with heavyweight but tried to make their own identity of a company which thought of filling a gap being existed for so long & which given more than value for money. Conception was not that difficult as was manufacturing a mobile phone & selling it to rural audience of India in a fiercely fought market with half a dozen big MNC players with big R&D budgets, economies of scale on their side complemented with a rich experience. And there were quite a few smaller players to add to their headache. A journey was started to bring a mobile phone that rural audience would be buying without heavy promotions & would be able to afford it at the same time against Nokia's affordable phones with a very reliable image (though it wasn't intended to compete with likes of Nokia directly).So they come up with a phones with a 30 day backup at an aggressive price range which was as much as 20-25% cheaper than the cheapest quality option available. Micromax has given what people wanted. Their 30 day battery backup phone succeeded because people in rural India wanted it. While Micromax has been innovating, they have never lost sight of value. Indians are value conscious consumers and Micromax has thus kept the prices affordable. The average sale price of a Micromax phone is around ₹ 2300. Yet at this price they are selling phone loaded with features. They done quite a few out of the box yet feasible things in the form of products like

I. Phone targeted only at women (Bling)
II. Phone which becomes a universal remote for all appliances
III. Phone which switches SIMcards by turning it upside down
IV. GSM and CDMA in one phone
V. Shake the phone and its SIM card changes
VI. Phone whose Bluetooth gets charged along with the phone

Thanks to all of this Micromax Mobile outscored LG Electronics in India in just a couple and a half years & its market share in India is close to a good 8%. Most importantly this much market share has been gained in just four years of operation. 80% of this market share comes from rural audience as per IDC report 2012. Micromax isn't only a product leader as far as phones for masses are concerned but a market leader in those kinds of phones as well.

ANALYSIS

The variable that differentiate in between two firms is the innovation centric approach. It has been proved in quite a few studies that companies that are customer centric are innovation centric as well. An organisation has to decide at outset the main theme of its operations because customer centric approach isn't something which is domain specific but it is, that governs the entire business effort. Quality needs to be enhanced at every level of value chain & not just one or two parts of it. A consistent effort at every step of value chain to add something which would enable customers to extract more value from a product is indeed the aim of organisations with innovative organisation culture. A specific organisation culture of this kind is a result of a long term proactive approach to be product leader which in turn gets translated into competiveness more often than not.

CONCLUSION AND MANAGERIAL IMPLICATIONS

Innovation normally is measured in terms of organisational growth but growth shouldn't always be measured in terms of numbers as human experience & efficiency are some other criterion as well. Innovation whether is in products or in the process would always lead to product leadership if that innovation is making some difference to lives of people at large. It can only be done if firms would direct their energy & efforts on identifying & filling gaps in between what is needed & available to customers. A mobile phone may have many features but these are not going to help if the basic feature which is a must have for a customer isn't there or partially there. For example bringing car at a price which can be afforded by someone who otherwise couldn't think of buying a car can be termed as an innovation despite having nothing new as far as functionality of the car is concerned. Job of a manager then becomes more of a solution provider to the problems faced by customers. Looking for a solution of customers problems requires ground work & some common sense & innovation is a byproduct of these two variables. Not every innovation gets converted into product leadership as it requires quite a few other types of resources that some organisations sometimes don't have. In the absence of these resources the process of innovation to product leadership to competitive advantage gets delayed but the difference in both the cases isn't very considerable.

BIBLIOGRAPHY

[1] Fagerberg, J., Mowery, D.C., Nelson, R.R., 2004. The Oxford Handbook of Innovation. Oxford University Press, USA.

[2] Geroski, P., 1995. Innovation and competitive advantage. Working Paper No. 159, OECD, Paris.

[3] Hamel G. and Prahalad C.K. (1994).Competing for the Future.Harvard Business SchoolPress. Boston, Massachusetts.

[4] Henderso, R. and Cockburn, I. (1994), 'Measuring competence? Exploring firm effectiveness in Pharmaceuticarle Search', Strategic Management Journal, volume 15, pp. 63-84.

[5] Hult, G.T., Snow, C.C., Kandemir, D., 2003. The role of entrepreneurship in building cultural competitiveness in different organizational types, Journal of Management 29 (3), 401–426.

[6] Ismail, AI, Rose, RC, Abdullah, H & Uli, J. (2010), 'The relationship between organisational competitiveadvantage and performance moderated by the age and size of firms', Asian Academy of Management Journal,volume 15, No. 2, pp. 157-173.

[7] Kuratko, D.F., Hodgetts, R.M., 1998. Entrepreneurship: A Contemporary Approach. Dryden Press,Fort WorthDrucker, P.F., 1985. Innovation and Entrepreneurship.Butterworth-Heinemann, Oxford.

[8] Markides C.C. and Williamson PJ. (1994). Related Diversification Core Competencies andCorporate Performance.Strategic Management Journal, 15,149-165.

[9] McAdam, R., Keogh, K., 2004. Transitioning towards creativity and innovation measurement in SMEs.Creativity and Innovation Management 13 (2), 126-141.

[10] Metcalfe, J. S., 1998. Evolutionary Economics and Creative Destruction. Routledge, London.

[11] Morgan, N.A., Kaleka, A. & Katsikeas, C.S., (2004), 'Antecedents of Export VenturePerformance: ATheoretical Model and Empirical Assessment', Journal of Marketing, volume 68, pp. 90-108.

[12] OECD, 2005. Oslo Manual: Proposed Guidelines for Collecting and Interpreting Technological Innovation Data. Paris.

[13] Porter M.E. (1985). Competitive Advantage: Creating and Sustaining Superior Performance.The Free Press, New York.

[14] Porter M. (1980). Competitive Strategy.The Free Press. New York.

[15] Raduan, C.R, U, J, A, H & I, A.I., (2009), 'Management, Strategic Management Theories and the Linkage withOrganizational Competitive Advantage from the Resource-Based View', European Journal of Social Sciences,volume 11, pp. 402-417.

[16] Raduan, C.R, U, J, A, H & I, A.I., (2009), 'A Conceptual Framework of the Relationship betweenOrganizational Resources, Capabilities, Systems, Competitive Advantage and Performance', Research Journalof Internatýonal Studýes, October, No. 12, pp. 45-58.

[17] Ray, G., Barney, J., Muhanna, W.A. (2004). "Capabilities, business processes and competitive advantage: choosing the dependent variable in empirical tests of the resource-based view". Strategic Management Journal, 25(1), pp.23-37.

[18] Wang, Y., &Lo., H.P, (2003), 'Customer-focused performance and the dynamic model for competence buildingand leveraging A resource-based view', Journal of Management Development, volume 22, pp. 483-526.

Role of Job Satisfaction in Insurance Industry

Matauddin Peerzada, J.K. Tandon and Lokesh Arora

Jaipur National University, Jaipur

ABSTRACT

HR practices are plans of action. Organizations need to evolve HR policies as they ensure consistency and uniformity in treating the people. They help and build loyalty, policies become benchmarks to compare and evaluate performance but sometimes it is seen that above mentioned aspect does not become possible when organization fails to understand employee's satisfaction level and simultaneously employee fails to understand vision of organization. Job satisfaction is closely associated with Human resource management and its policies, a management function that helps manager's recruit, select, train and develops members for an organization, the overall purpose of this article is to understand the various factors and its role with Job Satisfaction in Insurance Industry.

INTRODUCTION

The term Job Satisfaction describes a positive feeling about a job, resulting from an evaluation of its characteristics. A person with high level of job satisfaction holds positive feeling about his or her job, while a dis-satisfied person holds negative feelings. It is observed that when people speak of employees attitudes, they usually mean job satisfaction.

Various sectors have different HR policies and similarly Service/Insurance industry has also a HR policies which comprises of different HR aspects rules and regulation like Performance Appraisal (PMS), Recruitment & Selection , Pay roll, Compensation Management, Career Progression, Promotion, Training and Development, Human Resource Planning.

Above mentioned HR practices have direct or indirect relation as far as job satisfaction is concerned. There are many resources require to establish any business unit but among all the resources most important resource is to have a efficient and competent man power once having man power again most important part is to manage the man power by taking into consideration the individual's skills, for this formulation of effective HR policy is very essential as it also helps in retaining the employees.

HR practices are plans of action. Organizations need to evolve HR policies as they ensure consistency and uniformity in treating the people. They help and build loyalty, policies become benchmarks to compare and evaluate performance but sometimes it is seen that above mentioned aspect does not become possible when organization fails to understand employee's satisfaction level and simultaneously employee fails to understand vision of organization. It is very important to develop mutual understanding aspects from both ends which will result into ensuring the growth for both.

'It is said that happy employees are more productive, thus it is also important to identify the relationship of job satisfaction and productivity in the Insurance industry, David Carnomat has also said that how to grow the employee loyalty is challenging task and for the same the level of Job Satisfaction plays really a very important role'.

Apart from this Lisa M Moynihan from London School of Business has mentioned that the impacts of various Hr practices on Performance of Business unit and employee job satisfaction are different. Study says that job satisfaction levels in the United States, India and various other part of world are dropping down which is indeed a matter of concern for the corporate.

Job satisfaction is closely associated with Human resource management and its policies, a management function that helps manager's recruit, select, train and develops members for an organization. HRM is concerned with people's dimension in organizations. It refers to set of program, functions and activities designed and carry out in order to maximize both employee as well as organizational effectiveness.

'Organizations are not mere bricks, mortar, machineries or inventories. They are people. It is the people who staff and manage organizations'. HRM involves the application of management functions and principles. The functions and principles are applied to acquisitioning, developing, maintaining and remunerating employees in an organization.

Decisions relating to employees must be integrated. Decisions on different aspects of employees must be consistent with other human resource decisions must influence the effectiveness of an organization. Effectiveness of an organization must result in betterment of services to customers in the form of high-quality services at reasonable costs.HRM functions are not confined to business establishment only. They are applicable to non-business organizations, too, such as education, health care, recreation etc, in order to do understand the above aspect proposed study will be useful.

As far as Insurance sector and its Development in India is concerned according to various authentic sources like IRDA (Insurance Regulatory and Development Authority), 1818 saw the advent of life insurance business in India with the establishment of the Oriental Life Insurance Company in Calcutta. This Company however failed in 1834. In 1829, the Madras Equitable had begun transacting life insurance business in the Madras Presidency. 1870 saw the enactment of the British Insurance Act and in the last three decades of the nineteenth century, the Bombay Mutual (1871), Oriental (1874) and Empire of India (1897) were started in the Bombay Residency. This era, however, was dominated by foreign insurance offices which did good business in India, namely Albert Life Assurance, Royal Insurance, Liverpool and London Globe Insurance and the Indian offices were up for hard competition from the foreign companies.

In 1914, the Government of India started publishing returns of Insurance Companies in India. The Indian Life Assurance Companies Act, 1912 was the first statutory measure to regulate life business. In 1928, the Indian Insurance Companies Act was enacted to enable the Government to collect statistical information about both life and non-life business transacted in India by Indian and foreign insurers including provident insurance societies. In 1938, with a view to protecting the interest of the Insurance public, the earlier legislation was consolidated and amended by the Insurance Act, 1938 with comprehensive provisions for effective control over the activities of insurers.

An Ordinance was issued on 19th January, 1956 nationalizing the Life Insurance sector and Life Insurance Corporation came into existence in the same year. The LIC absorbed 154 Indian, 16 non-Indian insurers as also 75 provident societies—245 Indian and foreign insurers in all. The LIC had monopoly till the late 90s when the Insurance sector was reopened to the private sector.

In December, 2000, the subsidiaries of the General Insurance Corporation of India were restructured as independent companies and at the same time GIC was converted into a national re-insurer. Parliament passed a bill de-linking the four subsidiaries from GIC in July-2002, today there are 24 general insurance companies including the ECGC and Agriculture Insurance Corporation of India and 23 life insurance companies operating in the country.

The Insurance sector is a colossal (massive) one and is growing at a speedy rate of 15-20%. Together with banking services, insurance services add about 7% to the country's GDP. A well-developed and evolved insurance sector is a boon for economic development as it provides long- term funds for infrastructure development at the same time strengthening the risk taking ability of the country.

ICICI Prudential Life Insurance Company is a joint venture between ICICI Bank, which is one of India's foremost financial services companies, and Prudential plc, which is a leading international financial services group headquartered in the United Kingdom. ICICI Prudential began the operations in December 2000. Today, this company has over 2100 branches, which include 1,116 micro-offices, over 290,000 advisors and 18 banc assurance partners.

ICICI Prudential Life Insurance Company is the first life insurer in India that received a National Insurer Financial Strength rating of AAA from Fitch ratings. ICICI Prudential has been voted as India's Most Trusted Private Life Insurer for three consecutive years. ICICI Prudential Life Insurance Company has various insurance plans that have been designed for different individuals, as every individual has different insurance needs. Given below is a list of plans provided by ICICI Prudential Life Insurance Company.

As far as LIC in India is concerned Life Insurance Corporation of India was created on 1st September, 1956, with the objective of spreading life insurance much more widely and in particular to the rural areas with a view to reach all insurable persons in the country, providing them adequate financial cover at a reasonable cost.

LIC had 5 zonal offices, 33 divisional offices and 212 branch offices, apart from its corporate office in the year 1956. Since life insurance contracts are long term contracts and during the currency of the policy it requires a variety of services need was felt in the later years to expand the operations and place a branch office at each district headquarter. Re-organization of LIC took place and large numbers of new branch offices were opened. As a result of re-organization servicing functions were transferred to the branches, and branches were made accounting units. It worked wonders with the performance of the corporation. It may be seen that from about 200.00 crores of New Business in 1957 the corporation crossed 1000.00 crores only in the year 1969-70, and it took another 10 years for LIC to cross 2000.00 crore mark of new business. But with re-organization happening in the early eighties, by 1985-86 LIC had already crossed 7000.00 crore Sum Assured on new policies.

Today LIC functions with 2048 fully computerized branch offices, 109 divisional offices, 8 zonal offices, 992 satellite offices and the corporate office. LIC's Wide Area Network covers 109 divisional offices and connects all the branches through a Metro Area Network. LIC has tied up with some Banks and Service providers to offer on-line premium collection facility in selected cities. LIC's ECS and ATM premium payment facility is an addition to customer convenience. Apart from on-line Kiosks and IVRS, Info Centre have been commissioned at Mumbai, Ahmedabad, Bangalore, Chennai, Hyderabad, Kolkata, New Delhi, Pune and many other cities. With a vision of providing easy access to its policyholders, LIC has launched its SATELLITE SAMPARK offices. The satellite offices are smaller, leaner and closer to the customer. The digitalized records of the satellite offices will facilitate anywhere servicing and many other conveniences in the future.

LIC continues to be the dominant life insurer even in the liberalized scenario of Indian insurance and is moving fast on a new growth trajectory surpassing its own past records. LIC has issued over one crore policies during the current year. It has crossed the milestone of issuing 1,01,32,955 new policies by 15th Oct, 2005, posting a healthy growth rate of 16.67% over the corresponding period of the previous year.

From then to now, LIC has crossed many milestones and has set unprecedented performance records in various aspects of life insurance business. The same motives which inspired our forefathers to bring insurance into existence in this country inspire us at LIC to take this message of protection to light the lamps of security in as many homes as possible and to help the people in providing security to their families.

Job Satisfaction is very important aspect as far as any industry is concerned, to identify the levels of Job Satisfaction there are certain aspects of HR need to understand, "Existing level of Job Satisfaction of Employee in Organization, as far as this area is concerned it is very essential to understand the employees perception on various aspects of HR policies, working systems, environment and the culture in the existing Industry.

LITERATURE REVIEW

The body of Research examining the relationship between HR practices and firm performance has grown exponentially over the past few years. The seminal work in this area was produced by Huselid (1995), who examined the relationship between HR practices and corporate turnover, profitability and Job satisfaction. Huselid (1995) surveyed senior HR executives in a sample of 968 publicly traded corporations in the US regarding the percentage of employees who were covered by a set of HR practices generally considered representative of a High-Performance Work System (HPWS).

After controlling for a number of variables, he found that his HR index was significantly related to the gross rate of return on assets (a measure of profitability) and Tobin's Q (the ratio of the market value of a firm to its book value). This study provided the foundation for much of the research that followed. (Patrick M. Wright, Cornell University)

Delery and Doty (1996) examined the relationship between HR practices and profitability in a sample of banks in the US. In testing universalistic, contingency and configurationally approaches to HRM, they found that in general, HR practices were positively related to profitability.

Guthrie (2001) examined the impact of HR practices on Job-Satisfaction and firm productivity among a sample of firms in New Zealand. He noted that HR practices had an impact on turnover, and that the relationship between retention and productivity was positive when firms implemented high-involvement HR practices. (Timothy M. Gardner, Brigham Young University)

Two major studies at the plant level have been conducted examining the relationship between HR practices and firm performance. McDuffie (1995) found that the HR practice 'bundles' he measured were related to quality and productivity on auto assembly lines. Meanwhile, Youndt *et al* (1996) discovered that human capital enhancing HR practices were related to operational performance among a sample of manufacturing plants.

While much of the research on the relationship between HR practices and performance has somewhat consistently revealed a significant relationship, some recent debates have emerged regarding the value of different approaches to studying this phenomenon. Debates have arisen regarding the proper sources for gaining the most valid reports of HR practice measures, the proper level of analysis and proximity of performance measures, and the timing of measurement.

From previous study of Job Satisfaction, it has been observed that earlier many research studies have been done on different aspects of HR practices and various factors of job satisfaction; simultaneously the identification of various levels of Job Satisfaction is equally important for service/any other sector.

CONCLUSION

Job Satisfaction being a most important concern for employer and employee, it is very important to identify the levels of Job Satisfaction in Service/Insurance Sector, along with the same there are certain aspects mentioned above should be emphasized upon in order to reduce the perplexity of the concern.

Here at the same time understanding employee's perception on various aspects of HR policies, working systems, environment and the culture in the existing Industry is equally important. Identification of factors that motivate the employees related to various aspects of Job Satisfaction helps in dealing with primary corporate concern like Attrition, Retention, Job Rotation and Job Satisfaction as well.

Employees Social, Organizational, Functional and personal objectives should be given importance while formulation and reviewing the policies regarding the given area and testing the same through various methods and tools within regular interval can help in long term to employer and employee with regards to various challenges and its outcomes, thus this path of the growth can be developed even further by identifying the actual inside of the most important asset of an organization called 'employees'.

REFERENCES

[1] C.B. Mamoria (2002), Personnel Management, Himalaya Publications.

[2] C.R. Kothari Research Methodology, New Age International Publishers.

[3] D.S. Saini (2000), Human Resource Management: Perspective for the New Era, New Delhi.

[4] Human Resource Management (2006), ICFAI Press, Hyderabad.

[5] K. Aswathappa (2005), Human Resource Management & Personnel Management, Tata McGraw-Hill Publication.

[6] N.P. Podsakoff (2007), "Differential Challenges with Job Attitudes, Turn over ad Withdrawal Behavior, A Journal of Applied Psychology, pp. 883-891.

[7] N.W.Van (2003), "Fatigued and Dissatisfied or Fatigue and satisfied", Academy of Management Journal, pp. 339-348.

[8] R. Lines (2004), "Influence of participation in strategic change, Resistance, organizational Commitment and goal achievement", Journal of Change Management, September, pp. 193-213.

[9] Robin Stiphen/Seema Sanghvi (2006), Organizational Behavior, Pearson Education.

[10] Slocum/Hellriegel, Fundamentals of organizational behavior, Cengage India Private Ltd.

[11] Strategic Human Resource Management, ICFAI Center for management research.

[12] T.V. Rao (1999), HRD Audit: Evaluating the Human Resource Function for Business Improvement, New Delhi.

[13] www.irda.gov.in

[14] www.rbi.gov.in

Six Sigma as a Competitive Operations Strategy

Anuradha R Chetiya

Ramjas College, University of Delhi, Delhi

ABSTRACT

The measurement and improvement of processes is essential to achieve operational excellence and the ideals of total quality. This paper examines the role of the six sigma metrics in enhancing competitive advantage of various firms thereby holding this initiative as a competitive operations strategy. It discusses the improvements in operational metrics as a result of implementing the six sigma methodology. The paper also examines adoption of six sigma in the Indian corporate scenario. It concludes that improving the six sigma metrics can bring about improvement in effectiveness and efficiency of processes creating a competitive advantage in total business performance.

INTRODUCTION

The measurement and improvement of processes is essential to achieve operational excellence and the ideals of total quality. It is very important for organizations to choose the right metrics, which focus on the processes and not the products, to achieve the best results. According to Breyfogle (2001), however there is no 'one-size-fits-all' metric that will work for all organizations or for that matter even within any organization. What may prove to be appropriate in a particular product or process may not fit into another. It is thus a question of choosing the right metric to fit the right activity that will result in long-term strategic benefit. This paper examines the role of the Six Sigma metrics in enhancing competitive advantage of various firms thereby holding Six Sigma initiative as a competitive operations strategy.

SIX SIGMA METRICS FOR OPERATIONAL EXCELLENCE

A principal element of Six Sigma is the Six Sigma metrics or measures. These are the numerical performance measures for measuring operational performances. It is important to choose the right metric for the right purpose to ensure success of Six Sigma efforts. Organizations should consider using only those Six Sigma metrics that are appropriate for each situation Improperly chosen metrics lead to sub-optimal behavior and can lead people away from the organization's goals instead of towards them (Pyzdek, 2001).

Harry and Schroeder (2005) are also of the opinion that Six Sigma is basically about changing what companies' measure. According to them two important aspects of metrics are:

(i) It is not only important to measure customer opinion but even more important to link these measurements to the quality and efficiency of their processes to manufacture higher quality products at a lower costs.

(ii) Secondly, organizations also need to establish statistical correlation between metrics. For example how the metric 'first time yield' correlates to costs or how the 'rolled throughput yield' correlates to costs.

Thus, 'metrics create a common language for communication and allow process measurements to be communicated openly and candidly'. Harry & Schroeder (2005) have given a number of reasons as to why metrics are necessary in any quality improvement initiative, in particular, the Six Sigma methodology, some of which are stated here:

(i) To establish the differences between perception, intuition and reality.

(ii) To gather the facts for good decision making and provide the basis for sound implementation of those decisions.

(iii) To identify and verify problem areas or bottlenecks that have remained undetected.

(iv) To better understand the processes and determine which factors are important and which are not.

(v) Validate the processes and determine whether they are performing within the required specifications.

(vi) Evaluate customer satisfaction and establish the links to the key processes.

(vii) Document the processes and then communicate them to others.

(viii) Provide a baseline for process performance and cost correlation.

(ix) To check if the processes are improving and retain the gains for those that are.

According to Eckes (2001), measurements or metrics should focus on two key elements of any business – effectiveness (output measures of customer requirements) and efficiency (measures of amount of time or cost or labor etc). Further Pyzdek (2001) states that 'once chosen, the metrics must be communicated to the members of the organization'. To be useful, the employee must be able to influence the metric through his performance and it must be clear precisely how the employee's performance influences the metric'.

The commonly used Six Sigma metrics are:

1. Defect Per Unit (DPU)
2. Defect Per Million Opportunities (DPMO)
3. Process Capability

4. Rolled Throughput Yield (RTY)
5. Cost of Quality (COQ)

Defect Per Unit (DPU)

Six Sigma differentiates between a defect and a defective. Defect Per Unit (DPU) takes into consideration the actual number of defects found in each unit and not just the defective units while measuring product quality. A Defect Per Unit (DPU) is simply the ratio of the number of defects observed to the number of units produced.

$$\text{DPU} = \frac{\text{Number of defects discovered}}{\text{Number of units produced}}$$

For example, in a lot size of 60 printed circuit boards (PCB), if 5 of them fail testing, the Defects Per Unit (DPU) is 8.3%.

According to Harry (1997),focusing on total defects per unit

(a) Reduces the cycle time per unit
(b) Reduces WIP inventory carrying costs
(c) Reduces delivered defects
(d) Reduces early life failure rate
(e) Reduces defect analysis and repair cost per unit

Defects Per Million Opportunities (DPMO)

DPMO includes the total number of opportunities for failure and thus can give additional insights into a process.

$$\text{DPMO} = \frac{\text{DPU}}{\text{Opportunities for error}} \times 10^6$$

Breyfogle et al (2001) are of the opinion that a DPMO rate can serve as a useful link between a product metric and a process metric. This is because this metric, by considering the number of opportunities in a product can be used to measure products of varying degrees of complexity. Harry & Schroeder (2005) calls this kind of comparison 'quantitative benchmarking'. Quantitative benchmarking involves the following elements

(i) First, it determines the yield or defect rate for a particular product, service or transaction and
(ii) Secondly, it reveals how many opportunities for defects exist in that product service or transaction
(iii) A comparison is then possible by using the metric average yield per opportunity or the DPMO.

At Asea Brown Boveri for example, when Six Sigma was at the early implementation stage, each plant identified key processes and product characteristics and reported DPMO values to the headquarters. This allowed specific processes in one plant to be compared to similar processes in other plants.

Table 1. Six Sigma and DPMO

DPMO	*Sigma Level*
697700	1
308700	2
66810	3
6210	4
233	5
3.4	6

Source: Managing Six Sigma, Breyfogle III, Cuppelo, Meadows, 2001

In Six Sigma, it is possible to benchmark the quality of similar processes producing dissimilar products despite different yields and the number of opportunities for defects. The DPMO can be converted to sigma levels,assuming a process mean shift of 1.5 sigma ,asshown in the Table 1.

For manufacturing operations, defining a defect and hence calculating the DPMO is not very difficult. A defect is usually something that does not conform to specification or tolerances. In service processes it may not be very easy, but is certainly possible and care needs to be exercised. Six Sigma is equally applicable in solving quality problems involving soft areas-service, invoicing, packaging & so on (Harry & Schroeder, 2005). In fact GE was the first company to successfully apply Six Sigma to transactions and services. By applying the Six Sigma Breakthrough Strategy, GE Capital Services for example, generated over a billion dollars in net income in one year.

Process Capability

This is the most commonly used metric in Six Sigma. It is defined as the ability of a process to manufacture products well within the design specification limits. A process capability index compares the natural variability of a process and the process specification limits to determine whether a process is 'capable' or not. A process is defined to be at Six Sigma level if six standard deviations can fit in between the target value and the specification limits, provided the process is centered. An alternative way of looking at this, is to compare the total process width and the design width. Design specifications are expressed as a target and a tolerance above or below the nominal value is referred to as the upper specification limit (USL) and the lower specification limit (LSL). The process must be capable of producing the product within these specifications to rule out the possibility of defective products, keeping in mind that capabilities of processes are subject to constant equipment changes, shifting technologies, and difficult to measure variations. If the design width is twice that of the process width, we have a Six Sigma process.

The process capability index defined simply as the ratio of the specification spread to the process spread.

$$C_p = \frac{Design Width}{Process Width} = \frac{(USL - LSL)}{6\sigma}$$

USL = Upper Specification Limit

LSL = Lower Specification Limit

σ = Process Standard Deviation

For a three sigma process, the design width is same as the natural tolerance of the process, which is always assumed to be 6σ thereby implying that $C_p = 1$. For a Six Sigma process, the design width is twice (i.e. 12σ) that of the process width (i.e.6σ) thereby implying that $C_p = 2$.

Other measures of process capability can be found in the work of Pyzdek(2001).

Rolled Throughput Yield (RTY)

Most organizations report the throughput yield of a process as the percentage of units that pass the final test relative to the number of units that entered the process. Products or services are created in multiple steps and each process step may have different throughput yield values. While calculating throughput at a process step, previous process steps are not considered. Thus, throughput yield represents first time right quality at that step only. However it does not quantify the units that do not pass the process because they contain defects. Out of these some need rework and some become scrap. This operation is called the 'hidden factory'. The rolled throughput yield (RTY) however is applied to the entire process. It is the probability of a unit of product passing through all the process steps without any defects. It is computed by multiplying the throughput yield for each process step. Thus, the RTY can expose the location and the magnitude of the hidden factory.

Mathematically, Rolled Throughput Yield (RTY) for an 'm' stage process is computed as follows:

$$Y_{RT} = \underset{i=1}{P}\ Y_{tpi}$$

where Y_{tpi} is the throughput yield at the ith step of the process.

The throughput yield, by taking into consideration rework and scrap etc on the units can expose the so-called hidden factory operations and hence the RTY gives more insight into the overall process performance. The Six Sigma approach thus puts greater emphasis on achieving Six Sigma performance at each step in the process to achieve a high RTY.

LG for example had divided Six Sigma into three parts: manufacturing 6s, R & D 6s and transactional 6s. And in manufacturing area, improving RTY was the major focus of the projects and the know-how of RTY improvement was transferred to all subsidiaries.

Costs of Quality (COQ)

Quality Cost Accounting forms an important function in most modern organizations. Quality cost systems help management plan for quality improvement by identifying opportunities for greatest return on investment (Pyzdek, 2001).

Traditionally, quality related costs were limited to inspection and testing. However, as time passed, managers began to define and isolate quality related costs. Gyrna (1988), stated three facts about quality related costs –

(i) Quality related costs are generally in the range of 20 to 40 percent of sales.

(ii) Quality related costs are not only limited to manufacturing operations, but to ancillary services such as purchasing and customer service departments.

(iii) Individually, most of the costs resulting from poor quality were avoidable.

The traditional view of quality has been that 'quality is a cost' whereas, the modern view is that quality is not a cost. Six Sigma has shown that the highest quality producer is the lowest cost producer (Harry, 1997). Pyzdek, along with Harrington and Gryna used the term 'cost of poor quality (COPQ)', to emphasize that quality is not a cost, however poor quality is a cost. And over the years, many companies have utilized the cost of poor quality metric as a leading indicator of how well they are performing in the quality arena(Harry & Schroeder, 2005*)*.

For most organizations, quality costs are hidden costs, often referred to as 'the Hidden Factory' and are a result of adhoc systems and processes, for example rework set up to correct errors made during the manufacturing process. They take up unnecessary space, longer cycle times, increased costs and inefficient use of resourcesand cannot be identified unless specific quality cost identification efforts are in place. As a result of unmeasured quality, costs often escalate and revenues tend to come down triggering a multiplier effect, sometimes threatening the very existence of the company. Harry (1997) summarizes the essence of cost of poor quality as:

- The hidden cost of failing to meet customer expectations the first time
- The hidden loss in production capacity
- The hidden opportunity for increased efficiency
- The hidden potential for higher profits
- The hidden loss in market share
- The hidden increase in production cycle time

One of the characteristics of Six Sigma management is that it exposes the previously invisible Cost of Poor Quality (Lee & Choi, 2006). Wisely applied Six Sigma techniques can help eliminate or reduce many of the issues that affect overall Cost of Poor Quality (Park, 2003).

In the Korean company *Samsung SDI*, for example, the quality cost in 1999 was \$ 0.38 billion or 11.3 % of sales. However, due to intensive Six Sigma project activities, by 2000, the quality cost was reduced to \$0.30 billion, which translated to 5.6 % of the total sales.

Table 2 shows the interrelationship between sigma level, DPMO and cost of quality:

Table 2. Interrelationship Between Sigma Level, DPMO and Cost of Quality

Sigma Level	*Defects Per Million Opportunities*	*Cost of Quality*
2	308,537 (Noncompetitive companies)	Not applicable
3	66,807	25 – 40 % of Sales
4	6,210 (Industry Average)	15 – 25 % of Sales
5	233	5 – 15 % of Sales
6	3.4 (World Class)	< 1 % of Sales
Each sigma shift provides a 10 percent net income improvement		

Source: Six Sigma -The Breakthrough Management Strategy Revolutionizing the World's Top Corporations, Harry & Schroeder, 2005.

Relationship Between the Metrics

Trying to establish a link between the various metrics and determining correlation between them, if any, would perhaps be beneficial in identifying which are the areas that need more focus (Harry & Schroeder, 2005). Another aspect that Eckes (2001) talks about in the light of establishing relationships between metrics is what he calls the concept of '*double-dipping*'. Double dipping is said to occur when one measure accomplishes two things. For example if the process is room service, a metric like 'amount of time consumed in a delivery' constitutes an output measure (i.e. a measure of the effectiveness of the process) as well as a process measure (measure of efficiency of the process). Harry (1997) has done an empirical analysis of the relation between process capability and the rolled throughput yield. A Pareto analysis indicated that 84% of the variation in rolled throughput yield could be explained by the process capability. This research clearly indicates the need to focus on improving the metric process capability. He has also shown that the cycle time and the defects per unit are positively correlated. As the DPU increases, the cycle time also increases and as the sigma levels go up the cycle time shows a downward trend.

SIX SIGMA: IMPROVING THE OPERATIONAL METRICS

Adopting Six Sigma in an organization can bring about significant improvements in all the performance metrics and more. The benefits of operational excellence would reflect in all the other metrics introduced at the beginning of this paper like the RTY, the DPMO and the cost of quality. Harry & Schroeder (2005) estimated the COQ of three sigma companies at 25-40 % of sales and of world class six sigma companies to be at less than 1%.

Juran Institute's implementation of lean and Six Sigma initiatives in companies like AT&T, DuPont, Microsoft, Nokia and Hutchinson Sealing Systems has reportedly produced the following significant results

(a) Reduction in the level of inventories by 95%

(b) Reduction in lead times by 78%

(c) Reduction of shop floor requirement by 85%

(d) Reduction of waste by 33%

A look at the improvements in operational metrics reported by some of the world-class organizations reveals significant results.

Texas Instruments

Six Sigma initiative at Texas Instruments yielded following results between 1988 and 1993.

(a) Reduced cost of quality from 40.1% to 7.40%

(b) Reduced the Defects per unit from 0.104 to 0.009

(c) Brought down Cycle Time from 10.6 weeks to 3.9 weeks

(d) Improved the Rolled Throughput Yield from 84.3% to 98.9%

(e) Reduced Scrap from $3.0 million to $0.3 Million

General Electric

General Electric between 1995 and 1999:

(a) Achieved company wide savings of over $1billion.

(b) Had an estimated savings of $ 2 billion in 1999 alone.

(c) Increased the operations ROI fourfold.

(d) Cut down on operations costs by half.

(e) GE plastics improved the quality of a product used in CD ROMS from 3.8 to 5.7 and captured a significant amount of business from Sony.

(f) Achieved a 400% improvement on ROI in its industrial diamond business.

Motorola

The Six Sigma initiative, which started in 1987 in Motorola produced following results-

(a) Reduced manufacturing costs by \$1.4 billion and

(b) Increased shareholder value by fourfold.

(c) For a pager the cycle time from order entry to shipment time reduced from a 1.5 months to 1 hour.

Citibank

In services, Citibank group has reported the following success rates-

(a) Reduction of internal callbacks by 80%.

(b) Decrease in the credit processing time by 50 %.

(c) Cycle times of processing statements from 28 days to 15 days.

SIX SIGMA IN INDIAN CORPORATE SCENARIO

The Six Sigma wave in Indian companies began way back in the late 90's. Some of the companies who were early on to this program are Godrej – GE, Bajaj Auto, Hero Motors, Modi Xerox and Wipro. Wipro was the first Indian company to adopt this methodology in 1997 and since then the list is diverse and is growing. The automotive industry, consumer durables industry, software industry, banks, BPOs and public sector undertakings (PSUs) in India are known to have adopted the Six Sigma methodology.

The automobile industry seems to be clearly leading the way as far as adopting Six Sigma is concerned. Maruti for example rolled out the first Six Sigma pilot project in its spares department, and since then has been consistently applying it. Hyundai and Honda are also known to be following Six Sigma. Tata Motors launched their Six Sigma program under the umbrella of the Tata Business Excellence Model (TBEM) and since then has reaped rich dividends. It is one of the key factors of the company recovering from a loss of Rs 500 crore in the year ended March 2001, to a profit of Rs 28 crore in the first quarter of 2002 – 03. Overall quality improvement for the first year of the Six Sigma project was reported to be 80% and since then has been between 65 percent to 75 percent each year. Some of the operational results reported werereduction in costs of manufacturing, less rejection, less rework, smoother process flows and less cycle time.

IT majors such as Wipro, Infosys and Satyam, are pushing Six Sigma practices across all levels and training hundreds of their employees. Wipro is generally recognized as the first company to have adopted it in 1997. Wipro also claims that their cost of quality is on par with Six Sigma levels i.e. below 1%.

Consumer durables major Samsung India Electronics began the rollout by launching the program named TWIN (Together Win with Six Sigma). It aimed to develop vendor productivity by 30 % and reduce the defect ratio by over 30 % by using Six Sigma tools. LG Electronics India (LGEIL) started with a Six Sigma training initiative by training 12 Black Belts and 35 green belts among shop floor level workers. Apart from the manufacturing sector, the six-sigma initiative at LG extends into non-manufacturing and R&D sectors and the company had 60 Six Sigma projects in the areas of production, purchase and HR within a year of launching the program. Whirlpool India launched its program named OPEX- Renewed Commitment to Operational Excellence to transform the organization into a globally competitive entity.

Six Sigma is now increasingly being applied in public sector undertakings (PSUs) to reduce operational costs and improve services offered by the organization. Government and Public Sector Organizations in India like Bharat Heavy Electricals Limited (BHEL), Bharat Electronics Limited (BEL) and Oil and Natural Gas Company (ONGC) are not far behind when it comes to deploying Six Sigma. A case in point is Bharat Electronics Limited (BEL). BEL launched their capability upgradation program named *'Six Sigma Characterization and Optimization'*.BEL launched Six Sigma by starting a joint venture with General Electric called GE-BEL . Around 20 key executives including the CMD underwent training and also completed a project each. Subsequently BEL developed its own training institute called Bharat Electronics Quality Institute (BEQI) in Bangalore where Six Sigma courses were started. Executives in BEL have completed many projects bringing about a lot of improvement and cost savings to the company. ONGC began using Six Sigma in its R&D division in 2001. In one of their testing processes, the cycle time used to be 12 to 120 days. After the first Six Sigma intervention, the average was brought down to 24 days.

CONCLUSION

To compete in the world market, Indian companies have to move towards higher levels of operational performance. Some of the key benefits from adoptionof Six Sigma in terms of improved operations are –increase in production capacity and capability without running into problems of capacity constraints and additional capital investments, flexibility and space utilization in layout, smoothness in work flows and traffic, less need for inspection and supervision for workers, reduced transportation, traffic and turn-around times, less time in inspecting materials, reduced set -up costs , drastic reduction in WIP levels and overall reduction in cycle time. The benefits from the point of view of the customer would be - reduction in the number of complaints from internal customers, reduction in the number of complaints from end users, improvement in the customer delivery time, problem resolution time,reduction in the number of claims ultimately resulting in decrease in the cost of warranty claims.

For organizations currently operating at 3 to 4 sigma, moving towards Six Sigma capability would mean improvements in the critical –to-quality (CTQ) or special processes through which key functional quality results. It is not possible to follow Six Sigma across all processes. So it is an imperative exercise to identify core operational processes in the organization that affects the metrics of measurement for quality like process capability indices, RTY and COQ. Also, the CTQ variables or characteristics must be clearly defined at the outset. This must be supplemented by a regular assessment of process capabilities of all quality critical processes. It is undoubtedly clear that Six Sigma approach in addition to operational excellence can also bring about improvement in effectiveness and efficiency of processes creating a competitive advantage in total business performance by the corporate.

REFERENCES

[1] BregfoyleF.W.III , James M. C., Beki M. (2001). Managing Six Sigma, John Wiley and Sons,New York.

[2] De F., Joseph A. B., William W. (2005).Juran Institute's Six Sigma Breakthrough and Beyond, Tata McGraw Hill.

[3] Eckes, G. (2001). The Six Sigma Revolution, New York: John Wiley & Sons.

[4] Evans J. R., Lindsay, M. W. (2005). The Management and Control of Quality, Sixth Edition, Thomson South-Western.

[5] Gryna, Frank (1988). Quality Improvement, Juran's Quality Control Handbook. 4th Edition, McGraw-Hill.

[6] Harry, M.J, (1987), The Nature of Six Sigma Quality, Motorola University Press.

[7] Harry, M.J., Schroeder R. (2005). Six Sigma – The Breakthrough Management Strategy Revolutionizing the World's Top Corporations, Currency, New York.

[8] Kennedy S.(2003).Six Sigma at Ford Revisited, *Quality Digest.*

[9] Lee Kun – Chang, Choi Bong (2006).' Six Sigma Management Activities and their Influence on Corporate Competitiveness', Total Quality Management, Vol. 17, No 7, pp 893 – 911.

[10] Park, Sung H (2003).Six Sigma for Quality Improvement and Productivity. Asian Productivity Organization. Tokyo.

[11] Phillip B. C. (1980). Quality Is Free, Penguin Group.

[12] Pyzdek, T. (2001). The Complete Guide to Six Sigma, Quality Publishing, Arizona.

[13] Sharma,S. and Chetiya A. (2009). 'Organising and Implementing Six Sigma in a Lean Environment;A Casestudy of a PSU', Selected Papers of the 7th AIMS International Conference,IIM Bangalore,Publishedby AIMS,Houston,Texas,USA, pp 146-155.

[14] Six Sigma Characterization (2001). Volume I, BEQI, Bangalore.

[15] Tadikamalla, P. R. (1994). 'The Confusion over Six Sigma Quality', *Quality Progress.*

Internet Resources

[1] *www.wipro.com.*

Social Entrepreneurship: A Modern Approach of Sustainable Social Change

Satish C. Sharma, Harshila Bagoria[1] and Savio Howard[1]

Maharaja Group of Colleges, Udaipur, Rajasthan
[1] *Maharaja College of Management, Udaipur, Rajasthan*

ABSTRACT

Social entrepreneurship *is the recognition of a social problem and the uses of entrepreneurial principles to organize, create and manage a social venture to achieve a desired social change. While a business entrepreneur typically measures performance in profit and return, a social entrepreneur also measures positive returns to society. Thus, the main aim of social entrepreneurship is to further broaden social, cultural, and environmental goals. Social entrepreneurs are commonly associated with the voluntary and not-for-profit sectors, but this need not preclude making a profit. Social entrepreneurship signals the imperative to drive social change, and it is that potential payoff, with its lasting, transformational benefit to society, that sets the field and its practitioners apart.*

The paper suggests factors associated with successful social entrepreneurship, particularly with social entrepreneurship that leads to significant changes in the social, political, and economic contexts for poor and marginalized groups. It generates propositions about core innovations, leadership and organization, and scaling up in social entrepreneurship that produces societal transformation. This paper also provides certain cases of social entrepreneurship that have been widely recognized as successful.

DEFINING SOCIAL ENTREPRENEURSHIP

Social entrepreneurship refers to the practice of combining innovation, resourcefulness and opportunity to address critical social and environmental challenges. Social entrepreneurs focus on transforming systems and practices that are the root causes of poverty, marginalization, environmental deterioration and accompanying loss of human dignity. In so doing, they may set up for-profit or not-for-profit organizations, and in either case, their primary objective is to create sustainable systems change.

The key characteristics of social entrepreneurship are:

- **Sociality**: a context, process and/or set of outputs that are for public benefit.

- **Innovation:** the creation of new ideas and models that address social or environmental issues This can be manifested in three ways: a new product or service (institutional innovation); the use of existing goods and services in new, more socially productive ways (incremental innovation); and/or the reframing of norms to redefine social problems and suggest new solutions (disruptive innovation).
- **Market orientation:** the performance-driven, competitive, outlook that drives greater accountability and co-operation across sectors. Market-orientation can include anything from conventional competitive markets to the exchange of social and/or environmental value.

THE DIFFERENCES BETWEEN "ENTREPRENEURSHIP" AND "SOCIAL ENTREPRENEURSHIP"

A social entrepreneur is any person, in any sector, who uses earned income strategies to pursue a social objective, and a social entrepreneur differs from a traditional entrepreneur in two important ways:

- Traditional entrepreneurs frequently act in a socially responsible manner: They donate money to nonprofits; they refuse to engage in certain types of businesses; they use environmentally safe materials and practices; they treat their employees with dignity and respect. All of this is admirable, but their efforts are only *indirectly* attached to social problems. Social entrepreneurs are different because their earned income strategies are tied *directly* to their mission: They either employ people who are developmentally disabled, chronically mentally ill, physically challenged, poverty stricken or otherwise disadvantaged; or they sell mission-driven products and services that have a direct impact on a specific social problem (*e.g.*, working with potential dropouts to keep them in school, manufacturing assistive devices for people with physical disabilities, providing home care services that help elderly people stay out of nursing homes, developing and selling curricula).
- Secondly, traditional entrepreneurs are ultimately measured by financial results: The success or failure of their companies is determined by their ability to generate profits for their owners. On the other hand, social entrepreneurs are driven by a *double* bottom line, a virtual *blend* of financial and social returns. Profitability is still a goal, but it is not the only goal, and profits are re-invested in the mission rather than being distributed to shareholders.

WHO ARE SOCIAL ENTREPRENEURS?

Society's Change Agent: Pioneer of Innovations that Benefit Humanity

Social entrepreneurs are drivers of change. Together with institutions, networks, and communities, social entrepreneurs create solutions that are efficient, sustainable, transparent, and have measurable impact.

A few examples of social entrepreneurs and their systems-changing solutions include:

- **Muhammad Yunus (Bangladesh)**: started Grameen Bank which spearheaded microfinance globally.
- **Carlo Petrini (Italy)**: "Slow food movement" which currently has 100,000 member in 132 countries committed to rescuing cultural traditions and the preserving biodiversity.
- **Susan B. Anthony (U.S.)**: Fought for Women's Rights in the United States, including the right to control property and helped spearhead adoption of the 19th amendment.
- **Vinoba Bhave (India)**: Founder and leader of the Land Gift Movement, he caused the redistribution of more than 7,000,000 acres of land to aid India's untouchables and landless.
- **Florence Nightingale (U.K.)**: Founder of modern nursing, she established the first school for nurses and fought to improve hospital conditions.
- **John Muir (U.S.)**: Naturalist and conservationist, he established the National Park System and helped found The Sierra Club.
- **Jean Monnet (France)**: Responsible for the reconstruction of the French economy following World War II, including the establishment of the European Coal and Steel Community (ECSC). The ECSC and the European Common Market were direct precursors of the European Union.
- **Anita Ahuja (India)**: Addressed problems of waste, sanitation, and unemployment into a social entrepreneurial organization. Her business produces high-end accessories, such as wallets and purses, out of plastic waste.
- **Manish Sankla (India)**: Creating "consciousness" amongst young minds about their social responsibilities towards the wider community through Health, Education and Social activities.
- **Jiten Agrawal (India)**: Conserving environment by planting trees. TREES are planted by taking individual unique click through its website.

Social entrepreneurs are united by their ability to:

- Adopt a mission to create and sustain social value (not just commercial value)
- Recognize and relentlessly pursue new opportunities to serve that mission
- Engage in a process of continuous innovation, adaptation, and learning
- Act boldly without being limited by resources currently in hand, and
- Exhibit a heightened sense of accountability to the constituencies served and for the outcomes created.

SOCIAL ENTREPRENEURS IN INDIA (YEAR '06–'11)

India is not far behind in creating **social entrepreneurship** compared to the developed nations. In fact, India is home to a significant number of world's leading social entrepreneurs.

The Schwab Foundation is a platform (both at regional and global level) for social entrepreneurs to feature their models of sustainable social innovation and development. The foundation identifies and highlights the world's leading social entrepreneurs through its "Social Entrepreneur of the Year" competitions conducted in several countries including India since 2005.

The winners from Year '06–'11 are discussed here, for their selfless dedication to the society in reducing poverty, raising standard of living and providing novel solutions to the society's pressing problems.

Case 1: Social Entrepreneur of the Year 2011

Neelam Chhiber

Founder, Indus Tree Crafts Foundation

Brand – Mother Earth, Bangalore

Mother Earth is a great initiative to bridge the gap between rural traditional craftsmanship and urban consumer markets. Indus Tree trains rural artisans and develop them into self-help enterprising groups, creates contemporary innovative products and market them with their chain of retail stores branded as Mother Earth. They produce life style products, organic foods and garments with a focus on environmental integrity and sustainability.

Case 2: Social Entrepreneur of the Year 2010

Rajiv Khandelwal & Krishnavtar Sharma

Founders, Aajeevika Bureau, Udaipur

India accounts for nearly 100 million seasonal, rural migrant workers every year and due to enormous gaps in policy at state and national level for migrant workers, this massive workforce faces various problems. Aajeevika came to their rescue by providing a range of services to the migrants and their households. Some of its core services are registration and photo id service, social security, financial services, skills training and employment. Aajeevika helps seasonal migrants build partnerships with local governments and businesses.

Case 3: Social Entrepreneur of the Year 2009

Due to growing number of social entrepreneurs in India, the Schwab Foundation board decided to pick three winners in 2009.

Rajendra Joshi

Founder, SAATH, Ahmedabad

SAATH develops public-private partnerships to improve the lives of people living in slums which caters to around 60 million people in India. SAATH runs programmes for men, women, youth and children in the areas of healthcare, education, employment, housing, etc.

Brij Kothari

President, PlanetRead, Mumbai

PlanetRead is an attempt to improve functional literacy (Reading ability) rates with the use of SLS (Same Language Sub-titling) in TV programs. Kothari and his team have innovated, researched and nationalized the use of SLS in Bollywood film songs on TV, for mass literacy in India.

Y.A Padmanabha Rao & Rama Rao

Staffs, RIVER, Andhra Pradesh

The primary schools in rural India lack proper methodologies, resources and support systems for both teachers and students. Padmanabha and Rama Rao have developed a practical and effective curriculum that not only provides an enjoyable and sustainable learning environment for rural children but re-engages teachers in their responsibility as educators. Their success has led to replication of the model in over 75,000 schools as a part of Sarva Shiksha Abhiyan.

Case 4: Social Entrepreneur Of The Year 2008

Arbind Singh

Founder & Director, Nidan, Patna

Started in 1995, in Bihar, Nidan is an initiative to help and improve the living of informal sector workers – construction laborers, domestic helpers, micro-farmers, street traders and vendors, waste workers and other marginalized occupation groups, by creating sustainable businesses and collective enterprises owned and controlled by these members of the informal sector. Nidan facilitates education, health and livelihood of the poor men and women or protection of children involved in the informal sector. Presently, it is working in six states in India.

Case 5: Social Entrepreneur of the Year 2007

Harish Hande

Co-founder and Managing Director, SELCO, Bangalore

SELCO is aimed towards providing solar electrification to the below poverty line rural families. It facilitates sustainable and customized energy solutions by understanding the needs of its different users and thereby helping in enhancing the life of the poor. It facilitates financing through co-operative societies, commercial banks and micro finance institutions.

Case 6: Social Entrepreneur of the Year 2006

Vikram Akula

Founder & CEO, SKS Microfinance, Hyderabad

Started as an NGO in 1998, SKS is now a for-profit NBFC regulated by RBI. It uses microfinance as an important tool to eradicate poverty by giving access to financial services, like credit and insurance, to poor women. It helps women start small businesses that range from raising of goats and cows to sell milk, to opening of small shops so that they become financially free. SKS offer credit based on a simple group lending model where the women guarantee each other's loan.

CHALLENGES FACED BY SOCIAL ENTREPRENEURS

One major challenge is financing, and in particular, obtaining growth capital. Most social entrepreneurs have less trouble financing a new idea than financing the growth of their organization. Government funding is less than ideal because of the difficulty involved in complying with government reporting requirements.

The current preferred funding source for most social entrepreneurs is philanthropy, but with so much fragmentation and little standardization, this method can be time consuming and not conducive to building great institutions. Impact investors, investors who seek financial goals as well as social impact, are an important source of capital for social enterprises, but markets for impact investing are still young and undeveloped. Many social entrepreneurs are also exploring earned revenues, through social enterprises, as a way to finance large scale change.

Financing Social Ventures

Social entrepreneurs finance social organizations from a variety of sources. They often start with people close to them – family, friends, classmates and professional contacts. Social entrepreneurs also turn to corporations, public foundations, social venture competitions, impact investors and Web-based intermediaries. Web-based intermediaries such as Kiva have made it possible for social entrepreneurs to receive small donations from many individuals, i.e. micro-contributors. The Obama campaign proved that this approach can be highly effective. Fellowships and prize programs directed specifically at social entrepreneurs are another source of funding (a few examples include Echoing Green, the Skoll Foundation, and Ashoka). Though the organizations are not numerous they comprise the current key pipelines of support and recognition.

Achieving Social and Financial Objectives

Social entrepreneurs are increasingly seeing strong results through complementary nonprofit, business, and hybrid enterprises. The term "blended value" refers to the commingling of social and financial objectives, and an increasing number of organizations are working in this gray area, using a combination of business methods and philanthropy. Social enterprise, a combination of business and philanthropy, is a promising strategy because it allows a social organization to benefit from the strategies of traditional business entrepreneurs. These developments bring challenges. As the line between sectors blurs, a new form of financing will be necessary. Blended value or impact investors, investors who cross the lines between philanthropy, business and the public sector, will be increasingly important.

Cultivating Talent

Another challenge social entrepreneur faces is attracting talent. Social entrepreneurs must recruit talent without the ability to offer compensation that is comparable to business. Instead, social organizations rely on attracting people by promising meaningful work. The social sector also lacks a structured system to nurture talent; when combined with financial inhibitors, this makes retaining talent difficult. More people have chosen social organizations over other opportunities following the economic downturn, probably because comparable salaries in the private sector have dropped. Social entrepreneurs in the near future will have to determine the tipping point in compensation in order to redirect talent from other sectors.

Impact Measurements

Yet another challenge social entrepreneur faces is deciding how to measure their organization results and evaluate their impact. Effective measurement of results and impact requires a combination of data and storytelling tailored appropriately to the organizations work and its goals. In an environment where mediocrity often trumps excellence, and where money is not distributed competitively, it is important for organizations to measure results accurately so that we may begin to distinguish – and provide appropriate funding for – those programs that are achieving change. Efforts have been made to calculate a "social return on investment, similar to return on investment calculated by businesses, by groups such as the Roberts Enterprise

Development Fund in the 1990s and, more recently, the Global Impact Investing Network. Another example is the Pulse reporting system. More such efforts to create standards and rating agencies would help the process of accurately identifying successful organizations.

Scaling Impact vs. Scaling the Organization

When measuring growth and success, it is important to distinguish between the scale of an organization and the scale of its impact. The size of an organization is less important than the reach of its work; successful organizations will focus time and energy on effecting change beyond their immediate reach. Similarly, sustainability must be considered in terms of ideas in-stead of the organization itself. A field is truly sustainable when its institutions can be readily renewed and improved upon because the organizations ideas have lasting power.

Over specialization, and the divisions between fields and social groups, can be another hindrance to social change. Society is comprised of specialized fields that rarely overlap, people move vertically throughout their career paths, and many people live in homogenous communities. All of these factors result in significant blind spots within society while tending to reinforce preexisting beliefs. In order to achieve innovation and change, society needs a recombination of knowledge. Social entrepreneurs are the creative combiners who can help with this. They can carve out space in society to foster whole solutions and bring people together who would not coalesce naturally. When it comes to solving social problems, the integration of labor, rather than the division of labor, is likely the way forward.

CONCLUSION

Social entrepreneurship is emerging as an innovative approach for dealing with complex social needs and provide social service with non-profit social mission. The success of social entrepreneurship relies not only on the relocation of resources but also on the personality and social network of social entrepreneurs. **Social Entrepreneurs** are innovators who implement practical and sustainable solutions to address challenges in numerous areas including health, education, environment, access to technology and job creation. Whether they are set up as for profit entities, hybrid social ventures or not for profit organizations, their primary focus is transformational social change. Social entrepreneurs develop a revenue stream through the sale of products, services, fees or develop key partnerships to achieve sustainability. Social entrepreneurs function as the agents of change, questioning the status quo, grabbing the new yet overlooked opportunities, and changing the world for the better. Today, they are making up for the shortcomings of the bureaucracies and government. While business entrepreneurs aim to generate profits, social entrepreneurs aim to improve social values. But they differ from non-governmental organizations in that they aim to make broad-based, long-term changes, instead of few immediate small-time results. They recognize when a section of the society is stuck and offer innovative ways to break out of its stagnant state. They find out the things that don't work and alter the system to solve the problems. They detect resources while others see problems. They consider the affected people as part of the solution and not as passive beneficiaries. They propagate the solution and persuade the whole society to adopt it.

BIBLIOGRAPHY

[1] Bornstein, David. *How to Change the World: Social Entrepreneurs and the Power of New Ideas*. New York: Oxford University Press, 2004.

[2] Brock, Debbi. D., and Ashoka's Global Academy for Social Entrepreneurship. *Social Entrepreneurship Teaching Resources Handbook: For Faculty Engaged in Teaching and Research in Social Entrepreneurship*. Arlington, Virginia: Ashoka, 2008.

[3] Davis, Susan M. "Social Entrepreneurship: Towards an Entrepreneurial Culture for Social and Economic Development." Abstract, Social Science Research Network

[4] Dees, J. Greg. "The Meaning of Social Entrepreneurship," 1998

[5] Dees, J. Greg, Beth Anderson, and Jane Wei-Skillern, "Scaling Social Impact," *Stanford Social Innovation Review*, Spring 2004, pp.24-32.

[6] Dees, J. Greg. *Strategic Tools for Social Entrepreneurs: Enhancing the Performance of Your Enterprising Nonprofit*, with co-editors Jed Emerson and Peter Economy San Francisco: Wiley, 2002.

[7] Emerson, Jed, Tim Freundlich and Jim Fruchterman. "Nothing Ventured, Nothing Gained, Addressing The Critical Gaps In Risk-Taking Capital For Social Enterprise," Skoll Centre for Social Entrepreneurship, 2007

[8] Elkington, John and Pamela Hartigan. *The Power of Unreasonable People: How Social Entrepreneurs Create Markets That Change the World*. Cambridge, Mass.: Harvard Business School Press, 2008.

[9] Light, Paul C. *The Search for Social Entrepreneurship*. Washington D.C.: Brookings Institute Press, 2008.

[10] Martin, Roger, and Sally Osberg, "Social Entrepreneurship: The Case for Definition," *Stanford Social Innovation Review*, Spring, 2007.

[11] Trelstad, Brian, "Simple Measures for Social Enterprise," *Innovations*, Summer 2008.

[12] Wolk, Andrew, "Advancing Social Entrepreneurship: Recommendations for Policy Makers and Government Agencies," Aspen Institute, Root Cause, 2008.

Strategies for Launching Successful Private Labels in India

Sandeep Puri and Bhawana Sharma[1] and Harsh Dwivedi[2]

IMT, Ghaziabad
[1]Jaipur National University, Jaipur
[2]R.A. Podar Institute of Management, University of Rajasthan, Jaipur

ABSTRACT

The key to success for today's retailers isto understand the contribution and role oftheir private labels in the long-term businessstrategy and marketing mix of the retail store. The views of shoppers toward the brands have changed over the last few years. Private labels are no longer a feature primarily of retailers in the developed countries, as was the case for decades. Private labels have emerged as a key weapon for retailers and have started to play a vital role in the battle for control of the distribution channel and customer loyalty. This paper seeks to investigate the strategies for launching private label brands in the India. There are a number of factors explaining the substantial development of private labels in the Indian retailing.

INTRODUCTION

Kumar and Steenkamp (2007) have defined private label brands to be any brand that is owned by the retailer or distributor and is sold only in its own outlets. Lincoln and Thomassen (2008) define private label simply as, "brands owned and sold by the retailer and distributed by the retailer."

Private label products are capturing an increasing share of Indian retailing on the back of booming economy, rising inflation, retail consolidation and an improved image. Private labels have emerged as a key weapon for retailers and have started to play a vital role in the battle for control of the distribution channel and customer loyalty.

According to the Private Label Manufacturers' Association (PLMA), Private labels encompass all merchandise sold under a retailer's brand. That brand can be the retailer's own name or a name created exclusively by that retailer. The two distinct advantages derived from the adoption of private labels by retailers are: better margins, and increased store loyalty (Fontenelle 1996).

Key benefits for a retailer of having their private label brands are:

- **Higher margins in comparison to national brands:** Retailers' gross margins on private labels are usually 25 to 30 percent higher than those on national brands.
- **Greater leverage:** Presence of private labels in the portfolio allows the retailer better negotiating power with the national brand manufacturers.
- **Opportunities to launch new innovative products**: Private labels offer retailers to launch new innovative products. Private labels can help them to have a broader range of products at various price points. Retailers can also use private labels to provide variety to the customers.
- **Creation of strong customer loyalty:** Private labels help to differentiate the products of one retailer from those of others, resulting in increased customer loyalty towards a particular retail chain.
- **Greater control on the supply chain:** Retailers can have a greater control on the supply chain with their own private labels. They can have less stock outs and better customer satisfaction leading to improved customer loyalty.

Private label brands which were first introduced almost 100 years ago in few product categories, had seen an extraordinary growth in past few decades (Tarzijan, 2004). Private label brands are no longer a feature primarily of retailers in the developed countries, as was the case for decades. The marketing efforts of retailers across the world, and their competition with local manufacturers, have introduced private labels in almost every product category, and have made them available in both developed and emerging markets. It appears today that Europe and North America have maintained their position as the most vital markets, with an aggregated private label share of sales reaching 23 and 16 percent respectively, but with a moderate growth rate (5 percent). In comparison, private labels in emerging markets have achieved growth of up to 11 percent, and currently account for 6 percent of sales. As a general observation, the level of concentration of the retail industry and the market share of private labels are positively correlated. Moreover, in almost all categories, private labels now compete with national brands.

Private labels share is usually strongest in goods categories like milk, eggs, rice, wheat, cereals and sugar or in those with little differentiation. Private labels share is the lowest among product categories where there is strong marketing support for national brands (e.g., noodles, toothpastes, chocolates, cold drinks) and in those which require a high-level of innovation (e.g., soaps, washing powders, and cosmetics).

Private labels have emerged as a key armament for retailers and have started to play a vital role in the battle for control of the distribution channel and customer loyalty. There are a number of reasons explaining the substantial development of private labels all over the world. Among other benefits, private labels add diversity to a retailer's product line in a category; a retailer utilizes them as a measure of exclusivity to differentiate from manufacturers' brands;

and the retailer gross margins on their private labels are higher than those obtained on national brands. Apart from providing higher retail margins in comparison to national brands (Ashley, 1998), private labels added diversity to the product line in a retail category (Raju et al. 1995). Authors studied the reasons for the increased growth of private labels in the global retailing.

INDIAN RETAIL INDUSTRY

Retailing in India is booming in line with InfoTech and is becoming a key contributor to service economy. As per AT Kearney's report 2010, India's retail market is US$ 410 billion and is expected to rise to US$ 833 billion by 2013 and to US$ 1.3 trillion by 2018, at a compound annual growth rate (CAGR) of 10 per cent. The share of retail trade in the country's gross domestic product (GDP) is currently around 12 per cent, and is likely to reach 25 per cent by 2012. Yet, the industry is to un-tap the huge potential in Indian soil as the market witnesses a tremendous change in consumer preferences, tastes, abandoning life style. India's market offers tremendous promise because of its huge population base.

A greater proportion of retail industry in India is being occupied by unorganized sector with only 5% share of organized retail meaning opportunity for organized retailing is immense in India. Many retailers like Reliance, Big Bazaar, MORE, Westside, Shopper's Stop are stretching their strengths to increase their share in the organized sector. At present, it has emerged as a super organization by accumulating its own consumer base, who are ready to buy whatever retailers sell irrespective of brands (Big Bazaar, Reliance, Spencer, Vishal , More, Shoppers Stop, Life style, West End, Food world, EasyDay etc. to name a few). This poses a serious threat to existence of national brands of all FMCG and Life style products as most of the mega retailers have started selling their own private labels brands, which restricts the shelf space for national brands in their stores. This is also forcing national brand manufactures to increase their promotional spend.

REVIEW OF LITERATURE

Research on private label brands has been of considerable interest to the retailers, brand managers and academicians. One stream of research in this area deals with the factors associated with the adoption of private label brands by consumers. Cunningham (1961) examined the relationship between store loyalty and the purchase of private label brands for a sample of 16 products. Using purchase history data for 50 families, Cunningham measured the percentage of grocery expenditures devoted to store brands and calculated a store loyalty index, which he defined as the proportionate number of times a housewife visited the same store consecutively to purchase a product.

Sundel (1974) used a taste test and measured whether consumers perceive differences in quality between nationally and regionally distributed store brands of bread and canned corn. No significant differences were found. These results suggest that consumers regard store brands to be largely undifferentiated in the market. Sundel noted, however, that national brands were perceived to be superior to regional or local private labels.

Also employing a taste test format, Richardson *et al.* (1994) assessed whether consumers' quality perceptions of two locally distributed store brands of five products differed. They found no difference in quality perceptions between the store brands even when real price differences were revealed and the ingredients of the competing store brands were disguised. These findings suggest that the competing store brands were perceived to be the same not only in terms of brand image but also in terms of real product quality.

The other major stream of research on private label brands deals with the competition between private label brands and national label brands. This stream of research has tried to identify that how either private label brands or national brands could differentiate from each other. Initial research identified quality, pricing, and advertising as main bases of competition. Hoch and Banerjee (1993) contested the general perception that a private label's primary attraction was the significant price discount relative to the national brands, at which they were sold. They emphasized the role of quality in the private label purchase decision. They found evidence to support the notion that perceived quality of a private label brand was much more important than the level of price discount in determining the private-label category share. Even as retailers made efforts for serious quality improvements (Baltas, 1997), the poor quality perception has continued with private label brands.

Quelch et al (1996) found that in the case of manufactured products being introduced under private labels, the characteristics that enable store brand introduction are: (a) inexpensive, easy, low risk purchase for customer (b) easy to make from commodity ingredients (c) perishable, therefore local supplies are favored (d) category sales are growing fast, enabling the private brand's garnering reasonably high volumes and (e) low number of national players dominating the category so the retailer feels the need to reduce dependency on them.

Chaniotakis et al (2010) showed that consumers' purchase intention is directly affected by consumers' attitudes towards private labels of olive oil, which in turn are influenced by consumers' perceived benefits, economic situation, brand loyalty and trust. Dhar et al (1997) predicted the three important key determinants of store brand share. They are consumer factors, Retailer factors and the Manufacturer factors. From this it can be deducted that both supply and demand factors determine the store brand effectiveness.

Raju et al (1995) suggest that retailer's profits will increase more likely in product categories consisting of a large number of national brands. They explain that the profitability of a store's brand depends more on the directness of high competition between the private brand and the leading national brand, as against a high competition among national brands which is detrimental to the store brand.

The strategic role of Private Labels to distributors and retailers has increased in importance throughout the 1990s. Once positioned on the basis of price or value for money, Private Labels are now marketed by many firms using a "quality" focus. The success of such a strategy is especially evident in Europe where retailers such as J. Sainsbury have achieved dominance over national brands (Fitzell, 1992). Research shows that the store brand market is largely depend on the degree to which retailers are successful in communicating a quality rather than a low price image to consumers (Richardson et al, 1994). Cunningham concluded that his results may suggest that there is a positive association between store loyalty and loyalty to the brands sponsored by the store. (Cunningham 1961)

Customers are more sensitive to price when it is easy to compare competitive offerings. So retailer try to store unique offerings whose prices cannot be compared and, therefore, they can charge higher prices. (Chetan Bajaj et al, 2005). Among consumers, one obvious reason for the popularity and growth of private labels is their price advantage over national brands (Batra and Sinha, 2000). However, high quality seems to be more important in determining private labels success than lower price (Hoch and Banerji, 1993; Sethuraman, 1992).

One of the interesting phenomena concerning private labels is the fact that their growth has been highly uneven across product categories (Hoch and Banerji, 1993). Though some of the studies have compared quality perceptions of private label brands with national brands (Bellizzi et al. 1981, Rosen 1984), there have been a few studies which examined the ways to improve the quality perceptions of private label brands. Apart from providing higher retail margins in comparison to national brands (Ashley, 1998), private labels added diversity to the product line in a retail category (Raju et al. 1995).

PRIVATE LABELS IN INDIA

Big Bazaar	*EasyDay*	*MORE*	*Reliance*
Tasty Treat	Great Value	More	Reliance Select
Fresh n Pure	Equate	Feasters	Reliance Value
CareMate	Mainstays	Kitchen's Promise	Dairy Life
CleanMate	Home Trends	Enriche	Good Life Moments
Sach		110%	Good Life
Premium Harvest			Dazzle
			Sudz

STRATEGIES FOR PRIVATE LABEL MARKETERS

Develop a Strong Private Labels Proposition

Private label brand promise should be defined as a holistic representation of resounding functional and emotional attributes and benefits to fulfill a salient customer need. By setting a differentiated value proposition, an effective private label marketer considers the approach that national brands practice to project a holistic benefit proposition. Private labels proposition should start with the needs that are important to customers and offers a strong point of difference from other brands. This furthers the private label brand promise that has been informed by the competitors, but is obviously not a "me-too" communication.

Point of parities (POPs) and Points of Differentiations (PODs) between Private Labels and National Brands

POPs and PODs with the National brand are critical consideration for Private label branding. Once the brand proposition of a particular private label is established in the mind of the customers, the brand architecture strategy can enable the retail marketers to promote this brand promise at the retail store level in order to create a sense of familiarity, recognition and trust among the customers. Also the retailer can put its private labels in a broader set of aisles than national brands. This make it even more important to differentiate the private labels attributes and benefits on an aisle, category and product basis than the national brands. Good brand architecture and design expression of private label can help the prospective customer to navigate the breadth of the private label brand portfolio and understand its depth of expertise in different areas of the retail store.

Packaging Linked to Quality

It is found that customers tend to link quality with the packaging. They consider good packaging as the first visible point of quality. Thus it becomes necessary for the retailers to consider how package design, nomenclature and product strategy can boost and support the sales of a private label. Successful marketing plans for private labels often go hand in hand with packaging design and branding initiatives. These help to visualize and verbalize what the private label stands for and demonstrate its POPS and PODs in various product categories.

Product quality and packaging are a necessary functional supports for private label branding. Yet, decorative packaging and fancy brand names of private labels are not enough for today's sophisticated customers. Good packaging may be the reason that a customer picks a specific private label off the shelf, but if the product does not live up to his or her expectations in terms of quality or taste then the customer may be less inclined to repurchase.

Leverage and Own the Customer Connection

Marketers of private labels can often transcend specific product categories because they use a customer focus rather than a product focus as their brand foundation. A successful private label has the ability to own the customer connection. It has the capacity to strike a chord with customers in multiple product categories. Private labels have the potential to be magnets that draw customers into a particular retail store over another. We can take examples from Big Bazaar's success with its private labels like Tasty Treat, Care Mate and EasyDay's success with its private labels like Mainstays. Great Value. These private labels inspire such trustworthiness and commitment from their loyal customers that Big Bazaar is their pre-decided retail store whenever they think of buying something in these categories. Thus Private labels not only reinforce enduring loyalty and positive feelings for the retail brand but also enable the retailer to capture a more significant share of the customers' wallet, heart, mind and lifestyle in comparison to national brands.

Tangibles in the Store

Retail marketers are becoming more conscious about how the different aspects of their marketing mix work together to create a strong, consistent brand message to the customers. By developing store ambience, in-store messaging like signage, merchandising systems, and packaging as well as external messaging like catalogs and advertising in a harmonious manner, the retailer can create an enduring impression in-store, at shelf, at the time of purchase and during usage.

Collaborative Partnerships with Manufacturers/ Suppliers of Private Labels

Develop a collaborative relationship with manufacturers and/or suppliers to strengthen the relationships for better and innovative private labels. Collaborative category management is critical for a retailer to realize its "private label" brand goals and aspirations. There should be collaboration in understanding and deciding how to augment the product lines and SKUs that will increase the private label category as a whole and determine plans and shelving scenarios to demonstrate the high degree of category interest and excitement among the customers. The retailer and trade partnership will become more about cooperation and less about the retailer negotiating with the manufacturer or supplier on price. By following this strategy, both the parties can solidify partnership and ensure that the private label category as a whole remains profitable and appealing to the customer.

CONCLUSION

Today, retailers are not marketing their private labels as the poor "me-too" cousins of national brands in comparison to the earlier days when private were sold at low price and low value. Private labels are in a position of power and are showing lot of potential to design meaningful change in the Indian retail environment. With improved product quality, Private Label products are grabbing the market share from National Brands, and this trend is likely to continue in the future. The greatest potential for private labels lies in developing markets like India where retail chains with well-developed private label ranges are growing rapidly.

There is a paradigm shift in the retailer's mindset about the role and requirements of private label brands. This new paradigm of private label marketing entails that retailers consider a cache of often-overlooked business and branding tools to further their success. The key to success for today's retailers is to understand the contribution and role of their private labels in the long-term business strategy and marketing mix of the retail store. Retailers need to nurture their private labels as they can be growth engines of the future because of high returns in terms of margins and profitability. There is a need to have strategic brand management for private labels to establish viable points of difference in each aisle and segment within the retail store.

The rapid development of Private label products offered by Retail chains is changing the "rules of the game" in the Indian retail industry. Retail marketers need to be more conscious about the different aspects of marketing mix that can work together to create a strong, consistent brand message to the customers. Retailers must understand the contribution and role of private labels within their business and also within the lives of their customers. Marketing communication and expressions should all be developed in accordance with this thinking. There is a need for retailers to develop collaborative relationships with manufacturers and/or suppliers to strengthen the relationships for better and innovative private labels.

REFERENCES

[1] Ashley, S. (1998). How to effectively compete against private-label brands.Journal of Advertising Research, Vol.38 No. 1, 75-82.

[2] ATKearney Publications, Global Retail Development Index 2010 .www.atkearney.com (Assessed on 27/1/2011).

[3] Baltas, G. (1997), "Determinants of store brand choice: A behavioral analysis", Journal of Product & Brand Management, Vol. 6 No.5, pp.315-24.

[4] Batra, R., Sinha, I. (2000), "Consumer-level factors moderating the success of private label brands", Journal of Retailing, Vol. 76 pp.175-91.

[5] Bellizzi, J.A., Kruckeberg, H.F., Hamilton, J.R., Martin, W.S. (1981), "Consumer perceptions of national, private and generic brands", Journal of Retailing, Vol. 57 pp.56-70.

[6] Chaniotakis, I. E., Lemperopoulos, C., Soureli, M., (2010), "Consumers' intentions of buying own-label premium food products". Journal of Product and Brand Management, Vol. 19/5, pp 327-334

[7] Cheng, J.M.-S., Chen, L.S.-L., Lin, J.Y.-C., Wang, E.S.-T. (2007), "Do consumers perceive differences among national brands, international private labels and local private labels? The case of Taiwan", *Journal of Product & Brand Management*, Vol. 16 No.6, pp.368-76.

[8] Chetan Bajaj, RajnishTuli, Nidhi V Srivastava (2005), "Retail Management", PP459-460, ISBN 0-19-566986-X.

[9] Corstjens, M., and Lal, R. (2000).Building store loyalty through store brands.Journal of Marketing Research, Vol.37 No.3, 281-291.

[10] Cunningham, R.M. (1961), "Customer loyalty to store and brand," Harvard Business Review, Vol. 39, pp. 127-37.

[11] Dobson, P.W. (1998), "The Economic Welfare Implications of Own Label Goods",mimeo, University of Nottingham.

[12] Fitzell, P. (1992), Private Label Marketing in the 1990s, Global Book Productions, New York, NY.

[13] Fontenelle, S.M (1996), "Private labels and consumer benefits- The Brazilian Experience",Advances in Consumer Research, 23, pp 97-103.

[14] Hoch, S.J. and Banerji, S. (1993), "When do private labels succeed?," Sloan Management Review, Summer, pp. 57-67.

[15] Invading Private Labels, Retail Biz, Sep. 2004, p. 19,

[16] Kumar, Nirmalya, &Steenkamp J. (2007) Private Label Strategy: How to meet the store brand challenge, Boston: Harvard Business School Press.

[17] Lamey, L., Deleersnyder, B., Dekimpe, M., &Steenkamp, J. (2007). How business cycles contribute to private-label success: Evidence from the United States and Europe. Journal of Marketing, 71(1), 1-15.

[18] Lincoln, K. and Thomassen, L. (2008), Private Label: Turning the Retail Brand into Your Biggest Opportunity, p. 6, Kogan Page, London.

[19] Puri, Sandeep; and De, Kalyan. "The Changing Face of Private Labels ", Progressive Grocer, March 2012, pp. 46-49.

[20] PLMA International, http: //www.plmainternational.com/en/private_label_en3.htm. (Assessed on 2/12/2010).

[21] Quelch, J.A. and Harding, D. (1996), "Brands versus private labels: fighting to win," Harvard Business Review, January-February, pp. 99-109.

[22] Raghuram G., Bibek Banerjee and Abraham Koshy, 1999."Food World (B)", Case, Indian Institute of Management, Ahmedabad, p. 5.

[23] Raju, J., Sethuraman, R., &Dhar, S. (1995). The introduction and performance of store brands.Management Science, 41(6), 957-978.

[24] Richardson, P., Dick A.S. and Jain, A.K. (1994), "Extrinsic and intrinsic cue effects on perceptions of store brand quality," Journal of Marketing, Vol. 58 No. 4, pp. 28-36.

[25] Rosen, D. (1984). Consumer perceptions of quality for generic grocery products: A comparison across categories. Journal of Retailing, 60(4), 64-80.

[26] Steiner, R.L. (2004), "The Nature and Benefits of National Brand/Private Label Competition", Review of Industrial Organization, 24, 105-127.

[27] Sundel, H.H. (1974), "An experimental analysis of consumer attitudes toward grocery products under manufacturer's brands, nationally distributed private brands, and locally distributed private brands," unpublished doctoral dissertation, Saint Louis University.

[28] Tarzijan, J., (2004). Strategic effects of private labels and horizontal integration, International Review of Retail, Distribution and Consumer Research, 14(3), 321-335.

[29] The Global Staying Power of Private Label (2010), http://blog.nielsen.com/nielsenwire/consumer/the-global-staying-power-of-private-label/ (Assessed on 2/5/2011).\

Study of a Successful PURA Model: A Situation Analysis of Chitrakoot

Ranjana Agarwal, Surinder Batra, Neeraj Awasthy and Harsh Ajmera

IMT, Ghaziabad

ABSTRACT

PURA, Providing Urban amenities in Rural Areas, is a model of rural development. Thismodel envisages economic empowerment to a cluster of villages by strengthening their physical, electronic and knowledge connectivity. The aim of this paper is toStudy the process of PURA model and Enterprise creation. The paper also highlights the case of Chitrakoot, which is deemed as a successful PURA Model. A survey was conducted in Chitrakoot, where a PURA model has been successfully implemented by Deendayal Research Institute (DRI). Based on Chitrakoot model, alocally relevant model of change is suggested which can be replicated in other areas.The study is exploratory in nature.

INTRODUCTION

Around 70% of Indian population resides in villages and agriculture remains a major employment provider for a significant portion of the workforce in rural India. Though India is one of the rapidly growing economies in the world, India has huge divide in society manifested through a perceptible gap in the development of rural and urban areas. People migrate to urban areas looking for jobs and a better standard of living. There exists a need to create an environment of inclusive development and growth in rural areas where everyone gets an opportunity to build capacity and generate income based on competencies. Forces need to be created in rural areas which create jobs, stem migration and lead to a higher standard of living.

PURA (Providing Urban amenities in Rural Areas) is a model of rural development suggested by former President of India, Dr. A.P. J. Abdul Kalam. PURA envisages economic empowerment to a cluster of villages by providing physical, electronic and knowledge connectivity (*www.presidentofindia.nic.in*). A neo-Gandhian model of development, PURA is about creating economic facilities and employment in rural India such that the need to migrate to urban areas is obviated (Dutt and Sundaram, 2011).

AIM

The Aim of this paper is to

1. Study the process of PURA model and Enterprise creation
2. Get insight into working of Chitrakoot PURA, which is deemed as a successful PURA Model

METHODOLOGY

The following broad steps were followed in conducting the Study[1]:

(a) Obtain a detailed understanding of the concept of PURA. This was done through an orientation sessions on PURA for the research team, led by Mr. Srijan Pal Singh from Dr. Kalam's Office. Reports obtained from them were the primary source of data.

(b) Secondary research based on existing published reports of various institutions and document available on the websites of Dr. Kalam, various Central and State Government Ministries and successful PURA models.

(c) A field study was conducted for the existing PURA model at Chitrakoot to obtain an overview of the processes and implementation of existing model. Questionnaires and interviews were the main source of data collection. A field visit was made to Chitrakoot during September 2011.

RELEVANCE OF THE STUDY

PURA clusters have been in existence in several places in India and they have made their mark as examples of successful planning and implementation of the PURA model. Well-known successful PURA clusters include among others, Chitrakoot in Madhya Pradesh, Periyar in Tamil Nadu and Loni (Ahmednagar) in Maharashtra. It was considered useful to study one of these successful PURA models to derive learning which can be carried forward to the Greenfield areas being studied.

The first part of the paper deals with processes of PURA and its implementation. Section II deals with Chitrakoot model of PURA and its learning outcomes.

---

1 A research team from IMT Ghaziabad undertook a situation analysis study, as part of an initiative of planning for implementation of PURA in Greenfield areas. The Study was in alignment with the overall approach for such initiatives suggested by the Office of Dr. Kalam, involving (a) situation analysis of greenfield areas; and (b) resource analysis, with a view to identify enterprises which can best fit the needs and resources of the area under consideration. The research team comprised of selected faculty members, researchers and PGDM students of IMT Ghaziabad under the auspices of CRICKET, a research Centre at IMT for Rural Innovation, Capacity Building, Knowledge Management, Entrepreneurship and Technology.

SECTION I

PURA

The mission of PURA is to achieve sustainable growth and welfare of rural and suburban regions of the nation. The goal is to reduce distress migration by generating a wider spectrum of jobs. Providing local employment through creation of local enterprises based on local resources is a key objective. PURA aims at harnessing the local potential and finding solutions to address specific needs of the cluster of villages under its focus. By addressing issues of education and healthcare in its focal area, PURA tries to create "knowledge societies, with unique value system" at the rural level.The model envisages striving for ccomprehensive development aimed at generating sustainable income and not just poverty alleviation, which will help in bridging the urban –rural divide. (Source: President's document)

Fig. 1. Aim of PURA (From Office of Dr. APJ Abdul Kalam)

Salient Features of PURA

Some of the salient features of the PURA model areas follows:

(a) PURA is an enterprise driven model. Enterprises are envisaged to be established by harnessing local resources. These enterprises have to be financially sustainable and an attractive business proposition for an entrepreneur.Vertically integration of enterprises is strived for.

(b) PURA is based on Private-Public-Community Partnership (PPCP) model. It involves the Government, private entrepreneur and community (PPCP) at all stages of planning and implementation

(c) PURA is based on research-based planning at the local level. It consciously attempts to dovetail existing government schemes in the local area into meaningful economic activities for the PURA enterprises

(d) Planning for PURA strives to identify and acquire appropriate technology relevant for the enterprises proposed to be established.

(e) The local community is expected to play a pivotal role in setting up a PURA.

(f) Programs aimed at capacity building and skill development of the local community on a continual basis are typically undertaken as a source of continual value addition.

(g) Performance evaluation of the economic activities under PURA is community-based.

(h) Contributions from academia and research institutes in planning for PURA are looked forward to. People with professional expertise, domain experts and even students can be engaged in short term assignments for establishment of PURA.

The scope of activities planned under a PURA model include creation of local enterprises and generation of employment in agro-processing, energy, traditional production services and ancillary units, with concurrent attention to skill development, education, healthcare and sanitation. The impact of these activities must be visible in terms of growth in the indicators of Human Development Index (HDI) including education, longevity, health and higher income levels.

The implementation strategy of PURA is pitched at different levels. Unskilled personsare required to betrained in different skill sets relevant to the planned economic activities. Provision issimultaneously made for microfinance, such that the trained persons can start their own enterprises with supplementary marketing support. Creation of employment opportunities for local population from these enterprises is expected to be the key outcome.

Types of Connectivity in PURA Model

PURA envisages four types of connectivity among clusters of villages. These are Physical, Electronic, Knowledge and Economic connectivity. Each of these is briefly described below:

Physical Connectivity

The PURA model envisages that the villages must be connected within themselves and with main towns and cities by good roads, waterways and railway lines, depending upon their geographic location. They must have appropriate facilities for education, health and other amenities, thereby enabling movement of people and goods and improving access to schools and health care centres. Physical connectivity reduces investments in distribution of power, water and communication networks at the local level.

Electronic Connectivity

PURA Model also envisages provision of electronic connectivity through Information and Communication Technology (ICT) such as Broadband/ Fibre/Satellite/Wireless/ Leased Lines/ and Public Call Offices (STD/ISD/ISDN). Provision of electronic connectivity will enable provision of services such as tele-education and tele–medicine to the local community as well as setting up of village internet kiosks, e–Government kiosks, e–market access, tele-training on -farming, e–banking and ATM centres, etc. for the villagers. Indigenous knowledge can be preserved and enhanced with the latest tools of technology, training and research. Villages can have access to good education from the best teachers, wherever they are. They can have the benefit of good medical treatment, and latest information on their livelihood pursuits such as agriculture, fishery, horticulture and food processing.

Knowledge Connectivity

Knowledge connectivity refers to the creation of opportunities for the local populace to enhance their individual and collective knowledge and utilize this knowledge for their common good. This can be achieved by establishing schools, vocational training facilities, and resources for water/forest/environment management, etc. Tele-education to educate students/farmers/workers is a key component of knowledge connectivity. This connectivity contributes to explicit and tacit benefits such as increasing productivity, utilisation of spare time, awareness of health welfare, ensuring markets for products, increasing quality consciousness, interacting with partners, getting the best equipment and increasing transparency, etc.

Economic Connectivity

Availability of physical, electronic and knowledge connectivity facilitatescreation of sustainable earning capacity, leading to economic connectivity. Economic connectivity is seen in the form of creation of employment, entrepreneurship and increase of income of the rural populace through setting up agro–based, small scale/ cottage manufacturing and service industries and an increase in the total output of villagers in terms of production of agriculture and non-agriculture items. This will lead to a creation of a vibrant economy where economic strength is based on value systemwith improved quality of life and women empowerment. This can also be instrumental in attracting investors andestablishing/ promoting microfinance institutions and small-scale industries.

PURA Implementation Plan

AProcess Flow Diagram for realization of PURA is presented at Figure 2. One can view PURA as the equivalent of a Special Economic Zone (SEZ) for the rural areas.

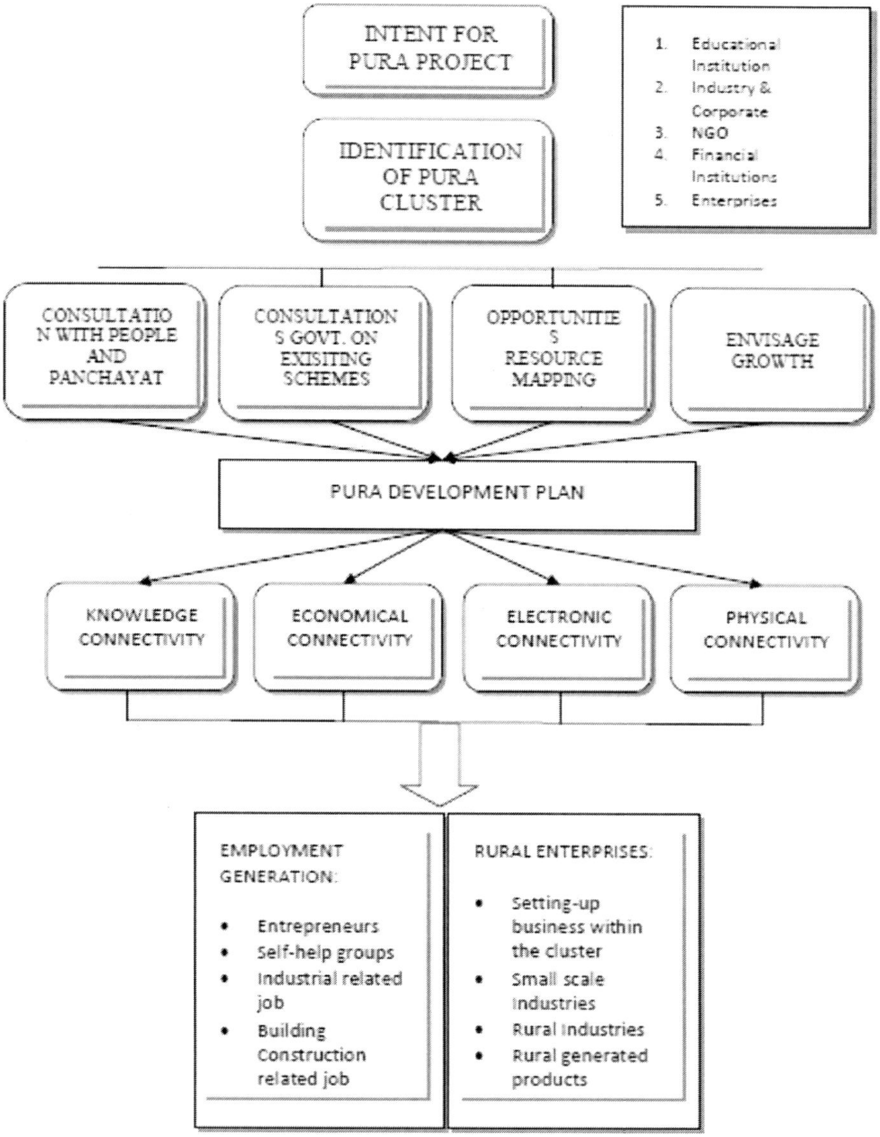

Fig. 2. PURA Implementation Plan
Source: President's document.pdf, www.presidentofindia.nic.in

After having identified the cluster of villages to be transformed into a PURA cluster, the first step involved is to identifyan institution such as educational institute/ industry/NGO/ financial institute/ small scale enterprise/ Government body, which intends to create a PURA cluster. As PURA is a research driven plan, the contribution of academia to PURA becomes significant.A PURA action group can be started by a management institution or an engineering institution available in that region.

SECTION II

UNDERSTANDING THE PURA CONCEPT THROUGH FIELD STUDY AT CHITRAKOOT

Chitrakoot PURA was set up by Deendayal Research Institute (DRI) under the leadership of Mr. Nanaji Deshmukh, an eminent social activist. The Chitrakoot PURA lies in District Chitrakuta of Uttar Pradesh as well as District Satna of Madhya Pradesh.This model is based on the "Integral Humanism Concept" of Pt. Deendayal Upadhyaya, which advocates the complimentary nature of the family, primary school and the local population in harnessing economic growth with values. Attaining self-reliance is the main goal of DRI.[2] The self-reliance campaign touches all sections of society, including the individual and his/her family. Self-reliance is sought to be achieved by addressing three key facets of village life, namely, (a) income generating activities; (b) health and hygiene; and (c) eradicating illiteracy and bringing in social consciousness.The facilitation for promoting these self-reliance activities is sought to be provided by the *Samaj Shilpi Dampattis,* also known as Social Architect Couple (SSDs).

Income Generation

The Chitrakoot Model covers both farm and non-farm sectors. In the farm sector, 1.5 acre model farms are developed which help in increasing the income of small and marginal farmers.[3] Watershed and soil management techniques have been introduced where necessary. DRI motivates farmers to take up multi-cropping, which also helps increase the income of farmers. In the non-farm sector, the model aims to enhance incomes through entrepreneur training and formation of income-generating Self Help Groups (SHGs). Keeping in mind issues of livelihood and self-reliance, an Entrepreneurial training Centre, Udyamita has been established to provide

---

2 A village is considered self-reliant if it satisfies criteria of having irrigation, health, drinking water, education, dispute free village and adequate roads. Every family in the village should have their own house, family income above Rs 18,000 per annum, no unemployed youth and no child should be out of school in age group 6 -14 years.

3 More than 80% of Indian farmers own 2.5 acres of land or less. A 2.5 and 1.5 acre horticulture- based farming model was formulated and tested at KVK, Satna using modern technologies. The 1.5 acre model provides beneficiaries a saving of about Rs. 10,000 to 14,000 in irrigated fields.

skill development training for stitching garments, embroidery and food processing etc., including special training to women in the skills of jam and jelly making, bakery, embroidery and cutting and tailoring, etc.

Health and Hygiene

Issues of health and hygiene are the second most important aspect of the campaign. Poor health and lack of adequate hygiene have the adverse effect of reducing the productivity of villagers and making them poor, since a large portion of their income tends to get spent on medical problems. The Chitrakoot modelemphasizes health solutions for the village people through Ayurveda and Naturopathy, enabling them to become self-reliant in health matters. A natural herbs pouch called, *Dadima ka Batua* consisting of 34 Ayurvedic local herbs has been developed, which is provided to in the villages of the Chitrakoot cluster to treat common ailments. The villagers are made aware of these herbs through specific campaigns. For treatment of major ailments, health facilities have been provided at Arogyadham, Deendayal Research Institute's Ayurvedic & Naturopathy Hospital & Research Centre at Chitrakoot. Dentistry facilities are also provided at Arogyadham.

Eradicating Illiteracy and Social Consciousness

An educational system based on the ancient *Gurukul Padati*has been set up in Chitrakoot to help eradicate illiteracy and promote social consciousness. Besides, *Gramodaya University*, proclaimed as world's first rural university, has beenestablishedand special schools have been set up to provide education to tribal girls in the cluster.

Samaj Shilpi Dampattis for Promoting Self Reliance

The key to campaign for self-reliance at Chitrakoot is the concept of *Samaj Shilpi Dampattis*(SSDs), also known as Social Architect Couple. These are young graduate couples introduced as change agents and acting as key functionaries in promoting all the three dimensions of self-reliance.These couples are required to stay in the rural area for four to five years and act as role model for the villagers. An SSD is allocated to each village in the cluster and assigned the responsibility of guiding the villagers in implementing the policies of DRI Chitrakoot in their group of villages through counseling and intervention. Working of SSDs starts from building of faith and confidence. These couples live within the community and, with passage of time, develop homely relations with all the villagers helping them in all spheres of their lives. Once the relationship develops, motivating the villagers to maintain cleanliness of their surroundings and settling their disputes within themselves, etc. become easy. These SSD couples organize skill development training in their respective villages. Owing to their being socially inclusive, the SSDs are successful as agents of change.

Success of the Self-Reliance Model

The self-reliance model of Chitrakoot is deemed quite successful. The self-reliance campaign launched in the year 2002 to develop 500 villages and conducted in two phases culminated in the year 2011, when all the 500 villages were declared self-reliant. This has gone a long way in empowering people in these villages both socially and economically. It can be argued that Chitrakoot can be a sustainable and replicable model for the holistic development of rural India.

LEARNINGS FROM CHITRAKOOT

(a) The key to promoting development is to promote education, which is the enabler of social change.

(b) Awareness creation is an important means to bring about change and progress in society

(c) There is a need to identify and create a locally relevant agent of change and to capitalize on social capital to bring about change, as is the case with SSDs in Chitrakoot. The SSDs are a prime example of how they managed to build social capital in the villages and how they leverage this social capital in their adopted villages.

(d) Agriculture continues to be the backbone of Indian economy. The progress in society takes place when agriculture and allied activities develop.

(e) Innovation is required in all dimensions of rural models. A key innovation in Chitrakoot is the adoption of 1.5 Acre model in agriculture and watershed management leading to better productivity in agriculture.

(f) Human capital formation through entrepreneurship, capacity building and local skill development is an important ingredient of rural development.

(g) Use of indigenous methods , resources and approaches is important. In the context of Chitrakoot, these include organic farming and *Dadi Ma Ka Batua*, among others

(h) Leadership can bring change, even in backward areas. Change has to be from within.

(i) Micro-financing is required for promoting entrepreneurship.

(j) Addressing the three key issues of income generation, education and health is important

(k) To pursue replication of the Chitrakoot model, it is important to identify a potential local agent of change within the community.

RECOMMENDATIONS

The way to development as seen in case of Chitrakoot model is to bring about change by spreading education and awareness. To promote change, there is a need to identify and create a locally relevant model/ agent of change similar to the case of SSD in Chitrakoot. The existing resources need to be targeted and a locally relevant model of change needs to be carved out.

After identifying the relevant model, steps need to be taken for mapping development activities and livelihood promotion. The relevant model of change would implement the activities to be undertaken.

CONCLUSIONS

This paper highlights the relevance of PURA model and studies a successful PURA model. The findings of Chitrakoot show how the studies of successful PURA model can be utilized to develop more such model.

REFERENCES

[1] Agarwal,R.,Batra,S.,Awasthy, N.(2012):*Planning for Implementation of PURA in Greenfield Areas- A Situation Analysis of Bahraich District*, Study sponsored by CRICKET, IMT Ghaziabad .

[2] Census of India: Vital Statistics. Available at: http://www.censusindia.gov.in/2011-*common/vitalstatistics.html*

[3[Chitrakoot Organization. Available at: *http://www.chitrakoot.org/html/index.htm*

[4] DRI(2011): *The Road to Self Reliance*, Deen Dayal Research Institute.

[5] Dutt, R. and Sundaram, K.P.M (2011): *Indian Economy*, S. Chand and Co, Delhi

[6] Government of India (2008): *Baseline Survey In The Minority Concentrated Districts Of U.P., (Report Of Bahraich District),* Study Sponsored by Ministry of Minority Affairs, Study Conducted by P.S.Garia, Giri Institute of Development Studies, Lucknow.

[7] Kalam, A.P.J A. and Singh, S.P. (2011) : *Target 3 Billion*, Penguin Books, Delhi

[8] Kalam, A.P.J. A. (2007): *PURA Mission to Reality*, Available at *www.presidentofindia.nic.in*

[9] "*Kalam praises RSS veteran Nanaji Deshmukh*" | 7933. Available at: *http://www.india-forums.com/news/national/7933-kalam-praises-rss-veteran-nanaji-deshmukh.htm*

[10] Singh, S. P. (2011): *Understanding PURA*, Presentation at Consultation Workshop on Knowledge Management at IMT Ghaziabad, March 2011

[11] Singh, S. P. (2010): *The PURA Action Group*, Office of Dr. A.P.J. Abdul Kalam.

Take the Big Leap – Innovate

Maninder S. Khalsa

Talent Acquisition & Field HR Management, Viom Networks Limited, Gurgaon

ABSTRACT

Changing market conditions are putting pressure on businesses and individuals to out-perform themselves continuously. This not only test their strategies and resource, but their ability to think, innovate and create a newer version of themselves as an organization and as an individual. This paper analyses the current challenges, which inhibit organizations to innovate and conclude with some practices of innovative organizations and leaders.

INTRODUCTION

Identify effective leaders and building talent pipeline is one of the top 3 business challenges. Competent and innovative leaders develop new products, new business models, identify new revenue streams, and create new rules and so on...

There are ample examples and case studies, where leaders have missed significant market trends and opportunities. Some examples are:

- "640K ought to be enough for anybody." – Bill Gates, 1981, rejecting proposal for larger computer memory.
- "We don't like their sound, and guitar music is on the way out." – Decca Recording Co. rejecting the Beatles, 1962.
- "Who the hell wants to hear actors talk?" – H.M. Warner (Warner Brothers) before rejecting proposal for movies with sound in 1927.
- "The concept is interesting and well-formed, but in order to earn better than a 'C,' the idea must be feasible." – A YALE UNIVERSITY professor in response to Fred Smith's paper proposing reliable overnight delivery service. (Smith went on to found Federal Express Corp.)
- "The wireless music box has no imaginable commercial value. Who would pay for a message sent to nobody in particular?" – David Sarnoff's Associates in rejecting a proposal for investment in the radio in the 1920s.
- When the movie camera was finally accepted and became main stream, the camera did not move! The actors would run around the static camera like the theatre or still camera.

The idea that the camera could move around the actors took a while to develop. To see great opportunities you need good leadership skills.

WHY INNOVATE

Great Leaders look beyond current practices and markets. Creativity is now considered by chief executives worldwide as the number one quality that leaders need to possess, with 60 per cent of them naming it as their top priority in an IBM study. ("Capitalising on Complexity", IBM, 2010).

The case for innovation is clear – 78 per cent of UK businesses now recognize that innovation is vital to their future survival and success. However, research ("Everyday Innovation", Nesta, 2009) shows that less than a third of British organizations (29 per cent) include innovation or creativity in any way in their recruitment selection criteria, which are primarily focused on operational effectiveness. The situation is not very different in India.

Organizations need to realize that creativity and innovation is no longer only needed in a select few industries. Employing creative, innovative staff is a necessity for all businesses, especially in these tough times when the development of new strategies, products and ways of working are so vital.

If the forecasts of the chief executives surveyed by IBM are correct, it is these creative individuals who will be particularly sought after as leaders in the future. Organizations would be well-advised to ensure they have such talented individuals in their workforce rising through the ranks sooner rather than later.

The director at the Harvard University Leadership Education Project, Ronald Heifetz, explains it as "Leaders of the future need to have the stomach for conflict and uncertainty - among their people and within themselves. That's why leaders of the future need to have an experimental mind-set." (1999)

Uday Kotak, 53, vice-chairman and managing director, Kotak Mahindra Bank says "leadership is about being disruptive and thinking out of the box. Great Leaders need not to be afraid to make mistakes. They need to have the confidence to take risks".

Mahatama Gandhi, was the smartest negotiator in the world. What negotiating leverage did he have when he went to the queen in a dhoti and yet, he shifted the negotiating leverage in his favour - as if saying that I am half naked because of what you have done to my country. The way Gandhi used fasts as a negotiating leverage, smartly, time and again, that too in era of no mobiles - he is the one of the smartest negotiators history has seen.

Innovation or Thinking Out of The box is defined as:

"The act of introducing something new" (the american heritage dictionary)

"A new idea, method or device" (Webster online)

"Change that creates a new dimension of performance" (Peter Drucker)

"The ability to deliver new value to a customer" (Jose Campos)

"Innovation is the way of transforming the resources of an enterprise through the creativity of people into new resources and wealth" (Paul Schumann)

"Innovation does not relate just to a new product that would come into the marketplace. Innovation can occur in processes and approaches to the marketplace" (David Schmittlen)

The process by which an idea or invention is translated into a good or service for which people will pay, or something that results from this process.

To be called an innovation, an idea must be replicable at an economical cost and must satisfy a specific need. (www.businessdictionary.com)

Thinking out of the Box is "explode the box" or "find a new box", it is thinking beyond the tried and true

Interestingly, "think outside the box" is assuming a box of conventional thinking and bringing our attention to it! If the goal is to think bigger and more creatively, then don't handicap your subconscious. Rather than thinking *about* the box.

APPLICATIONS OF INNOVATION

Innovation is applied at every facets of life. Innovation is beyond 'spray and pray', Innovation is about customized products / solutions for specific customers in a specific situation. Innovation is everywhere, expected of all in personal and professional life. The key question is do we innovate or someone will?

Some examples of innovation, which we say, that how come this does not strike me are :

- Customer engagement using social media like facebook or twitter by 3M, Subway, McDonald. Dell has made $6.5 Mn using twitter (http://www.nevillehobson.com/2010/01/02/five-examples-of-innovation-with-twitter).
- Rain water harvesting, used for first time was innovation
- Green building or energy stars
- Some product examples include microprocessor chips, personal and laptop computers, word processing software, microwave oven, spreadsheet software, The World Wide Web/ Internet, Email, Google search, iPod and iTunes, WiFi, even disposable baby diapers, and on and on

Is innovation all about big changes or small? Innovation spans across all aspects of corporate life - develop new products/services to serve customers, reduce cost, simplify organizational processes, reduce time to delivery, ensure mistake proofing, and improve employee productivity and engagement and many more.

Innovation is not only a corner stone for organizational success but also for individual success in today's era of relative ranking and bell-curve fitment. Each individual needs to demonstrate what additional value s/he add or demonstrate their effectiveness. Time of putting additional number of hours is history, now the organizations evaluate in terms of effectiveness, impact and value-add. It's innovation and innovation all the way:

- Changing demographics are forcing managers to innovate team engagement practices
- In the era of information overload and social networking, employees are innovating new ways to impressing their customers, bosses or colleagues
- New ways of presenting data are identified, with standardized templates from net
- Even impactful resumes with videos, reaching out to recruiters through social media and many more
- Some examples of work place innovations, which simplify things and reduce workplace stress are:
  - Week starts on Friday to ensure reporting every Monday
- Month starts from 21st to 20th to ensure availability of results
- FMCG has 13 months of 4 weeks each

We all have experienced, what is innovative and out of box today is quickly copied and replicated and many a times with much higher effectiveness.

Hence, Out of Box Thinking is a Journey, not a Destination.

Further, in today's market scenario, of internet, Gen Y or Z, 1-minute burger and 2-minute maggi, where globe is the play-field (as a market or for sourcing), shortening product lifecycle and increasing customer expectations, Out of Box Thinking is not a matter of choice either for individuals or for organizations, but necessity for survival. Individuals and organizations need to necessarily evolve and embrace this new skill, whether in the name of entrepreneurship or continuous improvement.

Before, evaluating the key enablers of Out of Box Thinking or innovative thinking, we need to create basic hygienic environment which does not inhibit innovation. Some examples of how our unconscious behavior kills innovative culture / initiatives:

- **Too much focus on efficiency and not on effectiveness**: Organizations are obsessed with efficiency and productivity. Focus on efficiency gives managers a comfort zone by focusing on activities and processes, which are more focused internally, though the cost may be effectiveness and deliverable. This result in increasing employee productivity, shorten cycle time or reduce cost. These incremental results are achieved by tightening process control, ensuring better process adherence and pushing the employees to be followers. There is little encouragement to thinking and more of better doing of same things. Some phrases often heard in corporate world reflect this patter:
  - Do as you are told
  - Its management decision

- Process to be followed / We cannot make changes
- Ensure adherence
- Report every hour

- **Follow the rules**: Managers have a tendency to think change is too risky, and price of change is change is too high. The safest option is to follow convention than implanting the change, which will require getting buy-in again and start, where I have to own the results.
- **Past Baggage**: Most leaders after bringing in abundant ideas to change and improve their businesses, *continue to have the impression* that they are still able to think radically different. This 'past baggage' actually doesn't push them enough to look at new ideas and thoughts.
- **Insufficiency in Concept:** Most leaders spend a lot of time in generating new ideas and concepts. However, their busy schedules often don't permit them to think-the-concept-through. This leads to an interesting situation where ideas are just thrown around without adequate checks and balances, and even taken up for implementation.
- **Fear of Failure:** The next challenge is the fear of failure. Definitions of failure could vary and so would the applicability of definitions to individual leaders. However, at the end of the day, nothing succeeds like success! And in today's world, failure is definitely a no-no for many leaders...
- **Politicking:** The biggest challenge to Out of Box Thinking is actually politicking within the organization. Unsupportive staff is the single largest reason for failure as it not only skews the culture, but also affects the very core of the productive organization. A leader who is unable to maneuver the political currents to bring out change, gets restricted to working 'within-the-box' rather than doing anything drastic. Defusing / Stripping off the political mines in an organization are hard work and require a controlled methodology to keep it contained, efficient and effective.

"The creative process is also the most terrifying part because you don't know exactly what's going to happen or where it is going to lead." Stephen Covey

Creating Culture of 'Out of Box Thinking'

Encouraging innovation is all about creating organization wide culture, setting up practices (consciously avoiding the word process), which encourage out of box thinking and innovation.

- ***Create a stretch:*** Necessity is mother of all inventions, people do not want to change – someone need to push them to innovate (Push them, not encourage), as this is the process to activate brain cells under stress not comfort. Give ambitious targets and share rewards.
- ***Focus on deliverable and results in a context:*** Change should be driven towards the desired results and employees need to understand the context of change. Once the desired outcome is commonly agreed, open arena should be provided to employees. Leaders can

at the most define the broad framework. Out of box thinking just for the sake of thinking differently produces only symbolic changes, which do not result in any significant transformation.

- ***Review and facilitate change:*** For a new idea or way of working to be successful and get the fruits, journey needs to be completed. These journeys unless sponsored and reviewed by leadership are abandoned mid-way, reinforcing the belief that change does not work here.
- ***Develop Learning Organization:*** Expand horizon of employees by creating a learning organization, enhance their experience by giving new exposure. New exposure could be by working with NGO (Many business schools have successfully initiated), bring in trainees, integration with academics, different roles or experience across various geographies. These experiences give different stimuli and situations forcing to think and explore. Different challenges. Anything done in past will not work. Need to take risk and encouraged to take path not travelled.
- **Diversity**: Diversity gives us a different perspective. Invariably diversity is discussed only from gender diversity, but remember to include gender diversity, experience, age and cultural diversity.
- ***Reward creativity:*** This may seem obvious, but if you want greater creativity, you first have to let people know it is important to you and then reward them for being creative. Rewards could be tangible, but don't have to be. Do people know you appreciate their ideas? Do you seek out and ask for bigger ideas regularly? This is a journey, not a quick fix. Asking or begging for big ideas today likely won't work if the long term feeling is that creativity doesn't really matter to you.
- ***Allow time:*** Every single person can be creative – but few, if anyone, can be creative on demand and to a deadline. For the issues, situations and problems that are most important to you and your organization, give people time to soak on and think about new ideas. Give their subconscious minds a chance to work.
- ***Provide a safety net:*** People often rein in their most creative ideas because they just aren't sure if they're going to work. Whether stated or not, people don't want to make mistakes. If you want more ideas and more bold ideas, you must get people past their fear of making mistakes. Acknowledge the risk that comes with innovation and encourage people to think about that risk *later* – the primary goal is to identify ideas!
- ***Provide varied stimuli:*** Our brains will create more and different ideas when they are stimulated in new ways. As a leader you can help people "think outside the box" by providing new stimuli.
- ***Model the behavior yourself:*** If you want others to create new, bold and big ideas, first take a look in the mirror. Are you doing it yourself?

KEY ACTIONABLE FOR INDIVIDUALS

While creating a culture of innovation will encourage more employee and help organizations benefit from all functions, levels, geographies and stake-holders. However, Out of Box Thinking is not only the responsibility of organizations, but of individuals for their own growth and ultimately resulting in organizational and national growth.

Being innovative is about achieving results with new ideas. **What matters is result, not necessarily source of idea**. Great Leaders think outside the box by displaying the following qualities:

- **Listening to others**: A basic human value, where we dispel our notions and focus on challenge at hand, with accumulated experience of all of us. An idea can come from anyone, with a famous concept of Pizza Delivery Boy. I have experienced a tea-delivery boy coming and suggested one of the most successful scheme at car dealership
- **Supporting others:** Support others, when they come up with new ideas and respecting them. Acknowledge their contribution
- Valuing new ideas and not being afraid to act on them
- Willingness to look at new perspectives to day to day work
- Openness to different things
- Openness to doing things differently
- Challenging your own assumptions can be the most difficult part of out of the box thinking. Just because something has always been one way, doesn't mean that it has to continue to be that way.

These are basic human values taught but we forgot to implement

Innovation is the key springboard to take a big leap, where individual need to collaborate to expand their horizons, continuously build on their capabilities and embrace change with open arms. While organizations are required to create an environment, where they can leverage the tacit knowledge of their people by creating a fearless and contributory culture.

Technomics of Food Grain Management in India

Srikanth Chintamaneni and Manjunath Kottur

Deloitte Consulting India Pvt Ltd, Hyderabad

ABSTRACT

In India, every year billions of dollars' worth grains are getting spoilt for various reasons. A country where around 40% of the total population falls below the international poverty line certainly cannot afford to let its food grain go waste. But it is unfortunate that the government officials have admitted to the fact that there is a lack of enough grain storage and distribution infrastructure in the major grain producing areas of the country to address this issue.

It is estimated that around 20-30% of the total food grain harvest is wasted due to inadequate storage capacity, regional imbalance in warehouses, lack of adequate scientific storage and inefficient logistic management in the country. It is said that each grain bag is handled at least six times before it is finally opened for processing which leads to higher storage & transportation charges and also increases to wastage of food grain during transit & handling.

This paper is an attempt to provide a solution using Business Intelligence and Data warehousing techniques to give visibility to the existing storage capacity and distribution facilities, keep track of the overall gross consumption figures and thereby, helps to store only what is in excess, instead of storing majority of the grains and depriving the people that are in need, analyze data to figure out the requirement of new storage facilities and most importantly helps in planning the distribution mechanism against unanticipated circumstances viz.weather disasters

INTRODUCTION

In India, every year billions of dollars' worth grains are getting spoilt for various reasons.A country where around 40% of the total population falls below the international poverty line certainly cannot afford to let its food grain go waste. But it is unfortunate that the government officials have admitted to the fact that there is a lack of sufficientgrain storage and distribution infrastructure in the major grain producing areas of the country to address this issue.

It is estimated that around 20-30% of the total food grain harvest is wasted due to inadequate storage capacity, regional imbalance in warehouses, lack of adequate scientific storage and

inefficient logistic management in the country. It is said that each grain bag is handled at least six times before it is finally opened for processing which leads to higher storage and transportation charges and also increases to wastage of food grain during transit and handling.

This paper is an attempt to provide a solution using Business Intelligence and Data warehousing techniques to give visibility to the existing storage capacity and distribution facilities, keep track of the overall gross consumption figures and thereby help to store only what is in excess, instead of storing majority of the grains and depriving the people that are in need, analyze data to figure out the requirement of new storage facilities and most importantly help in planning the distribution mechanism against unanticipated circumstances viz.weather disasters.

THE ECONOMICS OF FOOD GRAIN MANAGEMENT

India is expected to have a bumper crop this year per Government estimates and ironically it is also true we may see a higher percentage of wastage while in storage through rotting. International Food Policy and Research Institute ranked India's Global Hunger Index at 67th among 81 that were surveyed. The index measuring hunger levels as a percent of population ranks Sri Lanka, Myanmar, Nepal and Pakistan much better than India.

During the times of high inflation, like it happened in December 2009 with food-price inflation above 20% government decided to release wheat. However, the sales were not encouraging as it was priced at a premium (to offset the costs of storage and transportation) to the minimum support price at which the FCI had procured.

The reasons for not able to get the best out of our stocks stem from multiple reasons: usually it is one or more of the following:

Improper Storage Methods

Even though majority of the storage is covered in silos and godowns, there are still about 3.6 milliontons that are stored in open using an indigenous method called Cover andPlinth (CAP).

CAP storage is a term given to storage of food grains in the open with adequate precautions such as rat and damp proof plinths, use of Dunnage and covering of stacks with specially fabricated polythene covers etc.

Improper Facility Planning

Facility planning is an area that can help ease the overall logistics. Right now, the storage more or less indicates the surplus grains in the area where they are cultivated. While this makes excellent reason from a collection and initial transportation context, this will become a bottleneck when we have to shift them due to requirement at a faraway location. More often, we have a good sense of where we may need the grains most. For example, existing storage facilities indicate that the North East and the Eastern states combinedcan store only about 3 milliontons. Historically, these regions are frequently ravaged with floods and famine.

Large Intake Due to Bumper Harvest

Sometimes there is a problem arising out of excess production. While it is welcome to have a bumper crop, this poses problems of another nature having to ensure the growers get a fair price. An established process on how to handle excess stocks would be a very welcome practice.

Abnormal Weather Changes

Weather plays a very important role on the life of stocks that are stored. Further, this may be different for storage in silos to those in CAP. As more than 10% of the entire stock is held using the CAP method of open storage, any preventive action can be taken if there is an alert/ warning about the impending abnormal weather changes.

Decisions Making Leading to Delay in Procurement

There are different agencies involved in operating the ware houses. While FCI was set up in 1965 primarily to address the storage and distribution of food stocks, since then there are other agencies too involved in this. Of the total 35 milliontons capacity, FCI accounts for about 15.6 million tons, the State Warehousing Corp 11.2 million tons, and Central Warehousing corp. the state governments and some private owners contribute the rest 8.2 million tons. We need to have an independent body overseeing both procurement and distribution for effectively using the stocks.

BI/DW TECHNOLOGY IN FOOD GRAIN MANAGEMENT

India loses close to Rs.60,000 crore worth of agricultural food items due to lack of post harvesting infrastructure such as cold chains, transportation, and storage facilities. The inadequate storage facilities are resulting in rotting of tons of food grains and rendering it unfit for human consumption as well as for animals. India lost about two lakh metric tons of wheat and rice in April and May alone. The Food Corporation of India lacks adequate storage capacities in many states.

All this despite the fact that India ranks second worldwide, in farm output and the agriculture and allied sectors like forestry and logging. India is also the largest producer of milk, cashew nuts, coconuts, tea, ginger, turmeric, and black pepper in the world. It is the second largest producer of wheat, rice, sugar, groundnut, and inland fish. It is the third largest producer of tobacco and accounts for 10 percent share of the world fruit production, leading the world in the production of banana and sapota. Despite all these, we are yet to tap the complete potential of our yields. Food wastage and food processing are the two areas of concern.

The food processing sector—mainly comprising fruits and vegetables, milk and milk products, beer and alcoholic beverages, meat and poultry, marine products, grain processing, packaged or convenience food and packaged drinks—is a highly fragmented industry. The unorganized segment accounts for over 70 per-cent of the output in terms of volume and 50 percent in terms of value. Though the organized sector seems comparatively small, it is growing at a much faster pace.

The installed capacity of fruits and vegetables processing industry is about 2-3 million tons but the processing of fruits and vegetables is lesser than 3 percent share of the total production in the country.

India has the highest livestock population in the world and India's dairy industry is considered as one of the most successful sectors. The total milk processing in India is around 35 percent, of which the organized dairy industry accounts for 13 percent.

While the processing level of buffalo meat is estimated at 21 percent, poultry is estimated at 6 percent and marine products are estimated at 8 percent.

Processing of grain includes milling of wheat, rice, and pulses. We have over 91,000 huller rice mills and 45,000 sheller (modern) rice mills; nearly 1,000 roller flour mills and about 2.6 lakh small flour mills; dal mills number over 10,000. In the oilseeds-based industry, there are over 16,000 oil mills, nearly 800 solvent extraction plants, over 600 refineries and 200 vanaspati units. There are over 600 sugar facto-ries and 4,000 cotton ginning and pressing plants.

Some of the key constraints identified by the food processing industry include poor infrastructure in terms of cold storage and warehousing; inadequate quality control and testing infrastructure; inefficient supply chain and involvement of middlemen; high trans-portation and inventory carrying cost; and high packaging cost.

The broad questions to discuss include innovations that are needed to promote agriculture; the methods for advanced storage and distribution of food grains; use of technology for collection of data and prediction ahead of time, besides other things.

The key solution to this problem is to deploy planned and efficient supply chain management with a Data Warehouse that will minimize wastage and meet demands effectively. IT solutions in the area of supply chain management, demand planning, and business intelligence implemented at the national level are the key technologies that will help in resolving the problem.

THE SOLUTION

An appropriate Enterprise Data Warehousing Information System needsto be established which will serve as a good database asan early warning system in case of emergency and structural and development issues. The Warehousing Development and Regulation Act should oversee and monitor standardization of the warehousing activities in the country. Such a law –in the existence of proper food reserve and buffer stock policy- will help not only in keeping food grain reserves but would also facilitate efficient price discovery for stored commodities, which is fundamental feature in market competitiveness. To achieve both recommendations, the study suggests a consistent link between warehousing/storage and transport information systems.

The transport information system is important for availing data and information on road condition, pass ability; transporters, number/type of trucks etc. It will also be good if information on probable road blockages; probable events (festivals, football matches, etc.); risks and probability of incidents is obtained from traffic authorities. It is not far from being realized if information on traffic management (through SMS messages or radio for re-routing, closings, etc.) is kept on a unique database accessible to everybody interested in such type of information. Overall, transportinfrastructure, whether used for assembly or distribution of food, is an essential endeavor to development that will enhance and foster economic growth.

Fig 1. Data Warehousing Life Cycle

The BI/DW concepts can be applied to the existing, disparate data sources to help generate meaningful reports that:

- assist in pro-actively utilizing the available stocks
- generate reports the fastest way during natural calamity to address food shortage
- help in the long term solution of better facility planning

A Decision Support Enterprise Data Warehouse Information system enables knowledge workers to make strategic and tactical business decisions based on factual data stored in a business intelligence data warehouse. Decision support systems must allow users to intuitively, quickly, and flexibly manipulate data using familiar terms, in order to provide analytical insight.

Decision Support Data Warehouses are implementations of an informational database used to store sharable data sourced from an operational database-of-record. They are typically a subject database that allows users to tap into anorganization'svast store of operational data to track business trends, facilitate forecasting and data mining, respond to data patterns, aid planning efforts, and measure performance against strategic goals—all with the goal of aiding and supporting decision making.

Beyond Decision Support

The ultimate goal of any decision support data warehouse system is to improve corporate performance by providing decision makers with better information. Thus, relative success of any decision support system increases as more departments and users within the organization have access to relevant information to make better day-to-day decisions.

BUSINESS INTELLIGENCE - TECHNICAL REPORTS

Following are a few critical technical reports that can be generated using a BI/DW data model which helps in addressing grain storage problems

Region-wise Distribution of Storage Capacity

Storage / warehousing and distribution components form an important link in the entirelogistics chain.They are required to be stored temporarily, before they can be transported to the end customers. Storage facilities are usuallyrequired for a short period of time to ensure faster delivery to customers and to reduce theoverall logistics costs. A business intelligence report on region wise distribution of storage capacity will provide an insight into storage units of Product by Region in tons and also will help in performing Capacity planning analysis.

Following are the sample reports that can be generated based on the Storage capacity data for Government of Karnataka.

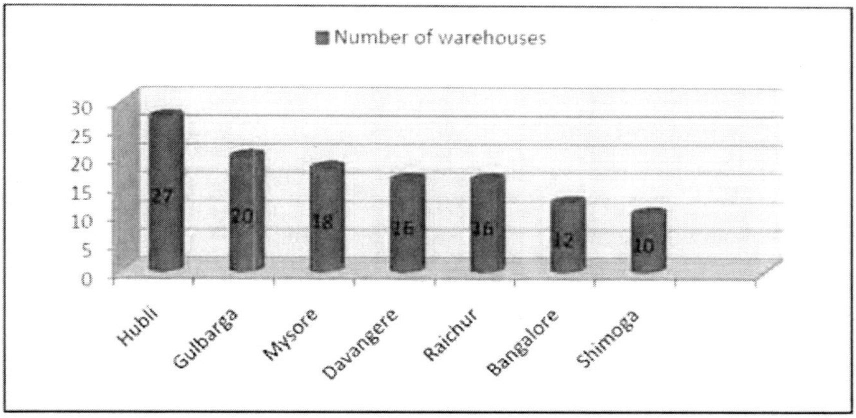

Fig 2. Region Wise Warehouse Distribution

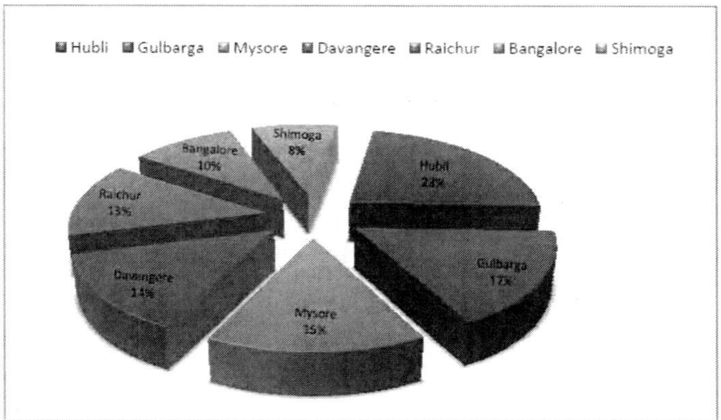

Fig 3. Percentages of Warehouse in Regions

Forecasting Reports

The BI/DW technical solution will provide an ability to perform estimation and project demand and supply of food grain products.

Demand and Supply Projections of Food upto 2020

There have been many studies on demand and supply projections. Government of India projected demand for rice at 84.2 million tons for 2011, 96.4 million tons for 2021, and 101.5 million tons for 2026. The corresponding supply projections are 95.7, 105.8, and 111.2 million tons respectively, envisaging a surplus of 11.46, 9.38, and 9.73 million tons respectively. Mittal's projections for wheat demand are 59.8, 66.1, and 68.1 million tons for the above mentioned years as compared to the supply projections of 80.2, 91.6, and 97.9 million tons indicating surpluses of 20.41, 25.53, and 29.84 million tons. For total cereals, the projected surpluses are 27.59, 12.76, and 4.63 million tons.

Rosegrant etal used demand elasticity and technical coefficients synthesized from other sources, primarily from past studies, and projected demand for total cereals at 237.3 million tons for the year 2020. Hanchate &Dyson projected demand and supply for total cereals for 2026 at 217.6 million tons and 265.8 million tons respectively. These estimates are based on the IMPACT model and assume a GDP growth of 7.5-7.7 per cent.

Projections given in Table below also show that India would be self-sufficient in food grains in future. In the case of pulses and oilseeds, the country would have to depend on imports, even by 2020. According to some projections, the household demand for milk and milk products would increase from 64 million tons in 2000 to 166 million tons in 2020, and fruits and vegetables from 48 million tons to 113 million tons. Given the shifts in consumption patterns, towards non-cereal food, and even to non-food, we feel that the demand projections of the Ministry of Agriculture on food grains of around 250 million tons for 2020 are reasonable. There would be enough supply to meet the demand for food grains by 2020.

Table 1: Estimated Production and Projected Demand of Food Grains

Crop	2008-09			2011-12			2020
	Projected Demand	Estimated Production	Surplus/ shortfall	Projected Demand	Projected production	Surplus/ shortfall	Projected Demand
Rice	92.87	99.15	6.28	98.79	104.21	5.42	111.9
Wheat	72.72	80.58	7.86	77.36	83.61	6.25	79.9
Coarse Cereals	35.9	39.48	3.58	38.19	35.75	-2.44	37.3
Pulses	17.51	14.66	-2.85	19.91	15.73	-4.18	23.8
Foodgrains	219.0	233.88	14.88	234.26	239.3	5.04	252.8
Sugarcane	275.9	271.25	-4.66	322.54	305.51	-17.03	--
Oilseeds	47.4	28.16	-19.27	53.39	27.53	-25.86	--

Source: Ministry of Agriculture

CONCLUSION

The problems India faces in managing the food grains are very specific to it. Regional variations in the crop output, a gigantic Public Distribution System, Infrastructure deficiencies, unorganized nature of food processing industry, natural disasters all add to the complexity. Repeated bumper harvests, increased expenditure on the infrastructure have not resulted in reducing the problems.

BI/DW technologies can certainly help on multiple fronts ranging from, identifying the issues, providing the solutions and finally in the implementation to help improving the overall food grain management in India.

REFERENCES

[1] Towards strategic planning in Food grain Warehousing – Khartoum.

[2] Farmers' Post-Harvest Grain Management Choices under Liquidity Constraints and Impending Risks: Abiebe H Gabriel.

[3) Implications for Achieving Food Security Objectives: Abiebe H Gabriel.

[4] Foodgrains Policy and Management in India - Responding to Today's Challenges and Opportunities - A. Ganesh-Kumar, Ashok Gulati, and Ralph Cummings Jr.

[5] Food Security in India: Performance, Challenges and Policies – Oxfam India - S. Mahendra Dev and Alakh N. Sharma.

[6] Integrated Information System for Food grains Management – IISFM - RanjnaNagpal.

[7) Agriculture – Saving the Food by Technology Review India website.

[8] Developing Indian grain supplychain cost model: a systemdynamics approach – Written by AmitSachan, B.S. Sahay and Dinesh Sharma.

[9] Decision Support Data Warehouse – BI Topics from Microstrategy.

[10[International Food Policy and Research Institute (http://www.ifpri.org).

[11] The Economics of Food grain Management in India - Kaushik Basu.

[12] Food Corporation of India (http://fciweb.nic.in/).

Unrelated Diversification: How Green and Efficient It Is? Conglomerates & Unrelated Diversification

Ankita Mishra, Deepak Joshi and Shalini Rahul Tiwari

Mt, Ghaziabad

ABSTRACT

A vast array of industries can cause pollution contrary to the perception that a chemical industry can only cause pollution. IT, Telecom sector, Petro-chemical, textile, transport, sugar etc. are directly impacting the environment via air, water, noise, solid waste and other types of pollution. [1]The subsidiaries of conglomerates with diversified interests were found to exhibit higher pollution levels for direct emissions than those of firms pursuing more related diversification strategies in US chemical industry. This paper proposes a similar study examining the relationship between corporate diversification strategy and the pollution activity of subsidiaries. The study will show the impact on the environment and analyze if the subsidiaries of conglomerates were found to exhibit higher pollution levels for direct emissions than those of firms who are parent in the sector. The conclusion on basis of analysis can vary in both the direction. It can be in favor of conglomerates having unrelated diversification strategy portraying that they have better resource utilization capacity or their practices are more environmental friendly, or it can be in favor of conglomerates and the companies having focused interest depicting their experience and expertise in that sector.

DIVERSIFICATION STRATEGY

The diversification strategy is successful and adapted by myriad of companies; the effect of diversification on firm performance has received an enormous amount of attention, probably more than any other empirical relation in the field of strategy. In early 1970's the diversification was done with a minor motive of enhancing shareholder's wealth (Bradley, Desai and Kim, 1988) but lately this strategy have been used to enhance firm's value e.g. GE, Reliance etc.

---

[1] Are Conglomerates Less Environmentally Responsible? By RobertS.Dooley, GeraldE.Fryxell.

[2] Causes and Effects of Multimarket Activity from theory to Empirical Analysis by Davide Vannoni.

[2]Montgomery (1994) provides a brief and perceptive review of three leading theories of diversification market power, agency, and firm resources, along with their predictions about its effect on firm performance. The notion is that firms diversify to exploit their excess capacity in resources. Though these resources are imperfectly tradable outside of the firm, there is a probability of them being used more productively across different businesses within the firm. With a new perspective and taking cues from other researches done in the field this paper plans to add a new dimension to it as "how diversification strategy of a company is correlated to its pollution excretion?" Though seems unrelated but a study done in early 90's titled "Are conglomerates less environmentally Responsible?" by Mr. Robert S. Dooley and Mr. Gerald E. Fryxell says that the subsidiaries of conglomerates with diversified interests were found to exhibit higher pollution levels for direct emissions than those of firms pursuing more related diversification strategies in US chemical industry.

UNRELATED AND RELATED DIVERSIFICATION STRATEGY

[3]Rumelt (1974) was the first to find that effect is contingent on the degree and type of relatedness across a firm's businesses. In essence, related diversification is good for firm profits while unrelated or conglomerate diversification is not. This finding has been widely replicated by many subsequent studies using many different samples and measures. [4]Jacquemin and Berry (1979) devised a continuous measure of diversification labeled "entropy" that allows a more objective separation between related and unrelated diversification and has been very widely used. Standard Industrial Classification (SIC) system, which is arguably not ideal for this purpose is a very common critique to most measures of relatedness; however several studies have come up with clever and objective measures of relatedness that do not rely on SIC codes: Lemelin (1982) uses input-output tables to classify relationships between pairs of industries as vertical or complementary in either inputs or outputs. Farjoun (1998) uses data from the Bureau of Labor Statistics about the distribution of job categories across industries to construct measures of skill-based relatedness.

[5]Related diversification is when a business adds or expands its existing product lines or markets. It comes with the advantage of understanding the business and of knowing what the industry opportunities and threats are; yet a number of related acquisitions fail to provide the benefits or returns originally predicted, usually because the diversification analysis under-estimates the cost of some of the softer issues: change management, integrating two cultures, handling employees – layoffs and terminations, promotions, and even recruitment. On the other hand when a business adds new, or unrelated, product lines or markets its unrelated

[3] Diversification and firm Performance: An Empirical Evaluation by Anil M. Pandya and Narendar V. Rao.

[4] Entropy Measure of Diversification and Corporate Growth by Alexis P. Jacquemin and Charles H. Berry.

[5] The Costs of Related Diversification: The Impact of the Core Business on the Productivity of Related Segments by Shyam Kumar.

diversification. Why would a company want to engage in unrelated diversification? Because there may be cost efficiencies or the acquisition might provide an offsetting cash flow during a seasonal lull. The driver for this acquisition decision is profit – it needs to be a low risk investment, with high potential for return.

CURRENT ENVIRONMENT NORMS

After all the Go green chaos for around two decade now many steps and acts have been passed by Government of India to keep a check on environmental pollution. In July 2008, the Indian government released its first National Action Plan on Climate Change (NAPCC) ([6]GOI, 2008a). The plan stresses the need to maintain high economic growth while effectively addressing climate change. [7]The NAPCC defines eight core national missions for the development and use of new technologies. Two of these, the National Mission on Enhanced Energy Efficiency (NMEEE) and the Jawaharlal Nehru National Solar Mission, focus specifically on the energy sector. The NAPCC also proposes that nationally 5% of the electricity purchased should be from renewable sources in 2009/10. This share should increase by 1% per year for the next ten years. In July 2010, India introduced a carbon tax on coal, at the rate of INR 50/t (USD 1.07/t), which will apply to both domestic and imported coal. For coal used in power generation, this tax represents a price increase in the order of 5% to 10% based on runofmine prices in October 2010, depending on the coal quality. [8]The income from the tax goes into a National Clean Energy Fund for funding research, innovative projects in clean energy technologies, and programs to repair environmental damage. Earnings from this tax for 2010/11 are estimated to be around INR 22.5 billion (USD 500 million). Within the Copenhagen Accord, India has pledged to reduce the emission intensity of its GDP by 20% to 25% by 2020 relative to 2005 levels. As India's pledge refers to articles in the United Nations Framework Convention on Climate Change (UNFCCC) related to the Provision of financial resources and technology transfer from developed countries, it is unclear whether India regards this technology cooperation as a precondition for pursuing its reduction efforts. The pledge explicitly excludes emissions from agriculture, but it is also not clear whether the target refers to CO^2 or GHG emissions. If it is taken to refer to energyrelated CO^2 emissions excluding agriculture, the target would be achieved within the less ambitious ETP 2010 Baseline Scenario, in which India's CO^2 intensity would fall by 30% compared to 2005 levels (IEA, 2010a.).

With the relevant actions and targets set by GOI the Corporates have started investing in R&D and new technologies to commit to environment protection as a corporate objective.[9] ACC has won accolades for environment friendly measures taken at its plants and mines, ITC

---

[6] GOI stands for Government of India.

[7] "Clean Technology Fund Investment Plan For India" http://envfor.nic.in

[8] http://www.cleanenergyfuture.gov.au

[9] Individual company sites to validate the information of stated top 10 green companies.

introduced 'ozone-treated elemental chlorine free' bleaching technology for the first time in India which resulted in environmentally friendly multi-purpose paper that is less polluting than its traditional counterpart, Tamil Nadu Newsprint and Paper Limited (TNPL) introduced two Clean Development Mechanism projects and a wind farm project that helped generate 2,30,323 Carbon Emission Reductions earning ₹ 17.40 crore.

SOCIETAL IMPACT OF DIVERSIFICATION

CSR is the procedure of assessing an organization's impact on society and evaluating their responsibilities. It begins with an assessment of the following aspects of each business customers, Suppliers, Environment, Communities and Employees. [10]CSR plans take organizations ahead of compliance with legislation and lead them to respect moral values and respect people, communities and the natural environment. Corporate social responsibility is sustainable involving activities that an organization can uphold without negatively affecting the business goals. For example, a more comprehensive method of development is adopted by some corporations such as Bharat Petroleum Corporation Limited, Maruti Suzuki India Limited, and Hindustan Unilever Limited. Provision of improved medical and sanitation facilities, building schools and houses, and empowering the villagers and in process making them more self-reliant by providing vocational training and a knowledge of business operations are the facilities that these corporations focus on. On the other hand, the CSR programs of corporations like GlaxoSmithKline Pharmaceuticals' focus on the health aspect of the community. They set up health camps in tribal villages which offer medical check-ups and treatment and undertake health awareness programs. Similarly few of the companies work in environment centric directions as cited previously. Today with the increase in awareness of the environmental check by the government as well as the corporates states the need of the separate Corporate Environment responsibility (CER) which has a separate entity from CSR. This would help the corporates to channel their resources with a clear approach to give the environment priority unlike CSR where the view might clutter with the others. CER may also help government to keep a check on the environmental contribution and the technology adopted by them to make the process clean and pollution free.

Power sector was chosen to study the impact of the diversification strategy and the contribution of the carbon gases due to the following reasons:

a. There is a dependency of Indian economy on Fossil fuel power generation which leads to the carbon emission adding to the [11]GHG.

b. Data availability was an issue, as there are multiple gasses other that CO^2 which

---

[10] Corporate Social Responsibility (CSR) in Asia: A Seven-Country Study of CSR Web Site Reporting by Wendy Chapple and Jeremy Moon.

[11] GHG stands for Greenhouse gasses.

contribute to air pollution, but relevant data for such emissions is mostly unavailable in sufficient quantities. Only data that was found to be relevant was on CARMA.org which has CO[2] emission data for a sample of companies like cement, sugar, paper mills, and electricity (thermal, hydro, solar etc.) in India which are into power generation or have captive power plants. Power generation plants were chosen excluding the one having captive plants (sugar, cement etc.) due to sufficient availability of data.

Greenhouse Gas Emissions of Carbon Dioxide Equivalent from Various Sectors in India 2008	
Sector	**(In Million Tons of CO_2 Equivalent)**
Electricity	719.3
Transport	142.04
Residential	137.84
Other Energy	100.87
Cement	129.92
Iron & Steel	117.32
Other Industry	165.31

[12]**Fig. 1.**

HYPOTHESIS

With main objective of the paper being to answer the question "Are Well diversified Conglomerates Less Environmentally Responsible?" following hypothesis were made:

H0: Subsidiaries of broadly diversified firms will exhibit same environmental performance as subsidiaries of narrowly diversified firms.

H1: Subsidiaries of broadly diversified firms will exhibit poorer environmental performance than subsidiaries of narrowly diversified firms.

H0 represents the null hypothesis, this presumes that their does not exist any statistically significant difference between the two sets of companies, that is the unrelatedly diversified and the relatedly diversified plant are the same in terms of environment friendliness. The same will be testes using single factor one-way ANOVA. Rejection of null hypothesis will lead to acceptance of alternative hypothesis that is the H1, which suggests that plants with parent companies being more unrelatedly diversified exhibit poorer environment performance, determined on the basis of post-hoc analysis, post one-way ANOVA.

METHODOLOGY

The method involves 3 steps:

[12] INCCA: Indian Network for Climate change assessment.

First Step:

Collection of Data was done through Carma.org (carbon monitoring for action) which is a website dealing with information about the electricity production and emissions of corporate entities involved in power generation. Every plant in the CARMA database is assigned to a company. The vast majority of that information comes from a proprietary, commercial database underpinning CARMA. (Cited from Carma.org). Data was taken of geographic region of India from this source.

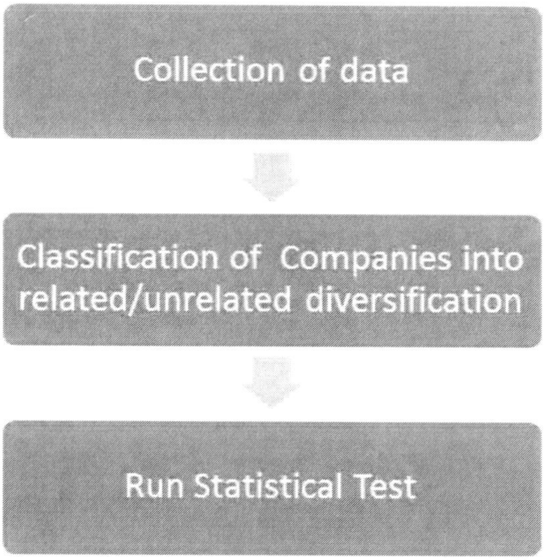

Fig. 2.

Sample: The sample is comprised of 385 facilities under various conglomerates in the Indian Power industry in 2009. These were further classified into 180 facilities being under parent companies with unrelated diversification strategies and rest 205 being under parent companies having dominant or related diversification strategy. Each of these companies is annually required to report the volume of carbon discharged by each of its facilities. The data is organized in below fields as:

- **Plant id:** It's the unique identification number of each power generating facility in India.
- **Carbon_2009:** It's the total carbon emission by a company in terms of CO^2 Kg's.
- **Energy_2009:** It's the total energy generated by the plant.
- **Intensity_2009:** It's the amount of carbon released per unit of electricity produced

The data collected consisted of carbon (CO^2 Kg's) released by each firm. Carbon released is chosen to be the determinant factor for environment friendliness because of multiple reasons; firstly about 60% of global electricity generation relies upon fossil fuels to generate the heat needed to power steam-driven turbines. Burning these fuels results in the production of carbon dioxide (CO^2) – the primary heat-trapping, "greenhouse gas" responsible for global warming., secondly the other sources of pollutant from a power facility include the toxic waste dumps, the residual fossil burnt etc. but the data most readily available is of its carbon emission which it has to report on an annual basis.

Second Step:

Classification of companies: For our research the set of power generating companies need to be classified into two broad categories Related and Unrelated, based on the diversification strategy of parent company. So, on the basis of researcher's understanding validated through secondary research of company websites, NSE, BSE enough information was garnered to put them in their respective category.

Third Step:

Statistical Test: post classification our task was to determine if there exist any statistically significant distinction between two categories of the companies or not?

ANALYSIS

Our hypothesis which tested whether the unrelated and related firms are the same when it comes to environment friendliness has a single independent variable that is the carbon credits released by the plant and dependent variable consisted of two categorical variable of one being related and other being unrelated, hence, Single Factor: One-way ANOVA was used to test whether there is any difference in the samples of related and unrelated they are the same in terms of carbon credits emitted. The confidence interval chosen was 95% hence alpha being 0.05.

The results of ANOVA came out to be as expected the p value of 0.000102 being less than 0.05 alpha significance level demonstrates that the two set of data are different in terms of their environmental performance. The F value being 15.4, much more than critical F value of 3.86 confirms it as shown in table II. The mean shows that the unrelatedly diversified companies tend to release as much as 13.53% more carbon in the air as compared to relatedly diversified companies; Figure III also details the same.

SUMMARY

Groups	*Count*	*Sum*	*Average*	*Variance*
Related	205	188.3099	0.918585	0.105751
Unrelated	180	187.7237	1.042909	0.085085

ANOVA

Source of Variation	*SS*	*df*	*MS*	*F*	*P-value*	*F crit*
Between Groups	1.481429	1	1.481429	15.41667	0.000102	3.865853
Within Groups	36.80348	383	0.096093			
Total	38.28491	384				

Fig. 3.

LIMITATIONS AND ASSUMPTIONS

Our first limitation would be the method of classification of the facilities, done on the basis of related and unrelated diversification strategy of the parent company. This classification is done on the basis of researcher's understanding and validated through secondary research of company websites and industry data such as [13]BSE, NSE. Though validated thoroughly this classification may wary according to researcher's discretion.

Second would be the availability of data which was available for 2009 only and restricted to power sector which gain most of it was the companies having captive power. Though the concept remains new but was reserved to one sector only due to unavailability of data.

Third would be the factor used is only CO_2 which again can be extended to other toxic pollutants in the sector due to the reasons cited earlier.

CONCLUSION

The results conclude that the facilities with parent having the related or dominant strategy companies contribute less to the environmental pollution, the factors which lead to such results include better resource capitalization, learning curve etc.. Whereas the companies with unrelated or broader diversification model are relatively less environmental friendly and the factor include experimentation, lack of experience in the sector, etc. The companies with broader diversification strategies aim at short term profits, which prohibits them to invest huge amounts for facility and technology up-gradation, hence leading to less environment friendly whereas the companies

[13] Bombay Stock Exchange and National Stock Exchange

having related diversification strategy aim at long term goals and hence tries to build more sustainable facility.

In conclusion, we feel this study has an important implication for organizational researchers, as well as for organizations and regulatory policymakers. Further research can be pursued in other sectors such as chemical, sugar, paper mills, IT etc. taking into account other polluting factors not just air but also water, radiation, noise etc. It is hoped that the current work will be the impetus for future investigations of how other organizational factors influence environmental performance. The findings raise concerns about the lack of centralized regulatory body across sectors which should keep a regular track of the on-going practices of the facilities and do not limit the role to initial sanctioning of the permissions to map it with environmental norms.

REFERENCES

[1] Alexis P. Jacquemin and Charles H. Berry "Entropy Measure of Diversification and Corporate Growth"

[2] Anil M. Pandya and Narendar V. Rao "Diversification and firm performance: an empirical evaluation"

[3] BSE (*http://www.bseindia.com/*) and NSE(*http://www.nseindia.com/*) websites

[4] Carma.org for datasets

[5] "Clean technology fund investment plan for India" *http://envfor.nic.in*

[6] Davide Vannoni "Causes and effects of multimarket activity from theory to empirical analysis"

[7] Government initiative on climate control *http://www.cleanenergyfuture.gov.au*

[8] INCCA: Indian Network for Climate change assessment

[9] Individual company sites to validate the information of stated top 10 green companies.

[10] Robert S. Dooley, Gerald E. Fryxell "Are Conglomerates Less Environmentally Responsible?" '

[11] Shyam Kumar "The costs of related diversification: the impact of the core business on the productivity of related segments"

[12] Wendy Chapple and Jeremy Moon "Corporate Social Responsibility (CSR) in Asia: A Seven-Country Study of CSR Web Site Reporting"

Vendor Managed Inventory System to Maximize Supply Chain Efficiency

Shruti Shah and Vikas Marwaha

IMT Ghaziabad

ABSTRACT

In today's flat world, it is important for the companies to go global and act local. It is equally important for the MNCs to integrate their supply chain in a way to increase the productivity and minimize the cost. However; in doing so companies often faced problems which make supply chain very rigid. It's needless to say that in this competitive world any of the firm just cannot afford to lose on SCM efficiency.

Vendor Managed Inventory (VMI) is an approach which provides solution to all the above discussed problems and addresses the need of current business scenarios. Vendor Managed Inventory (VMI) system transfers complete control of Inventory at distributors site back to vendor. By transferring the ownership of inventory to distributor, not only reduces the costs in SCM but also forms a symbiotic relation between supplier and distributer. Thus by automating the order build and order record system, VMI is opening up new doors and is providing the companies with an opportunity to drastically improve efficiency of SCM and hence making their venture more profitable and competitive. Careful application of this system is bound to yield high results in terms of lower costs, higher profits, increased efficiency, stronger supplier-retailer relation and increased competitive advantage.

This paper evaluates the benefits and limitations of implementing the VMI for supply chain efficiency.

INTRODUCTION

To understand the problems faced in Supply Chain Management, first of all we should have a basic understanding of supply chain and its management. Hence a Supply Chain can be defined as: "a network of facilities and distribution options that performs the functions of procurement of materials, transformation of these materials into intermediate and finished products, and the distribution of these finished products to customers. Supply chains exist in both service and manufacturing organizations, although the complexity of the chain may vary greatly from industry to industry and firm to firm."

Yet another definition for supply chain is:" A supply chain is a system of organizations, people, technology, activities, information and resources involved in moving a product or service from supplier to customer. Supply chain activities transform natural resources, raw materials and components into a finished product that is delivered to the end customer. "

The management of supply chain for increased productivity and minimised cost is known as Supply Chain Management (SCM). Now as we know the basics of supply chain and SCM, we will discuss the various issues which are being faced in Supply Chain Management in present. The major problems in SCM are as follows:

- Problem of over/under stocking at distributors end.
- The front end staff at distributor's end often lacks in the core/detailed knowledge of products being displayed.
- Distributor is deemed to be solely responsible for the cost incurred for unsold inventory.
- No connection between vendor and distributor.
- Often distributors are not able to predict the demand of product accurately due to lack of market info and conditions.
- Distributors often loose on competitiveness with decreasing efficiency of SCM.
- Vendor and Distributor work to increase their individual profits and hence
  - Vendor tries to sell maximum stock to distributor without caring for its needs.
  - Distributor tries to minimize the stock purchases and delay the payment for as long as he can.
- Distributors can create a virtual scarcity of any item by not sharing the status of inventory for any product with vendor.

All of the above are some of the many problems which are faced in current scenario in SCM. These issues are all critical in nature and need to be handled with utmost care and accuracy in order to boost the efficiency of supply chain. It's needless to say that in this competitive world any of the firm just cannot afford to lose on SCM efficiency. Managing supply chain can be a matter of Sustaining and losing a complete market.

We have several of the real world examples which demonstrate the importance of SCM and how drastic is the impact of SCM is on business:

- In the year 1995 Nokia got into a situation which changed the entire company and its logistics processes: "Despite strong sales growth, Nokia Mobile Phones profitability was adversely affected by a number of factors during the year. The principal factor affecting profitability was the difficulty of meeting the challenges created by the business group's rapid growth. Profitability was also affected by interruptions in the supply of certain components, as well as logistical issues. (Nokia annual report, 1995) Nokia learned and changed the logistics concept.

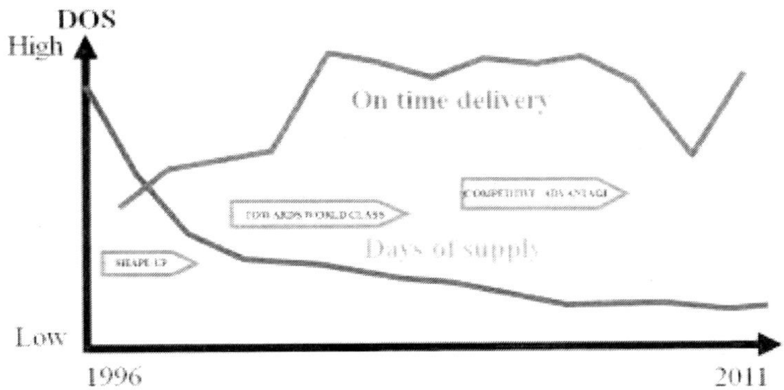

Fig. 1. Nokia Customer Service and Inventories Development of Global Level

Source: Stoerkel, 2010

- In the late 1990s, Boeing had to temporarily shut some of its assembly lines, and took billions of dollars in charges, when bottlenecks and quality issues arose after it tried to expand production too quickly. More recently, in 2008, inadequate training of new mechanics and supply-chain glitches led to quality problems at its 737 plant.(The Wall Street Journal ,Friday, December 30,2011)

Hence we see how crucial it is to manage supply chain. Vendor Managed Inventory (VMI) approach gives solution to all the above discussed problems and addresses the need of current business scenarios. VMI is not a mathematical tool but is an approach which provides a business level solution to effectively manage supply chain.

VENDOR MANAGED INVENTORY

Vendor Managed Inventory (VMI) system transfers complete control of Inventory at Distributors site back to vendor. The goods/inventory remains at distributor's warehouse/store/premises but are managed & owned by vendor based on exchange of sales information from distributor to vendor. In this system a Vendor can initiate re-order/purchase order of inventory on the behalf of retailer as soon as it senses a need for it. The ownership of inventory passes on from vendor to distributor as soon as the sale of inventory takes place.

Vendor-managed inventory (VMI) systems are a proven technique for improving the efficiency of supply chain operations. VMI is made possible by the implementation of an electronic means of exchanging inventory information between the buyers and sellers of products. These electronic links eliminate many of the built-in delays associated with traditional ordering systems and enable the establishment of collaborative inventory management systems. Experience has shown that improvements in these two areas can result in the elimination of between 20% and 30% of the previously required supply chain inventory. However, in order to achieve this level of success, it is critical for those companies that have not yet implemented VMI to follow a best practice approach. Successful VMI programs take advantage of a key supply chain relationship that has been reaffirmed many times over.

For the distributor, it means less work and less risk. For the supplier, it means inventory is set up how and where you want it, and you have the opportunity to educate associates and employees about your wares. It also means more risk.

According to Industry Week's Best Plants 2006 Statistical Profile, 56% of the top 25 plants between 2002 and 2006 have used "resident suppliers" to manage or replenish inventory. However, the average percentage of purchased materials and components (dollar volume) managed by on-site suppliers is only 13.7%.

In addition, there is a certain amount of IT integration that has to go on in order to make the VMI relationship work.

"For suppliers, they need to be able to get your forecasts on a regular basis, make intelligence out of them and have visibility into your inventory levels on an on-going basis," says Banker. "Turning that into useable intelligence is kind of difficult. Small and midsized companies often don't have the dedicated IT resources to make that happen, so they struggle."

VMI can drive more business, but sometimes it is implemented in a way where it affects cash flow. The supplier to the manufacturer ends up owning inventory for longer periods of time and ends up carrying more inventory risk. That often is a trade-off for gaining more business.

STRUCTURE OF VMI

VMI is a process where the supplier generates orders for the customer based on demand information sent by the customer. During this process the supplier is guided by mutually agreed to objectives for inventory levels, fill rates and transaction costs.

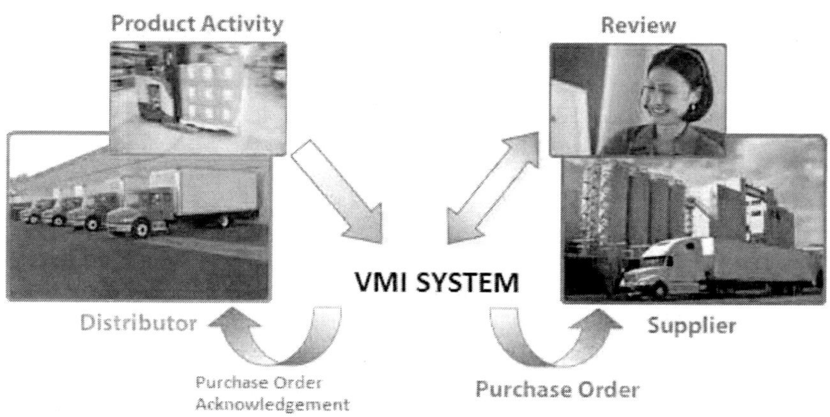

There are two EDI transactions at the heart of the process. The first is the Product Activity Record, frequently referred to as an 852. The data contained in this document are sales and inventory information. The inventory data is typically segmented into various groups such as on hand, on order, committed, back ordered and so forth. This transaction is the backbone of VMI and is sent by the customer on a prearranged schedule, typically, daily. The decision to order is based on this data.

The business process fed by this data is relatively simple. The supplier reviews the information that has been sent in by the customer on the 852 to determine if an order is needed. This review of the data varies by supplier and the software being used, but, many things are consistent.

- The first step is to verify the data as accurate and meaningful. Depending on the software, much of this verification is automated.
- On a scheduled basis, the software calculates a reorder point for each item based on the movement data and any overrides contributed by the customer or supplier. These overrides might include information such as promotions, projects, seasonality, new items and so forth.
- The VMI software compares the quantity available at the customer with the reorder point for each item at each location. This determines if an order is needed.
- The order quantities are then calculated. Typically calculation of order quantities takes into account such issues as carton quantities and transaction costs.

This completes the order build process. The second VMI transaction informs the customer what product to expect from the supplier. There are two transactions being used for this function. The most frequently used is the purchase order acknowledgment, referred to as the 855. This document contains the product numbers and quantities ordered by the supplier on the customer's behalf. A few customers skip the 855 and rely on the advance ship notice (856) to alert them to the order and shipment. This document differs from the 855 in both timing and content. The 856 is sent after the shipment has been made instead of at the time of the order. The 856 contains only the part numbers shipped as well as additional information such as carrier and waybill information. For the purposes of VMI, either of these documents works well if properly implemented.

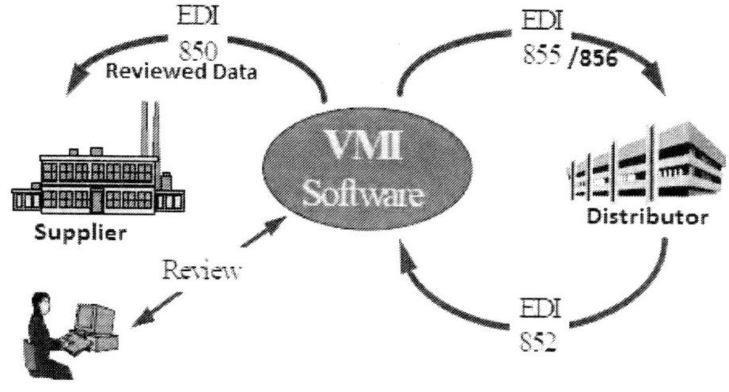

VMI IMPLEMENTATION CHALLENGES

VMI can be made to work, but the problem is not just one of logistics. VMI often encounters resistance from the sales force and distributors. At issue are roles and skills, trust, and power shifts. Some of the sales force concerns are:

- Loss of control
- Effect on compensation
- Possible loss of job
- Scepticism that it will function well - technical problems
- Concern that reduced inventory will result in less shelf space and therefore loss of market share.

Distributors also may have concerns about vendor managed inventory, like:

- Inventory will be pushed on them
- No more promotions, discounts, and forward buying
- With less inventory, more risk of disruptions due to strikes, adverse weather, etc.
- The vendor enjoys the benefits while the distributor gives up its only lever of power - data on what the retailers want.
- Danger of being replaced - vendor may decide to forward integrate.

ADDRESSING CONCERNS

For a VMI system to work, the concerns of distributors and the sales force must be addressed. They can be at least partially addressed by the following:

- Transform the sales role into one of marketing. For example, bonuses can be given based on the number of new clients.
- Distributor scepticism can be addressed by implementing a pilot program with vendor-owned warehouses in order to demonstrate that the system works. Introduce system in distributor-owned warehouses on a pilot basis.
- Engage a neutral consultant in meetings among the vendor, distributor, and sales force.
- Allow some manufacturer promotions in the transition.
- Extensively simulate the system off-line before implementing.
- Don't exaggerate the benefits of VMI; otherwise, any delay in realizing the benefits may cause the supply chain to lose faith in the system.

CONDITIONS UNDER WHICH VMI CAN WORK SUCCESSFULLY

VMI approach is highly dependent on a symbiotic relation between Vendor and Distributor. They need to work very closely and should align their goals in same direction. Mutual cooperation and trust is of crucial importance in order to have a successful VMI implementation.

Some of the other conditions which are critical for a successful VMI implementation are as follows:

- *COMMUNICATE* expectations of all parties. Customers and suppliers must make the effort to sit down and discuss the goals and objectives of implementing VMI.
- Customer must commit to sharing *PRECISE* information.
- Suppliers must ensure *RELIABLE* transmission, receipt, and use of information.
- Expect implementation to be a *PROCESS* not a project.

BENEFITS OF VMI

Supply Chain

- Lower inventory level at total supply chain level.
- Less overhead & increased sales.
- Reduces human data entry errors.

Vendors

- Better Insights in customer demand.
- Improved communication with customers.
- Increased sales via lower Stock out Rate. Opportunity for category management.

Distributors

- Reduced replenishment times & hence lowering of inventory cost.
- Increased sales through reduced number of stock outs. Hence uncertainty reduction.
- Building of symbiotic relationship between vendor and distributor. Sharing of risk.
- Training of sales force at distributor's site.
- Complete focus on sales & growth than on inventory management.

LIMITATIONS ASSOCIATED WITH VMI

Success of VMI initiative depends on the strength of relationship between Vendors and Distributors. Due to this increased dependency between vendor & distributor the switching (to a new vendor/distributor) cost for both of them is on the higher end of spectrum. Other concerns w.r.t to VMI are:

- Lack of trust in information exchange can result in an ineffective system.
- Costs of setting up VMI system. Also vendors will be reluctant to support distributors who contribute only a small part in vendor's revenue.

- Increased vulnerability with unavoidable/non-foreseeable risks like natural calamity, strikes as inventory levels will be very low.

Hence we can see that above are the limitations and points we should keep in mind while implementation of VMI. Every process and system has its pros and cons but its up-to us how to mitigate the risks and harness maximum benefits.

ANALYSIS OF FIRMS WHICH CAN BENEFIT FROM VMI AND FIRMS WHERE VMI SHOULD BE AVOIDED

VMI is not at all a generic business solution applicable to every sort of business. Its specific in nature and hence is tailor-made for organizations/businesses with certain definite traits.

It is usually successful for businesses with following traits:

- Industries with steady and high volumes(retail, consumer products etc.)
- Industries with high value inventory and a high level of demand unpredictability.
- Industries with long term partnerships between vendor & distributor (Automotive).
- Industries which bear severe consequences in case of stock out(Pharmaceutical).

Vendors & distributors should only consider VMI for trading partners that are important to them (e.g. Partners who have a high contribution to revenues or possess growth potential.)

CONCLUSION

Companies around the world are adopting VMI approach to manage supply chain and boost its efficiency. VMI is opening up new doors and is providing us with opportunity to drastically improve efficiency of SCM and hence making our venture more profitable and competitive. Careful application of this system is bound to yield high results in terms of lower costs, higher profits, increased efficiency, stronger supplier-retailer relation and increased competitive advantage.

VMI implementation should always be preferred in presence of experienced guidance. It should be realized that VMI is not a generic and one time solution, but in-fact it is a continuous process. It has the potential to radically boost the efficiency of supply chain of any business compatible to it. It will be apt to say that VMI opens the door to highly effective supply chain and provides competitive advantage to the firms implementing it.

REFERENCES

[1] Duncan, R., "State of a New Art." Manufacturing Systems, Logistics: Trading Places. Engineering (1996) pp. 2-10.

[2} Latamore G. B, Customers, Suppliers Drawing Closer through VMI Relationships, APICS - The Performance Advantage, July 1999, Volume 12, pp. 7-12.

[3] Mallman, L., "The strategic role of suppliers in manufacturing strategies", proceeding of the 2nd international symposium on logistics, Nottingham, 1995, pp. 3-8.

[4] Heck A, Stoerkel M, Global trends and practical examples of supply chain Management within the mobile telecommunications industry, International journal of social sciences and humanity studies (2011), Vol 3, pp 217-226.

[5] "Vendor Managed Inventory", retrieved on October 1,2012 from http://www.quickmba.com/ops/vendor-managed-inventory/

[6] Traci Purdum (February 7, 2007), "Vendor-Managed Inventory: Size Matters" , The Industry Week, retrieved on August 28,2012 from http://www.industryweek.com/procurement/vendor-managed-inventory-size-matters

[7] Shailesh Mishra (January 29, 2008), "Lean Manufacturing: Losing weight through VMI", retrieved on August 20,2012 from http://rising-entropy.blogspot.in/2008/01/lean-manufacturing-losing-weight.html

[8] Carl Hall, "Vendor Managed Inventory- Promising Value for the Truck Parts Industry" retrived on August 28, 2012 from http://www.datalliance.com/value_truck_parts.pdf

[9] Scott Frahm (March 5, 2003) , "Vendor Managed Inventory (VMI): Three Steps in Making It Work", retrived on October 5,2012 from http://scm.ncsu.edu/scm-articles/article/vendor-managed-inventory-vmi-three-steps-in-making-it-work

[10] Mark K. Williams (nd), "Making Consignment and Vendor-Managed Inventory Work for You", retrieved on October 1, 2012 from http://www.vendormanagedinventory.com/article6.php

[11] Ganesh R, Harrison T, (May 22, 1995), "An Introduction to Supply Chain Management" , retrieved on August 28, 2012 from http://lcm.csa.iisc.ernet.in/scm/supply_chain_intro.html

[12] Margaret Rouse (July, 2010), "Supply Chain Management" retrieved on August 28, 2012 from http://searchmanufacturingerp.techtarget.com/definition/supply-chain-management

[13] Zenjiro Imaoka, "Understand Supply Chain Management through 100 words", retrieved on October 3 ,2012 from http://www.lean-manufacturing-japan.com/scm-terminology/vmi-vendor-managed-inventory.html

[14] Hotchman S, Reale K, "Keys to Success with Vendor Managed Inventory", retrieved on August 25, 2012 from http://www.datalliance.com/keystosuccess.html

[15] David Kesmodel, "Boeing Examines Supply Chain for Weak Links", retrieved on August 28, 2012 from http://online.wsj.com/article/SB1000142405297020405840457711109109543 8300.html

Author Index